Discover Ireland

Contents 

Throughout this book, we use these icons to highlight special recommendations:

The Best...
Lists for everything from bars to wildlife – to make sure you don't miss out

Don't Miss
A must-see – don't go home until you've been there

Local Knowledge Local experts reveal their top picks and secret highlights

Detour
Special places a little off the beaten track

If you like...
Lesser-known alternatives to world-famous attractions

These icons help you quickly identify reviews in the text and on the map:

Sights

Eating

Drinking

Sleeping

Information

This edition written and researched by

Fionn Davenport
Catherine Le Nevez, Etain O'Carroll,
Ryan Ver Berkmoes, Neil Wilson

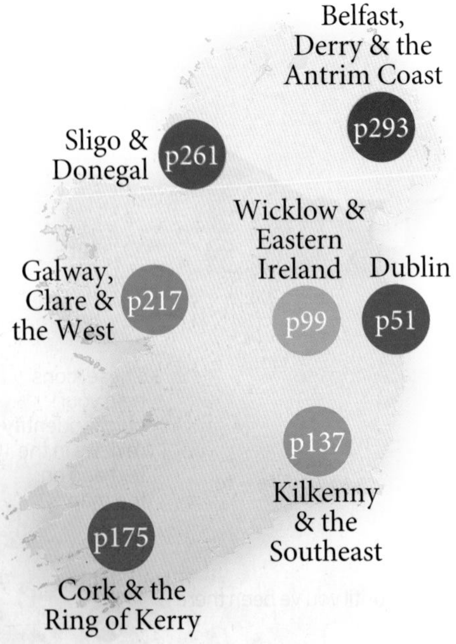

Belfast, Derry & the Antrim Coast
p293

Sligo & Donegal
p261

Wicklow & Eastern Ireland
p99

Dublin
p51

Galway, Clare & the West
p217

p137
Kilkenny & the Southeast

p175
Cork & the Ring of Kerry

Kilkenny & the Southeast

- Dungarvan
- Rock of Cashel
- Kilkenny City
- Walks on Hook Head
- Southeastern Kitchens
- National 1798 Rebellion Centre

Cork & the Ring of Kerry

- Killarney
- Skellig Michael
- The English Market
- Killarney National Park
- Kinsale
- Slea Head

Dublin

- Chester Beatty Library
- Trinity College
- Irish Museum of Modern Art
- Kilmainham Gaol
- A Pint of Plain
- Dublin Greenery

Wicklow & Eastern Ireland

- Brú na Bóinne
- Glendalough
- Powerscourt Estate
- Monasterboice
- Castletown House
- Old Mellifont Abbey

Galway, Clare & the West

- Trad Sessions in Clare
- Connemara
- Galway
- Music Festivals
- Cliffs of Moher
- Clonmacnoise
- Aran Islands

Contents

Plan Your Trip

On the Road

Contents

On the Road

Belfast, Derry & the Antrim Coast 293

In Focus

Survival Guide

This Is Ireland

For such a tiny country, Ireland gets a pretty big billing. Its praises are sung in song and described in prose; its many charms are evoked to delicious perfection by artists on canvas and poets in verse. They tell of a green landscape brushed with rain, a wild coastline tormented by a wind-blown sea... Hang on, can this idyll actually be real?

As it turns out, it is. You'll find this side of Ireland along the postcard-perfect peninsulas of the southwest, the brooding loneliness of Connemara and the dramatic wildness of County Donegal. Ireland may have modernised dramatically, but some things never change. Brave the raging Atlantic on a crossing to Skellig Michael or spend a summer's evening in the yard of a thatched cottage pub and you'll experience a country that has changed little in generations – this is most likely the Ireland you came to see.

Despite the trappings of modernity and the fickle hand of fortune, Ireland remains one of the world's most beautiful countries, and is worth every effort you make to explore it. And when we say Ireland, we mean the whole island – the North, for so long scarred by conflict, is now finally engaged in the process of recovery and is able once again to parade its stunning self to a world that for so long only knew of it through the stories on the evening news.

Céad míle fáilte – a hundred thousand welcomes. Why a hundred thousand when one is perfectly adequate everywhere else? Everyone has heard of Irish friendliness, and once you arrive you'll gladly discover it's not a myth. A bit of friendly banter and the offer of a helping hand – to read a map, make sense of garbled directions or share a pint (it's a sin to drink alone!) – are never far from the first hello, for the Irish consider hospitality to be their greatest asset. A hundred thousand welcomes. It seems excessive, but in Ireland, excess is fine, so long as it's practised in moderation. Friendly but never fawning.

“...postcard-perfect peninsulas, the brooding loneliness of Connemara and the wildness of Donegal”

Cliffs of Moher (p251), County Clare

Ireland

ELEVATION
700m
500m
300m
200m
100m
0

9°W
8°W
7°W
6°W
5°W
55°N
54°N
53°N

North Channel
Malin Head
Inishowen Peninsula
Giant's Causeway
Rathlin Island
Gare Loch
Tory Island
Ballyliffin
Clonmany
Culdaff
Port-stewart
Ballycastle
Dunfanaghy
Rosguill Peninsula
Fanad Peninsula
Portrush
Bushmills
17
Cushendun
Bloody Foreland
Glenveagh National Park
Buncrana
Coleraine
SCOTLAND
Gweedore
Limavady
ATLANTIC
OCEAN
Dunlewy
Lough Gartan
Letter-kenny
19
Derry/ Londonderry
Glens of Antrim
Dungloe
Ballymena
Larne
Strabane
DERRY
Slemish (438)
Kells
Ardara
Sperrin Mountains
Maghery
DONEGAL
Carrickfergus
Glencolumbcille
Loughrea Peninsula
Lough Eske
ANTRIM
Antrim
Bangor
Slieve League
20
Donegal
Holywood
Kilcar
Omagh
Lough Neagh
Belfast
15
Newtownards
Carrick
TYRONE
Rossnowlagh
Lower Lough Erne
Lisburn
Ards Peninsula
Craigavon
Mullaghmore
Bundoran
Portadown
Lurgan
Inishmurray
FERMANAGH
Rosses Point
Links Golf
7
Enniskillen
Armagh
Banbridge
Downpatrick
Ballycastle
Killala Bay
Easkey
Lough Macnean
Monaghan
ARMAGH
DOWN
Lecale Peninsula
Pollatomish
Sligo
Upper Lough Erne
Rossmore Forest Park
Newry
Killala
Strandhill
Lower
Mullet Peninsula
Bangor Erris
Enniscrone
Carrowmore Megalithic Cemetery
Cuilcagh Mountain (667)
Clones
Mourne Mountains
MAYO
Ballina
Ballycroy National Park
MONAGHAN
Carlingford
SLIGO
Achill Island
LEITRIM
Boyle
Dundalk
Cavan
Carrick-macross
Carrowkeel Megalithic Cemetery
Carrick-on-Shannon
Irish Sea
Newport
CAVAN
LOUTH
Clare Island
Clew Bay
Castlebar
Loughcrew Cairns
Battle of Boyne Site
21
Monasterboice
Westport
Knock
Strokestown
Kells
Slane
Drogheda
Inishturk
Croagh Patrick (765m)
9
Killary Harbour
LONGFORD
Navan
Inishbofin
Doolough Valley
Roscommon
Brú na Bóinne
Letterfrack
Leenane
Tara
Lough Ree
WESTMEATH
Trim
Cong
Claddaghduff
4
Connemara National Park
ROSCOMMON
Mullingar
Clifden
Lough Inagh
MEATH
Malahide
Cashel
GALWAY
Athlone
Howth
Roundstone
Oughterard
Maynooth
Kilbeggan
1
DUBLIN
Mace Head
Athenry
Ballinasloe
6
Durrow Abbey
Straffan
Galway
8
Tullamore
DUBLIN
Dalkey
Clonmacnoise
Kilcolgan
Newbridge
Blessington
10
Powerscourt Estate
Loughrea
KILDARE
Inishmór
25
Ballyvaughan
Burren
Kinvara
Mountmellick
Kildare
Wicklow Mountains
Aran Islands
Inishmaan
Inisheer
Doolin
Gort
OFFALY
Birr
Glendalough
3
Wicklow

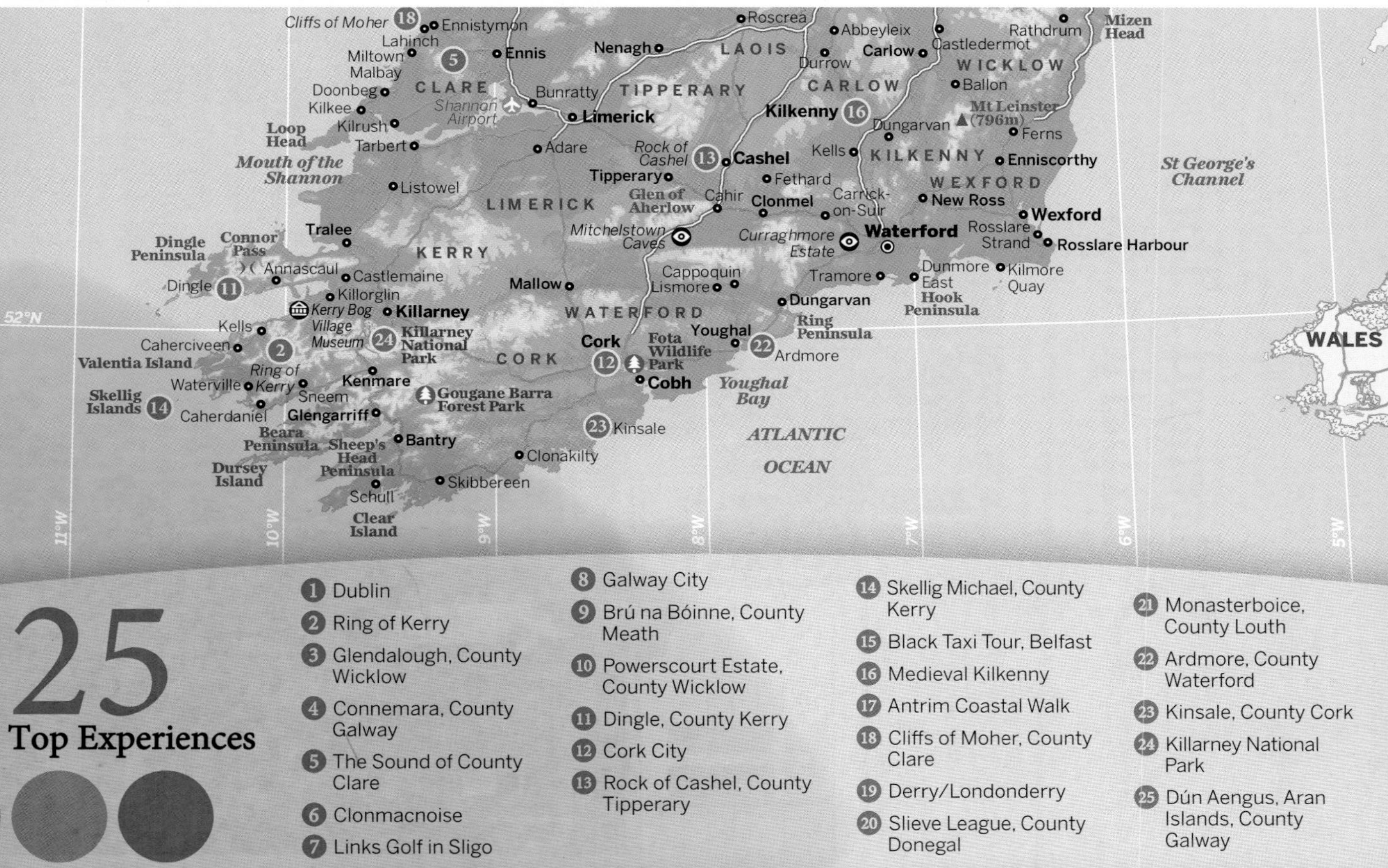

25 Top Experiences

1. Dublin
2. Ring of Kerry
3. Glendalough, County Wicklow
4. Connemara, County Galway
5. The Sound of County Clare
6. Clonmacnoise
7. Links Golf in Sligo
8. Galway City
9. Brú na Bóinne, County Meath
10. Powerscourt Estate, County Wicklow
11. Dingle, County Kerry
12. Cork City
13. Rock of Cashel, County Tipperary
14. Skellig Michael, County Kerry
15. Black Taxi Tour, Belfast
16. Medieval Kilkenny
17. Antrim Coastal Walk
18. Cliffs of Moher, County Clare
19. Derry/Londonderry
20. Slieve League, County Donegal
21. Monasterboice, County Louth
22. Ardmore, County Waterford
23. Kinsale, County Cork
24. Killarney National Park
25. Dún Aengus, Aran Islands, County Galway

25 Ireland's Top Experiences

Dublin

Ireland's capital, Dublin (p51), is the main gateway into the country, and it has enough distractions to keep visitors mesmerised for at least a few days. It has all the baubles of a major international metropolis, but the real clincher is the kindness of Dubliners themselves, who are friendlier and more easy-going than the burghers of virtually any other European capital. The Dublin Spire, on O'Connell St, designed by Ian Ritchie Architects

1

RICHARD I'ANSON / LONELY PLANET IMAGES ©

MARK DAFFEY / LONELY PLANET IMAGES ©

2

Ring of Kerry

Yes, it's popular. And yes, it's always choked with bus traffic, especially in summer. But there are about 1000 reasons why the Ring of Kerry (p204) is the tourist charm bracelet it is, and you'll find most of them around the Iveragh Peninsula just west of Killarney; do it counter-clockwise unless you want to get stuck behind a caravan of tour buses! Jaunting cars, County Kerry

Glendalough, County Wicklow

Once one of Ireland's most dynamic universities, the monastic ruins of Glendalough (p112), founded by St Kevin as a spiritual retreat, are now one of the country's most beautiful ruined sites. The remains of the settlement (including an intact round tower), coupled with the stunning scenery, are unforgettable and are the perfect spot for a mountain hike. St Kevin's Church and round tower, Glendalough

3

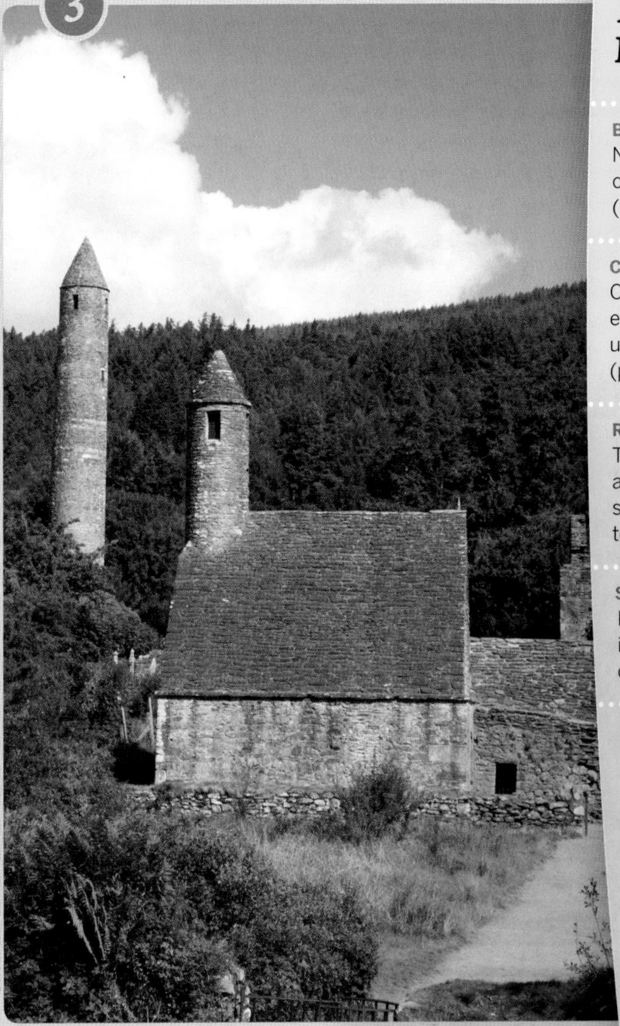

The Best... Ancient Monuments

BRÚ NA BÓINNE
Neolithic passage graves older than the pyramids. (p125)

CLONMACNOISE
Once one of Europe's greatest universities...before universities even existed. (p242)

ROCK OF CASHEL
Thousand-year-old castle, abbey and cathedral straddling a rock above the town. (p169)

SKELLIG MICHAEL
Monastic settlement dating from the 6th century clinging to a rock. (p209)

GLENDALOUGH
Beautiful monastic ruins in the serenest of settings. (p112)

The Best...
Places for Irish History

KILMAINHAM GAOL
Blood, guts and gore behind prison walls. (p75)

NATIONAL 1798 REBELLION CENTRE
The history of rebellion in bloody and magnificent detail. (p156)

DUNBRODY FAMINE SHIP
Full-scale replica of a 19th-century 'famine ship'. (p155)

ULSTER FOLK MUSEUM
The fascinating lives of ordinary people in 18th and 19th century Ulster. (p316)

LEFT: GARETH MCCORMACK / LONELY PLANET IMAGES © TOP: RICHARD CUMMINS / LONELY PLANET IMAGES ©

Connemara, County Galway

Welcome to Connemara (p237) one of Europe's most stunning corners. This kaleidoscope of rusty bogs, lonely valleys and enticing seaside hamlets is laid across a patchwork of narrow country roads punctuated by the odd inviting country pub. It evokes the timelessness of the very best of Irish scenery and the country itself, unsullied by centuries of history and transformation. **Left:** Connemara coast; **Above right:** Store on Main St, Clifden, Connemara

5 The Sound of County Clare

Traditional music finds its spiritual home in the crowded boozers of the county capital, Ennis (p244), as much as in the atmospheric small pubs of Ennistymon, Doolin and Kilfenora. The annual Willie Clancy Irish Music Festival in Miltown Malbay (p250) is also an unmissable treat for die-hard fans and aficionados.

Musicians at O'Connor's pub, Doolin

JOHN ELK III / LONELY PLANET IMAGES ©

GARETH MCCORMACK / LONELY PLANET IMAGES ©

6 Clonmacnoise, County Offaly

The once-enormous ecclesiastical city of Clonmacnoise (p242) may be long past its pre-medieval prime, but these magnificent ruins, in the ideal location overlooking the River Shannon, still pay a fine tribute to its former glory. This was one of Europe's premier universities, attracting scholars from all over Europe and giving credence to Ireland's reputation as the 'isle of saints and scholars'.

Links Golf in Sligo

Ireland's golf links are the scenic highlight of a round on the island, and a fine example is the breathtaking County Sligo Golf Club (p274). Most of the 18 holes are played in the shadow of the magnificent Benbulben, the mountain that so inspired WB Yeats that he was buried in view of it. Your challenge is to keep your head down on those putts! County Sligo Golf Club, Rosses Point

The Best... Traditional Pubs

KEHOE'S
The classic Dublin pub. (p89)

TYNAN'S BRIDGE HOUSE
A rural country pub in the middle of a big town. (p151)

TATLER JACK'S
No better place in Ireland to learn the lore of Gaelic football. (p199)

SÉHÁN UA NEÁCHTAIN
Galway's most celebrated pub. (p233)

OLDE GLEN BAR & RESTAURANT
A perfect boozer in a remote corner of the country. (p287)

Galway City

Storied, sung-about and snug, Galway (p230) is one of Ireland's great pleasures, so much so that it's full of people who came, saw and still haven't managed to leave. Wandering the tuneful streets and narrow alleys and refuelling in any of the city's great pubs will keep you busy for a month's worth of nights. Watch out, though, as before you know it you'll be putting down roots and never leaving.

8

The Best... Scenic Drives

SKY ROAD
A spectacular Connemara loop. (p239)

RING OF KERRY
Ireland's most popular drive. (p204)

THE HEALY PASS
Spectacular border crossing between Cork and Kerry. (p194)

LOUGH INAGH VALLEY
In the shadow of the brooding Twelve Bens. (p241)

GLEN GESH PASS
A touch of the Alps in Donegal. (p284)

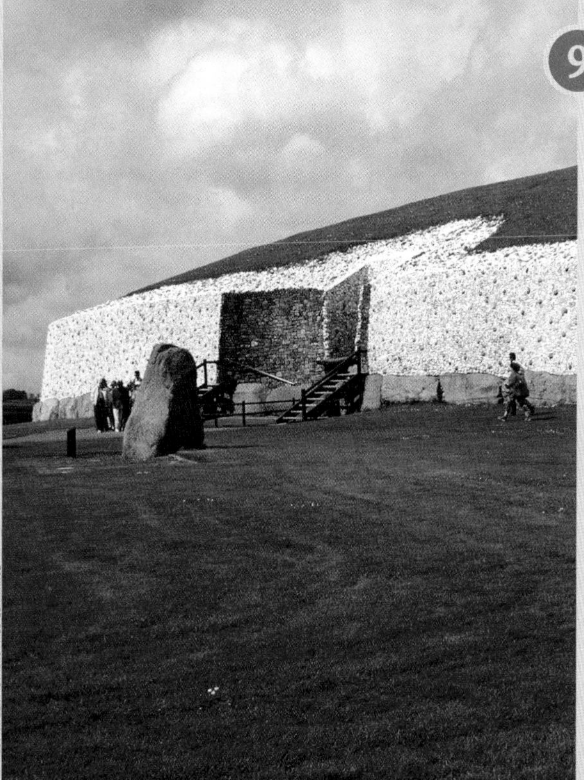

TONY WHEELER / LONELY PLANET IMAGES ©

9 Brú na Bóinne, County Meath

The vast Neolithic necropolis of Brú na Bóinne (p125) in County Meath is 600 years older than the pyramids, 1000 years older than Stonehenge and as magnificent an example of prehistoric genius as you'll find anywhere in the world. The passage is designed with a mathematical precision that would have confounded the ancient Greeks. A visit here is a must, especially to see the simulated winter sunrise that illuminates the main burial chamber. The Newgrange Stone Age passage tomb, Brú na Bóinne

10 Powerscourt Estate, County Wicklow

Most of the stunning Palladian mansion at the heart of the Powerscourt Estate (p116) is, alas, off limits due to a devastating fire that gutted the interior. But you'll be more than compensated by an amble through the sheltered woods and exquisite Italianate gardens, landscaped to perfection in the shadow of the Wicklow Mountains' most distinctive peak, the Sugarloaf. Italian gardens at Powerscourt Estate

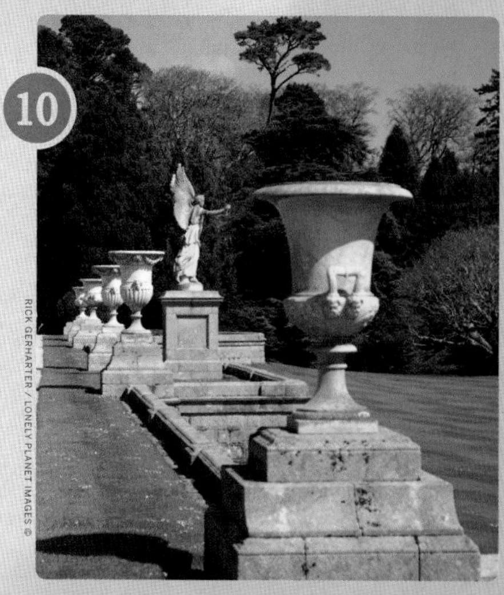

RICK GERHARTER / LONELY PLANET IMAGES ©

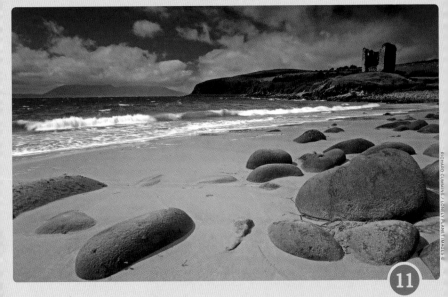

11 Dingle, County Kerry

Everybody has heard of Dingle (p211) and it seems that everybody wants to go there. Luckily, this is one place that transcends the crowds with its allure. Sure you may be stuck behind a bus, but this rocky, striated land that seems to dissolve into the sea has a history as compelling as its beauty, not to mention a collection of prehistoric monuments, scenic spots and fabulous pubs to make you wonder why you'd ever leave. Beach on the Dingle Peninsula

12 Cork City

An appealing waterfront location, some of the best food you'll find anywhere in the country, lively craic and a vibrant 'Dublin? Where's that?' dynamic make Ireland's second city, Cork (p186), hard to resist. Surprises abound on its busy narrow streets, weaving around the River Lee and its canals. Don't be surprised if the locals convince you it's the 'real' capital! Olives at the English Market, Cork

Rock of Cashel, County Tipperary

The Rock of Cashel (p169) never ceases to startle when first seen rising from the otherwise mundane plains of Tipperary. And this ancient fortified home of kings is just the tip of the iceberg, literally, as moody and forlorn ruins are hidden away in the surrounding green expanse, set neatly atop a rock overlooking the pretty town of Cashel.

13

JOHN ELK III / LONELY PLANET IMAGES ©

The Best... Local Activities

CLIMB CROAGH PATRICK
A three-hour climb rewards with superb views and a touch of spiritual enlightenment. (p257)

CATCH A DONEGAL WAVE
Test your skills and try your luck on 'the Peak', Ireland's most famous wave. (p281)

COOKING IN CORK
Learn the nuances of fine Irish cuisine at the country's most famous cooking school. (p193)

CATCH A FISH
Tackle the sea with some angling off the coast of Kilmore Quay. (p152)

TEE OFF IN SLIGO
Go for par on one of Ireland's most beautiful links, in the shadow of Benbulben. (p273)

The Best...
Festival Frolics

KILKENNY ARTS FESTIVAL
Medieval Kilkenny shows its artistic side. (p149)

CAT LAUGHS COMEDY FESTIVAL
Comics from the world over descend upon Kilkenny every year for fits and giggles. (p149)

WILLIE CLANCY IRISH MUSIC FESTIVAL
You'll hear some of the best traditional music in the world at this annual festival on the Clare coast. (p250)

GALWAY ARTS FESTIVAL
The city goes arts-and-fun crazy for two weeks. (p235)

GALWAY INTERNATIONAL OYSTER FESTIVAL
Locally fished oysters washed down with Guinness to a lively musical soundtrack. (p235)

GARETH McCORMACK / LONELY PLANET IMAGES ©

14 Skellig Michael, County Kerry

Brace yourself for the experience of a lifetime as you brave the choppy crossing to clamber about the jagged rocks of Skellig Michael (p209), where early Christian monks lived in splendid isolation from the 6th to the 12th centuries, perched 150m above the raging sea in bare, beehive cells. The only difference now is the monks are gone and a small guard rail is in place. Stone stairway leading to Skellig Michael monastic settlement

© ANDREW McCONNELL / ALAMY

15 Black Taxi Tour, Belfast

Learn about Northern Ireland's recent troubled history as you tour the political murals and peace lines of West Belfast's divided neighbourhoods of the Falls and the Shankill in the back of a black taxi (p313). The tour is leavened with a touch of black humour from the wise-cracking driver, who encourages questions, comments and debate: it's one of the liveliest history lessons you'll get in Ireland.

Medieval Kilkenny

16

Fulfil your fantasies of historic Ireland by soaking up some of iconic Kilkenny City (p148), from the incredible 12th-century castle to the medieval alleyways lined with colourfully painted shopfronts. Cultural events include its famous comedy bash and arts festival, as well as the cracking traditional music sessions. Make sure you sample its superb beer, best enjoyed in one of the city's huge collection of atmospheric, traditional bars. High St, Kilkenny

RICHARD CUMMINS / LONELY PLANET IMAGES ©

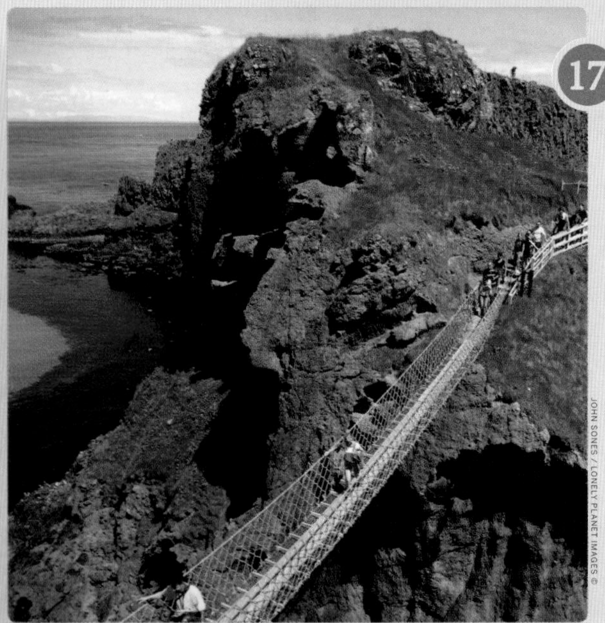

JOHN SONES / LONELY PLANET IMAGES ©

Antrim Coastal Walk

17

Put on your walking boots, shoulder your rucksack loaded with sandwiches and tea, and set off along one of Ireland's finest coastal walks. The Antrim Coastal Walk stretches for 16 scenic kilometres between the swaying rope bridge of Carrick-a-Rede (p320) and the grand geological flourish of the Giant's Causeway (p321), Northern Ireland's most popular attraction. Carrick-a-Rede Rope Bridge

Cliffs of Moher, County Clare

Bathed in the golden glow of the late afternoon sun, the iconic Cliffs of Moher (p251) are one of the splendours of the west coast. Witnessed from a boat bobbing below, the towering stone faces have a jaw-dropping, dramatic beauty that is enlivened by scores of sea birds, including cute little puffins. Cliffs of Moher, between Doolin and Lahinch

The Best... Leg Stretchers

MOURNE MOUNTAINS
The most scenic walks in Northern Ireland are around these famed mountains. (p316)

GLENDALOUGH
Fabulous walks around this monastic site are part of the 117km Wicklow Way. (p121)

KILLARNEY NATIONAL PARK
You've seen these views on a thousand postcards – now you can see them for yourself. (p200)

DUBLIN CITY CENTRE
Who says you need greenery for a good walk? Try Dublin's Georgian architecture instead. (p62)

ARDMORE CLIFFS
Walk part of the ancient St Declan's Way across green fields and alongside stunning cliff views. (p165)

The Best... Seaside Villages

KILMORE QUAY
Great spot to relax and watch the fishermen pull in their nets. (p152)

DUNFANAGHY
Elegant village fronted by a huge strand. (p284)

ROUNDSTONE
Colourful terrace houses and a boat-filled harbour complete this Connemara gem. (p239)

CUSHENDUN
Cornish-style houses make this one of the delights of the Antrim Coast. (p322)

ARDMORE
Quiet and relatively undiscovered, Ardmore's beach is a well-kept secret. (p165)

19 Derry/ Londonderry

Northern Ireland's second city might have a disputed name, but no one will dispute that Derry (or Londonderry) (p322) is worth a visit. Its superb – and intact – city walls and neighbourhoods are fascinating, especially the Bogside, a hardscrabble district that has borne the brunt of violence but still comes up smiling and is only too happy to show visitors around. Derry's *Hands Across the Divide* peace monument by artist Maurice Harron

GARETH McCORMACK / LONELY PLANET IMAGES ©

SIMON GREENWOOD / LONELY PLANET IMAGES ©

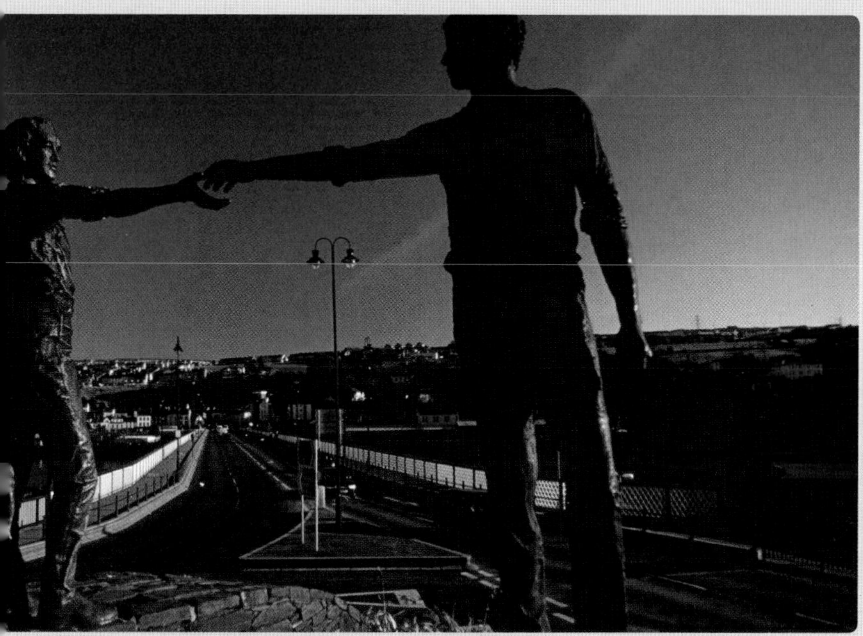

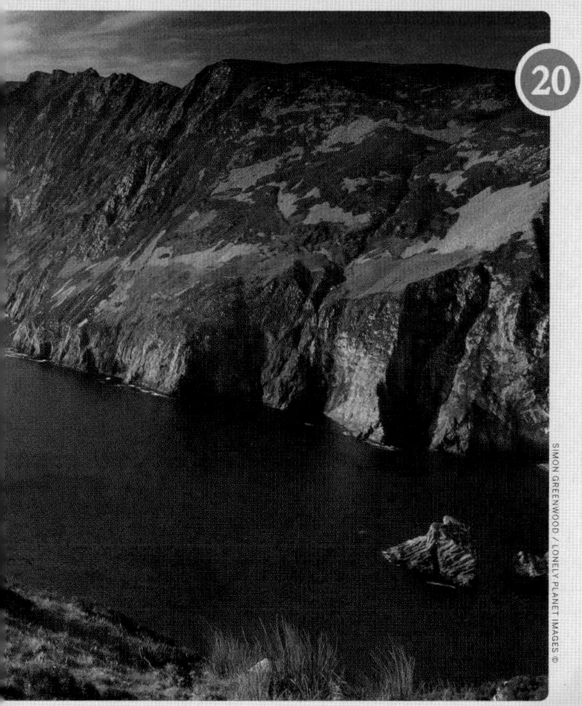

20 Slieve League, County Donegal

The Cliffs of Moher may be more famous and get all the tourist kudos, but the cliffs at Slieve League (p282) in County Donegal are taller – the highest in Europe in fact. Sail beneath them aboard a diminutive 12-seater boat, or head up to the top to see the stark, otherworldly rock face tumbling into the Atlantic Ocean.

Monasterboice, County Louth

21

Home to two of the finest Celtic High Crosses in the country, an imposing round tower and a pair of church ruins, the remains of the 5th-century monastery at Monasterboice (p135) have retained the air of monastic stillness that once encouraged the contemplative life.

High Cross, Monasterboice cemetery

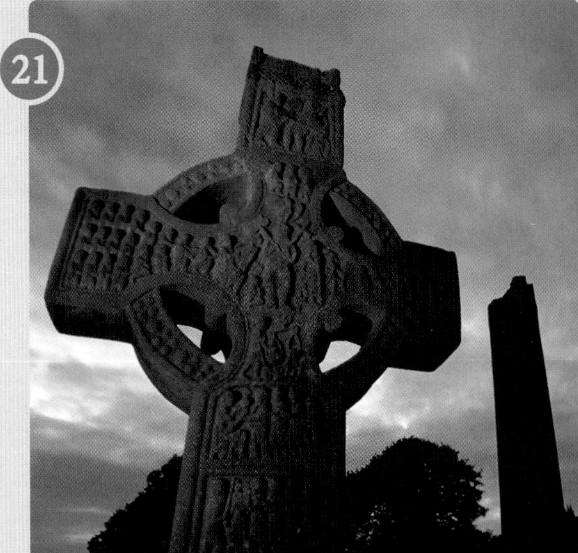

22

Ardmore, County Waterford

The quiet seaside village of Ardmore (p164) in County Waterford is blessed by the wide, ranging arc of a superb beach, a magnificent headland that makes for a fabulous hike and one of the finest hotels in the country. And all of this beauty remains largely undiscovered!

Kinsale, County Cork

Made famous by the ill-fated attempts of a Spanish fleet to land here in 1601, Kinsale's (p191) reputation today is more gourmet than gunships. Its narrow, winding streets are home to some of the country's best eateries, from mouth-watering pub grub to simply exquisite fish restaurants

23

The Best... Places for Food

DUBLIN
The capital's range of cuisines is the best in the country. (p84)

BELFAST
From pub grub to gourmet feasts, Belfast's foodie rep is growing. (p313)

CORK CITY
Gourmet capital of Ireland, Cork is renowned for its emphasis on local produce. (p187)

KINSALE
Kinsale has two of the best seafood restaurants in Ireland – although the food is superb everywhere else, too. (p198)

DUNGARVAN
Great farmers' markets provide local restaurateurs with the raw ingredients to fashion their magic. (p163)

Killarney National Park, County Kerry

Surrounding the peaty waters of three stunning lakes is the equally beautiful expanse of Killarney National Park (p200), 10,000-odd hectares of such beauty that they've gotten the Unesco stamp of protection. Inside, you'll find castle ruins, stately homes, restorative walks and Ireland's only wild herd of red deer. Ross Castle, Killarney National Park

The Best... Places to Stay

CLIFF HOUSE HOTEL
Modern refurb of an old hotel that has been an unqualified success. (p165)

PARKNASILLA RESORT & SPA
Fab setting and top-class service since 1895. (p210)

NUMBER 31
Modernist style and Georgian elegance combine for the perfect stay. (p81)

HOUSE HOTEL
Boutique style and a friendly welcome in Galway City. (p231)

RATHMULLAN HOUSE
Large and luxurious country house by a lake. (p287)

24

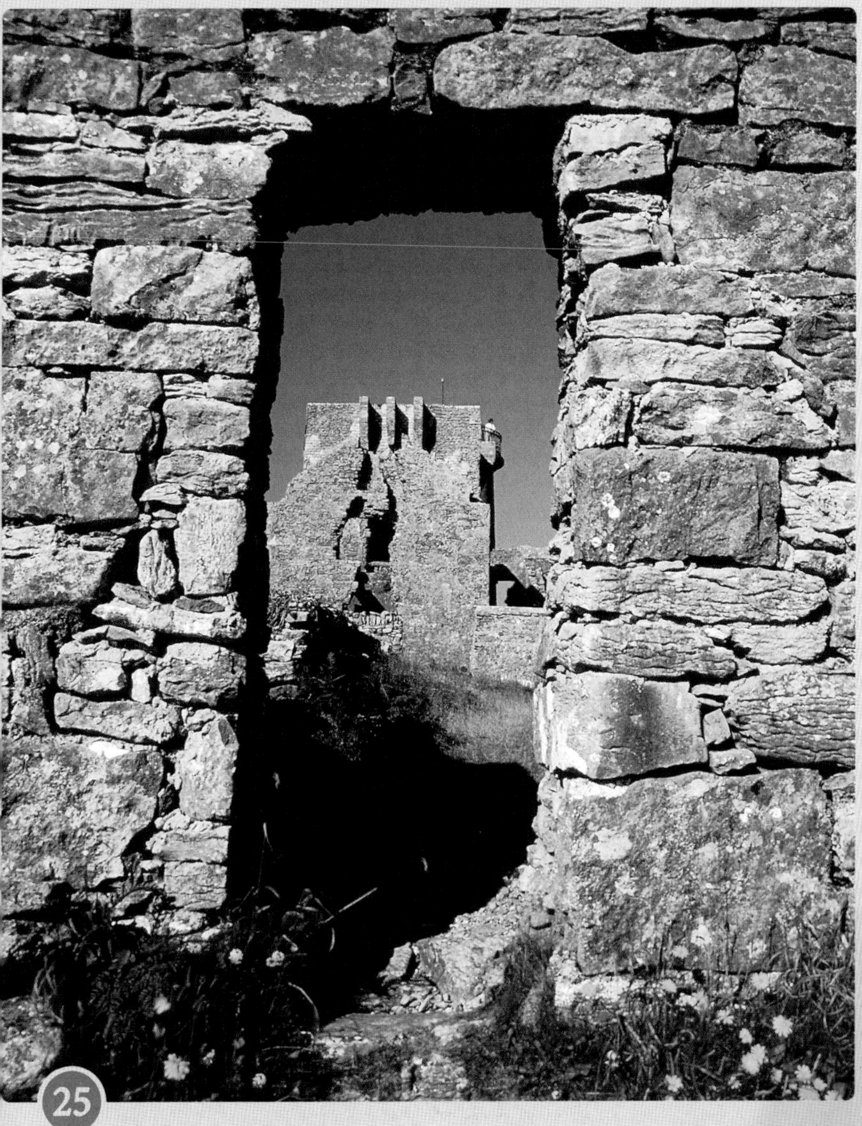

25

Dún Aengus, Aran Islands, County Galway

Perched perilously at the edge of a wind- and ocean-lashed cliff, the Iron Age fort of Dún Aengus (p237) is a tribute to the imagination, forbearance and building skills of its Celtic constructors. It has withstood both time and weather to remain standing after 2000 years.

Ireland's Top Itineraries

Dublin & Around Capital Highlights

5 DAYS

Short on time? Dublin has enough to entertain you for at least three days, leaving you two to devote to day trips from the capital – even on a quick trip here you'll see some of the country's top highlights.

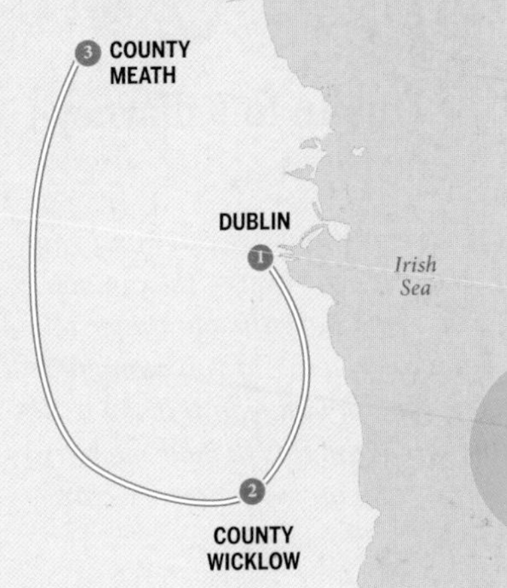

1 Dublin (p62)

Start with the city's big hitters – Trinity College, the **Book of Kells** and the **Guinness Storehouse**. Then, take in a collection or two: the **Chester Beatty Library** is worth an hour at least, as is the **National Museum – Archaeology & History**. On day two, amble through St Stephen's Green and Merrion Square before checking out the **National Gallery**; if you're with kids, skip it in favour of the **National History Museum** just down the road. In the afternoon, head west and visit the **Irish Museum of Modern Art** and/or the fabulous **Kilmainham Gaol**. On day three, explore the north side of the city – a walk down O'Connell St will lead you to the **Dublin City Gallery – Hugh Lane**. In the evening, take in a performance at either the **Abbey Theatre** or the **Gate**. All the while, be sure to sample the inside of one of the city's traditional **pubs**.

DUBLIN ➔ GLENDALOUGH

One hour Along M11, then right on R755
Four hours Organised bus tour from Dublin Tourism, includes Powerscourt

Forest covered in hoar frost, Glendalough (p112), County Wicklow

2 County Wicklow (p110)

Immediately south of Dublin is the wild countryside of County Wicklow. If you only have one day, we recommend a guided tour – you'll visit the county's showpiece attractions and be back in time for dinner. Top of the pile are the monastic ruins at **Glendalough** and the broad expanse of **Powerscourt House and Gardens** on the edge of the village of Enniskerry; along the way, you'll pass through the beautiful Wicklow Mountains.

DUBLIN ➔ BRÚ NA BÓINNE

One hour Along M1, left on N51 **Four hours** Organised bus tour from Dublin Tourism

3 County Meath (p125)

On day five, head north into County Meath and prehistory by visiting the stunning Neolithic passage grave complex of **Brú na Bóinne**, which predate Stonehenge and the pyramids of Egypt. If you're on an organised tour, you can also visit **Tara**, where the high kings of Ireland resided in Celtic times, and the **Battle of the Boyne site**, where the bloody showdown in 1690 between Protestant and Catholic forces would determine the course of Irish history for the next 300 years.

Dublin to Killarney
Ireland in a Nutshell

If you've only got five days and you must see the best of the country, you won't have time to linger too long anywhere – if you manage it correctly though, you'll leave with the top highlights in your memory and on your memory card.

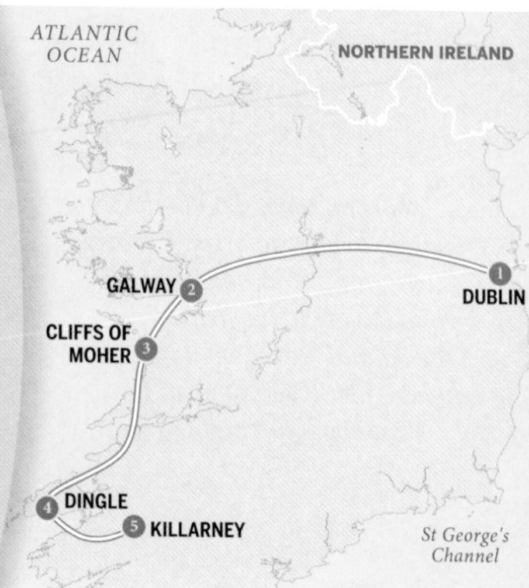

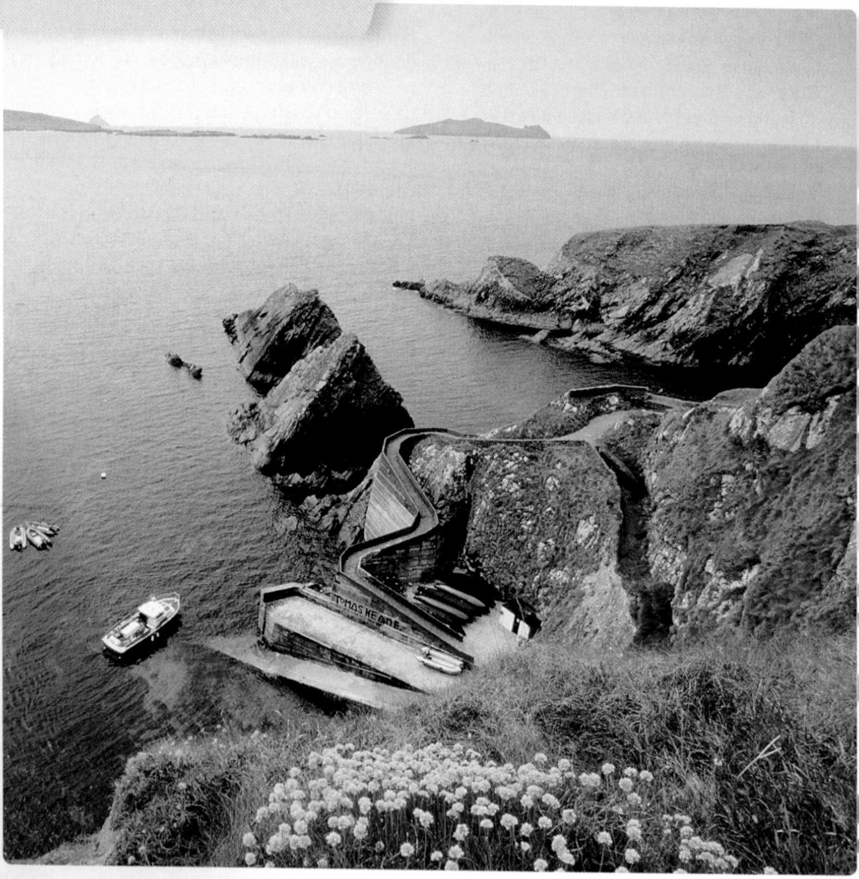

1 Dublin (p62)

A one-day whistle-stop tour of the capital should include visits to **Trinity College** and the **Book of Kells**, the **National Museum – Archaeology & History** and the **Guinness Storehouse**, although make sure you also sample a pint of Guinness in one of the city's collection of superb **pubs**.

DUBLIN ➲ GALWAY

Three hours Along M6 **Three hours, 30 minutes** From Dublin's Busaras to Galway Bus Station **Three hours** From Dublin's Heuston Station to Galway's Ceannt Station

2 Galway (p230)

On day two, cross the island and make for the capital of the west, **Galway City** – the journey should take no longer than three hours. Once settled in, take a drive into Connemara: you won't get far, but the drive to **Oughterard** will give you more than a taste of Connemara's stunning beauty. In the late afternoon, return to Galway and soak in the city's aesthetic delights: a meal followed by a drink (or four) and a live *céilidh* (session of traditional music and dancing) in a traditional old pub like **Tig Cóilí**.

GALWAY ➲ CLIFFS OF MOHER

One hour Along N18 **80 minutes** From Galway Bus Station to Ennis Bus Station **80 minutes** From Galway's Ceannt Station to Ennis Station

3 Cliffs of Moher (p251)

On day three, go south, through the **Burren** towards the **Cliffs of Moher**, where the crowds are a small price to pay for some of the most stunning views you'll see anywhere. A good base for the evening is **Ennis**, County Clare's largest town, where you'll find decent hotels and some excellent music bars – we recommend **Cíaran's Bar**, unassuming by day but it is livened up by traditional music at night.

CLIFFS OF MOHER ➲ DINGLE

Two hours, 30 minutes Along N18 to Limerick, N21 to Tralee and N86 to Dingle

4 Dingle (p211)

Moving south again, cross into County Kerry through the beautiful **Connor Pass** and make for **Dingle**, on its eponymous peninsula. The town itself has plenty to keep you there, but it would be a shame to miss the peninsula itself, especially **Slea Head** and its stunning prehistoric monuments – not to mention the views!

DINGLE ➲ KILLARNEY

80 minutes Along N86 to Tralee and N22 to Killarney

5 Killarney (p196)

On day five, head south once more to storied **Killarney**, which you should use as a base for the equally renowned **Ring of Kerry**, a much-trafficked loop around the Iveragh Peninsula. By day's end you should feel exhausted and in need of another holiday; the good news is that there's plenty more to see and do in Ireland when you next return.

Slea Head (p214), Dingle Peninsula, County Kerry

Dublin to Clare & Galway
East to West

Ten days is ample time to explore the country's midriff from east to west, beginning in Dublin and wending your way to the west coast, where Galway, Connemara and the natural and musical bounty of County Clare awaits.

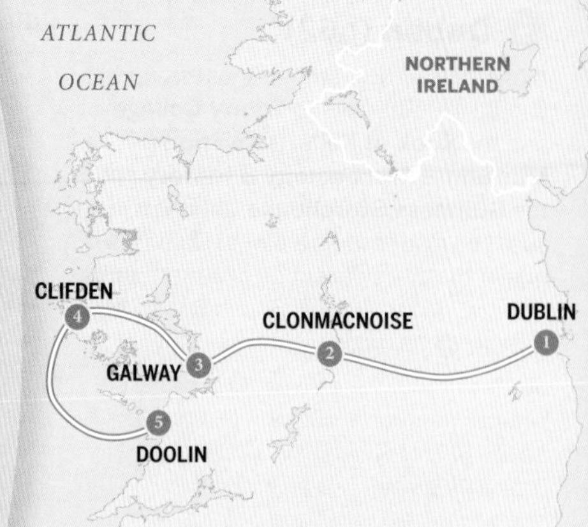

1 Dublin (p62)

Spend a couple of days in the capital visiting **Trinity College** and the **Book of Kells**, the **National Museum – Archaeology & History** and the **Guinness Storehouse**. On day two, be sure to visit the **Chester Beatty Library** and **St Patrick's Cathedral** before visiting the neighbouring attractions of the **Irish Museum of Modern Art** and **Kilmainham Gaol**.

DUBLIN ➔ CLONMACNOISE

90 minutes Along M4 and M6

2 Clonmacnoise (p242)

As you move westwards across the midlands, stop at the Neolithic passage graves at **Loughcrew** in County Meath, rarely visited but fascinating nonetheless. Then head for the 6th-century ruins of **Clonmacnoise**, majestically positioned overlooking the mighty Shannon – a fitting location for the country's most important monastic site. From here, cross into County Galway and head for Galway City.

CLONMACNOISE ➔ GALWAY

50 minutes Along M6

3 Galway (p230)

In **Galway City**, you can shop for Claddagh rings, enjoy the street life around Shop St and the Spanish Arch and, most memorably, the nightlife in one of the city's collection of outstanding traditional bars, where you will hear some terrific tunes. It's also the perfect base from which to explore Connemara and North Clare.

GALWAY ➔ CLIFDEN

75 minutes Along N59 **90 minutes** From Galway Bus Station to Clifden

Saturday market, Galway (p230)

4 Clifden (p239)

Head west, into the wilds of **Connemara**, exploring seaside villages like **Roundstone**, driving through scenic wonderlands like the **Lough Inagh Valley**, and sneaking some R & R in Victorian **Clifden** before perhaps making a daytrip to the Aran Islands. **Inishmór** is the most popular of the islands thanks to the presence of the prehistoric fort of Dún Aengus, but **Inishmaan** is just as beautiful if not nearly as visited.

CLIFDEN ➔ DOOLIN

75 minutes Along N18 to Kilcolgan and N67 to Doolin **90 minutes** From Galway Bus Station to Doolin Hostel **90 minutes** From Inishmór (Aran Islands)

5 Doolin (p254)

From the Aran Islands, you can hop on a boat across to **Doolin**, which is the perfect spot to begin exploring County Clare. If you're looking for authentic traditional music, Doolin, along with other villages like **Ennistymon** and **Miltown Malbay**, are some of the best places in the country to hear some outstanding musicians. Clare's other attractions are geographic: the **Cliffs of Moher** are justifiably one of the country's outstanding tourist attractions, while the lunar-like landscape of the **Burren** is a haven for birdlife.

Belfast to Donegal
Northern Delights

One of the benefits of a more peaceful Northern Ireland is that the province has been able to showcase its outstanding visitor attractions and superb scenery. Worth including on your travels is County Donegal, one of Ireland's most beautiful counties and a favourite with vacationing northerners.

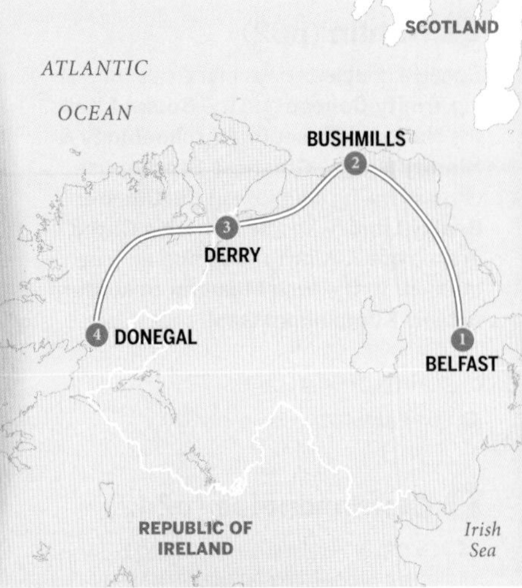

1 Belfast (p306)

Start in **Belfast**, where you should take a Black Taxi tour of West Belfast and then a boat tour to visit the docks (including the Titanic docks) before settling in to one of the city's top hotels. You should also be sure to pay a visit to one of the city's famed Victorian pubs – the most famous of them is the **Crown Liquor Saloon**. On your second day, visit the **Ulster Transport Museum** and the **Ulster Folk Museum** in the town of Holywood, just outside Belfast.

BELFAST ➔ BUSHMILLS

70 minutes Along Antrim Coast **Three hours** From Belfast Europa Bus Station via Portstewart, Portrush & Antrim Coast

2 Bushmills (p318)

Head north toward the Antrim Coast, visiting **Cushendun** before challenging your vertigo with a crossing of the **Carrick-a-Rede Rope Bridge** – it's a short but nail-biting walk across the bridge but the views are worth it. Nearby is the Unesco World Heritage **Giant's Causeway** – it shouldn't be missed by any visitor to Northern Ireland – and, just beyond it, the fascinating village of **Bushmills**, home to the famous distillery.

BUSHMILLS ➔ DERRY

One hour Along B17 to Coleraine and A2 to Derry **Two hours** Bushmills via Coleraine to Derry Foyle St

3 Derry (p322)

Derry City should be your next stop, where you should walk the city's 17th-century walls before exploring its more recent past with a visit to the Bogside neighbourhood, home to some of the most famous murals in Northern Ireland and a powerful example of the efforts of urban regeneration. Be sure to step in to the **Museum of Free Derry** for a full-bodied history of how the Troubles affected this storied district.

DERRY ➔ DONEGAL

One hour Along A38 to Lifford and N15 to Donegal Town **90 minutes** Derry Foyle St to Abbey Hotel, Donegal Town

4 Donegal (p277)

Cross the invisible border into the Republic by visiting County Donegal. Your first stop should be the **Inishowen Peninsula**; as you venture further west, the savage beauty of the land becomes ever more apparent as you skirt the coastline past handsome **Dunfanaghy**, imposing **Mount Errigal** and the beguiling **Poisoned Glen**. In Donegal's southwestern corner there are the surfing meccas of **Rossnowlagh** and **Bundoran**, as well as the weaving centre of **Ardara**, where you can observe genuine Irish woollens and tweeds being fashioned in front of your very eyes – and then you can buy them. Near here – through the lovely Glen Gesh Pass – are the stunning sea cliffs at **Slieve League**, the tallest in Europe.

The Crown Liquor Saloon (p307), Belfast
PHOTOGRAPHER: RICHARD CUMMINS / LONELY PLANET IMAGES ©

Belfast to Dublin

The Long Way Round

This tourist trail takes you past some of Ireland's most famous attractions and through spectacular countryside. It's only about 500km in length, so you could manage it in a few days, but what would be the point of rushing? You won't be disappointed on this route.

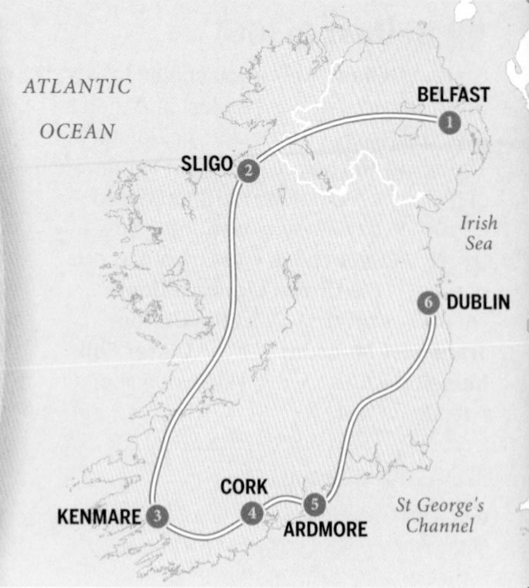

1 Belfast (p306)

Start your loop in **Dublin**, visiting the main attractions before heading north to the mind-blowing Neolithic necropolis at **Brú na Bóinne**, built before the Great Pyramids were even a twinkle in the Pharaoh's eye. Continue north to **Mellifont Abbey**, Ireland's first Cistercian abbey, before crossing the border in to Northern Ireland. Once you've landed in **Belfast**, you should take a Black Taxi tour and celebrate your arrival in one of the city's outstanding collection of Victorian pubs.

BELFAST ➜ SLIGO

Two hours, 30 minutes Along M1, via Enniskillen
Three hours, 30 minutes Belfast Europa Bus Station to Sligo Institute of Technology, via Enniskillen

2 Sligo (p272)

Go northwest along the Antrim Coast to the Unesco World Heritage site, the **Giant's Causeway**, best enjoyed at sunset but wonderful at any time of the day or year. Continue around the stunning coastline of north Donegal, stopping at gorgeous **Dunfanaghy** and then continuing on to beautiful **Glenveagh National Park**. Head south past the mighty sea cliffs of **Slieve League** and in to lively **Sligo**, from where you can climb the Stone Age passage grave **Carrowkeel** for panoramic views of Lough Arrow, or tee off in the shadow of Benbulben at the simply superb **County Sligo Golf Club** at Rosses Point.

SLIGO ➜ KENMARE

Five hours Along N17 & N18 via the Burren (p252), to N71

3 Kenmare (p210)

Make your way to the southwest via **Connemara**, visiting at least one of the **Aran Islands** as you go. Marvel at the **Burren** and check out some lively traditional music in **Doolin** before crossing into County Kerry and setting up base in **Dingle** to explore the **Dingle Peninsula**. Go through **Killarney** on your way round the **Ring of Kerry**, and step offshore and into a different century with a visit to **Skellig Michael**. Make your camp in handsome **Kenmare**, which is not quite as popular as Killarney but that little bit prettier.

Wildflowers on the Beara Peninsula (p196), County Cork
PHOTOGRAPHER: TRISH PUNCH / LONELY PLANET IMAGES ©

KENMARE ➜ CORK

🚗 **90 minutes** Along R569 & N22 🚌 **Four hours** Darcy's in Kenmare to Parnell Place, Cork

4 Cork (p186)

Explore the north side of **Beara Peninsula**, particularly the scenic stretch between Eyeries and Lauragh. Test the county's foodie credentials by buying some black pudding in **Clonakilty** and sampling the fine dining in the gourmet capital of **Kinsale** – a love of seafood is definitely a plus. Wind your way east and explore Ireland's second city, **Cork**, making sure to pay a visit to the Victorian English Market. From Cork, head east to **Midleton** for a picnic and a visit to the **Old Jameson Distillery**.

CORK ➜ ARDMORE

🚗 **Two hours, 45 minutes** Along N25 via Dungarvan (p162) & R676/696

5 Ardmore (p164)

Explore the often-ignored beauty of County Waterford from the handsome seaside village of **Ardmore**. Visit **Dungarvan Castle**, with its unusual 12th-century shell and then pay a visit to the recently renovated **Waterford Museum of Treasures**. Cross the border into County Wexford and explore Irish history in **Enniscorthy** (p156), home of the 1798 Rebellion Centre. Go northwards through Thomastown and visit medieval **Kilkenny**, whose narrow streets are dominated by an imposing castle and cathedral.

ARDMORE ➜ DUBLIN

🚗 **90 minutes** Along M9 🚌 **Two hours, 30 minutes** Ormonde Rd, Kilkenny to Busaras, Dublin 🚆 **Two hours** MacDonagh Station, Kilkenny to Heuston Station, Dublin

6 Dublin (p62)

Visit **Castletown House** in County Kildare before cutting east through the Wicklow Mountains to visit stunning **Glendalough** in the middle of **Wicklow Mountains National Park**. Head back to Dublin and settle in to a well-deserved pint of Guinness at the **Long Hall** to toast the end to your Irish adventure.

Ireland Month by Month

Top Events

Dublin International Film Festival, February

St Patrick's Day, March

Galway Arts Festival, July

Willie Clancy Irish Music Festival, July

Féile An Phobail, August

February

Dublin International Film Festival

Sponsored by Jameson, the island's biggest film festival (www.dubliniff.com) runs during the last two weeks of February, offering a mix of local flicks, arty international films and advance releases of mainstream movies.

March

St Patrick's Day

Ireland erupts into one giant celebration on March 17 (www.stpatricksday.ie), but Dublin throws a five-day party around the parade (attended by 600,000), with gigs and festivities that leaves the city with a giant hangover.

April

Circuit of Ireland International Rally

Northern Ireland's most prestigious rally race – known locally as the 'Circuit' (www.circuitofireland.net) – sees over 130 competitors throttle and turn through some 550km of Northern Ireland and parts of the Republic over two days at Easter.

Irish Grand National

Ireland loves horse racing; the most beloved race, the Grand National (www.fairhouseracecourse.ie), is the showcase of the national hunt season, running at Fairyhouse in County Meath on Easter Monday.

World Irish Dancing Championships

There's far more to Irish dancing than Riverdance. Every April, some

March Face painting, St Patrick's Day parade

PHOTOGRAPHER: IAN CONNELLAN / LONELY PLANET IMAGES ©

4500 competitors from all over the world gather to test their steps and skills against the very best. The location varies from year to year; see www.worldirishdancing.com for details.

May

Cork International Choral Festival

The winners of this, one of Europe's premier choral festivals (www.corkchoral.ie), go on to the Fleischmann International Trophy Competition; it's held over four days from the first Monday of May.

NorthWest 200

Ireland's most famous road race (www.northwest200.org) is also the country's biggest outdoor sporting event; 150,000-plus people line the triangular route to cheer on some of the biggest names in motorcycle racing. Held in mid-May.

Fleadh Nua

The third week of May sees the cream of the traditional music crop come to Ennis, County Clare, for one of the country's most important festivals (www.comhaltas.ie).

June

Cat Laughs

Kilkenny gets very, very funny in early June with the country's premier comedy festival (www.thecatlaughs.com), which draws comedians both known and unknown from the four corners of the globe.

Irish Derby

Racing fans pack their wallets and ladies don their fancy hats for the best flat-race festival in Ireland (www.curragh.ie), run during the first week of the month.

Bloomsday

Edwardian dress and breakfast of 'the inner organs of beast and fowl' are but two of the elements of the Dublin festival celebrating June 16th, the day on which Joyce's *Ulysses* takes place; the real highlight is retracing Leopold Bloom's daily steps.

July

Willie Clancy Irish Music Festival

Inaugurated to celebrate the memory of a famed local piper, this exceptional festival of traditional music sees the world's best players show up for gigs, pub sessions and workshops over 10 days in Miltown Malbay, County Clare (for more information, see p250).

Galway Arts Festival

Music, drama and a host of artistic endeavours are on the menu at the most important arts festival in the country, which sees Galway go merriment mad for the last two weeks of the month.

Galway Film Fleadh

Irish and international releases make up the program at one of the country's premier film festivals, held in early July.

Oxegen

Ireland's answer to Glastonbury is a three-day supergig in mid-July at Punchestown Racecourse in County Kildare, featuring some of the big names in rock and pop.

Killarney Summerfest

From kayaking to street theatre and gigs by international artists, this weeklong extravaganza (www.killarneysummerfest.com) in late July has something for everybody.

August

Féile An Phobail, West Belfast

The name translates simply as the 'people's festival' and it is just that: Europe's largest community arts festival takes place on the Falls Rd in West Belfast over two weeks.

Fleadh Cheoil nah Éireann

The mother of all Irish music festivals (www.comhaltas.ie) attracts in excess of 250,000 music-lovers/revellers to whichever town is playing host (usually at the end of the month) – there's some great music amid the drinking.

Galway Races

The biggest horse racing festival west of the Shannon is not just about the horses, it's a celebration of Irish culture, sporting gambles and elaborate hats (p235).

Mary From Dungloe

Ireland's second-most-important beauty pageant takes place in Dungloe, County Donegal, at the beginning of the month – although it's really an excuse for a giant party, the young women genuinely want to be crowned the year's 'Mary'.

Puck Fair

Ireland's quirkiest premise for a festival: crown a goat king and celebrate for three days. Quirky idea, brilliant festival; it takes place in Killorglin (p205) in mid-August.

Rose of Tralee

The foremost Irish beauty pageant (www.roseoftralee.ie) sees wannabe Roses plucked from Irish communities throughout the world competing for the ultimate prize. For everyone else, it's a big party.

September

Galway International Oyster Festival

Galway kicks off its oyster season with a festival (www.galwayoysterfest.com) celebrating the local catch. Music and beer have been the accompaniment since its inception in 1953.

Dublin Fringe Festival

Upwards of 100 different performances take the stage, the street, the bar and the car in the fringe festival (www.fringefest.com) that is unquestionably more innovative than the main theatre festival that follows it.

All-Ireland Finals

The second and fourth Sundays of the month see the finals of the hurling and Gaelic football championships, respectively, with 80,000-plus thronging into Dublin's

Croke Park for the biggest sporting days of the year.

October

Dublin Theatre Festival

The most prestigious theatre festival (www.dublintheatrefestival.com) in the country sees new work and new versions of old work staged in theatres and venues throughout the capital.

Wexford Opera Festival

Opera fans gather in the atmospheric grounds of Johnstown Castle to enjoy Ireland's premier festival of opera (www.wexfordopera.com), which eschews the big hits in favour of lesser-known works.

Cork Jazz Festival

Ireland's best-known jazz festival (www.corkjazzfestival.com) sees Cork taken over by over 1000 musicians and their multitude of fans during the last weekend of the month.

Belfast Festival at Queen's

Northern Ireland's top arts festival (www.belfastfestival.com) attracts performers from all over the world for the second half of the month; everything from visual arts to dance is on offer.

December

Christmas

This is a quiet affair in the countryside, though on 26 December (St Stephen's Day), the ancient custom of Wren Boys is re-enacted, most notably in Dingle, County Kerry, when groups of children dress up and go about singing hymns.

Far left: September Hurling stick and ball
Below: July All dressed up for the Galway Races

PHOTOGRAPHERS: (FAR LEFT) OLIVIER CIRENDINI / LONELY PLANET IMAGES © (LEFT) HOLGER LEUE / LONELY PLANET IMAGES ©

What's New

For this new edition of Discover Ireland, *our authors hunted down the fresh, the revamped, the transformed, the hot and the happening. Here are some of our favourites. For up-to-the-minute recommendations, see lonelyplanet.com/ireland.*

1 **NATIONAL MUSEUM OF IRELAND – NATURAL HISTORY** Following the collapse of its central staircase, the 150-year-old 'Dead Zoo' was forced to close for a major revamp. Thankfully, it has now reopened and we can gawk once again at the two-million-odd exhibits from all over the world in a grand old building that doesn't seem to have changed much since Dr Livingstone cut the ribbon in 1857 (p73).

2 **TITANIC QUARTER** The long overdue construction of the 'iconic visitor attraction', centred on the construction of the world's most famous sunken ship, is scheduled for completion in April 2012 (p307).

3 **WATERFORD MUSEUM OF TREASURES** The interactive museum detailing Waterford's 1000-year history moved to the newly renovated Bishop's Palace, an 18th-century stunner on the Mall (p158).

4 **PEACE BRIDGE** An elegant new footbridge is the most visible sign of Derry City's makeover, just in time for its starring role as UK City of Culture in 2013 (p322).

5 **THE LITTLE MUSEUM OF DUBLIN** Excellent new museum that aims to serve as a 'biography of the city' and whose myriad exhibits have all been donated by Dubliners (p73).

6 **TEMPLE HOUSE FESTIVAL** A three-day festival featuring an eclectic line-up of music, arts, workshops and woodland crafts is the west's answer to Electric Picnic (p273).

Get Inspired

Books

- **Dubliners** (James Joyce, 1914) Classic short stories about Joyce's hometown.
- **The Book of Evidence** (John Banville, 1989) Psychological portrait of a killer, based on true events.
- **The Butcher Boy** (Patrick McCabe, 1992) Boy retreats into a violent fantasy life as his small-town world collapses.
- **Paddy Clarke Ha Ha Ha** (Roddy Doyle, 1993) Booker Prize winner about the trials of a Dublin child.
- **Angela's Ashes** (Frank McCourt, 1996) Legendary memoir of working-class Limerick.

Films

- **Bloody Sunday** (Paul Greengrass, 2002) Superb film about the events of 30 January 1972.
- **The Dead** (John Huston, 1987) Based on Joyce's fantastic *Dubliners* story.
- **Garage** (Lenny Abrahamson, 2007) A lonely man attempts to come out of his shell.
- **The Crying Game** (Neil Jordan, 1992) A classic that explores violence, gender and the IRA.
- **The Magdalene Sisters** (Peter Mullan, 2002) Harrowing portrayal of life in the infamous asylum.

Popular Music

- **Boy** (U2) Best Irish debut album ever?
- **I Do Not Want What I Haven't Got** (Sinead O'Connor) Powerful album by a superb singer.
- **Becoming a Jackal** (Villagers) The band's knockout debut album.
- **St Dominic's Preview** (Van Morrison) Lesser known but still brilliant.
- **Live & Dangerous** (Thin Lizzy) Excellent live album by beloved Irish rockers.

Websites

- **Fáilte Ireland** (www.discoverireland.ie) The Republic's tourist site has practical info and a huge accommodation database.
- **Irish Times** (www.irishtimes.com) Ireland's newspaper of record.
- **Lonely Planet** (www.lonelyplanet.com) Comprehensive travel information and advice.
- **Northern Ireland Tourism** (www.discovernorthernireland.com) Official tourist information site, with activities and accommodation.

Short on time?

This list will give you an instant insight into the country.

Read *Angela's Ashes* painted a sorry picture of Limerick but did wonders for the author!

Watch *Bloody Sunday*, Paul Greengrass' documentary-style drama is gripping.

Listen *Becoming a Jackal* is a great record by Conor O'Brien, one of Ireland's top contemporary musicians.

Log on www.discoverireland.ie for everything you need for your Irish holiday.

James Joyce statue, St Stephen's Green (p74), Dublin

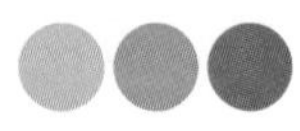

Need to Know

Currency

Republic of Ireland: Euro (€); Northern Ireland: Pound Sterling (£)

Language

English, Irish

ATMs

Widely available.

Credit Cards

Widely accepted.

Visas

Not required for most citizens of Europe, Australia, NZ, USA and Canada.

Mobile Phones

Most foreign phones work in Ireland (beware roaming charges). Local SIM cards cost from €10; SIM and a basic phone from €40.

Wi-Fi

Free in many hotels, cafes and restaurants; charges apply for trains and airports.

Internet Access

Most towns have an internet cafe (€4–8 per hour).

Driving

Drive on the left (steering wheel on the right). Most hire cars have manual gears.

Tipping

Not required, but 10–15% is expected for good service.

When to Go

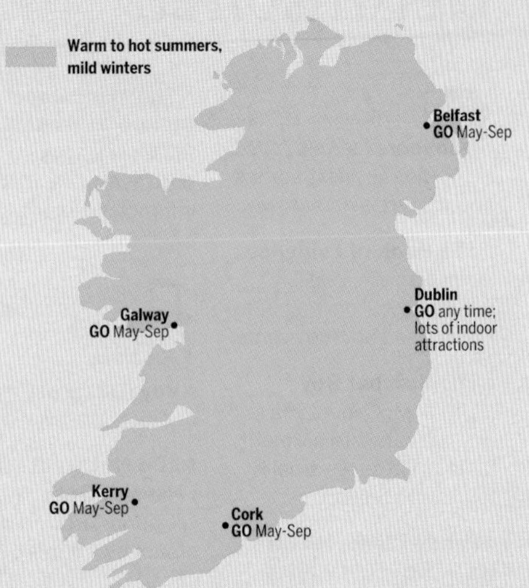

High Season

(Jun–Aug)

- Ireland's weather at its best.
- Accommodations rates at their highest (especially August).
- Tourist peak in Dublin, Kerry, southern and western coasts.

Shoulder

(Easter to end May, mid-Sep to end Oct)

- Weather often good, sun and rain in May. 'Indian summers' often warm September.
- Crowds and accommodation rates drop off.

Low Season

(Nov–Feb)

- Reduced opening hours October to Easter; some places shut down.
- Cold, wet, foggy weather throughout the country.
- Sights in big cities (Dublin, Cork, Galway, Belfast) operate as normal.

Advance Planning

- **Two months ahead** Book accommodation and any special activities.
- **One month ahead** Book your rental car and make reservations for top-end restaurants.
- **Two weeks ahead** Confirm opening times and prices for visitor attractions.
- **One week ahead** Check the weather forecast (but plan for it to be wrong).

Your Daily Budget

Budget Less than €60

- Dorm beds €12–20
- Cheap meals in cafes and pubs €6–12
- Intercity bus travel €12–25 for 200km journey
- Pint €4.50

Midrange €60–120

- Midrange hotel or B&B €40–100 (Dublin €60–130) per double room
- Main course in midrange restaurant €10–18
- Car rental from €40 per day
- Three-hour train journey €65

Top End Over €120

- Accommodation in four-star hotel from €150
- Three-course meal in good restaurant around €50 per person
- Round of golf at respected course from €80 midweek

Exchange Rates

Australia	A$1	€0.75
Canada	C$1	€0.71
Japan	¥100	€0.94
New Zealand	NZ$1	€0.57
UK	£1	€1.15
USA	US$1	€0.72

For current exchange rates see www.xe.com

What to Bring

- **Good walking shoes** Rubber soles and weatherproof uppers an advantage.
- **Rain jacket** It really could rain at any minute.
- **UK/Ireland electrical adapter** Those three-pin plugs are quite devilish!
- **A good sense of humour** The Irish express affection by making fun of each other – and you.
- **A hollow leg** How else can you last the night in a pub?

Arriving in Ireland

- **Dublin Airport**

Private coach Every 15 minutes to city centre (€7).

Taxi Allow 30–45 minutes to city centre (€20–25).

- **Dun Laoghaire Ferry Port**

Bus Public bus about 45 minutes to city centre.

DART (suburban rail) About 25 minutes to city centre.

- **Dublin Port Terminal**

Bus Timed to meet arrivals and departures (€2.50).

Getting Around

- **Air** Besides the main hubs, Donegal, Kerry, Knock and Waterford have regional airports.
- **Bus** Bus Éireann has the most extensive network; local operators offer regular – and often cheaper – regional services.
- **Train** The train network is limited and expensive, but the easiest way to travel between major urban centres.
- **Car** Your own car will let you reach those out-of-the-way spots; petrol is expensive and traffic can be challenging.

Accommodation

- **B&Bs** Ubiquitous and varying in standard. Many rural ones accept only cash.
- **Guesthouses** Large family homes with boutique-hotel comfort. Most accept credit cards.
- **Hotels** Ranging from local pubs to five-star castles; priced accordingly. Business chain hotels are clean, comfortable and characterless.

Be Forewarned

- **Public holidays** Banks and businesses close on bank holidays; *everything* (including pubs) closes on Good Friday and Christmas Day in the Republic; not much opens on 26 December and New Year's Day. Avoid Northern Ireland on 12 July, the climax of the Loyalist marching season.
- **Pub restrictions** Under 16s aren't allowed in pubs after 7pm, even if accompanied by parents (enforced less strictly in rural areas).
- **Traffic jams** A fact of life in big towns and cities during rush hours.

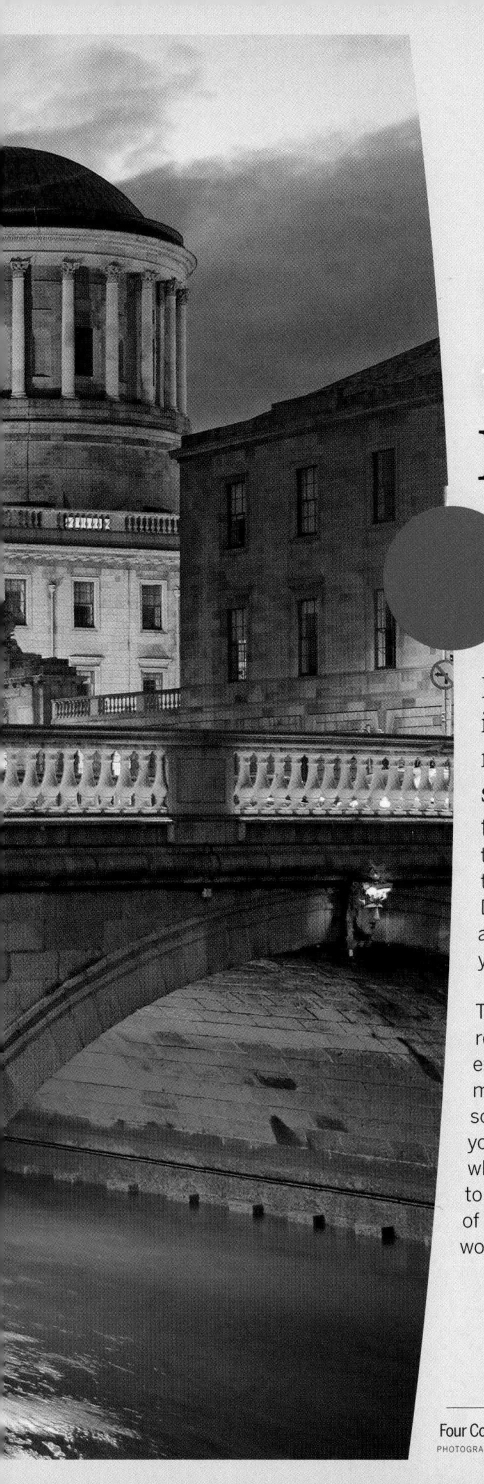

Dublin

Form is temporary, but class is permanent: the good times may have gone, but Dublin still knows how to have a good time. From its music, art and literature to the legendary nightlife that has inspired those same musicians, artists and writers, Dublin has always known how to have fun and does it with deadly seriousness. As you'll soon find out.

There are world-class museums, superb restaurants and the best collection of entertainment in the country: from rock music to classical concerts there's always something on, and should there not be, you'll always have its 1000-or-so pubs to while away an evening. And should you wish to get away from it all, the city has a handful of seaside towns at its edges that make for wonderful day trips.

Four Courts (p79) and bridge over the River Liffey, Dublin

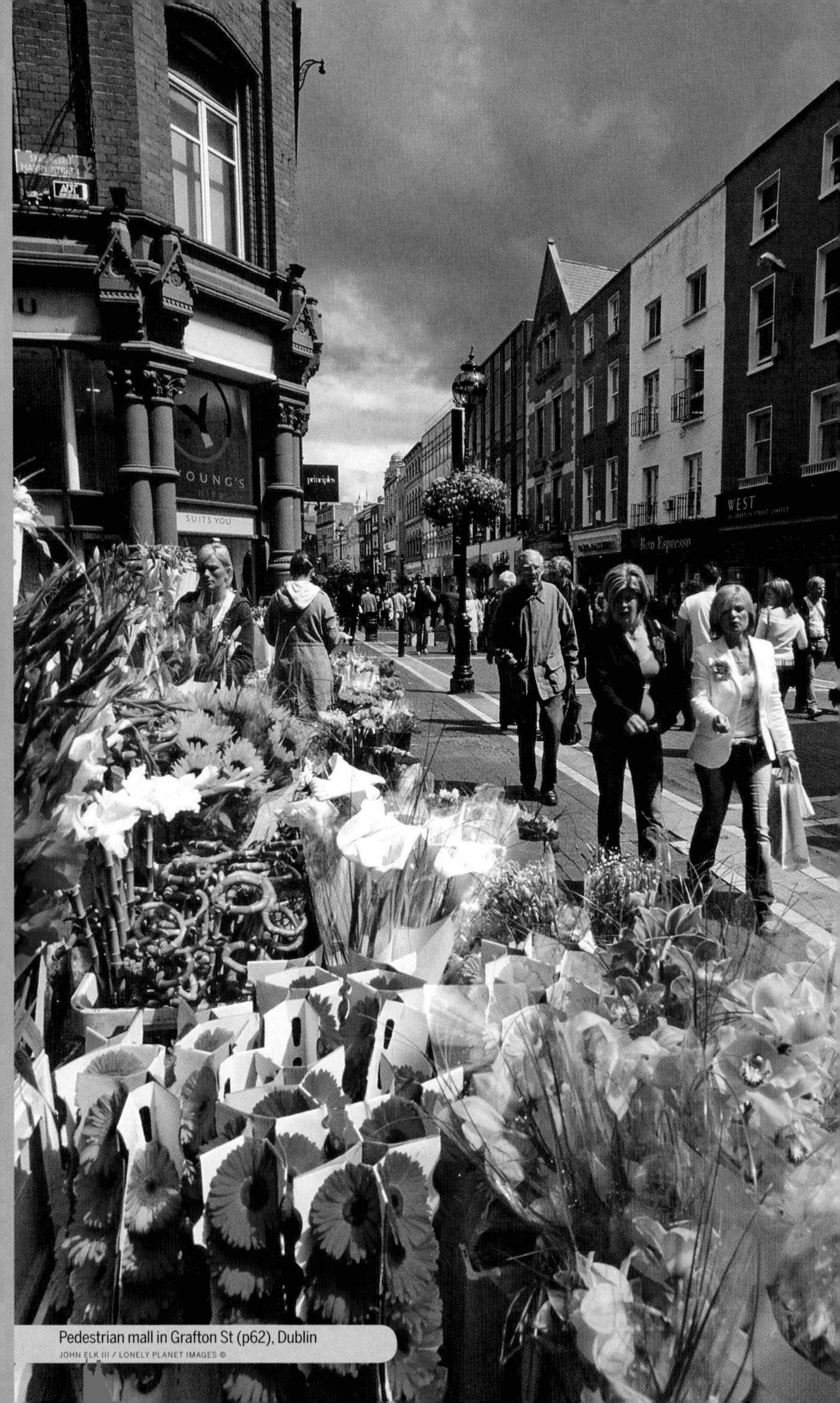

Pedestrian mall in Grafton St (p62), Dublin

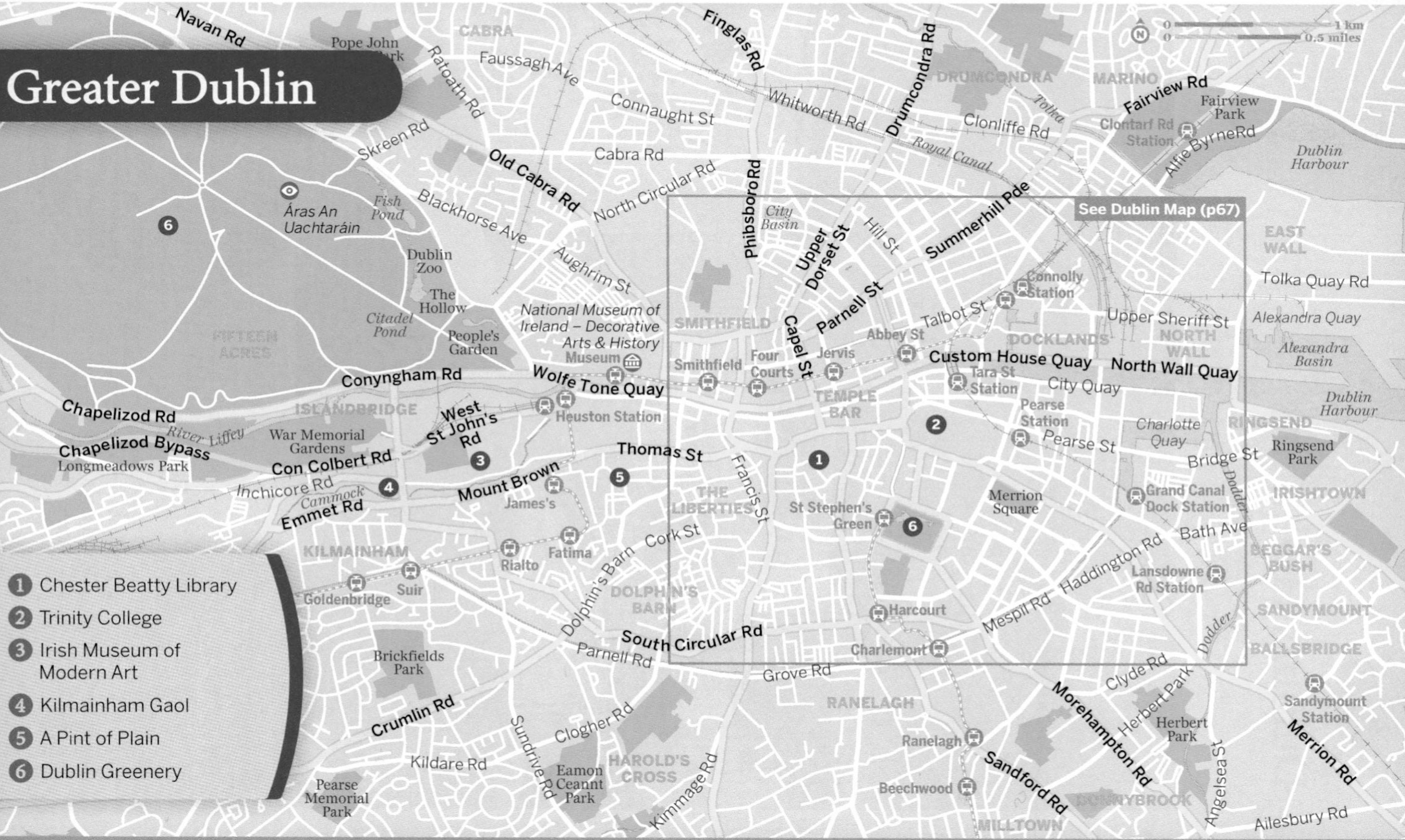
Greater Dublin
1 Chester Beatty Library
2 Trinity College
3 Irish Museum of Modern Art
4 Kilmainham Gaol
5 A Pint of Plain
6 Dublin Greenery
See Dublin Map (p67)
0 1 km
0 0.5 miles
Navan Rd
Finglas Rd
Drumcondra Rd
Fairview Rd
Fairview Park
Clontarf Rd Station
Alfie Byrne Rd
Dublin Harbour
Pope John Paul
CABRA
DRUMCONDRA
MARINO
Ratoath Rd
Faussagh Ave
Connaught St
Whitworth Rd
Clonliffe Rd
Tolka
Royal Canal
Skreen Rd
Old Cabra Rd
Cabra Rd
North Circular Rd
Phibsboro Rd
Blackhorse Ave
Áras An Uachtaráin
Fish Pond
Dublin Zoo
The Hollow
Citadel Pond
People's Garden
FIFTEEN ACRES
Aughrim St
National Museum of Ireland – Decorative Arts & History Museum
City Basin
Upper Dorset St
Hill St
Summerhill Pde
Parnell St
Capel St
EAST WALL
Tolka Quay Rd
Connolly Station
Talbot St
Upper Sheriff St
Alexandra Quay
Alexandra Basin
SMITHFIELD
Smithfield
Four Courts
Jervis
Abbey St
DOCKLANDS
NORTH WALL
Custom House Quay
North Wall Quay
Conyngham Rd
Wolfe Tone Quay
Tara St Station
City Quay
TEMPLE BAR
Chapelizod Rd
ISLANDBRIDGE
West St John's Rd
Heuston Station
Pearse Station
Charlotte Quay
RINGSEND
Ringsend Park
River Liffey
War Memorial Gardens
Chapelizod Bypass
Longmeadows Park
Con Colbert Rd
Thomas St
Francis St
Pearse St
Bridge St
Dodder
Inchicore Rd
Cammock
Mount Brown
James's
THE LIBERTIES
St Stephen's Green
Merrion Square
Grand Canal Dock Station
IRISHTOWN
Emmet Rd
Cork St
Bath Ave
KILMAINHAM
Rialto
Fatima
Haddington Rd
Lansdowne Rd Station
BEGGAR'S BUSH
Goldenbridge
Suir
Dolphin's Barn
DOLPHIN'S BARN
Harcourt
Mespil Rd
SANDYMOUNT
South Circular Rd
Parnell Rd
Charlemont
BALLSBRIDGE
Brickfields Park
Grove Rd
Clyde Rd
RANELAGH
Crumlin Rd
Sundrive Rd
Clogher Rd
Morehampton Rd
Herbert Park
Sandymount Station
Merrion Rd
Ranelagh
Kildare Rd
Eamon Ceannt Park
HAROLD'S CROSS
Kimmage Rd
Sandford Rd
Beechwood
DONNYBROOK
Angelsea St
Pearse Memorial Park
MILLTOWN
Ailesbury Rd

Dublin's Highlights

1

Chester Beatty Library

The Chester Beatty Library was originally the private library of its founder, Alfred Chester Beatty: today it is one of Ireland's national cultural icons. A selection of the Library's remarkable treasures is on display in two permanent exhibition galleries, and occasional temporary exhibitions are held throughout the year. Eastern Religions display at the Chester Beatty Library

Need to Know

Best Time to Visit Open every day from May to September; closed Monday rest of year. **How Long Will I Need?** A couple of hours. **Top Tips** Great gift shop. **For further coverage, see p81.**

Local Knowledge

Chester Beatty Library Don't Miss List

BY FIONNUALA CROKE, DIRECTOR OF THE CHESTER BEATTY LIBRARY

1 SACRED TRADITIONS GALLERY

This 2nd floor gallery exhibits sacred texts, illuminated manuscripts and miniature paintings from Christianity, Islam and Buddhism, with smaller displays on Confucianism, Taoism, Sikhism and Jainism. Of particular note are the biblical papyri, which include some of the earliest copies of the Christian New Testament and other biblical texts.

2 THE ISLAMIC COLLECTION

The Islamic Collections are among the finest in existence. They derive primarily – though not exclusively – from the Arab world of Iran, Turkey and India, and include some of the greatest documents of Islamic art and culture. The Library holds more than 260 Qur'ans and Qur'an fragments dating from the 9th to 19th centuries, which comprises one of the most important collections outside the Middle East.

3 THE ARTS OF THE BOOK EXHIBITION

This permanent exhibition on the 1st floor contains spectacular displays of illustrated manuscripts and printed books from many different cultures. Visitors can view books from the ancient world including Egyptian Books of the Dead, beautifully illuminated European and Islamic manuscripts, Chinese and Japanese painted scrolls and albums and Old Master prints.

4 THE EAST ASIAN EXHIBITION

Of particular beauty here are rare Burmese and Thai manuscripts on the life of the Buddha, a rare collection of inscribed jade books dating from the eighteenth century and the beautifully painted scroll 'The Song of Everlasting Regret' by the seventeenth-century Japanese artist Kano Sansetsu.

5 SILK ROAD CAFÉ

Cafes aren't usually a highlight of a museum visit, but this is the exception – the food is suitably Middle Eastern, and of a very high standard.

Trinity College

Ireland's most prestigious university is also its most beautiful, a 16-hectare masterpiece of Victorian architecture and landscaping. Trinity College (p62) was granted its charter in 1592 by Queen Elizabeth I in the hope that the city's youth would not be 'infected with popery', and indeed it remained exclusively Protestant until 1793. No such exclusions exist today, which has helped cement its reputation as one of the best universities in the world. Regent House entrance to Trinity College on College Green

2

4

Kilmainham Gaol

Ireland's tempestuous and torturous path to independence is vividly documented in the former prison (p75), whose list of (reluctant) residents reads like a roll call of Irish patriots and revolutionaries. A visit here is as close to Irish history as you can get in Dublin, especially when standing in the yard where the leaders of the 1916 Rising were executed.

MARTIN MOOS / LONELY PLANET IMAGES ©

MARTIN MOOS / LONELY PLANET IMAGES ©

Irish Museum of Modern Art 3

Whatever you happen to think of modern art, a visit to the Irish Museum of Modern Art (p76) in Kilmainham should leave you thoroughly satisfied – if not for the magnificent range of contemporary art hanging on its walls, then for the exquisite surroundings of its building, styled after Les Invalides in Paris. It was also once used as a hospital for veterans.

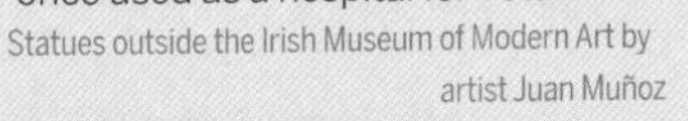

Statues outside the Irish Museum of Modern Art by artist Juan Muñoz

OLIVIER CIRENDINI / LONELY PLANET IMAGES ©

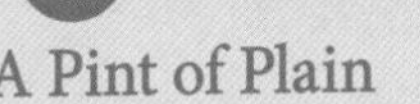

5 A Pint of Plain

Go on, admit it: there's a good likelihood that you came to Dublin in the hope of tasting the magic that is Guinness in its native home. The Guinness Storehouse (p74), on the grounds of the famous brewery, isn't a bad place to start, but a pint is best enjoyed in the surroundings of a good pub – try the Stag's Head (p89) or Kehoe's (p89) on for size.

6 Dublin Greenery

From the well-trodden paths of St Stephen's Green (p74) to the elegant folds of Merrion Square (p75), Dublin's green spaces are more than just a place to breathe some fresh air and revel in the aroma of freshly cut grass; they're the ideal spot to appreciate the grandeur of the Georgian experiment. If you want real green, go west and lose yourself in the massive expanse of Phoenix Park (p90). Jogger in Phoenix Park

Dublin's Best...

Things for Free

- Visit one of Dublin's four national **museums** – entrance is free at all of them.
- Have a picnic in **St Stephen's Green** (p74).
- Explore the wonders of the **Chester Beatty Library** (p81).
- Window-shop on **Grafton St** (p62) – it won't cost you a penny.
- Enjoy sport, walks, museums and a herd of red deer at **Phoenix Park** (p90).

Spots to Wet Your Beak

- **Long Hall** (p89) Tipple in Victorian treasure.
- **Sin É** (p90) For beats and beatniks.
- **Cobblestone** (p91) For fiddles and bodhráns.
- **O'Donoghue's** (p90) For mixing with Dubliners.
- **No Name Bar** (p89) To see and be seen.

Uniquely Dublin

- **Bloomsday** (p82) Get Edwardian every 16 June.
- **Guinness Storehouse** (p74) Home of the world's most famous beer.
- **Ha'Penny Bridge** (p62) Get a snap of Dublin's most iconic bridge.
- **Little Museum of Dublin** (p73) Museum devoted to the city's history.
- **St Patrick's Cathedral** (p75) Visit Jonathan Swift's tomb.

Georgian Classics

- **Leinster House** (p72) Ireland's parliament was once the city's most handsome residence.
- **Custom House** (p79) James Gandon's first Irish masterpiece.
- **Four Courts** (p79) Gandon's greatest building is an appellant's nightmare.
- **Merrion** (p82) The Duke of Wellington's birthplace is now a top hotel.
- **Áras an Uachtaráin** (p90) The official residence of the President inspired the White House.

Left: Interior of St Patrick's Cathedral (p75); **Above:** St Stephen's Green pond (p74)

Need to Know

ADVANCE PLANNING

- **Two months before** Sort out your hotel room.
- **Two weeks before** Work on your hollow leg.
- **One week before** Make restaurant reservations.

RESOURCES

- **Visit Dublin** (www.visitdublin.com) The main event.
- **Dublin Links** (www.dublinks.com) One-stop guide for all manner of goings-on.
- **Le Cool** (www.lecool.com/cities/dublin) Listings, reviews and events.

EMERGENCY NUMBERS

- **Police/Fire/Ambulance** (☎999)
- **Samaritans** (☎1850 609 090)

GETTING AROUND

- **Bus** Good for sightseeing; not good for traffic.
- **Walk** The easiest way to get around town.
- **Cycle** If you're not overly worried about cars.
- **Luas** The best way to visit the southern suburbs.

BE FOREWARNED

- **Sightseeing** Cut costs on entrance charges and skip the queues with the **Dublin Pass** (see boxed text, p73).
- **Restaurants** You'll need to book for top-end establishments.
- **Public transport** You'll need exact change if you're getting a bus.
- **Rounds system** In the pub, you take it in turns to buy rounds of drinks for your party.

The Dublin Crawl Walking Tour

Dubliners of old would assure their 'bitter halves' that they were 'going to see a man about a dog' before beating a retreat to the nearest watering hole. Treat this walking tour as a sociological study...and with great care!

WALK FACTS

- **Start** Lower Camden St
- **Finish** Ormond Quay
- **Distance** 2.5km
- **Duration** One hour to two days

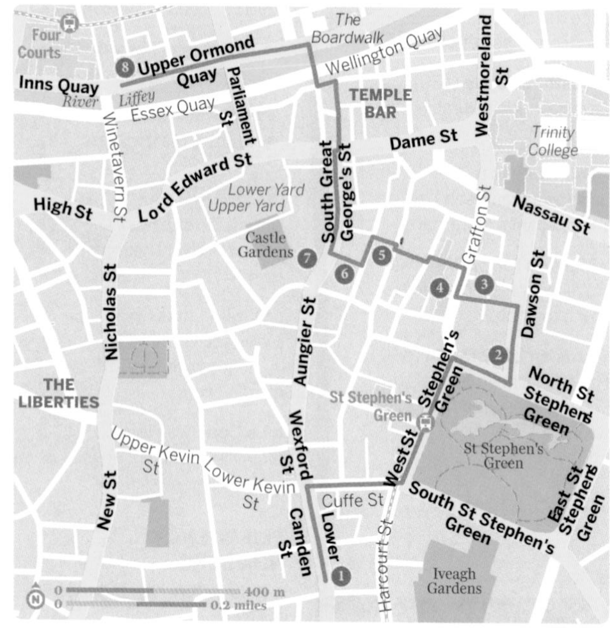

1 Anseo

Start in the always excellent **Anseo** on Camden St, where hipsters rub shoulders with the hoi polloi and everyone toe-taps to the great bag of DJ tunes.

2 Dawson Lounge

Head deep into the city centre and stop for one at Dublin's smallest pub, which serves a superb pint of Guinness.

3 Kehoe's

Sink an equally glorious pint of plain in the snug at South Anne St's **Kehoe's**, one of the city centre's most atmospheric bars, and a must-stop for all visitors to the city.

4 Bruxelles

Find a spot out the front of **Bruxelles**: the bronze statue of Thin Lizzy's Phil Lynott outside is testament to the bar's reputation as a great spot for rock music, even if these days it's just on the stereo.

5 Grogan's Castle Lounge

Discuss the merits of that unwritten masterpiece with a clutch of frustrated writers and artists in **Grogan's Castle Lounge** on Castle Market, a traditional haunt that admirably refuses to modernise.

6 No Name Bar

A couple of streets away is one of the latest contenders for coolest bar in town, the appropriately named **No Name Bar**; there's no sign but it's up the stairs from the doorway next door to L'Gueuleton restaurant. Occuyping the upstairs floor of an old townhouse, this is one of the city centre's most pleasant and handsome watering holes.

7 Long Hall

If it's more conversation you require, make your way to the **Long Hall**, where the vicissitudes of life are discussed in a sombre Victorian setting.

8 Sin É

Cross the Liffey and make a beeline for Ormond Quay and **Sin É**, a small bar with a big reputation for top-class music and a terrific night out. If you've followed the tour correctly, it's unlikely that you'd now be referring to this guide. How many fingers?

Dublin In…

TWO DAYS

If you've only got two days, start with **Trinity College** and the **Book of Kells** before venturing into the Georgian heartland – amble through **St Stephen's Green** and **Merrion Sq**, but be sure to visit both the **National Museum** and the **National Gallery**. In the evening, try an authentic Dublin pub – **Kehoe's** off Grafton St will do nicely. The next day go west, stopping at the **Chester Beatty Library** on your way to the **Guinness Storehouse**; if you still have legs for it, the **Irish Museum of Modern Art** and **Kilmainham Gaol** will round off your day perfectly. Take in a traditional Irish music session at the **Cobblestone**.

FOUR DAYS

Follow the two-day itinerary, but stretch it out between refuelling stops at some of the city's better pubs. Visit the **Dublin City Gallery – The Hugh Lane**. Become a whiskey expert at the **Old Jameson Distillery** and a literary (or beer) one with a **Dublin Literary Pub Crawl**. Oh, and don't forget **Temple Bar** – there are distractions there for every taste.

Sphere within a Sphere sculpture by Arnaldo Pomodoro, Trinity College (p62)

Discover Dublin

At a Glance

- **Grafton St & Around** The heart of Georgian Dublin: beautiful squares and fine homes.
- **North of the Liffey** Home to the city's grandest boulevard, the north side is where you'll find the biggest mix of ethnicities.
- **Temple Bar** Dublin's cultural quarter, offering a mix of heritage, history and plenty of hedonism.

Temple Bar

Sights

Grafton St & Around

TRINITY COLLEGE University

(Map p66; walking tours 01-896 1827; www.tcd.ie; tour €10; tours every 30min 10.15am-3.40pm Mon-Sat, 10.15am-3pm Sun mid-May–Sep) On a summer's evening, when the bustling crowds have gone for the day, there's hardly a more delightful place in Dublin than the grounds of Ireland's most prestigious **university**, a masterpiece of architecture and landscaping beautifully preserved in Georgian aspic. Not only is it Dublin's most attractive bit of historical real estate but it's also home to one of the world's most famous – and most beautiful – books, the gloriously illuminated Book of Kells. There is no charge to wander around the gardens on your own between 8am and 10pm.

Trinity's greatest treasures are kept in the Old Library's stunning 65m **Long Room** **(East Pavilion, Library Colonnades; adult/student/child €9/8/free; 9.30am-5pm Mon-Sat year-round, noon-4.30pm Sun Oct-Apr, 9.30am-4.30pm Sun May-Sep)**, which houses about 250,000 of the library's oldest volumes, including the breathtaking **Book of Kells** (see the boxed text, p69). Your entry ticket includes admission to temporary exhibitions on display in the East Pavilion.

TEMPLE BAR Neighbourhood

There's been many a wild night had within the cobbled precincts of Temple Bar, Dublin's most visited neighbourhood, a maze of streets and alleys sandwiched between

County Dublin

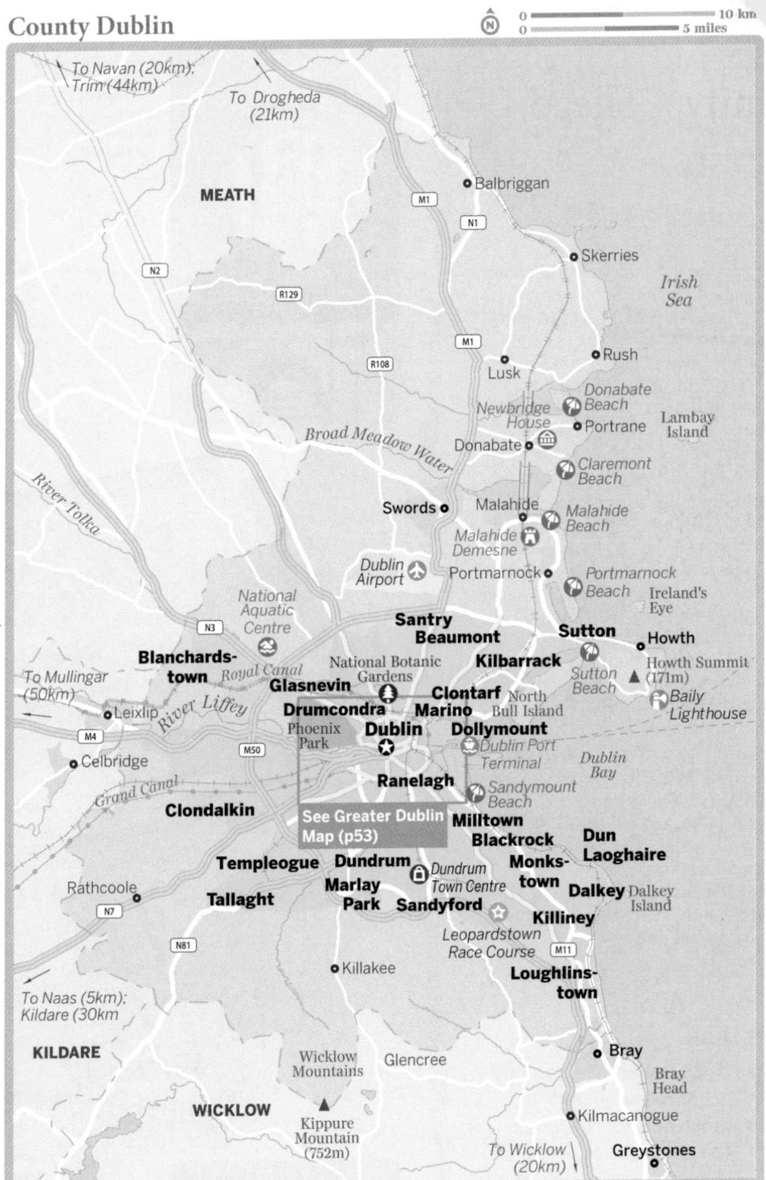

Dame St and the Liffey, running from Trinity College to Christ Church Cathedral.

During the day and on weekday nights Temple Bar does have something of a bohemian bent about it – if you ignore the crappy tourist shops and dreadful restaurants serving bland, overpriced food – but at weekends, when the party really gets going, it can get very sloppy. The huge, characterless bars crank up the sounds and throw their doors open to the tens of thousands of punters looking to

College, Dublin

Step into the Past

Ireland's most prestigious university, founded on the order of Queen Elizabeth I in 1592, is an architectural masterpiece, a cordial retreat from the bustle of modern life in the middle of the city. Step through its main entrance and you step back in time, the cobbled stones transporting you to another era, when the elite discussed philosophy and argued passionately in favour of empire.

Standing in Front Square, the 30m-high **Campanile** 1 is directly in front of you with the **Dining Hall** 2 to your left. On the far side of the square is the Old Library building, the centrepiece of which is the magnificent **Long Room** 3, which was the inspiration for the computer-generated imagery of the Jedi Archive in *Star Wars Episode II: Attack of the Clones*. Here you'll find the university's greatest treasure, the **Book of Kells** 4. You'll probably have to queue to see this masterpiece, and then only for a brief visit, but it's very much worth it.

Just beyond the Old Library is the very modern **Berkeley Library** 5, which nevertheless fits perfectly into the campus' overall aesthetic: directly in front of it is the distinctive ***Sphere Within a Sphere*** 6, the most elegant of the university's sculptures.

DON'T MISS

Douglas Hyde Gallery, the campus' designated modern art museum.

Cricket match on pitch, the most elegant of pastimes.

Pint in the Pavilion Bar, preferably while watching the cricket.

Visit to the Science Gallery, where science is made completely relevant.

© FIONN DAVENPORT

Campanile
Trinity College's most iconic bit of masonry was designed in the mid-19th century by Sir Charles Lanyon; the attached sculptures were created by Thomas Kirk.

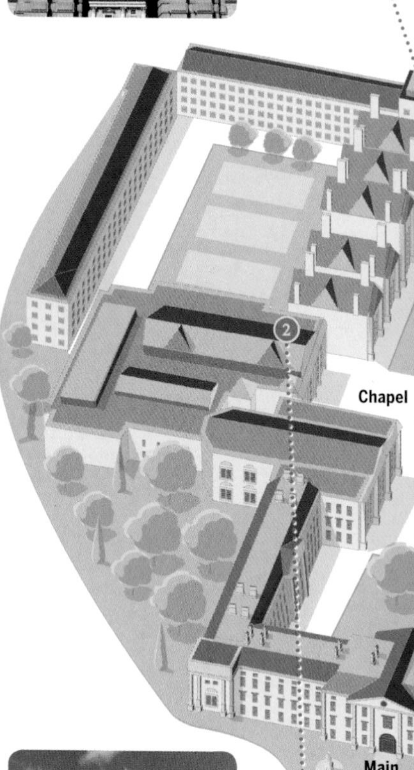

© FIONN DAVENPORT

Dining Hall
Richard Cassels' original building was designed to mirror the Examination Hall directly opposite on Front Square: the hall collapsed twice and was rebuilt from scratch in 1761.

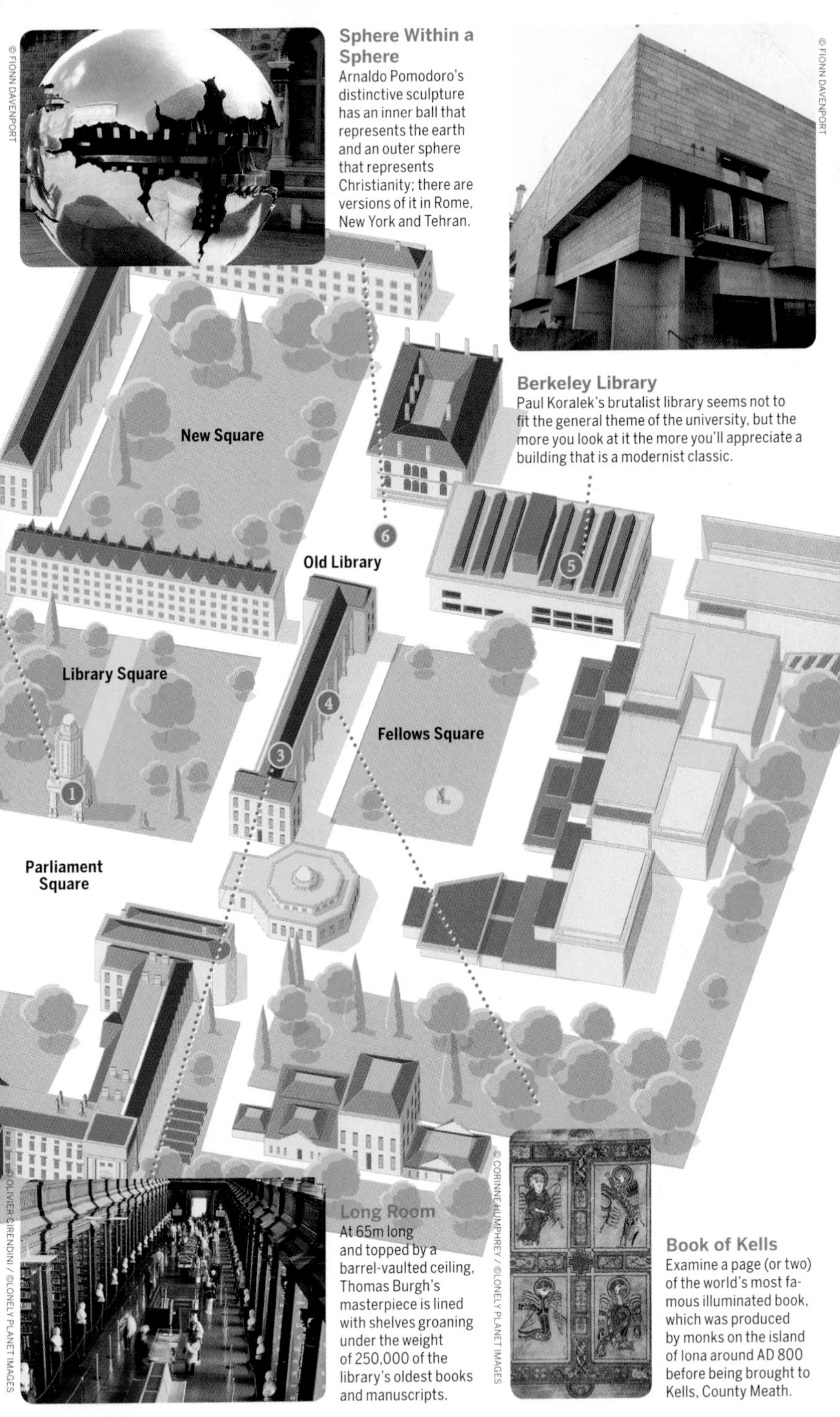

Sphere Within a Sphere
Arnaldo Pomodoro's distinctive sculpture has an inner ball that represents the earth and an outer sphere that represents Christianity; there are versions of it in Rome, New York and Tehran.

Berkeley Library
Paul Koralek's brutalist library seems not to fit the general theme of the university, but the more you look at it the more you'll appreciate a building that is a modernist classic.

Long Room
At 65m long and topped by a barrel-vaulted ceiling, Thomas Burgh's masterpiece is lined with shelves groaning under the weight of 250,000 of the library's oldest books and manuscripts.

Book of Kells
Examine a page (or two) of the world's most famous illuminated book, which was produced by monks on the island of Iona around AD 800 before being brought to Kells, County Meath.

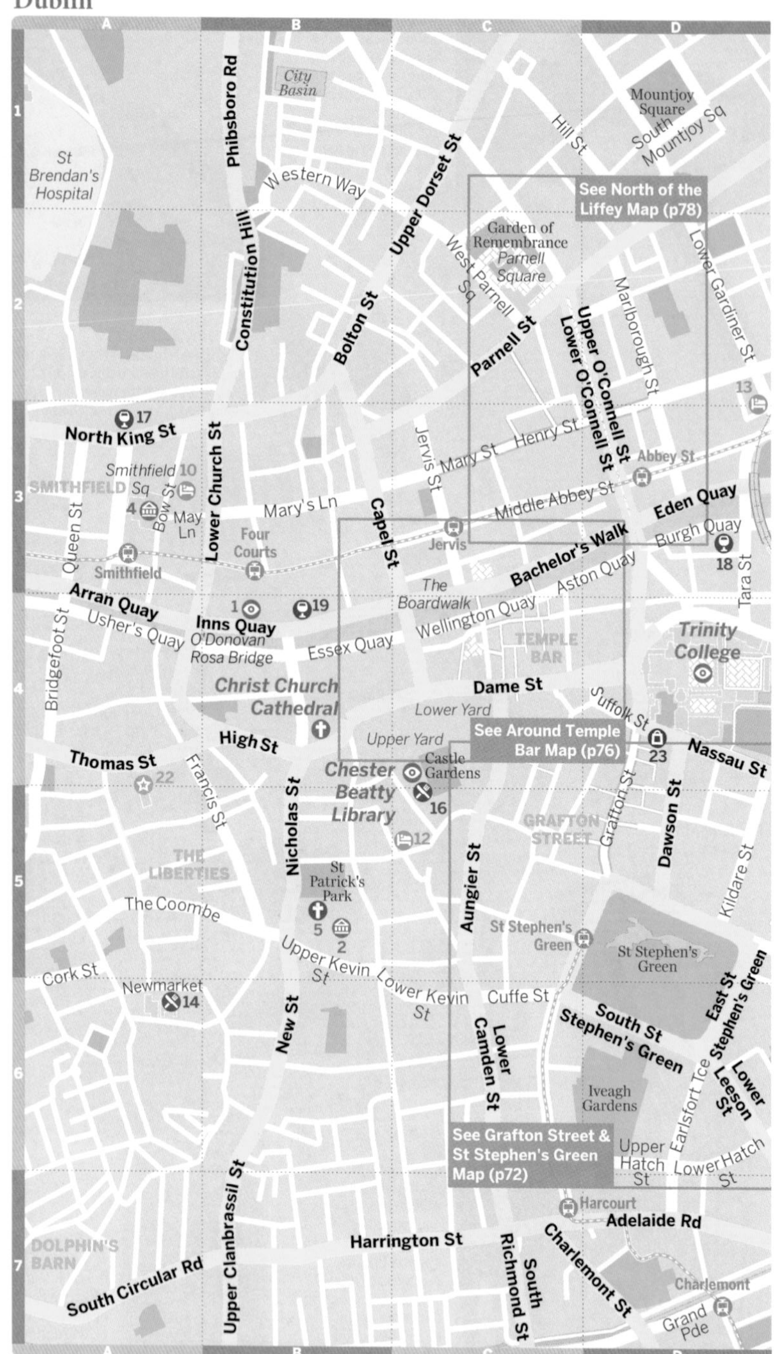

A
B
C
D
1
2
3
4
5
6
7
City Basin
Mountjoy Square
South Mountjoy Sq
Hill St
St Brendan's Hospital
Phibsboro Rd
Western Way
Upper Dorset St
See North of the Liffey Map (p78)
Garden of Remembrance
Parnell Square
West Parnell Sq
Lower Gardiner St
Constitution Hill
Bolton St
Parnell St
Upper O'Connell St
Lower O'Connell St
Marlborough St
13
17
North King St
Lower Church St
Jervis St
Mary St
Henry St
Abbey St
Smithfield
10
SMITHFIELD
Sq
Bow St
4
May Ln
Mary's Ln
Capel St
Middle Abbey St
Eden Quay
Queen St
Four Courts
Jervis
Bachelor's Walk
Burgh Quay
18
Tara St
Smithfield
Aston Quay
The Boardwalk
Arran Quay
1
19
Wellington Quay
Usher's Quay
Inns Quay
O'Donovan Rosa Bridge
Essex Quay
TEMPLE BAR
Trinity College
Bridgefoot St
Christ Church Cathedral
Dame St
Suffolk St
Lower Yard
See Around Temple Bar Map (p76)
23
Nassau St
High St
Upper Yard
Castle Gardens
Thomas St
Francis St
Chester Beatty Library
22
16
Nicholas St
Grafton St
Dawson St
GRAFTON STREET
12
THE LIBERTIES
St Patrick's Park
Aungier St
Kildare St
The Coombe
5
2
St Stephen's Green
St Stephen's Green
Upper Kevin St
Lower Kevin St
Cork St
Newmarket
14
Cuffe St
New St
Lower Camden St
South St Stephen's Green
East St Stephen's Green
Earlsfort Tce
Lower Leeson St
Iveagh Gardens
See Grafton Street & St Stephen's Green Map (p72)
Upper Hatch St
Lower Hatch St
Harcourt
Adelaide Rd
Upper Clanbrassil St
Harrington St
DOLPHIN'S BARN
South Richmond St
Charlemont St
South Circular Rd
Charlemont
Grand Pde

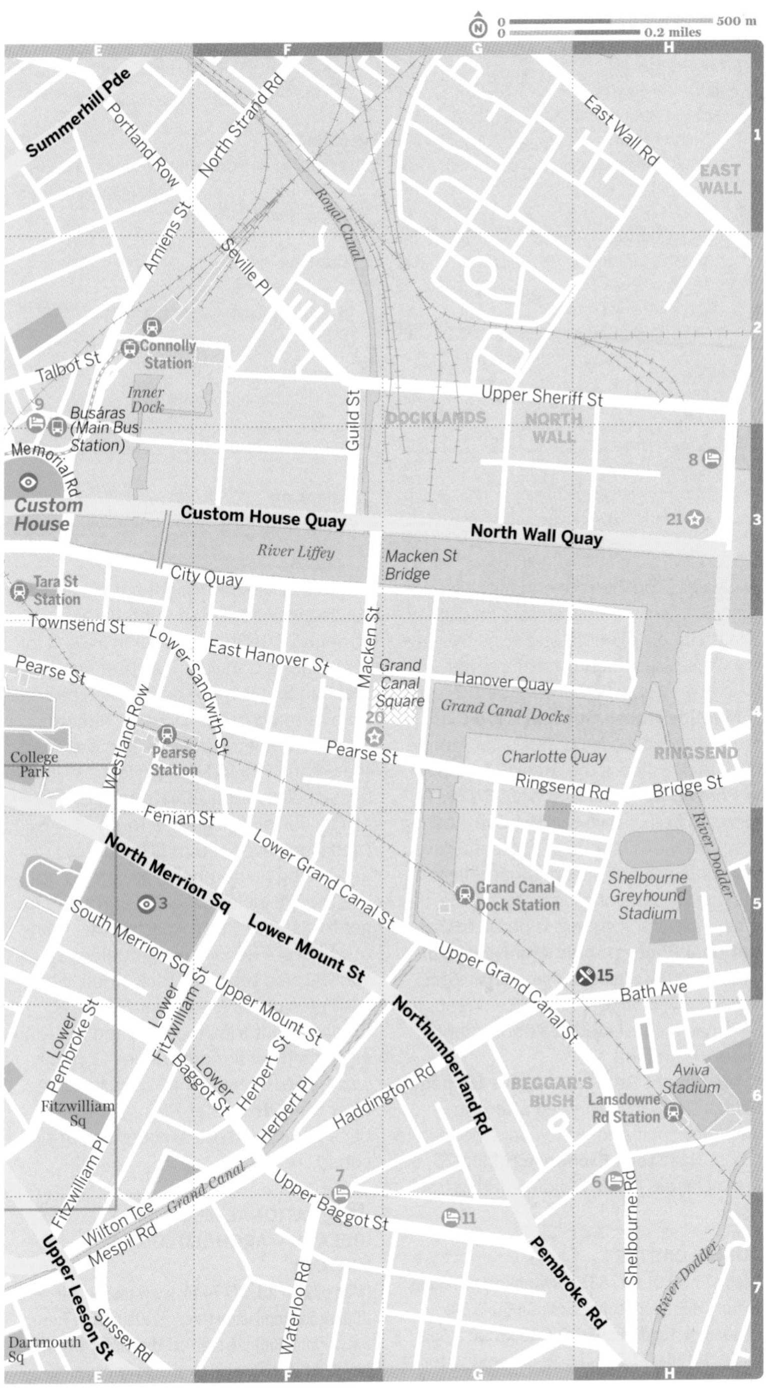
0 500 m
0 0.2 miles
Summerhill Pde
Portland Row
North Strand Rd
East Wall Rd
EAST WALL
Amiens St
Seville Pl
Royal Canal
Connolly Station
Talbot St
Inner Dock
Busáras (Main Bus Station)
Memorial Rd
Custom House
Guild St
Upper Sheriff St
DOCKLANDS
NORTH WALL
Custom House Quay
North Wall Quay
River Liffey
Macken St Bridge
City Quay
Tara St Station
Townsend St
Lower Sandwith St
East Hanover St
Macken St
Grand Canal Square
Hanover Quay
Grand Canal Docks
Pearse St
Westland Row
Pearse Station
College Park
Charlotte Quay
RINGSEND
Ringsend Rd
Bridge St
Fenian St
Lower Grand Canal St
North Merrion Sq
Grand Canal Dock Station
Shelbourne Greyhound Stadium
River Dodder
South Merrion Sq
Lower Mount St
Upper Grand Canal St
Bath Ave
Lower Fitzwilliam St
Upper Mount St
Northumberland Rd
Lower Pembroke St
Lower Baggot St
Herbert St
Herbert Pl
Haddington Rd
BEGGAR'S BUSH
Lansdowne Rd Station
Aviva Stadium
Fitzwilliam Sq
Fitzwilliam Pl
Grand Canal
Upper Baggot St
Wilton Tce
Mespil Rd
Shelbourne Rd
Pembroke Rd
Upper Leeson St
Sussex Rd
Waterloo Rd
Dartmouth Sq

Dublin

Top Sights

	Chester Beatty Library	C4
	Christ Church Cathedral	B4
	Custom House	E3
	Trinity College	D4

Sights

1	Four Courts	B4
2	Marsh's Library	B5
3	Merrion Square	E5
4	Old Jameson Distillery	A3
5	St Patrick's Cathedral	B5

Sleeping

6	Ariel House	H6
7	Dylan	F6
8	Gibson Hotel	H3
9	Isaacs Hostel	E2
10	Maldron Hotel Smithfield	A3
11	Pembroke Townhouse	G7
12	Radisson Blu Royal Hotel	C5
13	Townhouse	D2

Eating

14	Dublin Food Co-op	A6
15	Juniors	H5
16	Silk Road Café	C5

Drinking

17	Cobblestone	A3
18	John Mulligan's	D3
19	Sin É	B4

Entertainment

20	Grand Canal Theatre	F4
21	O2	H3
22	Vicar St	A4

Shopping

23	DesignYard	D4

drink and score like the end of the world is nigh. By 3am, the only culture on display is in the pools of vomit and urine that give the whole area the aroma of a sewer – welcome to Temple Barf.

Meeting House Square (Map p76) is one of the real success stories of Temple Bar. On one side is the excellent **Gallery of Photography** (Map p76; ☎01-671 4653; admission free; ⏰11am-6pm Mon-Sat), hosting temporary exhibitions of contemporary local and international photographers. Staying with the photography theme, the other side of the square is home to the **National Photographic Archive** (Map p76; ☎01-671 0073; admission free; ⏰11am-6pm Mon-Sat, 2-6pm Sun), a magnificent resource for anyone interested in a photographic history of Ireland.

Merchant's Arch leads to the **Ha'penny Bridge** (Map p76), named after the ha'penny (half-penny) toll once needed to cross. The **Stock Exchange** (Map p76) is on Anglesea St, in a building dating from 1878.

DUBLIN CASTLE — Castle

(Map p76; ☎01-645 8813; www.heritageireland.ie; Cork Hill; adult/concession €4.50/3.50; ⏰10am-4.45pm Mon-Fri, 2-4.45pm Sat & Sun; 🚌50, 54, 56a, 77, 77a) If you're looking for a medieval castle straight out of central casting you'll be disappointed; the stronghold of British power in Ireland for 700 years is principally an 18th-century creation that is more hotchpotch palace than turreted castle. Only the **Record Tower**, completed in 1258, survives from the original Anglo-Norman fortress commissioned by King John from 1204.

The 45-minute guided tours (departing every 20 to 30 minutes, depending on numbers) are pretty dry, but they're included in the entry fee. You get to visit the State Apartments, many of which are decorated in dubious taste. You will also see St Patrick's Hall, where Irish presidents are inaugurated and foreign dignitaries toasted, and the room in which the wounded James Connolly was tied to a chair while convalescing after the 1916 Easter Rising – brought back to health to be executed by firing squad.

FREE NATIONAL MUSEUM OF IRELAND – ARCHAEOLOGY & HISTORY — Museum

(Map p72; ☎01-677 7444; www.museum.ie; Kildare St; admission free; ⏰10am-5pm Tue-Sat, 2-5pm Sun) Designed by Sir Thomas Newenham Deane and completed in

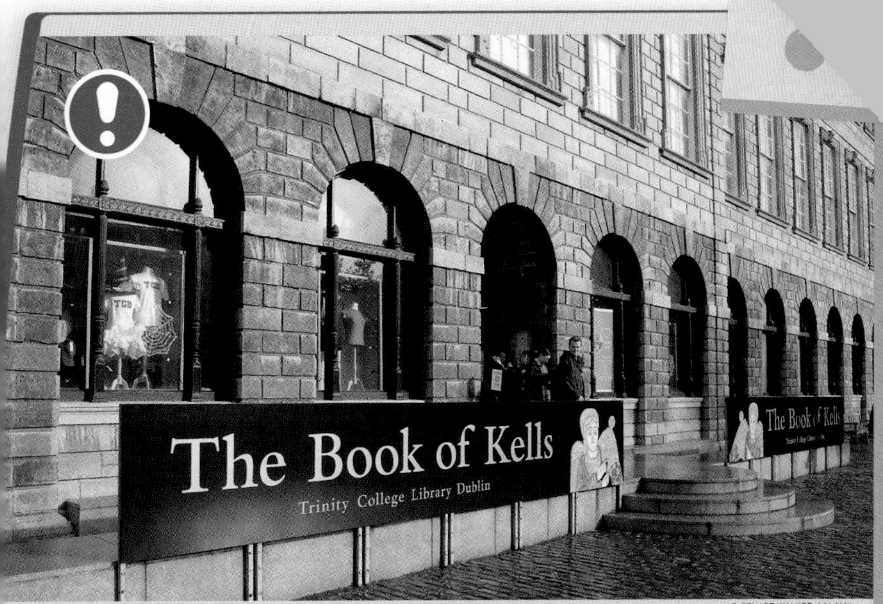

© STUART WALKER / ALAMY

Don't Miss The Book of Kells

More than half a million visitors stop in each year to see Trinity's top show-stopper, the world-famous **Book of Kells**. This illuminated manuscript, dating from around AD 800 and therefore one of the oldest books in the world, was probably produced by monks at St Colmcille's Monastery on the remote island of Iona, off the western coast of Scotland. Repeated looting by marauding Vikings forced the monks to flee to the temporary safety of Kells, County Meath, in AD 806, along with their masterpiece. Around 850 years later, the book was brought to the college for safekeeping and has remained here since.

To really appreciate the book, you can get your own reproduction copy for a mere €22,000. Failing that, the library bookshop stocks a plethora of souvenirs and other memorabilia, including Otto Simm's excellent *Exploring the Book of Kells* (€12.95), a thorough guide with attractive colour plates, and a popular DVD-ROM (€31.95) showing all 800 pages. Kids looking for something a little less stuffy might enjoy the animated *Secret of Kells* (2009), which is more fun than accurate in its portrayal of how the gospel was actually put together.

1890, the star attraction of this branch of the **National Museum of Ireland** is the Treasury, home to the finest collection of Bronze Age and Iron Age gold artefacts in the world, and the world's most complete collection of medieval Celtic metalwork.

FREE NATIONAL GALLERY Gallery

(Map p72; ☎01-661 5133; www.nationalgallery.ie; West Merrion Sq; admission free; ⏲9.30am-5.30pm Mon-Wed, Fri & Sat, 9.30am-8.30pm Thu, noon-5.30pm Sun) A magnificent Caravaggio and a breathtaking collection of works by Jack B Yeats – William Butler's younger brother – are the main reasons to visit the National Gallery, but not the only ones. Its excellent collection is strong in Irish art, but there are also high-quality collections of every major European school of painting. There are free tours at 3pm on Saturdays and at 2pm, 3pm and 4pm on Sundays.

National Museum of Ireland

National Treasures

Ireland's most important cultural institution is the National Museum, and its most important branch is the original one, housed in this fine neoclassical (or Victorian Palladian) building designed by Sir Thomas Newenham Deane and finished in 1890. Squeezed in between the rear entrance of Leinster House – the Irish parliament – and a nondescript building from the 1960s, it's easy to pass by the museum. But within its fairly cramped confines you'll find the most extensive collection of Bronze and Iron Age gold artefacts in Europe and the extraordinary collection of the Treasury. This includes the stunning **Ardagh Chalice** 1 and the delicately crafted **Tara Brooch** 2. Amid all the lustre, look out for the **Broighter Gold Collar** 3 and the impressively crafted **Loughnashade War Trumpet** 4, both extraordinary examples of Celtic art. Finally, pay a visit to the exquisite **Cross of Cong** 5, which was created after the other pieces but is just as beautiful.

As you visit these treasures – all created after the arrival of Christianity in the 5th century – bear in mind that they were produced with the most rudimentary of instruments.

VIKING DUBLIN

Archaeological excavations in Dublin between 1961 and 1981 unearthed evidence of a Viking town and cemeteries along the banks of the River Liffey. The graves contained weapons such as swords and spears, together with jewellery and personal items. Craftsmen's tools, weights and scales, silver ingots and coins show that the Vikings, as well as marauding and raiding, were also engaged in commercial activities. The Viking artefacts are now part of the National Museum's collection.

Lunch Break

Enjoy homemade pasta along with a nice glass of Italian red at the very authentic Dunne & Crescenzi (14–16 South Frederick St), or a pancake on the go from Lemon (Dawson St).

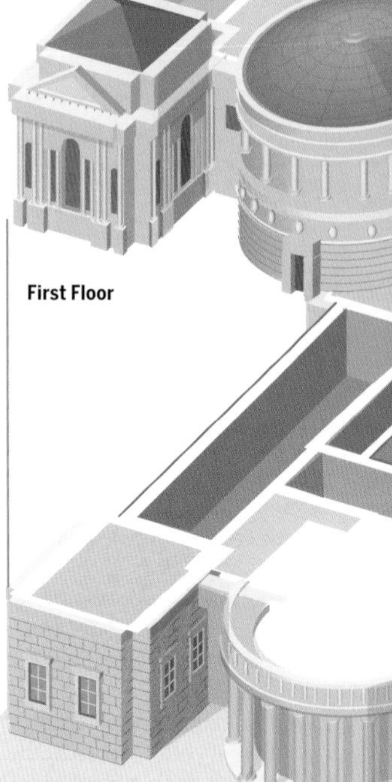

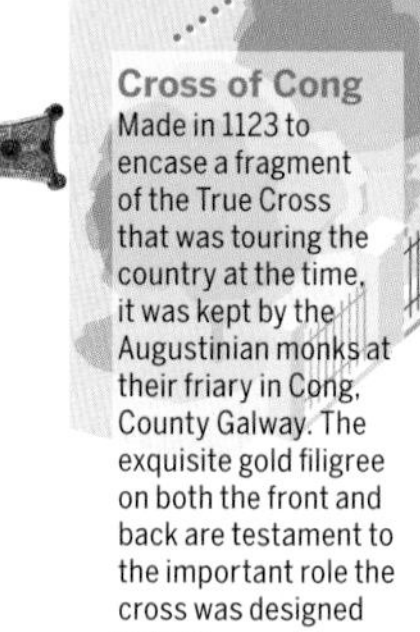

Cross of Cong
Made in 1123 to encase a fragment of the True Cross that was touring the country at the time, it was kept by the Augustinian monks at their friary in Cong, County Galway. The exquisite gold filigree on both the front and back are testament to the important role the cross was designed to have.

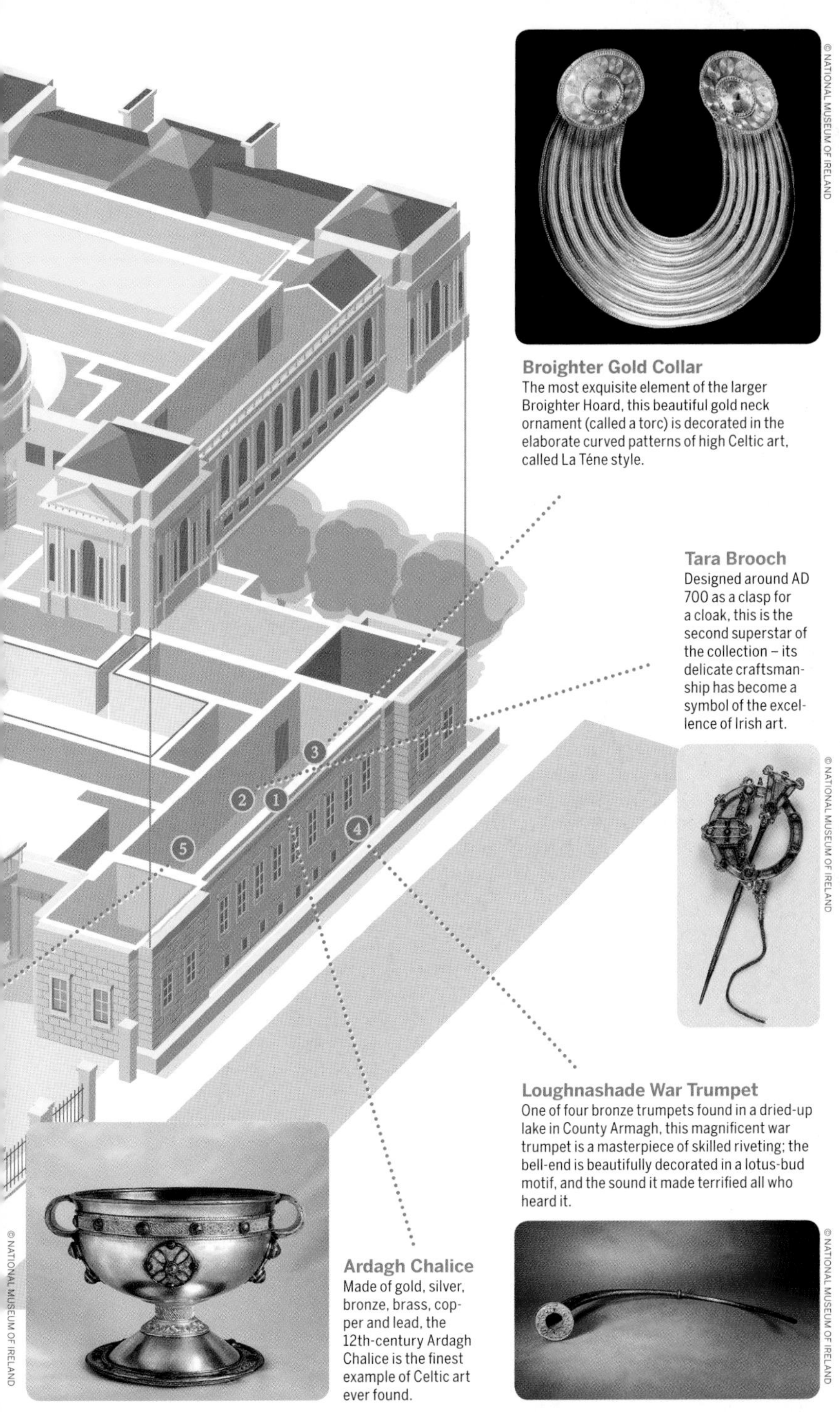

Broighter Gold Collar
The most exquisite element of the larger Broighter Hoard, this beautiful gold neck ornament (called a torc) is decorated in the elaborate curved patterns of high Celtic art, called La Téne style.

Tara Brooch
Designed around AD 700 as a clasp for a cloak, this is the second superstar of the collection – its delicate craftsmanship has become a symbol of the excellence of Irish art.

Loughnashade War Trumpet
One of four bronze trumpets found in a dried-up lake in County Armagh, this magnificent war trumpet is a masterpiece of skilled riveting; the bell-end is beautifully decorated in a lotus-bud motif, and the sound it made terrified all who heard it.

Ardagh Chalice
Made of gold, silver, bronze, brass, copper and lead, the 12th-century Ardagh Chalice is the finest example of Celtic art ever found.

Grafton Street & St Stephen's Green

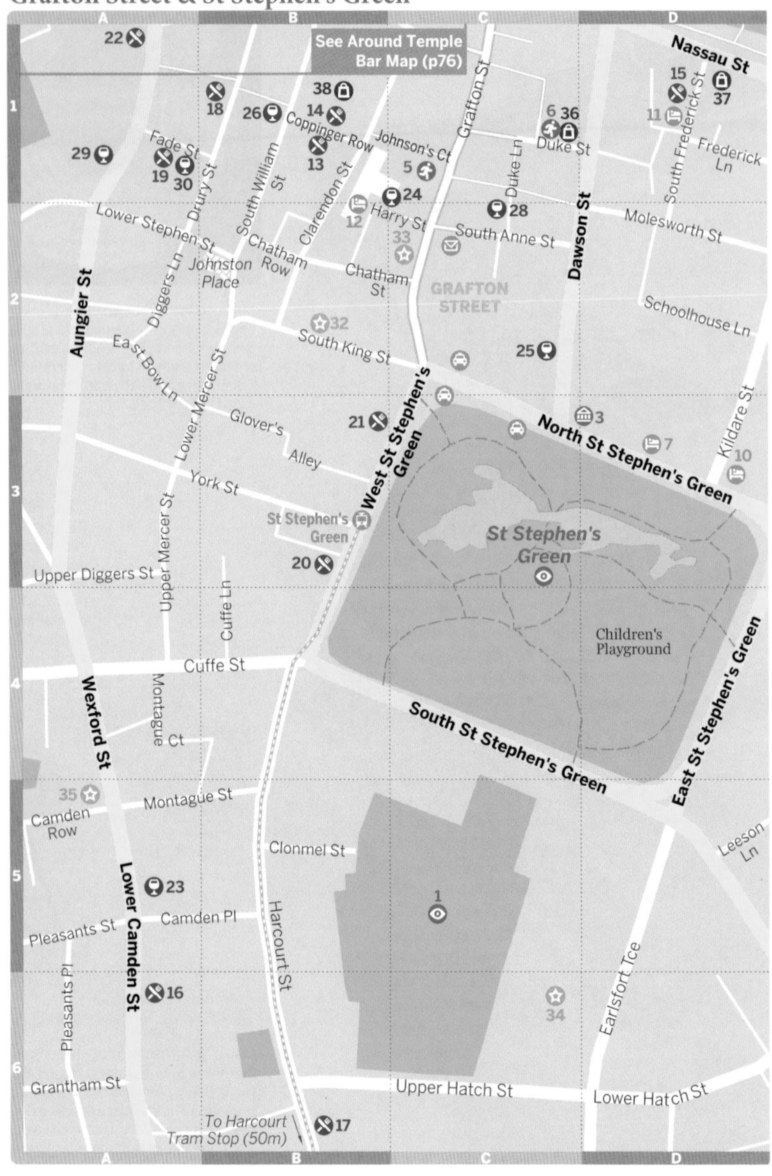

FREE **LEINSTER HOUSE** Parliament Building

(Map p72; ☎01-618 3000, tour information 618 3271; www.oireachtas.ie; Kildare St; admission free; ⊙observation gallery 2.30-8.30pm Tue, 10.30am-8.30pm Wed, 10.30am-5.30pm Thu Nov-May, tours 10.30am, 11.30am, 2.30pm & 3.30pm Mon-Fri when parliament is not in session) Dublin's grandest Georgian home, built by Richard Cassels between 1745 and 1748 for the very grand James Fitzgerald,

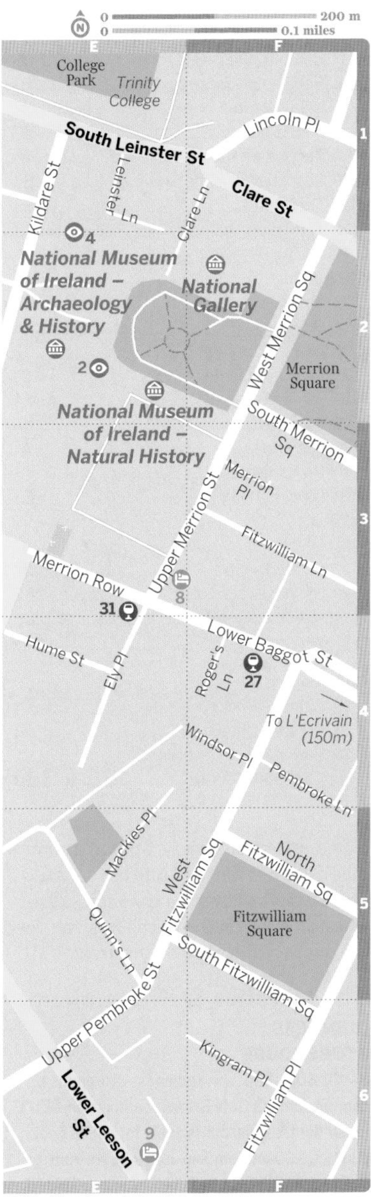

Earl of Kildare, is now the seat of both houses of the Oireachtas na Éireann (Irish Parliament) – the Dáil (Lower House) and Seanad (Upper House).

When Parliament is sitting, visitors are admitted to an observation gallery. You'll get an entry ticket from the Kildare St entrance on production of some identification.

The Dublin Pass

If you're planning some heavy-duty sightseeing, you'll save a packet by investing in the **Dublin Pass (adult/child 1-day €35/19, 2-day €55/31, 3-day €65/39, 6-day €95/49)**. Not only do you gain free entry to 32 attractions but you also can skip whatever queue there is by presenting your card; it also includes free transfer to and from the airport on the Aircoach (see p95). The Dublin Pass is available from any of the Dublin Tourism offices (p94).

LITTLE MUSEUM OF DUBLIN Museum

(Map p72; (☎01-661 1000; www.littlemuseum.ie; 15 St Stephen's Green N; admission €6.95; ⏲10am-5pm Mon-Fri) The idea is ingeniously simple: a museum, spread across two rooms of an elegant Georgian building, devoted to the history of Dublin in the 20th century, made up of memorabilia contributed by the general public. Only open since summer 2011, the contributions have been impressive – amid the nostalgic posters, time-worn bric-a-brac and wonderful photographs of personages and cityscapes of yesteryear are some extraordinary finds, including an original copy of the fateful letter given to the Irish envoys to the treaty negotiations of 1921, whose contradictory instructions were at the heart of the split that resulted in the Civil War. But you don't need to know anything about Irish history or Dublin to appreciate it: visits are by guided tour and everyone is presented with a handsome booklet on the history of the city.

FREE **NATIONAL MUSEUM OF IRELAND – NATURAL HISTORY** Museum

(Map p72; www.museum.ie; Merrion St; ⏲10am-5pm Tue-Sat, 2-5pm Sun) Dusty, weird and

Grafton Street & St Stephen's Green

Top Sights
National Gallery ... F2
National Museum of Ireland – Archaeology & History ... E2
National Museum of Ireland – Natural History ... E2
St Stephen's Green ... C3

Sights
1 Iveagh Gardens ... C5
2 Leinster House ... E2
3 Little Museum of Dublin ... D3
4 National Library ... E2

Activities, Courses & Tours
5 Dublin Footsteps Walking Tours ... C1
6 Dublin Literary Pub Crawl ... C1

Sleeping
7 Cliff Townhouse ... D3
8 Merrion ... E3
9 Number 31 ... E6
10 Shelbourne ... D3
11 Trinity Lodge ... D1
12 Westbury Hotel ... B2

Eating
13 Coppinger Row ... B1
14 Coppinger Row Market ... B1
15 Dunne & Crescenzi ... D1
16 Green Nineteen ... A6
17 Harcourt St Food Market ... B6
18 Honest to Goodness ... B1
19 L'Gueuleton ... A1
Pepperpot ... (see 38)
Restaurant Patrick Guilbaud ... (see 8)
20 Shanahan's on the Green ... B3
21 Thornton's ... B3
22 Yamamori ... A1

Drinking
23 Anseo ... A5
24 Bruxelles ... C1
25 Dawson Lounge ... C2
26 Grogan's Castle Lounge ... B1
27 James Toner's ... F4
28 Kehoe's ... C2
29 Long Hall ... A1
30 No Name Bar ... A1
31 O'Donoghue's ... E3

Entertainment
32 Gaiety Theatre ... B2
33 HMV ... C2
34 National Concert Hall ... C6
35 Whelan's ... A5

Shopping
36 Cathach Books ... C1
37 Kilkenny Shop ... D1
38 Powerscourt Townhouse Shopping Centre ... B1

utterly compelling, this window into Victorian times has barely changed since Scottish explorer Dr David Livingstone opened it in 1857 – before disappearing off into the African jungle for a meeting with Henry Stanley.

Compared to the multimedia, interactive this and that of virtually every modern museum, this is a beautifully preserved example of Victorian charm and scientific wonderment.

ST STEPHEN'S GREEN & AROUND Park
(Map p72; admission free; dawn-dusk) While enjoying the nine gorgeous, landscaped hectares of Dublin's most popular square, consider that once upon a time it was an open common used for public whippings, beatings and hangings. Activities in the green have quieted since then and are generally confined to the lunchtime picnic-and-stroll variety. Still, on a summer's day it is the favourite retreat of office workers, lovers and visitors alike, who come to breathe a little fresh air, feed the ducks and cuddle on the grass.

The Liberties & Kilmainham

GUINNESS STOREHOUSE Brewery, Museum
(01-408 4800; www.guinness-storehouse.com; St James's Gate Brewery; admission €15/11, under 6yr free, discounts apply for online bookings; 9.30am-5pm Sep-Jun, 9.30am-7pm Jul-Aug; 51b, 78a, 123; St James'; 21A, 78 ir 78A from Fleet St) The most popular visit in town is the beer-lover's Disneyland, a multimedia bells-and-whistles homage to the country's most famous export and the city's most enduring symbol. The old grain storehouse, the only part of the massive, 26-hectare St James's Gate

Brewery open to the public, is a suitable cathedral in which to worship the black gold; shaped like a giant pint of Guinness, it rises seven impressive storeys high around a stunning central atrium. At the top is the head, represented by the **Gravity Bar**, with a panoramic view of Dublin.

ST PATRICK'S CATHEDRAL Church

(Map p66; ☎01-475 4817; www.stpatrickscathedral.ie; St Patrick's Close; adult/senior & student/child €5.50/4.50/free; ⏰9am-6pm Mon-Sat, 9-11am, 12.45-3pm & 4.15-6pm Sun Mar-Oct, 9am-6pm Mon-Fri, 9am-5pm Sat, 10-11am & 12.45-3pm Sun Nov-Feb; 🚌50, 50A or 56A from Aston Quay or 54 or 54A from Burgh Quay) It was at this cathedral, reputedly, that St Paddy himself dunked the Irish heathens into the waters of a well, so the church that bears his name stands on one of the earliest Christian sites in the city and a pretty sacred piece of turf. Although there's been a church here since the 5th century, the present building dates from 1190 or 1225 (opinions differ) and it has been altered several times, most notably in 1864 when the flying buttresses were added, thanks to the neo-Gothic craze that swept the nation.

CHRIST CHURCH CATHEDRAL Church

(Church of the Holy Trinity; Map p66; ☎01-677 8099; www.cccdub.ie; Christ Church Pl; adult/senior/student €6/4/3; ⏰9.45am-4.15pm Mon-Sat, 12.30-2.30pm Sun Sep-May, 9.45am-6.15pm Mon-Tue & Fri, to 4.15pm Wed-Thu & Sat, 12.30-2.30pm & 4.30-6.15pm Sun Jun–mid-Jul, 9.45am-6.15pm Mon-Fri, to 4.15pm Sat, 12.30-2.30pm & 4.30-6.15pm Sun mid-Jul-Aug; 🚌50, 50A or 56A from Aston Quay or 54 or 54A from Burgh Quay) Its hilltop location and eye-catching flying buttresses make this the most photogenic by far of Dublin's three cathedrals as well as one of the capital's most recognisable symbols.

Throughout much of its history, Christ Church vied for supremacy with nearby St Patrick's Cathedral but, like its neighbour, it also fell on hard times in the 18th and 19th centuries – earlier, the nave had been used as a market and the crypt had housed taverns – and was virtually derelict by the time restoration took place. Today, both Church of Ireland cathedrals are outsiders in a largely Catholic nation.

If You Like... Gardens

If you like the pastoral charms of St Stephen's Green, you'll enjoy the following green oases:

1 **IVEAGH GARDENS**
(Map p66; admission free; ⏰dawn-dusk year-round) Behind the imposing walls is one of the city's loveliest spots to relax in on a summer's day.

2 **MERRION SQUARE**
(Map p72; admission free; ⏰dawn-dusk) Beautifully tended flower beds are just one of the features of this tranquil square.

3 **WAR MEMORIAL GARDENS**
(www.heritageireland.ie; South Circular Rd, Islandbridge; admission free; ⏰8am-dusk Mon-Fri, from 10am Sat & Sun) By our reckoning, these gardens are the city's most beautiful, if only because they're as tranquil a spot as any you'll find in the city. Designed by Sir Edwin Lutyens, this patch of landscaped beauty was designed to commemorate the dead of WWI.

KILMAINHAM GAOL Museum

(☎01-453 5984; www.heritageireland.com; Inchicore Rd; adult/student/child €6/2/2; ⏰9.30am-5pm Apr-Oct, 9.30am-4pm Mon-Sat, 10am-4pm Sun Nov-Mar; 🚌23, 51, 51A, 78 or 79 from Aston Quay) If you have *any* desire at all to understand Irish history – especially the juicy bits about resistance to English rule – then a visit to this former prison is an absolute must. This threatening grey building, built between 1792 and 1795, has played a role in virtually every act of Ireland's painful path to independence.

The uprisings of 1798, 1803, 1848, 1867 and 1916 ended with the leaders'

Around Temple Bar

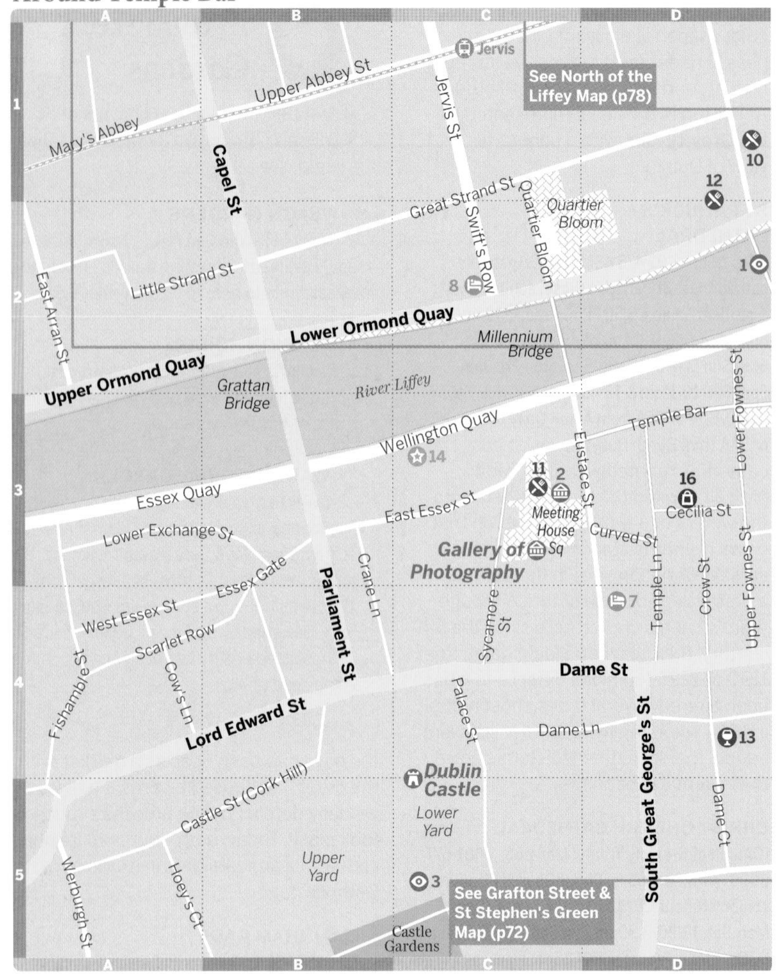

confinement here. Of the 15 executions that took place between 3 May and 12 May after the revolt, 14 were conducted here.

An excellent audiovisual introduction to the building is followed by a thought-provoking tour of the eerie prison, the largest unoccupied building of its kind in Europe. Sitting incongruously outside in the yard is the *Asgard*, the ship that successfully ran the British blockade to deliver arms to Nationalist forces in 1914. The tour finishes in the gloomy yard where the 1916 executions took place.

FREE IRISH MUSEUM OF MODERN ART Art Gallery

(IMMA; 01-612 9900; www.imma.ie; Military Rd; admission free; 10am-5.30pm Tue-Sat, noon-5.30pm Sun; Heuston) Ireland's most important collection of modern and contemporary Irish art is housed in the elegant, airy expanse of the Royal Hospital at Kilmainham, which in 1991 became a magnificent exhibition space.

There are free guided tours (2.30pm Wednesday, Friday and Sunday) of the museum's exhibits throughout the year,

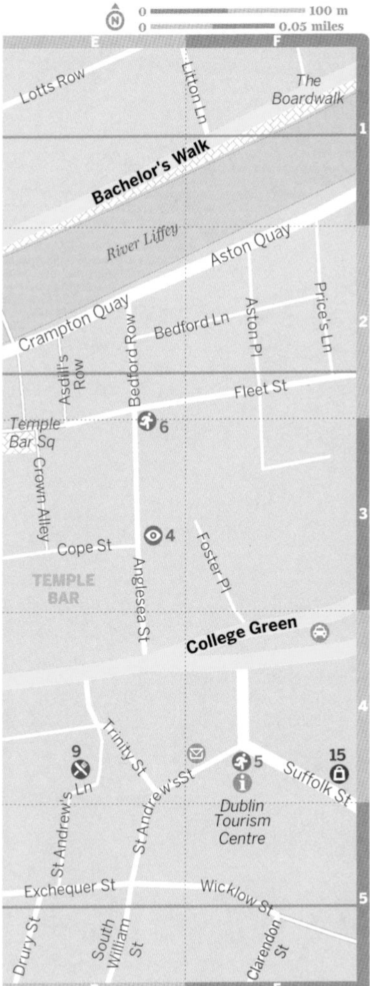

Around Temple Bar

but we strongly recommend the free seasonal heritage **tours (50 mins; hourly 11am-4pm Tue-Sat, 1-4pm Sun Jun-Sep)** of the building itself, which run from July through to September.

North of the Liffey

FREE DUBLIN CITY GALLERY – THE HUGH LANE Art Gallery

(Map p78; 01-874 1903; www.hughlane.ie; 22 North Parnell Sq; admission free; 10am-6pm Tue-Thu, 10am-5pm Fri & Sat, 11am-5pm Sun) Whatever reputation Dublin has as a repository of world-class art has a lot to do with the simply stunning collection housed within this exquisite gallery, which is not only home to works by some of the brightest stars in the modern and contemporary art world both foreign and domestic but is also where you'll find one of the most singular exhibitions to be seen anywhere: the actual studio of one of the 20th century's truly iconic artists, Francis Bacon.

All the big names of French Impressionism and early-20th-century Irish art are here. Sculptures by Rodin and Degas, and paintings by Corot, Courbet, Manet and Monet sit alongside works by Irish greats Jack B Yeats, William Leech and Nathaniel Hone.

OLD JAMESON DISTILLERY Museum

(Map p66; 01-807 2355; www.jamesonwhiskey.com; Bow St; adult/child/student €13.50/8/11;

North of the Liffey

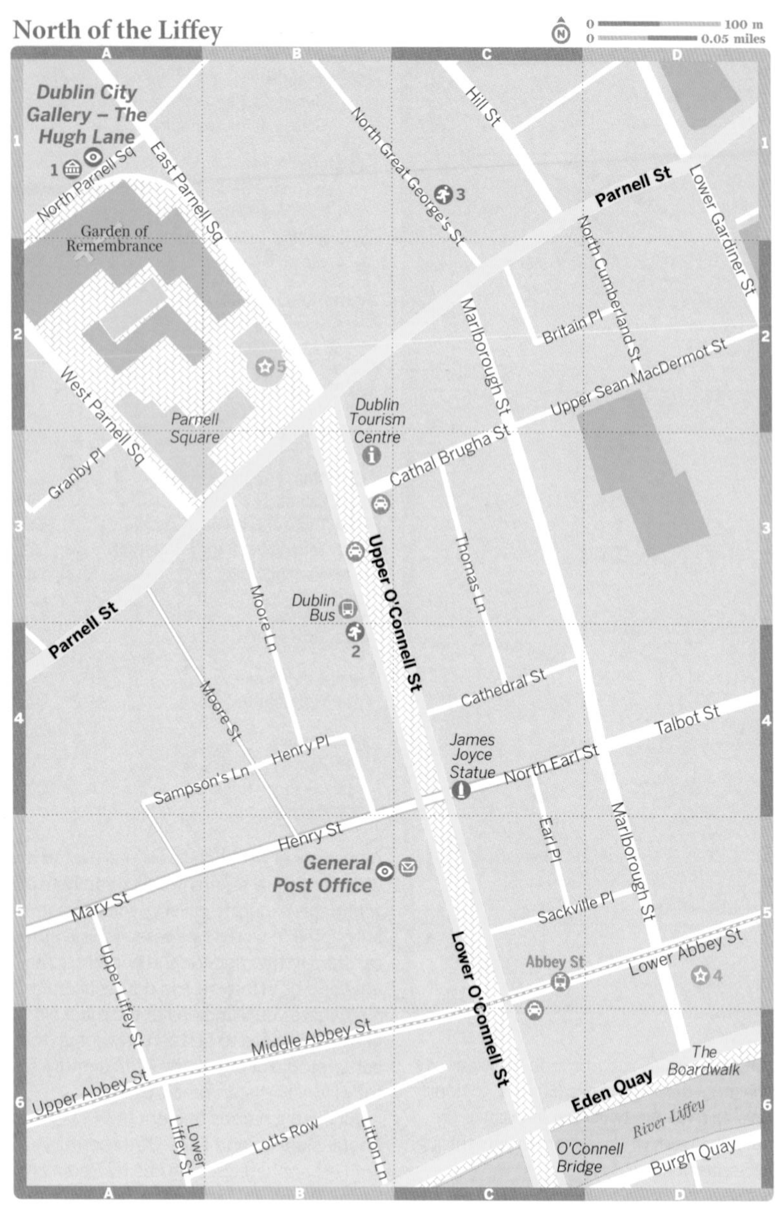

tours every 35min 9am-5.30pm) Smithfield's biggest draw is this converted distillery, now a huge museum devoted to *uisce beatha* (the water of life). Beginning with a short film, the tour runs through the whole process of distilling, from grain to bottle. There are plenty of interesting titbits, such as what makes a single malt, where whiskey gets its colour and bouquet, and what the difference is between Irish whiskey and Scotch.

North of the Liffey

If you're buying whiskey, go for the stuff you can't buy at home, such as the excellent Red Breast or the super-exclusive Midleton, a very limited reserve that is appropriately expensive.

FREE NATIONAL MUSEUM OF IRELAND – DECORATIVE ARTS & HISTORY Museum

(**01-677 7444; www.museum.ie; Benburb St; admission free; 10am-5pm Tue-Sat, 2-5pm Sun)** Known colloquially as Collins Barracks, the decorative arts and history annexe of the National Museum of Ireland is housed within one of the most beautiful buildings in the whole city, built in 1704 on the orders of Queen Anne and at one time the largest military barracks in the world. At its heart is the huge central square surrounded by arcaded colonnades and blocks linked by walking bridges.

The museum itself offers a glimpse of Ireland's social, economic and military history over the last millennium. It's a big ask – too big, say its critics – but well-designed displays, interactive multimedia and a dizzying array of disparate artefacts make for an interesting and valiant effort.

GENERAL POST OFFICE Post Office

(Map p78; 01-705 7000; www.anpost.ie; O'Connell St; 8am-8pm Mon-Sat) Talk about going postal. The country's most important post office will forever be linked to the dramatic and tragic events of Easter Week 1916, when Pádraig Pearse, James Connolly and the other leaders of the Easter Rising read their proclamation from the front steps and made the building their headquarters. Since its reopening in 1929 it has lived through quieter times, but its central role in the history of independent Ireland has made it a prime site for everything from official parades to personal protests.

FREE FOUR COURTS Courts

(Map p66; 01-872 5555; Inns Quay; admission free; 9am-5pm Mon-Fri) Appellants quake and the accused may shiver, but visitors are only likely to be amazed by James Gandon's imposing Four Courts, Ireland's uppermost courts of law. Gandon's Georgian masterpiece is a mammoth structure incorporating a 130m-long facade and a collection of statuary. The Corinthian-columned central block, connected to flanking wings with enclosed quadrangles, was begun in 1786 and not completed until 1802. The original four courts (Exchequer, Common Pleas, King's Bench and Chancery) all branch off the central rotunda.

Docklands

CUSTOM HOUSE Museum

(Map p66) James Gandon (1743–1823) announced his arrival on the Dublin scene with the stunning, glistening white building that is the Custom House, one of the city's finest Georgian monuments. It was constructed between 1781 and 1791, in spite of opposition from city merchants and dockers at the original Custom House, upriver in Temple Bar.

Beneath the dome is the **Custom House Visitor Centre** (**01-888 2538; Custom House Quay; admission €1; 10am-12.30pm Mon-Fri, 2-5pm Sat & Sun mid-Mar–Oct, closed Mon-Tue & Sat Nov–mid-Mar)**, which features a small museum on Gandon himself, as well as information on the history of the building.

If You Like… Libraries

If you like the books at the Chester Beatty Library, you'll enjoy the following repositories of the written word:

1 **DUBLIN WRITERS MUSEUM**
(Map p66; ☎01-872 2077; www.writersmuseum.com; 18 North Parnell Sq; adult/child/student €7.50/4.70/6.30; ⏱10am-5pm Mon-Sat Sep-May, to 6pm Jun-Aug, 11am-5pm Sun year-round) Interesting collection of vaguely literary ephemera associated with some of the city's most recognisable names (Samuel Beckett's phone; Brendan Behan's union card).

2 **MARSH'S LIBRARY**
(Map p66; ☎01-454 3511; www.marsh library.ie; St Patrick's Close; adult/child/student €2.50/free/1.50; ⏱10am-1pm & 2-5pm Mon & Wed-Fri, 10.30am-1pm Sat) A barely visited antique library with over 25,000 books dating from the 16th to early 18th centuries.

3 **NATIONAL LIBRARY**
(Map p72; ☎01-603 0200; www.nli.ie; Kildare St; admission free; ⏱9.30am-9pm Mon-Wed, 10am-5pm Thu & Fri, 10am-1pm Sat) The library's extensive collection has many valuable early manuscripts, first editions, maps and other items; its reading room is featured in James Joyce's *Ulysses*.

Tours

DUBLIN BUS TOURS Bus Tour
(www.dublinbus.ie; tours €16-26; ⏱tours daily) O'Connell St **(Map p78; ☎01-872 0000; 59 Upper O'Connell St)**; Suffolk St **(Map p76; Dublin Tourism Centre, St Andrew's Church, 2 Suffolk St)** Offers a variety of tours, including Dublin City Tour, Ghost Bus Tour, Coast and Castles Tour, and South Coast and Gardens Tour.

DUBLIN FOOTSTEPS WALKING TOURS Walking Tour
(Map p72; ☎01-496 0641; Bewley's Bldg, Grafton St; adult €11; ⏱10.30am Mon, Wed, Fri & Sat Jun-Sep) Departing from Bewley's on Grafton St, these excellent two-hour tours weave Georgian, literary and architectural Dublin into a fascinating walk.

DUBLIN LITERARY PUB CRAWL Walking Tour
(Map p72; ☎01-670 5602; www.dublinpubcrawl.com; The Duke, 9 Duke St; adult/student €12/10; ⏱7.30pm Mon-Sat, noon & 7.30pm Sun Apr-Nov, 7.30pm Thu-Sun Dec-Mar) An award-winning 2½-hour walk-and-performance tour led by two actors, exploring pubs with literary connections. There's plenty of drink taken, which makes it all the more popular; get to the Duke pub by 7pm to reserve a spot.

DUBLIN MUSICAL PUB CRAWL Walking Tour
(Map p76; ☎01-478 0193; www.discoverdublin.ie; Oliver St John Gogarty's, 58-59 Fleet St; adult/student €12/10; ⏱7.30pm Apr-Oct, 7.30pm Thu-Sat Nov-Mar) The story of Irish traditional music and its influence on contemporary styles is explained and demonstrated by two expert musicians in a number of Temple Bar pubs. Tours meet upstairs at Oliver St John Gogarty's and take 2½ hours.

JAMES JOYCE WALKING TOUR Walking Tour
(Map p78; ☎01-878 8547; James Joyce Cultural Centre, 35 North Great George's St; adult/student €10/8; ⏱2pm Tue, Thu & Sat) Excellent 1¼-hour walking tours of northside attractions associated with James Joyce, departing from James Joyce Cultural Centre.

Sleeping

Dublin gets busy in summer and it can be tough to get a central bed from around May to September.

You can pay anything from €80 to €200 for a quality guesthouse or midrange hotel, while the city's top digs usually start their rates at about €200; at the other end of the scale, a hostel bed may cost anything from €10 to as much as €34.

DOUG McKINLAY / LONELY PLANET IMAGES ©

Don't Miss Chester Beatty Library

The world-famous library, in the grounds of Dublin Castle, houses the collection of mining engineer Sir Alfred Chester Beatty (1875–1968), bequeathed to the Irish State on his death. And we're immensely grateful for Chester's patronage: spread over two floors, the breathtaking collection includes more than 20,000 manuscripts, rare books, miniature paintings, clay tablets, costumes and other objects of artistic, historical and aesthetic importance. The library runs tours at 1pm on Wednesdays and at 3pm and 4pm on Sundays.

Head for the collection of Qur'ans from the 9th to the 19th centuries, considered to be among the best illuminated Islamic texts. You'll also find ancient Egyptian papyrus texts (including Egyptian love poems from around 1100 BC), scrolls and exquisite artwork from Burma, Indonesia and Tibet – as well as the second-oldest biblical fragment ever found (after the Dead Sea Scrolls).

THINGS YOU NEED TO KNOW

Map p66; ☎407 0750; www.cbl.ie; Dublin Castle, Cork Hill; ⏰10am-5pm Mon-Fri, 11am-5pm Sat, 1-5pm Sun year-round, closed Mon Oct-Apr

Grafton St & Around

NUMBER 31 Guesthouse **€€**

(Map p72; ☎01-676 5011; www.number31.ie; 31 Leeson Close; s/d/tr from €100/140/240; 📶) This elegant slice of accommodation paradise is unquestionably the most distinctive of Dublin's hotels. Separated by a beautiful garden, its 21 bedrooms are split between the chichi coach house and the more gracious Georgian house, where rooms are individually furnished with French antiques and big beds. Gourmet breakfasts are served in the conservatory. Children under 10 are not permitted.

RADISSON BLU ROYAL HOTEL Hotel **€€**

(Map p66; ☎01-898 2900; www.radissonblu.ie/royalhotel-dublin; Golden Lane; r €160-220; P ❄ 📶) The stunning Dublin flagship of this well-respected Scandinavian group

Bloomsday

Bloomsday is a slightly gimmicky and touristy phenomenon that appeals almost exclusively to Joyce fanatics, but it's plenty of fun. Events are designed to follow Bloom's progress around town. In recent years festivities have expanded to continue over four days around 16 June. On Bloomsday proper you can kick things off with breakfast at the James Joyce Cultural Centre, where the 'inner organs of beast and fowl' come accompanied by celebratory readings.

is an excellent example of how sleek lines and muted colours can combine beautifully with luxury to make for a memorable night's stay: from the hugely impressive public areas (the bar alone is worth the visit) to the sophisticated bedrooms – each with flat-screen digital TVs embedded in the wall – this is bound to be one of the most popular options for the business traveller, or anyone looking for an elegant contemporary bed.

IRISH LANDMARK TRUST Historic Home **€€**
(Map p76; ☎01-670 4733; www.irishlandmark.com; 25 Eustace St; 1 night/week €300/1800)
If you're travelling in a group, instead of renting a bunch of doubles in a hotel that you'll barely remember a week after you've gone home, why not go for this fabulous 18th-century heritage house, gloriously restored to the highest standard by the Irish Landmark Trust? You'll have this unique house all to yourselves. It sleeps up to seven in its double, twin and triple bedrooms. Furnished with tasteful antiques, authentic furniture and fittings (including a grand piano in the drawing room), this kind of period rental accommodation is something really special. A €7 daily contribution to offset energy costs is included in the price.

TRINITY LODGE Guesthouse **€€**
(Map p72; ☎01-617 0900; www.trinitylodge.com; 12 South Frederick St; s/d from €130/170; [wifi] [family])
Martin Sheen's grin greets you on entering this cosy, award-winning guesthouse. Not that he's ditched movies for hospitality: he just enjoyed his stay (and full Irish breakfast, presumably) at this classically refurbished Georgian pad so much that he let them take a mugshot. Room 2 has a lovely bay window.

MERRION Hotel **€€€**
(Map p72; ☎01-603 0600; www.merrionhotel.com; Upper Merrion St; r from €455; [P] [@] [pool])
This is a resplendent five-star hotel set in a terrace of beautifully restored Georgian town houses. Try to get a room in the old house (which has the largest private art collection in the city) – rather than the newer wing – to sample the hotel's truly elegant comforts. Located opposite government buildings, its marble corridors are patronised by visiting dignitaries and the odd celeb. Even if you don't stay, come for the superb afternoon tea (€36), with endless cups of tea served out of silver pots near a raging fire.

WESTBURY HOTEL Hotel **€€€**
(Map p72; ☎01-679 1122; www.doylecollection.com; Grafton St; s/d from €218/245; [P] [@] [wifi])
The Westbury sits snugly on a small street just off Grafton St, which suits the high-powered business people and visiting celebs who favour the hotel's finer suites, where they can watch TV from the jacuzzi before retiring to a four-poster bed. Mere mortals tend to make do with the standard rooms, which are perfectly appointed but lack the sophisticated grandeur promised by the luxurious public spaces.

SHELBOURNE Hotel **€€€**
(Map p72; ☎01-676 6471; www.theshelbourne.ie; 27 North St Stephen's Green; r from €200;

P @ wifi) Dublin's most iconic hotel has long been the best address in town – it was good enough for the framers of the Irish Constitution – but since a major refurbishment and its acquisition by the Marriott group there has been steady grumbling that the hotel is not quite at the top of its five-star game. It *looks* pretty impressive, especially the Lord Mayor's Lounge, where afternoon tea is still one of the best experiences in town.

North of the Liffey

MORRISON HOTEL Hotel **€€€**

(Map p76; ☎01-887 2400; www.morrisonhotel.ie; Lower Ormond Quay; r from €195, ste from €255; @) Fashion designer John Rocha's loosely Oriental style is evident in the zenlike contemporary furnishings and exclusive use of muted earth colours. There's little doubt this place is cool and sophisticated, but it's starting to wear a little around the edges, a fact that no amount of iMac computers and iPod docking stations can hide. The rooms in the newer wing are by far your best option: the seven studio rooms have plenty of space and even a balcony. A great hotel that needs a once over.

MALDRON HOTEL SMITHFIELD Hotel **€€**

(Map p66; ☎01-485 0900; www.maldronhotels.com; Smithfield Village; r €140; @ wifi family) This modern hotel, with big bedrooms and plenty of earth tones to soften the contemporary edges, is your best bet in this part of town. We loved the floor-to-ceiling windows – great for checking out what's going on below in the square.

TOWNHOUSE

Guesthouse **€€**

(Map p66; ☎01-878 8808; www.townhouseofdublin.com; 47-48 Lower Gardiner St; s/d/tr from €60/80/120; wifi) The ghostly writing of Irish-Japanese author Lafcadio Hearn may have influenced the Gothic-style interior of his former home. A dark-walled, gilt-framed foyer with a jingling chandelier leads into 82 individually designed, comfy rooms. Some rooms in the new wing at the back are larger, with balconies overlooking the small Japanese garden.

Docklands

As a hive of activity, the Docklands isn't quite what the planners had hoped it would be, which means that you'll still be making your way west along the quays to get to the action. Still, the hotels here are all good in their respective categories.

GIBSON HOTEL Hotel **€€**

(Map p66; ☎01-618 5000; www.gibsonhotel.ie; Point Village; r from €99; tram Grand Canal Dock, bus 151 from city centre; P @ wifi) A sleek, brand-new hotel with 250-odd rooms all decked out in snazzy Respa beds, flat-screen TVs and internet workstations is the ideal stopping point for the business traveller looking to press the flesh in the Docklands – and for the performers

Wall mural at the James Joyce Cultural Centre (p80)

playing at the O2 Arena next door (p91). The hotel is owned by the same folks who own the arena, so there are some great deals if you're looking for tickets to a show and a bed for the night.

Beyond the Grand Canal

PEMBROKE TOWNHOUSE Guesthouse **€€**

(Map p66; 01-660 0277; www.pembroke townhouse.ie; 90 Pembroke Rd; s €90-195, d €115-290; 5, 7, 7A, 8, 18 or 45 from city centre; P) This superluxurious town house is a perfect example of what happens when traditional and modern combine to great effect. A classical Georgian house has been transformed into a superb boutique hotel, with each room carefully crafted and appointed to reflect the best of contemporary design and style, right down to the modern art on the walls and the handy lift to the upper floors. May we borrow your designer?

ARIEL HOUSE Guesthouse **€€**

(Map p66; 01-668 5512; www.ariel-house.net; 52 Lansdowne Rd; s/d €70/140; 5, 7, 7A, 8, 18 or 45 from city centre; P) Somewhere between a boutique hotel and a luxury B&B, this highly rated Victorian-era property has 28 rooms with private bathrooms, all individually decorated in period furniture, which lends the place an air of genuine luxury. A far better choice than most hotels.

DYLAN Hotel **€€€**

(Map p66; 01-660 3001; www.dylan.ie; Eastmoreland Pl; r from €200; 5, 7, 7A, 8, 18, 27X or 44 from city centre; @) A genuine contender for favourite celebrity stopover, the Dylan's designer OTT look – baroque meets Scandinavian sleek by way of neo–art nouveau and glammed-up 1940s art deco – has nevertheless been a big hit, a reflection perhaps of a time when too much was barely enough for the glitterati who signed contracts over cocktails before retiring to the crisp Frette linen sheets in the snazzily appointed rooms upstairs.

Eating

The most concentrated restaurant area is Temple Bar but, apart from a handful of good places, the bulk of eateries offer bland, unimaginative fodder and cheap set menus for tourists. Better food and service can usually be found on either side of Grafton St, while the top-end restaurants are clustered around Merrion Sq and Fitzwilliam Sq. Fast-food chains dominate the northside, though some fine cafes and eateries are finally appearing there too.

For many restaurants, particularly those in the centre, it's worth booking for Friday or Saturday nights to ensure a table.

A full Irish breakfast

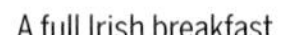

Grafton St & Around

GREEN NINETEEN Organic €€

(Map p72; ☎01-478 9626; 19 Lower Camden St; mains €10-12; ⏰10am-11pm Mon-Sat, noon-6pm Sun) Proof that good food doesn't have to be expensive resides in this sleek restaurant that specialises in locally sourced, organic grub. Braised lamb chump, corned beef, pot-roast chicken and the ubiquitous burger are but the meaty part of the menu that also includes salads and vegie options. We love it, but so does everybody else: book ahead.

COPPINGER ROW Mediterranean €€

(Map p72; ☎01-672 9884; www.coppingerrown.com; Coppinger Row; mains €12-17; ⏰noon-10pm; 👪) This new eatery comes up trumps – the chefs have created a tasty, unfussy menu of Mediterranean treats, to be enjoyed as main courses or as bar bites. We like the roast guinea fowl with borlotti beans but will settle for the meatball linguini.

SILK ROAD CAFÉ Middle Eastern €€

(Map p66; ☎01-407 0770; Chester Beatty Library, Dublin Castle; mains around €11; ⏰11am-4pm Mon-Fri) Museum cafes don't often make you salivate, but this vaguely Middle Eastern–North African–Mediterranean gem is the exception. On the ground floor of the Chester Beatty Library, it is the culinary extension of the superb collection upstairs, gathering together exotic flavours into one outstanding menu that is about two-thirds vegie. Complementing the house specialities like Greek moussaka and spinach lasagne are daily specials like *djaj mehshi* (chicken stuffed with spices, rice, dried fruit, almonds and pine nuts and served with okra and Greek yoghurt). For dessert, there's Lebanese baklava and coconut *kataifi*, or you could opt for the juiciest dates this side of Tyre. All dishes are halal and kosher.

DUNNE & CRESCENZI Italian €€

(Map p72; ☎01-677 3815; 14-16 South Frederick St; mains €9-20; ⏰9am-7pm Mon & Tue, to 10pm Wed-Sat) This exceptional Italian eatery delights its regulars with a basic menu of rustic pleasures: panini, a single pasta dish and a superb plate of mixed antipasti drizzled in olive oil. The shelves are stacked with wine, the coffee is perfect and the desserts are sinfully good.

HONEST TO GOODNESS Cafe €

(Map p72; ☎01-677 5373; George's St Arcade; mains €6.95; ⏰9am-6pm Mon-Sat, noon-4pm Sun) Wholesome sandwiches (made with freshly baked bread), tasty soups and a near-legendary Sloppy Joe, all made on the premises using produce sourced from local farmers, have earned this lovely spot in the George's St Arcade a bevy of loyal fans who want to keep it all to themselves.

RESTAURANT PATRICK GUILBAUD French €€€

(Map p72; ☎01-676 4192; www.restaurantpatrickguilbaud.ie; 21 Upper Merrion St; 2-/3-course set lunch €38/50, dinner mains €38-56; ⏰12.30-2.30pm & 7.30-10.30pm Tue-Sat) Handing out the title of 'Best in the Country' involves some amount of personal choice, but few disagree that this exceptional restaurant is a leading candidate, not least those good people at Michelin, who have put two stars in its crown. The reasons are self-evident: the service is formal but surprisingly friendly, the setting elegant but not stuffy, the wine list simply awesome and head chef Guillaume Lebrun's *haute cuisine* proudly French. The food is innovative without being fiddly, just beautifully cooked and superbly presented. The lunch menu is an absolute steal, at least in this stratosphere.

L'ECRIVAIN French €€€

(Map p72; ☎01-661 1919; www.lecrivain.com; 109A Lower Baggot St; 3-course lunch menu €25/35/45, dinner menu €65, mains €40-47; ⏰closed Sun & lunch Sat) A firm favourite with the bulk of the city's foodies, L'Ecrivain trundles along with just one Michelin star to its name, but the plaudits just keep coming. Head chef Derry Clarke is considered a gourmet god for the exquisite simplicity of his creations, which put the emphasis on flavour and the use of the best local ingredients – all given the French once over and turned into something that approaches divine dining.

Farmers & Organic Markets

Dublin Food Co-op (Map p66; 01-454 4258; www.dublinfoodcoop.com; 12 Newmarket; 2-8pm Thu, 9.30am-4.30pm Sat) A buzzing community market specialising in organic veg, homemade cheeses and organic wines; there's also a bakery.

Coppinger Row Market (Map p72; Coppinger Row; 9am-7pm Thu) It's small – only a handful of stalls – but it packs a proper organic punch, attracting punters with the waft of freshly baked breads, delicious hummus and other goodies.

Harcourt St Food Market (www.irishfarmersmarkets.ie; Park Pl, Station Bldgs, Upper Hatch St; 10am-4pm Thu) Organic vegies, cheeses, olives and meats made into dishes from all over the world.

Temple Bar Farmers Market (Map p76; Meeting House Sq; 9am-4.30pm Sat) This great little market is a fabulous place to while away a Saturday morning, sampling and munching on organic gourmet goodies.

For more info on local markets, check out www.irishfarmersmarkets.ie, www.irishvillagemarkets.com or local county council sites such as www.dlrcoco.ie/markets.

L'GUEULETON French €€
(Map p72; 01-675 3708; 1 Fade St; mains €12-25; noon-3pm & 6-11.30pm Mon-Sat) Dubliners have a devil of a time pronouncing the name (which means 'the Gluttonous Feast' in French) and have had their patience tested with the no-reservations, get-in-line-and-wait policy, but they just can't get enough of the restaurant's take on French rustic cuisine, which makes twisted tongues and sore feet a small price to pay. The steak is sensational, but the Toulouse sausages with *choucroute* (sauerkraut) and Lyonnaise potatoes is a timely reminder that when it comes to the pleasures of the palate, the French really know what they're doing.

PICHET French €€
(Map p76; 01-677 1060; www.pichet-restaurant.com; 14-15 Trinity St; mains €16-26; lunch & dinner) It's not the most obvious spot to open a fancy new restaurant, but that didn't stop Nick Munier, made famous on the English TV show *Hell's Kitchen*, and Stephen Gibson, formerly of L'Ecrivain, who've brought their version of modern French cuisine to this elongated dining room replete with leather blue chairs and lots of windows to stare out of. The result is pretty good indeed, the food excellent (we expected nothing less) and the service impeccable. Sit down the back – the atmosphere is better.

PEPPERPOT Cafe €
(Map p72; 087-790 3204; www.thepepperpot.ie; Powerscourt Townhouse; mains €5-8; 10am-6pm Mon-Wed & Fri, to 8pm Thu, 9am-6pm Sat & noon-6pm Sun) Everything is baked and made daily at the lovely cafe on the 1st-floor balcony of the Powerscourt Townhouse. The salads with homemade brown bread are delicious but the real treat is the soup of the day (€4.50).

YAMAMORI Japanese €€
(Map p72; 01-475 5001; 71 South Great George's St; mains €16-25, lunch bento €9.95; 12.30-11pm) Hip, inexpensive and generally pretty good, Yamamori rarely disappoints with its bubbly service and vivacious cooking that swoops from sushi and sashimi to whopping great plates of noodles. It's a great spot for a sociable group – including vegetarians – although you'll have to book

at the weekend. The lunch bento is one of the best deals in town.

SHANAHAN'S ON THE GREEN Steakhouse **€€€**

(Map p72; ☎01-407 0939; www.shanahans.ie; 119 West St Stephen's Green; mains €36-52; ⏰from 6pm Mon-Thu & Sat & Sun, from noon Fri) 'American-style steakhouse' hardly does justice to this elegant restaurant where JR Ewing and his cronies would happily have done business. Spread across three floors of a stunning Georgian building are four elegant dining areas, where impeccable service and a courteous bonhomie attract the great, the good and the not-so-good to its well-laid-out tables. Although the menu features seafood, this place is all about meat, notably the best cuts of impossibly juicy and tender Irish Angus beef you'll find anywhere on the island. The mountainous onion rings are the perfect accompaniment, while the sommeliers are among the best in the business.

THORNTON'S French **€€€**

(Map p72; ☎01-478 7000; www.thorntonsrestaurant.com; 128 St Stephen's Green; midweek 2-/3-course lunch €25/49, dinner tasting menus €79-125; ⏰12.30-2pm & 7-10pm Tue-Sat) Kevin Thornton shrugged his shoulders when Michelin saw fit to strip him of one of his two stars, and replied by ordering a refurb of his über-trendy room on the 1st floor of the Fitzwilliam Hotel overlooking St Stephen's Green. The food – a mouth-watering Irish interpretation of new French cuisine – remains as good as ever, offering a mix of succulent seafood and gamey dishes like roast woodcock. A nice touch is Kevin himself making a round of the tables, answering questions and explaining the dishes. He also offers an all-day masterclass (€200) on how to recreate his cuisine.

North of the Liffey

CHAPTER ONE Modern Irish **€€€**

(Map p78; ☎01-873 2266; www.chapterone restaurant.com; 18 North Parnell Sq; mains €32-72; ⏰12.30-2pm Tue-Fri, 6-11pm Tue-Sat) One of the best restaurants in Dublin, this venerable old trooper in the vaulted basement of the Dublin Writers Museum (p80) sets its ambitions no further than modern Irish cuisine, which it has realised so brilliantly that those Michelin lads saw fit to throw one of their sought-after stars its way. Menus change regularly but the

Menu at the Winding Stair (p88)

OLIVIER CIRENDINI / LONELY PLANET IMAGES ©

dishes are always top-notch, the service first class and the atmosphere reassuringly reserved – although its success means that you have to book well in advance to land a table. Get there between 6pm and 7.40pm for the three-course pretheatre special (€37.50).

WINDING STAIR Modern Irish **€€€**
(Map p76; ☎01-873 7320; 40 Lower Ormond Quay; mains €21-27; ⏰noon-4pm & 6-10pm Tue-Sat, 1-10pm Sun) Housed within a beautiful Georgian building that was once home to the city's most beloved bookshop (the ground floor still is one), the conversion to elegant restaurant has been faultless. The wonderful Irish menu – creamy fish pie, bacon and organic cabbage, steamed mussels, and Irish farmyard cheeses – coupled with an excellent wine list make for a memorable meal.

TASTE OF EMILIA Italian **€**
(☎01-878 8188; 28 Lower Liffey St; mains €4-10; ⏰7.30am-7pm Mon-Wed & Fri & Sat, to 9.30pm Thu) Half bar, half Italian deli, this warm, buzzing locale does a wonderful trade in cured meats and cheeses from all over Italy, paying particular attention to the produce of the true heartland of Italian cuisine, Emilia-Romagna. The sandwiches are made with homemade *piadina* bread or *tigelle,* and you can wash it down with a light sparkling wine from Northern Italy. Italians love the joint, and it's no wonder.

Beyond the Grand Canal

JUNIORS Italian **€€**
(Map p66; ☎01-664 3648; www.juniors.ie; 2 Bath Ave, Sandymount; mains €15-24; ⏰lunch & dinner) Cramped and easily mistaken for any old cafe, Juniors is anything but ordinary: designed to imitate a New York deli, the food (Italian-influenced, all locally sourced produce) is delicious, the atmosphere always buzzing (it's often hard to get a table) and the ethos top-notch, which is down to the two brothers who run the place.

Left: Interior of Patrick Guilbaud's restaurant (p85);
Below: Inside the Stag's Head pub

PHOTOGRAPHER: (LEFT) OLIVIER CIRENDINI / LONELY PLANET IMAGES ©; (BELOW) OLIVER STREWE / LONELY PLANET IMAGES ©

Drinking

Come hell or high water, Dubliners will always take a drink, and if you don't join them for at least one you will never crack the social code that makes this city tick – and you'll run the risk of being dismissed as a dry shite who really doesn't know how to enjoy themselves. No pressure, then.

Grafton St & Around

STAG'S HEAD Pub

(Map p76; ☎ 01-679 3701; 1 Dame Ct) The Stag's Head was built in 1770, remodelled in 1895 and thankfully not changed a bit since then. It's a superb pub: so picturesque that it often appears in films and also featured in a postage-stamp series on Irish bars. It's probable that some of the fitters that worked on this pub would have also worked on churches in the area, so the stained-wood-and-polished-brass similarities are no accident.

KEHOE'S Pub

(Map p72; ☎ 01-677 8312; 9 South Anne St) This is one of the most atmospheric pubs in the city centre and a real favourite with all kinds of Dubliners. It has a beautiful Victorian bar, a wonderful snug, and plenty of other little nooks and crannies. Upstairs, drinks are served in what was once the publican's living room. And it looks it!

LONG HALL Pub

(Map p72; ☎ 01-475 1590; 51 South Great George's St) Luxuriating in full Victorian splendour, this is one of the city's most beautiful and best-loved pubs. Check out the elegant chandeliers and the ornate carvings in the woodwork behind the bar. The bartenders are experts at their craft – an increasingly rare experience in Dublin these days.

NO NAME BAR Bar

(Map p72; ☎ 01-675 3708; 3 Fade St) A low-key entrance just next to L'Gueuleton leads

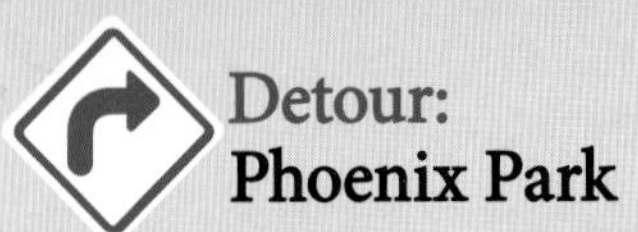

Detour: Phoenix Park

Measuring 709 glorious hectares, the **Phoenix Park** (admission free) is Europe's largest city park: a green lung that is more than double the size of New York's Central Park (a paltry 337 hectares), and larger than all of London's major parks put together.

Áras an Uachtaráin (01-617 1000; Phoenix Park; admission free; guided tours hourly 10.30am-4.30pm Sat), the residence of the Irish president, is a Palladian lodge that was built in 1751 and enlarged a couple of times since, most recently in 1816. Tickets for the free one-hour **tours** (hourly 10-4pm Sat) can be collected from the **Phoenix Park Visitor Centre** (01-677 0095; admission free; 10am-5.45pm Mar-Sep, 9.30-5.30pm Wed-Sun Oct-Feb), the converted former stables of the papal nunciate, where you'll see a 10-minute introductory video before being shuttled to the Áras itself to inspect five state rooms and the president's study.

To get to Dublin's beloved playground, take bus 10 from O'Connell St. The best way to get around the park is to hop on the **Phoenix Park Shuttle Bus** (hourly 7am-5pm Mon-Fri, 10am-5pm Sat & Sun; adult/child €2/1), which goes from just outside the main gate on Parkgate St and loops around to the visitor centre.

upstairs to one of the nicest bar spaces in town – three huge rooms in a restored Victorian town house plus a sizeable heated patio area for smokers. It gets its name from not having one.

JOHN MULLIGAN'S Pub

(Map p66; 01-677 5582; 8 Poolbeg St) Outside the eastern boundary of Temple Bar, John Mulligan's is another pub that has scarcely changed over the years. It featured as the local in the film *My Left Foot* and is also popular with journalists from the nearby newspaper offices. Mulligan's was established in 1782 and was long reputed to have the best Guinness in town, as well as a wonderfully varied collection of regulars.

JAMES TONER'S Pub

(Map p72; 01-676 3090; 139 Lower Baggot St) With its stone floor, Toner's is almost a country pub in the heart of the city, and the shelves and drawers are reminders that it once doubled as a grocery store. Not that its suit-wearing business crowd would ever have shopped here...

O'DONOGHUE'S Pub

(Map p72; 01-661 4303; 15 Merrion Row) The most famous traditional music bar in Dublin, O'Donoghue's is where world-famous folk group The Dubliners started off in the 1960s. On summer evenings a young, international crowd spills out into the courtyard beside the pub.

ANSEO Bar

(Map p72; 01-475 1321; 28 Lower Camden St) Unpretentious, unaffected and incredibly popular, this cosy alternative bar is a favourite with those who live by the credo that to try too hard is far worse than not trying at all. Wearing cool like a loose garment, the punters thrive on the mix of chat and terrific music.

North of the Liffey

SIN É Bar

(Map p66; 01-878 7009; 14-15 Upper Ormond Quay) This excellent quayside bar is proof that the most important quality for any pub is ambience. There's no real decor to speak of, but this place buzzes almost nightly with a terrific mix of students and professionals, the hip and the uncool. It helps that the DJs here are all uniformly excellent.

COBBLESTONE Pub
(Map p66; ☎01-872 1799; North King St) This pub is on the main square in Smithfield, an old northside marketplace. There's a great atmosphere in the cosy upstairs bar, where the nightly music sessions – both traditional and up-and-coming folk and singer-songwriter acts – are superb.

Entertainment

Rock & Pop

Dublin's love affair with popular music has made it one of the preferred touring stops for all kinds of musicians, who seem to relish the unfettered manner in which audiences embrace their favourite artists. There are venues of every size; bookings can be made either directly at the venues or through **HMV** (Map p72; ☎01-679 5334; 65 Grafton St) or **Ticketmaster** (☎0818 719 300, 01-456 9569; www.ticketmaster.ie), but they charge between 9% and 12.5% service charge *per ticket,* not per booking, on credit-card bookings.

WORKMAN'S CLUB Bar
(Map p76; ☎01-670 6692; www.theworkmansclub.com; 10 Wellington Quay) A 300-capacity venue and bar in the former working-men's club of Dublin, this new spot puts the emphasis on keeping away from the mainstream, which means a broad range of performers, from singer-songwriters to electronic cabaret.

VICAR STREET Venue
(☎01-454 5533; www.vicarstreet.com; 58-59 Thomas St) Smaller performances take place at this intimate venue, near Christ Church Cathedral. It has a capacity of 1000, spread between table-serviced group seating downstairs and a theatre-style balcony. It has a varied program of performers, with a strong emphasis on folk and jazz.

TOP CHOICE **02** Arena
(Map p66; ☎01-819 8888; www.theo2.ie; East Link Bridge, North Wall Quay) The premier indoor venue in the city has a capacity of around 10,000 and plays host to the very brightest stars in the firmament: Rihanna, Bryan Adams and the cast of Glee are just some of the acts that have brought their magic to its superb stage.

WHELAN'S Live Music
(Map p72; ☎01-478 0766; www.whelanslive.com; 25 Wexford St) Whelan's near-legendary status as the home of the sensitive, soul-searching singer – and where gigs are treated like semimystical experiences by their devoted fans – is inevitably the cause of much derision in some Dublin quarters, but there's no denying the venue's special place in the Dublin musical scene. It's a pretty intimate space, perfect if you're looking to 'connect' with

Cricket match at Phoenix Park
PHOTOGRAPHER: JONATHAN SMITH / LONELY PLANET IMAGES ©

Dublin for Children

Dublin has some good activities that parents and children can enjoy together. The National Museum (p68 and p79) and the Irish Museum of Modern Art (p76) run fun, educational programs for children at weekends.

All but a few hotels will provide cots, and most top-range hotels have baby-sitting services (€8 to €15 per hour). Restaurants are generally accommodating until 6pm, after which things can get difficult, especially for babies: check while making a booking.

your favourite artists, who will most likely be cadging drinks off fans in the bar afterwards.

Classical

GRAND CANAL THEATRE Theatre
(Map p66; ☎01-677 7999; www.grandcanaltheatre.ie; Grand Canal Sq) Daniel Liebeskind's masterful design is a three-tiered, 2000-capacity auditorium where you're as likely to be entertained by the Bolshoi or a touring state opera as you are to see Disney on Ice or Barbra Streisand. It's a magnificent venue – designed for classical, paid for by the classics.

NATIONAL CONCERT HALL Concert Hall
(Map p72; ☎01-417 0000; www.nch.ie; Earlsfort Tce) Ireland's premier orchestral hall hosts a variety of concerts year-round, including a series of lunchtime concerts from 1.05pm to 2pm on Tuesdays, June to August.

Theatre

Dublin's theatre scene is small but busy. Bookings can usually be made by quoting a credit-card number over the phone and tickets collected just before the performance.

GATE THEATRE Theatre
(Map p78; ☎01-874 4045; www.gatetheatre.ie; 1 Cavendish Row) To the north of the Liffey, the Gate Theatre specialises in international classics and older Irish works with a touch of comedy by playwrights such as Oscar Wilde, George Bernard Shaw and Oliver Goldsmith, although newer plays are sometimes staged too. Prices vary according to what's on, but they're usually around €20.

ABBEY THEATRE Theatre
(Map p78; ☎01-878 7222; www.abbey_theatre.ie; Lower Abbey St) Ireland's national theatre resides in a large concrete box by the river. It puts on new Irish works, as well as revivals of classic Irish plays by writers such as WB Yeats, JM Synge, Sean O'Casey, Brendan Behan and Samuel Beckett. Tickets for evening performances cost up to €25, except on Monday, when they're cheaper. The smaller **Peacock Theatre (☎01-878 7222)** is part of the same complex and stages more fringe work.

GAIETY THEATRE Theatre
(Map p72; ☎01-677 1717; www.gaietytheatre.com; South King St) Opened in 1871, this theatre is used for modern plays, TV shows, musical comedies and revues.

Shopping

British and US chains dominate the high street and major shopping centres, but there are also numerous small, independent shops selling high-quality, locally made goods. Irish designer clothing and streetwear, handmade jewellery, unusual homewares and crafts, and cheeses to die for are readily available if you know where to look.

Grafton St & Around

AVOCA HANDWEAVERS Irish Crafts
(Map p76; ☎01-677 4215; 11-13 Suffolk St) This contemporary craft shop is a treasure trove of interesting Irish and foreign products. The colourful shop is chock-a-block with woollen knits, ceramics, handcrafted gadgets and a wonderful toy selection – and not a tweed cap in sight.

POWERSCOURT TOWNHOUSE SHOPPING CENTRE Mall
(Map p72; ☎01-679 4144; 59 South William St) This gorgeous, stylish centre is in a carefully refurbished Georgian town house, originally built between 1741 and 1744. These days it's best known for its cafes and restaurants but it still does a top-end, selective trade in high fashion, art, exquisite handicrafts and other chichi sundries.

CLADDAGH RECORDS Irish Music
(Map p76; ☎01-677 0262; 2 Cecilia St) This shop sells a wide range of Irish traditional and folk music.

CATACH BOOKS Rare Books
(Map p72; ☎01-671 8676; www.rarebooks.ie; 10 Duke St) A rich and remarkable collection of rare and secondhand Irish-interest books, including first editions.

DESIGNYARD Crafts
(Map p66; ☎474 1011; 48-49 Nassau St) A high-end craft-as-art shop where everything you see – be it glass, batik, sculpture, painting – is one-off and handmade in Ireland. It also showcases contemporary jewellery from young international designers in its exhibition space.

KILKENNY SHOP Crafts
(Map p72; ☎01-677 7066; 6 Nassau St) This shop has a wonderful selection of finely made Irish crafts, featuring clothing, glassware, pottery, jewellery, crystal and silver from some of Ireland's best designers.

Information

Dangers & Annoyances

Dublin is generally quite a safe city, although petty crime of the bag-snatching, car break-in variety can be a low-level irritant. Be sensible: guard your belongings, don't leave anything in your car and consider the use of supervised car parks for overnight parking. Remember also that insurance policies often don't cover losses from cars.

The Powerscourt Townhouse Shopping Centre

DOUG McKINLAY / LONELY PLANET IMAGES ©

The only consistent trouble in Dublin is alcohol-related: where there are pubs and clubs there are worse-for-wear revellers looking to get home and/or get laid, and sometimes the frustrations of getting neither can result in a trip to the casualty department of the nearest hospital – hospitals are clogged to bursting with drink-related cases throughout the weekend.

When using ATMs, guard your PIN details carefully. Don't use one that looks like it's been tampered with as card cloning is a growing problem.

Tourist Information

You can book accommodation via www.visitdublin.ie or www.gulliver.ie, or via telephone: in Ireland call ☎1800 668 668; from Britain call ☎00800 6686 6866; from the rest of the world call ☎66-979 2030.

Dublin Tourism **(Map p76; ☎01-605 7700; www.visitdublin.com; St Andrew's Church, 2 Suffolk St; 9am-7pm Mon-Sat, 10.30am-3pm Sun Jul & Aug, 9am-5.30pm Mon-Sat Sep-Jun)** Main tourist office. There's a booking fee of €5 for serviced accommodation or €7 for self-catering accommodation, and a 10% deposit that is refunded through your hotel bill. Also Dublin Airport **(arrivals hall; 8am-10pm)**, Dun Laoghaire **(Dun Laoghaire ferry terminal; 10am-1pm & 2-6pm Mon-Sat)**, O'Connell Street **(Map p78; 14 Upper O'Connell St; 9am-5pm Mon-Sat)** and Wilton Terrace **(Wilton Tce; 9.30am-noon & 12.30-5.15pm Mon-Fri)**.

Getting There & Away

Air

Dublin Airport **(Map p63; ☎01-814 1111; www.dublinairport.com)** About 13km north of the centre is Ireland's major international gateway airport, with direct flights from Europe, North America and Asia.

Boat

Dublin has two ferry ports: the Dun Laoghaire ferry terminal **(☎01-280 1905; Dun Laoghaire)**, 13km southeast of the city, serves Holyhead in Wales and can be reached by DART to Dun Laoghaire, or bus 7, 7A or 8 from Burgh Quay or bus 46A from Trinity College; and the Dublin Port terminal **(Map p63; ☎01-855 2222; Alexandra Rd)**, 3km northeast of the city centre, serves Holyhead and Liverpool.

Buses from Busáras (p94) are timed to coincide with arrivals and departures: for the 9.45am ferry departure from Dublin Port, buses leave Busáras at 8.30am. For the 9.45pm departure, buses depart from Busáras at 8.30pm. For the 1am sailing to Liverpool, the bus departs from Busáras at 11.45pm. All bus trips cost adult/child €2.50/1.25.

See p379 for details of ferry journeys.

Bus

Busáras **(Map p66; ☎01-836 6111; www.buseireann.ie; Store St)** The main bus station is just north of the river behind Custom House, and serves as the main city stop for Bus Éireann **(www.buseireann.ie)**.

For information on fares, frequencies and durations to various destinations in the Republic and Northern Ireland, see p381.

Sunset sailing near Howth

Fare Saver Passes

The increasingly integrated public transport system offers a range of fare-saver passes, available from Dublin Bus and the tourist office.

- **Freedom Pass** (adult/child €26/10) offers three days of unlimited travel on all Dublin Bus services, including its Airlink, Xpresso and hop-on, hop-off tourist bus.
- **Rambler One-Day Family** (€10.50) One day unlimited travel for two adults and two children on all Dublin Bus services, including Airlink and Xpresso.
- **Family One-Day Short Hop** (€15.75) One day unlimited travel for two adults and two children on all Dublin Bus services, including Xpresso, DART and suburban rail services.

Train

For general train information, contact Iarnród Éireann Travel Centre (☎01-836 6222; www.irishrail.ie; 35 Lower Abbey St; ⏰9am-5pm Mon-Fri, 9am-1pm Sat). Connolly Station (Map p66; ☎01-836 3333), just north of the Liffey and the city centre, serves the north and northwest (including Belfast, Derry and Sligo). Heuston Station (Map p66; ☎01-836 5421), just south of the Liffey and west of the centre, serves all destinations to the south and west including Cork, Galway, Killarney, Limerick, Wexford and Waterford. See p385 for more information.

Getting Around

To/From the Airport

There is no train service to/from the airport, but there are bus and taxi options.

BUS

Aircoach (☎01-844 7118; www.aircoach.ie; one way/return €7/12) Private coach service with two routes from the airport to 18 destinations throughout the city, including the main streets of the city centre. Coaches run every 10 to 15 minutes between 6am and midnight, then hourly from midnight until 6am.

Airlink Express Coach (☎01-872 0000, 01-873 4222; www.dublinbus.ie; adult/child €6/3) Bus 747 runs every 10 to 20 minutes from 5.45am to 11.30pm between the airport, the central bus station (Busáras) and the Dublin Bus office on Upper O'Connell St; bus 748 runs every 15 to 30 minutes from 6.50am to 10.05pm between the airport and Heuston and Connolly Stations.

Dublin Bus (Map p78; ☎01-872 0000; www.dublinbus.ie; 59 Upper O'Connell St; adult/child €2.20/1) A number of buses serve the airport from various points in Dublin, including buses 16A (Rathfarnham), 746 (Dun Laoghaire) and 230 (Portmarnock); all cross the city centre on their way to the airport.

TAXI

There is a taxi rank directly outside the arrivals concourse. A taxi should cost about €20 from the airport to the city centre, including a supplementary charge of €2.50 (not applied going to the airport). Make sure the meter is switched on.

Bicycle

The blue bikes of Dublinbikes (www.dublinbikes.ie) have become a ubiquitous presence around the city centre, making this scheme one of the most successful transport initiatives of recent years. The pay-as-you-go service is straightforward: cyclists purchase a €10 Smart Card (as well as pay a credit card deposit of €150) – either online or at any of the 40 stations throughout the city centre – before 'freeing' a bike for use, which is then free for the first 30 minutes and 50c for each half hour thereafter.

Public Transport

BUS

The office of Dublin Bus (Map p78; ☎01-872 0000; www.dublinbus.ie; 59 Upper O'Connell St; ⏰9am-5.30pm Mon-Fri, 9am-2pm Sat) has free single-route timetables of all its services.

Buses run from around 6am (some start at 5.30am) to 11.30pm. You must use exact change for tickets when boarding buses; anything more and you will be given a receipt for reimbursement, which is possible only at the Dublin Bus main office. Avoid this by using a smartcard ticket, available at most Spar or Centra shops.

LUAS

The Luas (www.luas.ie; ⏰5.30am-12.30am Mon-Fri, from 6.30am Sat, 7am-11.30pm Sun) light-rail system has two lines: the Green Line (trains run every five to 15 minutes), which connects St Stephen's Green with Sandyford in south Dublin via Ranelagh and Dundrum; and the Red Line (trains run every 20 minutes), which runs from the Point Village in the Docklands to Tallaght via the north quays and Heuston Station. There are ticket machines at every stop or you can buy tickets from newsagencies throughout the city centre; a typical short-hop fare will cost you €1.80. Smartcard tickets can also be used.

TRAIN

The Dublin Area Rapid Transport (DART; ☎01-836 6222; www.irishrail.ie) provides quick train access to the coast as far north as Howth (about 30 minutes) and as far south as Greystones in County Wicklow.

Pearse Station (Map p66) is convenient for central Dublin south of the Liffey, and Connolly Station for north of the Liffey. There are services every 10 to 20 minutes, sometimes even more frequently, from around 6.30am to midnight Monday to Saturday; services are less frequent on Sunday. Dublin to Dun Laoghaire takes about 15 to 20 minutes. A one-way DART ticket from Dublin to Dun Laoghaire or Howth costs €2.30; to Bray it's €2.75.

There are also suburban rail services north as far as Dundalk, inland to Mullingar and south past Bray to Arklow.

Left: Luas light rail on Lower Abbey St;
Below: Georgian doorways near Merrion Square (p75)

PHOTOGRAPHERS: (LEFT) RICHARD CUMMINS / LONELY PLANET IMAGES © (BELOW) OLIVIER CIRENDINI / LONELY PLANET IMAGES ©

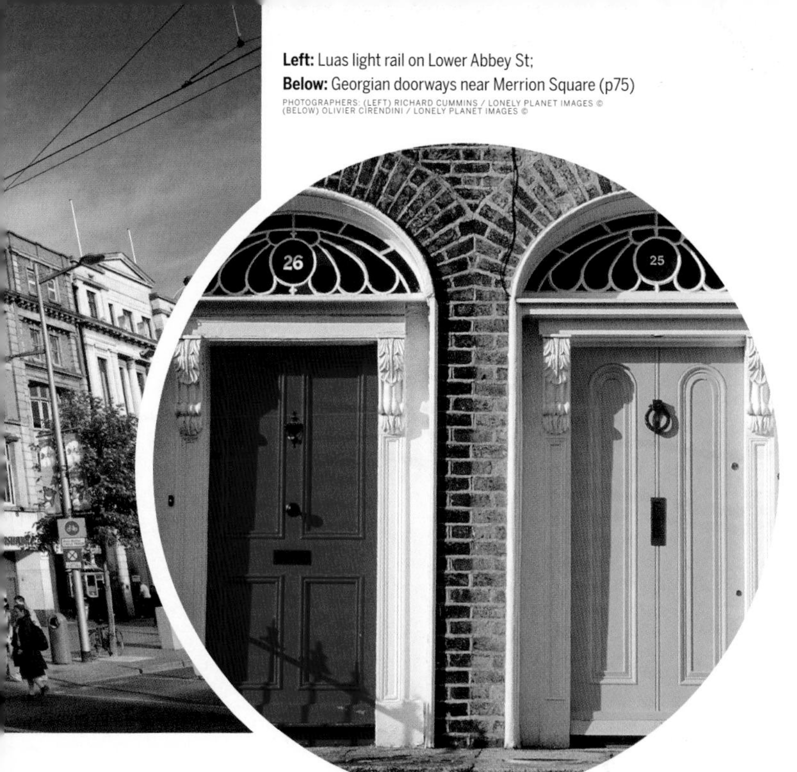

Taxi

From 8am to 10pm, taxi fares begin with a flagfall of €4.10, followed by around €1 per kilometre thereafter; from 10pm to 8am, it's €4.45 flagfall and €1.35 per kilometre. Extra charges include €1 for each extra passenger and €2 for telephone bookings; there is no charge for luggage.

Taxis can be hailed on the street and found at taxi ranks around the city, including O'Connell St, College Green (in front of Trinity College) and St Stephen's Green at the end of Grafton St. There are numerous taxi companies that will dispatch taxis by radio. Some options:

City Cabs (☎ 01-872 2688)

National Radio Cabs (☎ 01-677 2222)

Wicklow & Eastern Ireland

South of Dublin is Wicklow – scenic, stunning and wild.

Its most imposing natural feature is a gorse-and-bracken mountain spine that provides one of Ireland's most stunning landscapes, replete with dramatic glacial valleys, soaring mountain passes and some of the country's most important archaeological treasures, from breathtaking early-Christian sites to the elegant country homes of Ireland's 18th-century nobility.

To the west is pastoral Kildare, the home of Irish horse racing and some of Ireland's richest farmland; what it lacks in history it more than makes up for in beautiful countryside.

North and northwest of Dublin is Meath, once one of the five provinces of ancient Ireland. The 'Middle Kingdom' attracted Ireland's first settlers, who left their mark in the magnificent Neolithic monuments of the Boyne Valley. Slightly north again is the 'Wee County', but while Louth may be small, it still packs a scenic punch – the ruins of Mellifont and Monasterboice are but two of the county's big attractions.

Lough Dan (p112) in the Wicklow Mountains

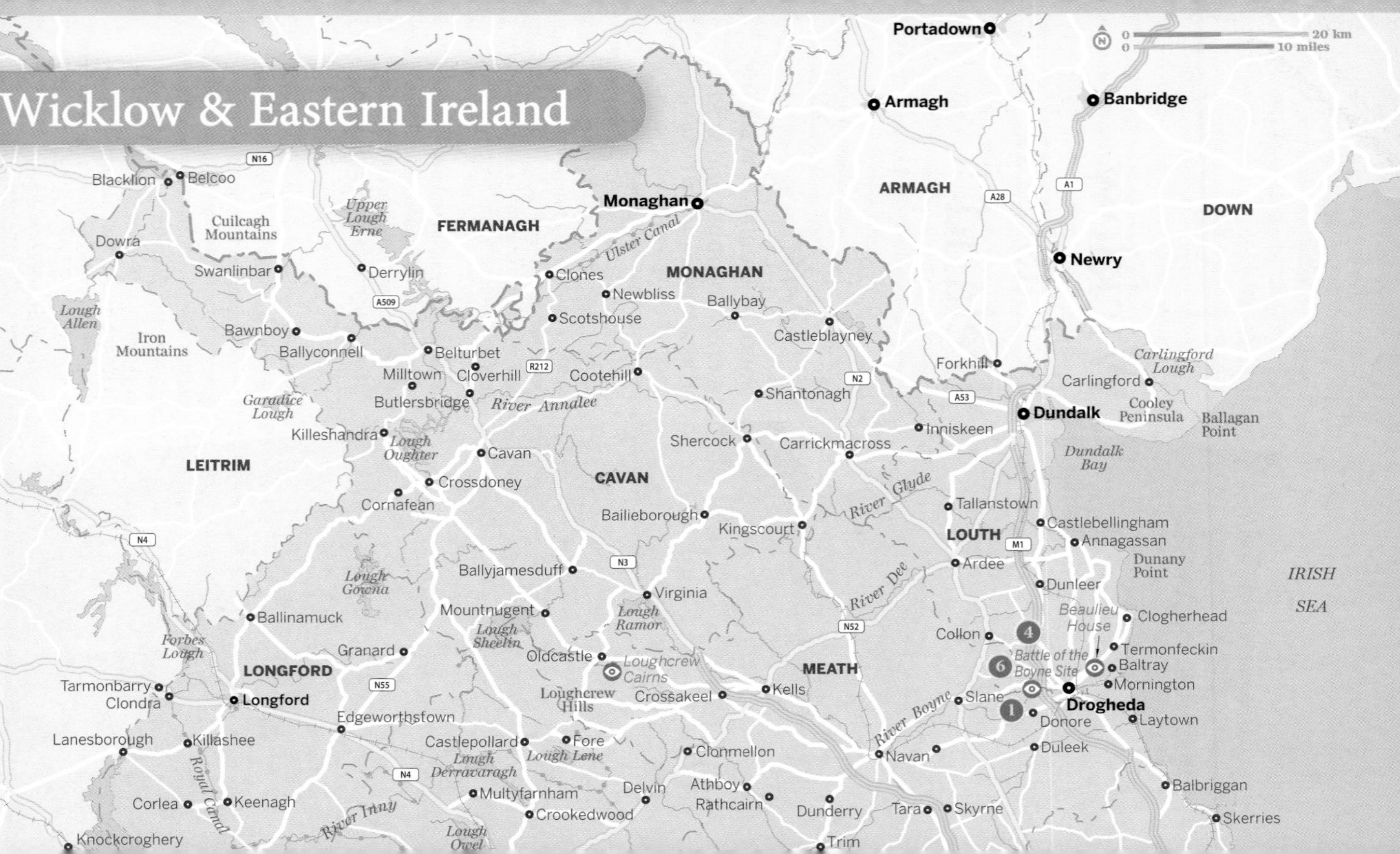

Wicklow & Eastern Ireland
0 20 km
0 10 miles
Portadown
Armagh
Banbridge
ARMAGH
DOWN
Newry
Monaghan
FERMANAGH
MONAGHAN
Blacklion
Belcoo
Cuilcagh Mountains
Upper Lough Erne
Dowra
Swanlinbar
Derrylin
Clones
Ulster Canal
Newbliss
Ballybay
Scotshouse
Castleblayney
Lough Allen
Iron Mountains
Bawnboy
Ballyconnell
Belturbet
Milltown
Cloverhill
Cootehill
Forkhill
Carlingford Lough
Carlingford
Cooley Peninsula
Ballagan Point
Shantonagh
Dundalk
Garadice Lough
Butlersbridge
River Annalee
Killeshandra
Lough Oughter
Inniskeen
Shercock
Carrickmacross
Dundalk Bay
Cavan
LEITRIM
Crossdoney
CAVAN
River Glyde
Cornafean
Tallanstown
Bailieborough
Kingscourt
Castlebellingham
LOUTH
Annagassan
Dunany Point
Ardee
Ballyjamesduff
Lough Gowna
Virginia
River Dee
Dunleer
IRISH SEA
Mountnugent
Lough Ramor
Ballinamuck
Beaulieu House
Clogherhead
Lough Sheelin
Collon
Forbes Lough
Granard
Termonfeckin
Oldcastle
Loughcrew Cairns
Battle of the Boyne Site
LONGFORD
MEATH
Baltray
Tarmonbarry
Mornington
Clondra
Longford
Loughcrew Hills
Crossakeel
Kells
Slane
Drogheda
Edgeworthstown
River Boyne
Donore
Laytown
Lanesborough
Killashee
Castlepollard
Fore
Lough Lene
Clonmellon
Navan
Duleek
Lough Derravaragh
Royal Canal
Athboy
Balbriggan
Multyfarnham
Delvin
Corlea
Keenagh
Rathcairn
Dunderry
Tara
Skyrne
River Inny
Crookedwood
Skerries
Lough Owel
Knockcroghery
Trim
N16
A509
R212
N2
A53
A28
A1
M1
N3
N4
N52
N55

1 Brú Na Bóinne
2 Glendalough
3 Powerscourt Estate
4 Monasterboice
5 Castletown House
6 Old Mellifont Abbey
ROSCOMMON
WESTMEATH
GALWAY
OFFALY
KILDARE
DUBLIN
LAOIS
WICKLOW
CARLOW
KILKENNY
WEXFORD
DUBLIN
Dun Laoghaire
Mullingar
Athlone
Tullamore
Portlaoise
Naas
Carlow
Arklow
Wicklow
Greystones
Bray
Howth
Swords
Ballymahon
Rathconrath
Glasson
Lough Ree
Lough Ennell
Coralstown
Kinnegad
Royal Canal
Laracor
Summerhill
Dunshaughlin
Ratoath
Ashbourne
Black Bull
Dunboyne
Lusk
Rush
Portrane
Lambay Island
Donabate
Malahide
Portmarnock
Dublin Airport
Moate
Horseleap
Kilbeggan
Clara
Ballinahown
River Shannon
Shannonbridge
Shannon Harbour
Banagher
Cloghan
Frankford
Rahan
Grand Canal
Daingean
Edenderry
Bog of Allen
Lullymore
Robertstown
Rathangan
Kilcock
Maynooth
Leixlip
Celbridge
Straffan
Clane
Sallins
Kill
Rathcoole
Clondalkin
Marlay Park
Killakee
Sandycove
Dalkey
Killiney
Loughlinstown
Kilmacanogue
Enniskerry
Glencree
Kilbride
Blessington
River Liffey
Newbridge
Kildare
Tully
The Curragh
Kilcullen
Monasterevin
Portarlington
River Barrow
Rosenallis
Mountmellick
Slieve Bloom Mountains
Ballyfin
Emo
Clonenagh
Stradbally
Athy
Timahoe
Old Town
Abbeyleix
Ballinakill
Durrow
Cullahill
Ballyragget
Killeshin
Castledermot
Kilkea
Baltinglass
Rathdangan
Knockanarrigan
Ballitore
Donard
Dunlavin
Hollywood
Poulaphouca Reservoir
Valleymount
Wicklow Mountains National Park
Wicklow Mountains
Sally Gap
Sraghmore
Kilpedder
Kilcoole
Roundwood
Devil's Glen
Annamoe
Glendalough
Laragh
Ashford
Rathnew
Glenealy
Wicklow Head
Lugnaquilla Mountain (924m)
Drumgoff
Derrynamuck
Rathdrum
Redcross
Brittas Bay
Mizen Head
Macreddin
River Avonbeg
Avoca
Aughrim
River Ow
Woodenbridge
St George's Channel
Kilmichael Point
Tinahely
Shillelagh
Carnew
River Slaney
River Bann
N55
N62
N52
N80
M6
M4
N41
N3
N2
M1
M50
N7
M7
N78
M9
R755
M11
N77

Wicklow & Eastern Ireland's Highlights

1

Brú na Bóinne

Newgrange and its surrounding tombs of Knowth and Dowth – known in Irish mythology as Brú na Bóinne, the home of the God Dagda and his wife Bóinne (the river Boyne) and later the burial place of the pagan kings of Tara – are one of only three World Heritage sites in Ireland. Winter solstice sunrise entrance, Newgrange

Need to Know

Best Time to Visit Midweek, outside of the summer months. **Advance Planning** Enter the Winter Solstice lottery before 25 September. **For further coverage, see p125.**

Local Knowledge

Brú na Bóinne Don't Miss List

BY MARY GIBBONS, HERITAGE TOUR SPECIALIST (WWW.HERITAGEIRELAND.IE)

1 GREAT STONE CIRCLE

The great stone circle surrounding Newgrange (p125) is the largest of its kind in Ireland; although only 12 are left, there were once 35-odd standing stones. It's believed to have been an astronomical calendar, with shadows dividing the year into times of planting and harvest.

2 THE KERBSTONES

The decorated kerbstones built into the outside of the great passage tomb are part of a Neolithic art tradition which spanned over a thousand years. The most magnificent is found at the entrance, forming a symbolic barrier between the living and the dead; a second decorated stone is diametrically opposite, perhaps marking a 'symbolic exit'.

3 THE PASSAGE

The 19m stone tunnel passage that leads into the mound has some of the most beautifully executed Neolithic art anywhere in the world. Individually decorated stones alternate with undecorated ones. Just before the inner chamber is one of the most famous pieces of Neolithic art in Ireland: a triple spiral framed by triple lines in a chevron pattern.

4 THE INNER CHAMBER

The inner chamber, rediscovered in 1699 by one of the victors of the Battle of the Boyne, is a corbelled, cruciform-shaped space over 6m high, with three heavily decorated recesses; one has a triple spiral regarded by Dr Geraldine Stout, the foremost authority on Newgrange, as 'the most exquisite carving to be found in the entire corpus of European megalithic art'.

5 WINTER SOLSTICE EVENT

For 17 minutes of magic on the morning of 21 December, the light of the rising sun funnels through a light box above the main passage entrance and illuminates the passageway and the main chamber to reveal one of the world's most extraordinary prehistoric art galleries. At other times of the year, visitors witness an inspiring re-creation of this singular event.

ugh

traordinary monastic remains at Glendalough (p112) are reason enough to but once you're there, you'll see why St Kevin chose this particular spot to stled in a tree-dotted glacial valley and bordered by two lakes, Glendalough ubt one of the most beautiful corners of the whole country. St Kevin's Church, Glendalough

2

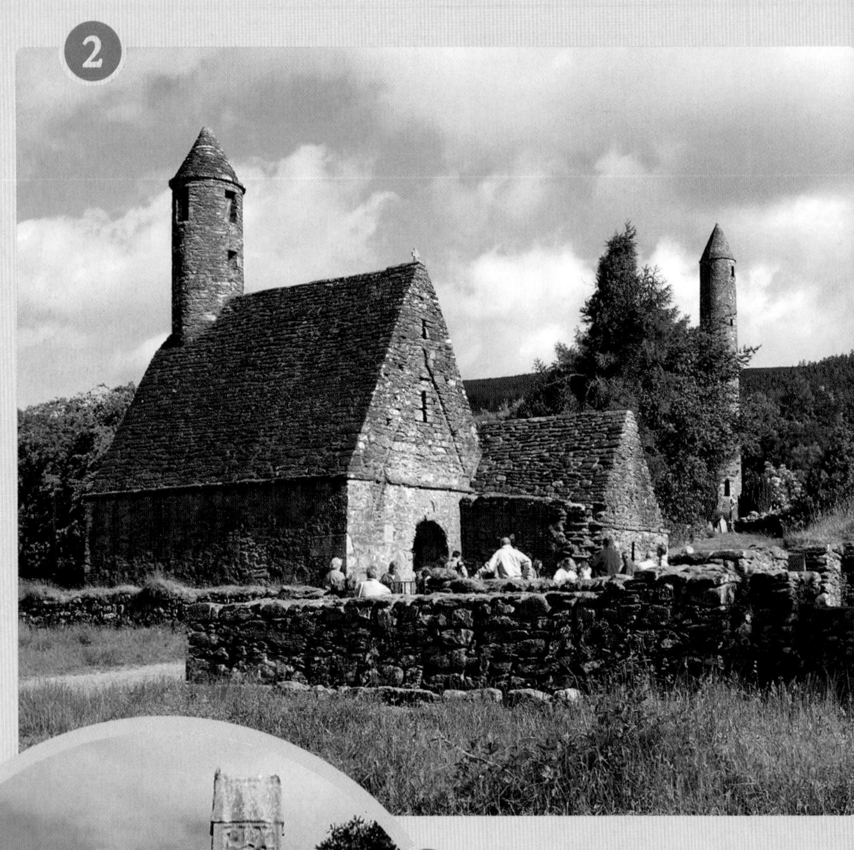

4

Monasterboice

Most Irish monastic sites are soaked in atmosphere, but Monasterboice (p135) has an extra-special hue. The ancient church ruins, the near-perfect round tower and the exquisite high crosses dotted around a grass-covered cemetery make this site at the end of a country lane one of Ireland's most beautiful. Best of all, it doesn't get nearly as many visitors as its competitors. An ancient High Cross Monasterboice cemetery

GARETH McCORMACK / LONELY PLANET IMAGES ©

Powerscourt Estate

3

For a sense of how well the powerful and mighty Anglo-Normans lived, wander the magnificent Italianate gardens of Powerscourt Estate (p116), soak up the superb views of nearby Sugarloaf and then peek inside the former home of the Power family. This isn't how the other half lived, but how the other half a percent lived. Gardens and forecourt of Powerscourt House

© PRISMA BILDAGENTUR AG / ALAMY

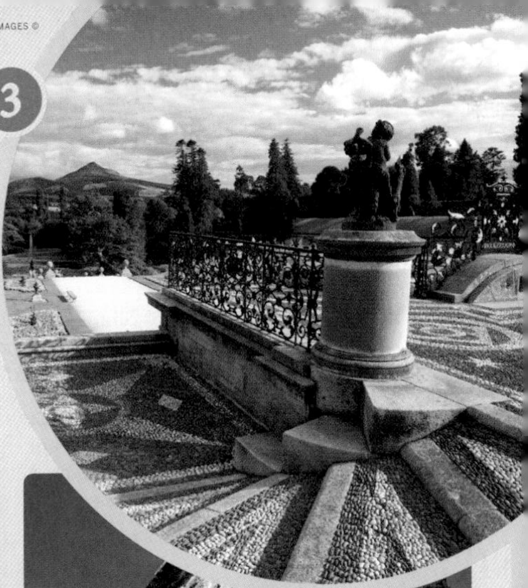

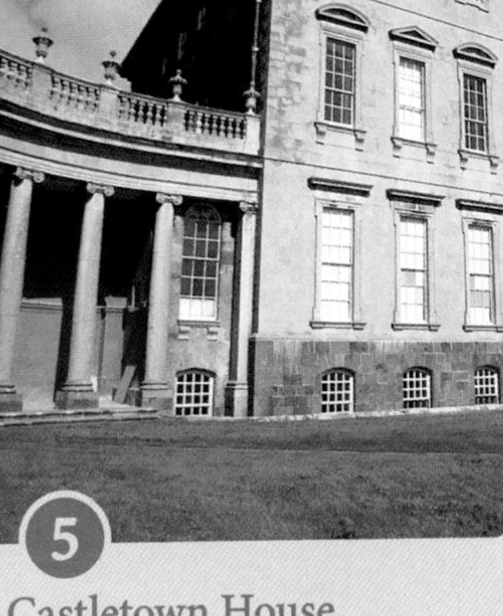

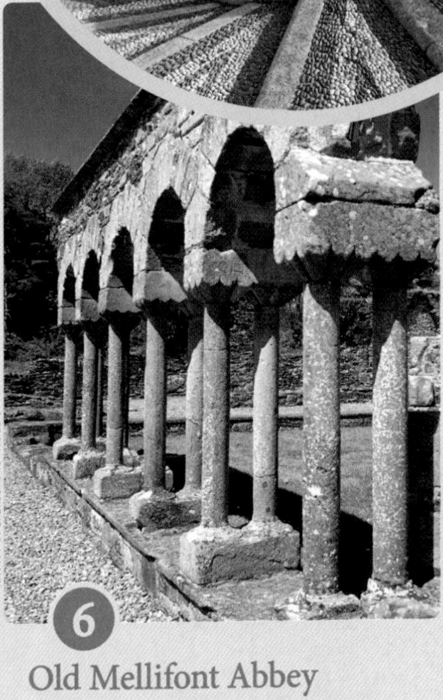

5

Castletown House

William Conolly was Speaker of the Irish House of Commons and, conveniently, Ireland's richest man, so he commissioned construction of a home to befit his elevated status – the breathtaking Castletown House (p124), near Maynooth, County Kildare. Its classical Palladian style would influence the architects of the soon-to-be-constructed Washington, DC. Castletown House facade

6

Old Mellifont Abbey

Of Ireland's one-time powerful abbeys, none is more evocative of its past than Old Mellifont Abbey (p133). Built by the Cistercians and once their most magnificent domicile, it is a home for 400 monks and a mother-house for 21 lesser monasteries spread throughout the country. The ruins are beautiful, and the adjacent rushing stream gives the whole place a romantic feel. Cloister ruins at Old Mellifont Abbey

Wicklow & Eastern Ireland's Best...

Beauty Spots

- **Sally Gap** (p112) Cut across the Wicklow Mountains.
- **Avondale House** (p121) Where Parnell would retreat to.
- **Powerscourt Estate** (p116) The most beautiful garden in Ireland?
- **Hill of Tara** (p129) Ireland's most sacred turf.
- **Loughcrew Cairns** (p132) Superb views from the top of the hill.

Gourmet Experiences

- **Ghan House** (p123) Superb restaurant, magnificent surroundings.
- **Tinakilly Country House & Restaurant** (p123) Fine Irish cuisine in Italianate mansion.
- **Rathsallagh House** (p120) Luxury, quality and style in a fine Palladian mansion.
- **Eastern Seaboard Bar & Grill** (p133) Drogheda's finest eatery.
- **Ballyknocken House** (p123) Learn to cook like a gourmet chef.

Historical Spots

- **Battle of the Boyne Site** (p127) King James got whupped here by his son-in-law, King William of Orange in 1690.
- **Hill of Tara** (p129) Home of the High Kings.
- **Monasterboice** (p135) One of Ireland's most important monasteries.
- **Avondale House** (p121) Charles Parnell's country pile.
- **Russborough House** (p119) A thieves' paradise?

Things for Free

- **Glendalough** (p112) Monastic magic in the valley.
- **Battle of the Boyne Site** (p127) The eye of Irish history's storm.
- **Mellifont Abbey** (p133) Handsome ruins of a mighty Cistercian abbey.
- **Monasterboice** (p135) Visit the marvellous high crosses.
- **Loughcrew Cairns** (p132) Little-visited Neolithic passage graves.

Left: Cycling in the Wicklow Mountains; **Above:** Standing stone, Hill of Tara (p129), County Meath

PHOTOGRAPHERS: (LEFT) © DAVID LYONS / ALAMY; (ABOVE) © GEORGE MUNDAY / ALAMY

Need to Know

ADVANCE PLANNING

- **Ten months before** Put your name into the Winter Solstice lottery at Brú na Bóinne.
- **Three months before** Book your spot at one of the cooking schools.
- **One month before** Sort out your accommodation.
- **Two weeks before** Check out the weather forecast. Then ignore it.

RESOURCES

- **Wicklow National Park** (www.wicklownationalpark.ie) All the info on the national park, including walks and visits to Glendalough.
- **Heritage Ireland** (www.heritageireland.ie) The Heritage Service is responsible for Glendalough, Brú na Bóinne and other sites of historical and archaeological importance.
- **Bus Eireann** (www.buseireann.ie) Official site for the national bus service, which is handy for getting around the region.
- **Battle of the Boyne** (www.battleoftheboyne.ie) Stacks of info on one of the most decisive battles of Irish history.

GETTING AROUND

- **Bus** Good bus networks cover most of the East Coast.
- **Train** Good service along the coast only – fine for coastal Wicklow and up to Drogheda.
- **Car** The best way of getting around; watch out for commuter traffic!

BE FOREWARNED

- **Crowds** Be prepared for summer crowds and traffic jams, especially in the Wicklow Mountains and the N11 south through Wicklow.
- **School Tours** Brú na Bóinne is not just spectacular but educational and very popular with school outings.
- **Weather** The Wicklow Mountains ain't high, but they can get very cold. Come prepared.

Wicklow & Eastern Ireland Itineraries

Counties Wicklow, Kildare and Meath each have a distinctive character and plenty to offer visitors, from active hiking to ancient history. You can stay overnight, but all make for easy day trips from Dublin, too.

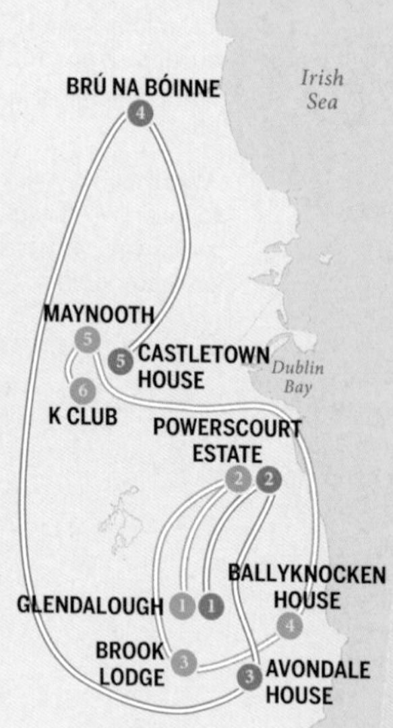

3 DAYS

GLENDALOUGH TO CASTLETOWN HOUSE

In & Out From Dublin

Start southward, in the Wicklow Mountains, taking in the glacial **(1) Glendalough** valley, home to 6th-century monastic ruins, a pair of beautiful lakes and some of the finest walks in the county. Then head over to **(2) Powerscourt Estate**, the one-time demesne of the Power family, now a favourite with garden and scenery lovers – the view of Wicklow's most distinctive peak, the Sugarloaf, is magnificent. Both can be visited in the morning; most organised tours take in both. In the afternoon, wend your way south to Rathdrum and pay a visit to **(3) Avondale House**, former home of the 'uncrowned king' of Ireland, the brilliant and damned Charles Stewart Parnell, one of the most important figures in Irish history (it's also accessible by public transport). On the second day, explore the magnificent Neolithic passage tomb of **(4) Brú na Bóinne** and marvel at the mathematical sophistication of its construction; be sure to take the tour that includes a simulation of the shaft of light illuminating the tomb on the winter solstice. On day three, visit Ireland's finest Palladian mansion, **(5) Castletown House**.

Top Left: Avondale House (p121), Rathdrum;
Top Right: St Patrick's College (p123), Maynooth

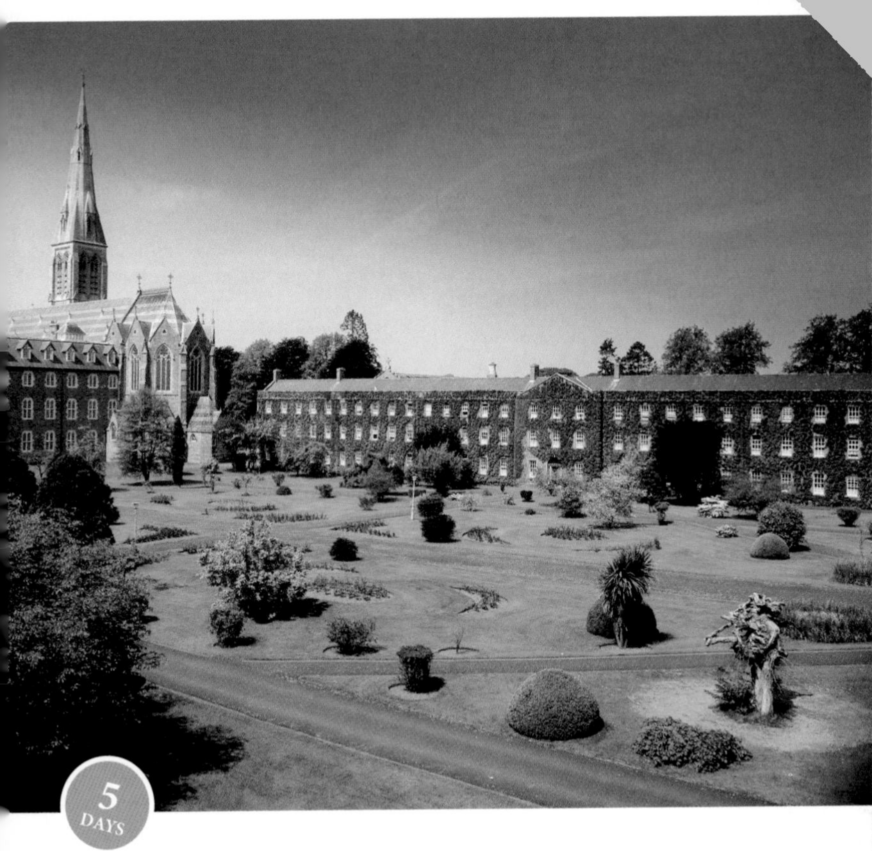

WICKLOW TO KILDARE

History & Hedonism

This five-day route explores the rich heritage that surrounds Dublin, but doesn't forget that interspersed with all that learning there should be a little bit of fun. When you're done exploring **(1) Glendalough** and **(2) Powerscourt Estate**, head south into Southern Wicklow to set up luxurious camp at **(3) Brook Lodge**. If you fancy a more hands-on rest, put on the apron at **(4) Ballyknocken House** and learn the essentials of Irish gourmet cooking. After a couple of days of R&R, cross into County Kildare to **(5) Maynooth**, visiting St Patrick's College before pitching your tent at Carton House, home to two exquisite golf courses. You can spend the rest of your time here, or if the golf bug has bitten, get over to the nearby **(6) K Club** in Straffan, and pretend that you too are playing in the Ryder Cup.

over Wicklow & Eastern Ireland

At a Glance

- **Glendalough** (p112) A monastic settlement nestled deep in a glacial valley.
- **Maynooth** (p123) Dynamic, tree-lined university town.
- **Brú na Bóinne** (p125) Vast Neolithic necropolis.
- **Tara** (p129) Ireland's most sacred site.
- **Loughcrew Cairns** (p132) Amazing Stone Age passage graves.

Wild heather on the Wicklow Mountains
PHOTOGRAPHER: CHRIS HILL / NATIONAL GEOGRAPHIC ©

COUNTY WICKLOW

As you leave Dublin and cross into Wicklow, the landscape changes dramatically. From Killakee, still in Dublin, the Military Rd begins a 30km southward journey across vast sweeps of gorse-, bracken- and heather-clad moors, bogs and mountains dotted with small corrie lakes.

The numbers and statistics aren't all that impressive. The highest peak in the range, Lugnaquilla (924m), is really more of a very large hill, but that hardly matters here. This vast granite intrusion, a welling-up of hot igneous rock that solidified some 400 million years ago, was shaped during the Ice Ages into the schist-capped mountains visible today. The peaks are marvellously desolate and as raw as only nature can be. Between the mountains are a number of deep glacial valleys, most notably Glenmacnass, Glenmalure and Glendalough; while corrie lakes such as Lough Bray Upper and Lower, gouged out by ice at the head of the glaciers, complete the wild topography.

The narrow Military Rd winds its way through the most remote parts of the mountains, offering some extraordinary views of the surrounding countryside. The best place to join it is at Glencree (from Enniskerry). It then runs south through the Sally Gap, Glenmacnass Valley and Laragh, then on to Glenmalure Valley and Aghavannagh.

Tours

BUS ÉIREANN Bus Tour
(**☎01-836 6111; www.buseireann.ie; Busáras; adult/child/student €28/22/25; ⏲10am mid-Mar-Oct**) A whole-day tour that takes in

Wicklow Mountains National Park

Wicklow Mountains National Park covers just over 200 sq km of mountainous blanket bogs and woodland. Within the boundaries of the protected area are two nature reserves, owned and managed by the Heritage Service and legally protected by the Wildlife Act 1976. The larger reserve, west of the Glendalough Visitor Centre, conserves the extensive heath and bog of the Glendalough Valley plus the Upper Lake and valley slopes on either side. The second, Glendalough Wood Nature Reserve, conserves oak woods stretching from the Upper Lake as far as the Rathdrum road to the east.

Most of Ireland's native mammal species can be found within the confines of the park. Large herds of deer roam on the open hill areas, though these were introduced in the 20th century as the native red-deer population became extinct during the first half of the 18th century. The uplands are the preserve of foxes, badgers and hares. Red squirrels are usually found in the pine woodlands – look out for them around the Upper Lake.

The bird population of the park is plentiful. Birds of prey abound, the most common being peregrine falcons, marlins, kestrels, hawks and sparrowhawks. Hen harriers are a rarer sight, though they too live in the park. Moorland birds found in the area include meadow pipits and skylarks. Less common birds such as whinchats, ring ouzels and dippers can be spotted, as can red grouse, whose numbers are quickly disappearing in other parts of Ireland. For information, call in or contact the **National Park Information Point** (Map p113; 0404-45425; www.wicklownationalpark.ie; Bolger's Cottage, Miners' Rd, Upper Lake, Glendalough; 10am-6pm May-Sep, to dusk Sat & Sun Oct-Apr), off the Green Rd that runs by the Upper Lake, about 2km from the Glendalough Visitor Centre. There's usually someone on hand to help, but if you find it closed the staff may be out running guided walks. 'Exploring the Glendalough Valley' (Heritage Service; €2) is a good booklet on the trails in the area.

Powerscourt and Glendalough (all admissions included), departing from Busáras (Map p66).

DUBLIN BUS TOURS Bus Tour
(Map p66; 01-872 0000; www.dublinbus.ie; 59 Upper O'Connell St; adult/child €28/14; 11am) A visit to Powerscourt is included in the four-hour South Coast & Gardens tour, which takes in the stretch of coastline between Dun Laoghaire and Killiney before turning inland to Wicklow and on to Enniskerry. Admission to the gardens is included.

IRISH SIGHTSEEING TOURS Bus Tour
(Map p66; 01-872 9010; www.irishcitytours.com; Gresham Hotel, O'Connell St; adult/student/child €32/30/25; 10am Fri-Sun) Wicklow's big hits – Powerscourt, Glendalough and the lakes and a stop at Avoca, then Dun Laoghaire and Dalkey (includes admission to Glendalough visitor centre and Powerscourt, but not coffee).

Eating

JOHNNIE FOX Seafood €€
(01-295 5647; www.jfp.ie; Glencullen; seafood platter €29.95; noon-10pm) Busloads of tourists fill the place nightly throughout the summer, mostly for the knees-up, faux-Irish floorshow of music and dancing. But there's nothing contrived about the seafood, which is so damn good we'd happily sit through yet another chorus of *Danny Boy* and even consider joining in the jig. The pub is 3km northwest of Enniskerry in Glencullen.

Detour: Sally Gap

One of the two main east–west passes across the Wicklow Mountains, the Sally Gap is surrounded by some spectacular countryside. From the turn-off on the lower road (R755) between Roundwood and Kilmacanogue near Bray, the narrow road (R759) passes above the dark and dramatic Lough Tay, whose scree slopes slide into **Luggala** (Fancy Mountain). This almost fairy-tale estate is owned by one Garech de Brún, member of the Guinness family and founder of Claddagh Records, a leading producer of Irish traditional and folk music. The small River Cloghoge links Lough Tay with Lough Dan just to the south. It then heads up to the Sally Gap crossroads, where it cuts across the Military Rd and heads northwest for Kilbride and the N81, following the young River Liffey, still only a stream.

Getting There & Away

Enniskerry is 18km south of Dublin, just 3km west of the M11 along the R117. Getting to Powerscourt House under your own steam is not a problem (it's 500m from the town), but getting to the waterfall is tricky.

Dublin Bus (872 0000, 01-873 4222) Service 44 (€2.40, every 20 minutes) takes about 1¼ hours to get to Enniskerry from Hawkins St in Dublin. Alternatively, you can take the DART train to Bray (€2.90) and catch bus 185 (€1.60, hourly) from the station, which takes an extra 40 minutes.

Alpine Coaches (286 2547; www.alpinecoaches.ie) Runs a shuttle service between the DART station in Bray, Powerscourt Waterfall (€6 return) and the house (€4.50). Shuttles leave Bray at 11.05am (11.30am July and August), 12.30pm, 1.30pm (and 3.30pm September to June) Monday to Saturday, and 11am, noon and 1pm Sunday. The last departure from Powerscourt House is at 5.30pm.

Glendalough

POP 280

If you've come to Wicklow, chances are that a visit to Glendalough (Gleann dá Loch, 'Valley of the Two Lakes') is one of your main reasons for being here. And you're not wrong, for this is one of the most beautiful corners of the whole country and the epitome of the kind of rugged, romantic Ireland that probably drew you to the island in the first place.

The substantial remains of this important monastic settlement are certainly impressive, but the real draw is the splendid setting: two dark and mysterious lakes tucked into a deep valley covered in forest. It is, despite its immense popularity, a deeply tranquil and spiritual place, and you will have little difficulty in understanding why those solitude-seeking monks came here in the first place.

History

In AD 498 a young monk named Kevin arrived in the valley looking for somewhere to kick back, meditate and be at one with nature. He pitched up in what had been a Bronze Age tomb on the southern side of the Upper Lake, and for the next seven years slept on stones, wore animal skins, maintained a near-starvation diet and – according to the legend – became bosom buddies with the birds and animals. Kevin's ecofriendly lifestyle soon attracted a bunch of disciples, all seemingly unaware of the irony that they were flocking to hang out with a hermit who wanted to live as far away from other people as possible. Over the next couple of centuries his one-man operation mushroomed into a proper settlement

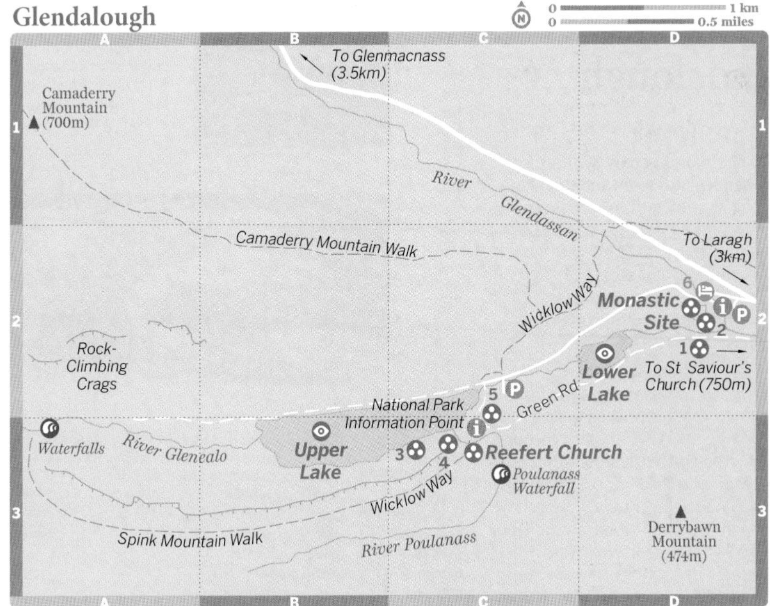

and by the 9th century Glendalough rivalled Clonmacnoise (p242) as the island's premier monastic city. Thousands of students studied and lived in a thriving community that was spread over a considerable area.

Inevitably, Glendalough's success made it a key target for Viking raiders, who sacked the monastery at least four times between 775 and 1071. The final blow came in 1398, when English forces from Dublin almost destroyed it. Efforts were made to rebuild and some life lingered on here as late as the 17th century when, under renewed repression, the monastery finally died.

Sights

UPPER LAKE

The original site of St Kevin's settlement, **Teampall na Skellig** is at the base of the cliffs towering over the southern side of the Upper Lake and is accessible only by boat; unfortunately, there's no boat service to the site and you'll have to settle for looking at it across the lake. The terraced shelf has the reconstructed ruins of a church and early graveyard. Rough wattle huts once stood on the raised ground

Glendalough

Top Sights

	Lower Lake	D2
	Monastic Site	D2
	Reefert Church	C3
	Upper Lake	B3

Sights

	Cathedral of St Peter & St Paul	(see 2)
1	Deer Stone	D2
	Graveyard	(see 2)
	Monastery Gatehouse	(see 2)
	Priest's House	(see 2)
2	Round Tower	D2
3	St Kevin's Bed	C3
4	St Kevin's Cell	C3
	St Kevin's Kitchen	(see 2)
	St Kieran's Church	(see 2)
	St Mary's Church	(see 2)
5	Stone Fort	C2
	Teampall na Skellig	(see 3)

Sleeping

6	Glendalough Hotel	D2

Glendalough

Walking Tour

A visit to Glendalough is a trip through ancient history and a refreshing hike in the hills. The ancient monastic settlement founded by St Kevin in the 5th century grew to be quite powerful by the 9th century, but it started falling into ruin from 1398 onwards. Still, you won't find more evocative clumps of stones anywhere.

Start at the **Main Gateway** ❶ to the monastic city, where you will find a cluster of important ruins, including the (nearly perfect) 10th-century **Round Tower** ❷, the **Cathedral** ❸ dedicated to **Sts Peter and Paul**, and **St Kevin's Kitchen** ❹, which is really a church. Cross the stream past the famous **Deer Stone** ❺, where Kevin was supposed to have milked a doe, and turn west along the path. It's a 1.5km walk to the **Upper Lake** ❻. On the lake's southern shore is another cluster of sites, including the **Reefert Church** ❼, a plain 11th-century Romanesque church where the powerful O'Toole family buried their kin, and **St Kevin's Cell** ❽, the remains of a beehive hut where Kevin is said to have lived.

ST KEVIN

St Kevin came to the valley as a young monk in AD 498, in search of a peaceful retreat. He was reportedly led by an angel to a Bronze Age tomb now known as St Kevin's Bed. For seven years he slept on stones, wore animal skins, survived on nettles and herbs and – according to legend – developed an affinity with the birds and animals. One legend has it that, when Kevin needed milk for two orphaned babies, a doe stood waiting at the Deer Stone to be milked.

Kevin soon attracted a group of disciples and the monastic settlement grew, until by the 9th century Glendalough rivalled Clomacnoise as Ireland's premier monastic city. According to legend Kevin lived to the age of 120. He was canonised in 1903.

St Kevin's Cell
This beehive hut is reputedly where St Kevin would go for prayer and meditation; not to be confused with St Kevin's Bed, a cave where he used to sleep.

Deer Stone
The spot where St Kevin is said to have truly become one with the animals is really just a large mortar called a *bullaun*, used for grinding food and medicine.

St Kevin's Kitchen
This small church (called the Priests' House) is unusual in that it has a round tower sticking out of the roof – it looks like a chimney, hence the church's nickname.

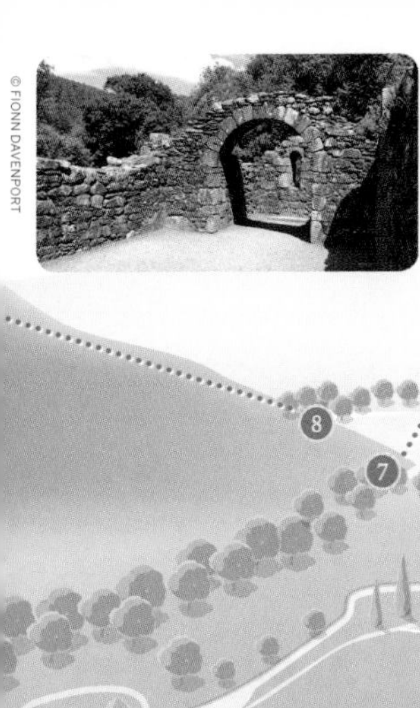

Reefert Church

Its name derives from the Irish *righ fearta*, which means 'burial place of the kings'. Seven princes of the powerful O'Toole family are buried in this simple structure.

Upper Lake

The site of St Kevin's original settlement is on the banks of the Upper Lake, one of the two lakes that gives Glendalough its name – the 'Valley of the Lakes'.

Round Tower

Glendalough's most famous landmark is the 33m-high Round Tower, which is exactly as it was when it was built a thousand years ago except for the roof; this was replaced in 1876 after a lightning strike.

Information

Halfway between the two lakes is the office of the National Parks Service, which has maps and information on the whole area, but no bathrooms! The grassy spot in front of the office is a popular picnic spot in summer.

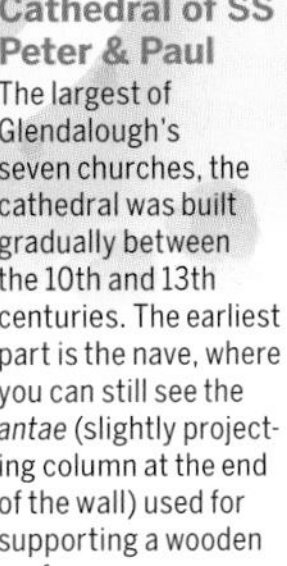

Cathedral of SS Peter & Paul

The largest of Glendalough's seven churches, the cathedral was built gradually between the 10th and 13th centuries. The earliest part is the nave, where you can still see the *antae* (slightly projecting column at the end of the wall) used for supporting a wooden roof.

Main Gateway

The only surviving entrance to the ecclesiastical settlement is a double-arch; notice that the inner arch rises higher than the outer one in order to compensate for the upward slope of the causeway.

RICK GERHARTER / LONELY PLANET IMAGES©

Don't Miss Enniskerry & Powerscourt Estate

The handsome village of Enniskerry is home to art galleries and all-organic gourmet cafes. The village is lovely, but the main reason for its popularity is the magnificent 64-sq-km **Powerscourt Estate**. The main entrance is 500m south of the village square.

The estate has existed more or less since 1300, when the LePoer (later anglicised to Power) family built themselves a castle here. The property changed Anglo-Norman hands a few times before coming into the possession of Richard Wingfield, newly appointed Marshall of Ireland, in 1603. His descendants were to live here for the next 350 years. In 1731 the Georgian wunderkind Richard Cassels (or Castle) was given the job of building a Palladian-style mansion around the core of the old castle. He finished the job in 1743, but an extra storey was added in 1787 and other alterations were made in the 19th century.

Easily the biggest drawcards of the whole pile are the simply magnificent 20-hectare formal gardens and the breathtaking views that accompany them. Originally laid out in the 1740s, the gardens were redesigned in the 19th century by Daniel Robinson. His largely informal style is a magnificent blend of landscaped gardens, sweeping terraces, statuary, ornamental lakes, secret hollows, rambling walks and walled enclosures with more than 200 types of trees and shrubs, all beneath the stunning natural backdrop of the Great Sugarloaf Mountain to the southeast. Tickets come with a map laying out 40-minute and hour-long tours of the gardens.

A 7km walk to a separate part of the estate takes you to the 130m **Powerscourt Waterfall**. It's the highest waterfall in Britain and Ireland, and is most impressive after heavy rain.

THINGS YOU NEED TO KNOW

Powerscourt Estate (☎01-204 6000; www.powerscourt.ie; adult/child/student €8/5/7; ⏰9.30am-5.30pm Feb-Oct, to 4.30pm Nov-Jan);

Powerscourt Waterfall (adult/child/student €5/3.50/4.50; ⏰9.30am-7pm May-Aug, 10.30am-5.30pm Mar-Apr & Sep-Oct, to 4.30pm Nov-Jan).

nearby. Scattered around are some early grave slabs and simple stone crosses.

Just east of here and 10m above the lake waters is the 2m-deep artificial cave called **St Kevin's Bed**, said to be where Kevin lived. The earliest human habitation of the cave was long before St Kevin's era – there's evidence that people lived in the valley for thousands of years before the monks arrived. In the green area just south of the car park is a large circular wall thought to be the remains of an early Christian **stone fort** *(caher)*.

Follow the lakeshore path southwest of the car park until you come to the considerable remains of **Reefert Church** above the tiny River Poulanass. It's a small, plain, 11th-century Romanesque nave-and-chancel church with some reassembled arches and walls. Traditionally, Reefert (literally 'Royal Burial Place') was the burial site of the chiefs of the local O'Toole family. The surrounding graveyard contains a number of rough stone crosses and slabs, most made of shiny mica schist.

Climb the steps at the back of the churchyard and follow the path to the west and you'll find, at the top of a rise overlooking the lake, the scant remains of **St Kevin's Cell**, a small beehive hut.

LOWER LAKE

While the Upper Lake has the best scenery, the most fascinating buildings lie in the lower part of the valley east of the Lower Lake, huddled together in the heart of the ancient monastic site.

Just round the bend from the Glendalough Hotel is the stone arch of the **monastery gatehouse**, the only surviving example of a monastic entrance way in the country. Just inside the entrance is a large slab with an incised cross.

Beyond that lies a **graveyard**, which is still in use. The 10th-century **round tower** is 33m tall and 16m in circumference at the base. The upper storeys and conical roof were reconstructed in 1876. Near the tower, to the southeast, is the **Cathedral of St Peter and St Paul** with a 10th-century nave. The chancel and sacristy date from the 12th century.

At the centre of the graveyard to the south of the round tower is the **Priest's House**. This odd building dates from 1170 but has been heavily reconstructed. It may have been the location of shrines of St Kevin. Later, during penal times, it became a burial site for local priests – hence the name. The 10th-century **St Mary's Church**, 140m southwest of the round tower, probably originally stood outside the walls of the monastery and belonged to local nuns. It has a lovely western doorway. A little to the east are the scant remains of **St Kieran's Church**, the smallest at Glendalough.

Glendalough's trademark is **St Kevin's Kitchen** or Church at the southern edge of the enclosure. This church, with a miniature round towerlike belfry, protruding sacristy and steep stone roof, is a masterpiece. How it came to be known as a kitchen is a mystery as there's no indication that it was anything other than a church. The oldest parts of the building date from the 11th century – the structure has been remodelled since but it's still a classic early Irish church.

At the junction with Green Rd as you cross the river just south of these two churches is the **Deer Stone** in the middle of a group of rocks. Legend claims that when St Kevin needed milk for two orphaned babies, a doe stood here waiting to be milked. The stone is actually a *bullaun* (a stone used as a mortar for grinding medicines or food). Many such stones are thought to be prehistoric, and they were widely regarded as having supernatural properties: women who bathed their faces with water from the hollow were supposed to keep their looks forever. The early churchmen brought the stones into their monasteries, perhaps hoping to inherit some of their powers.

The road east leads to **St Saviour's Church**, with its detailed Romanesque carvings. To the west, a nice woodland trail leads up the valley past the Lower Lake to the Upper Lake.

Tours

BUS ÉIREANN
(☎836 6111; www.buseireann.ie; Busáras; adult/child/student €29/23/25; ⏰departs 10am mid-Mar-Oct) Includes admission to the visitor centre and a visit to Powerscourt Estate in this whole-day tour, which returns to Dublin at about 5.45pm. The guides are good but impersonal.

WILD WICKLOW TOUR
(☎280 1899; www.discoverdublin.ie; adult/student & child €28/25; ⏰departs 9am) Award-winning tours of Glendalough, Avoca and the Sally Gap that never fail to generate rave reviews for atmosphere and all-round fun, but so much craic has made a casualty of informative depth. The first pick-up is at the Dublin Tourism office, but there are a variety of pick-up points throughout Dublin; check the point nearest you when booking. The tour returns to Dublin about 5.30pm.

Sleeping

GLENDALOUGH HOTEL
(☎0404-45135; www.glendaloughhotel.com; s/d €110/150; P @ ᯤ 👪) There's no mistaking Glendalough's best hotel, conveniently located next door to the visitor centre. There is no shortage of takers for its 44 fairly luxurious bedrooms.

Eating

Laragh's the place for a bit of grub, as there's only the Glendalough Hotel that serves food near the site.

Getting There & Away

St Kevin's Bus (☎0404-481; www.glendaloughbus.com) Departs from outside the Mansion House on Dawson St in Dublin at 11.30am and 6pm Monday to Saturday, and 11.30am and 7pm Sunday (one way/return €13/20, 1½ hours). It also stops at the Town Hall in Bray. Departures from Glendalough are at 7.15am and 4.30pm Monday to Saturday. During the week in July and

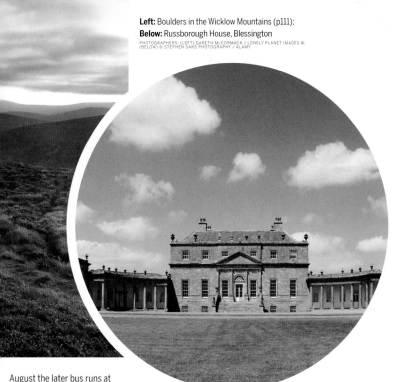

Left: Boulders in the Wicklow Mountains (p111);
Below: Russborough House, Blessington

PHOTOGRAPHERS: (LEFT) GARETH McCORMACK / LONELY PLANET IMAGES ©; (BELOW) © STEPHEN SAKS PHOTOGRAPHY / ALAMY

August the later bus runs at 5.30pm, and there is an additional service at 9.45am.

Blessington

POP 4018

There's little to see in Blessington; it's basically made up of a long row of pubs, shops and 17th- and 18th-century town houses. It's the main town in the area and as such makes a decent exploring base.

Sights

RUSSBOROUGH HOUSE Historic Building

(☎045-865 239; www.russborough.ie; Blessington; adult/child/student €10/5/8; 10am-6pm May-Sep, Sun & bank holidays only Apr & Oct, closed rest of year) Magnificent Russborough House is one of Ireland's finest stately homes, a Palladian pleasure palace built for Joseph Leeson (1705-83), later the first Earl of Milltown and, later still, Lord Russborough. It was built between 1741 and 1751 to the design of Richard Cassels, who was at the height of his fame as an architect. Poor old Richard didn't live to see it finished, but the job was well executed by Francis Bindon.

The house remained in the Leeson family until 1931. In 1952 it was sold to Sir Alfred Beit, the eponymous nephew of the cofounder of the de Beers diamond-mining company. Uncle Alfred was an obsessive art collector, and when he died his impressive haul – which includes works by Velázquez, Vermeer, Goya and Rubens – was passed on to his nephew, who brought it to Russborough House. The collection was to attract the interest of more than just art lovers.

In 1974 the IRA decided to get into the art business by stealing 16 of the paintings. They were eventually all recovered, but 10 years later the notorious Dublin criminal Martin Cahill (aka the General) masterminded another robbery, this time for Loyalist paramilitaries. On this occasion, however, only some of the works were recovered and of those, several were damaged beyond repair – a good thief does not a gentle curator make. In 1988 Beit got the picture and decided to hand over the most valuable of the paintings to the National Gallery; in return for the gift, the gallery agreed to lend other paintings to the collection as temporary exhibits. The sorry story didn't conclude there. In 2001 two thieves took the direct approach and drove a jeep through the front doors, making off with two paintings worth nearly €4 million, including a Gainsborough that had been stolen, and recovered, twice before. And then, to add abuse to the insult already added to injury, the house was broken into again in 2002, with the thieves taking five more paintings, including two by Rubens. Incredibly, however, both hauls were quickly recovered.

The admission price includes a 45-minute tour of the house, which is decorated in typical Georgian style, and all the important paintings, which, given the history, is a monumental exercise in staying positive. Whatever you do, make no sudden moves.

Sleeping & Eating

RATHSALLAGH HOUSE & COUNTRY CLUB Hotel **€€€**

(**045-403 112; www.rathsallaghhousehotel.com; Dunlavin; mains €33-42, s/d from €135/260**) About 20km south of Blessington, this fabulous country manor, converted from Queen Anne stables in 1798, is more than just a fancy hotel. Luxury is par for the course here, from the splendidly appointed rooms to the exquisite country-house dining (the food here is some of the best you'll eat anywhere in Ireland) and the marvellous golf course that surrounds the estate. Even the breakfast is extraordinary: it has won the National Breakfast Award three times. Is there anything Irish tourism doesn't have an award for?

Getting There & Away

Blessington is 35km southwest of Dublin on the N81. There are regular daily services by **Dublin Bus** (**01-872 0000, 01-873 4222**); catch bus 65 from Eden Quay in Dublin (€4.70, 1½ hours, every 1½ hours). **Bus Éireann** (**01-836 6111; www.buseireann.ie**) operates express bus 005 to and from Waterford, with stops in Blessington two or three times daily; from Dublin it's pick-up only and from Waterford drop-off only.

Southern Wicklow

South of Wicklow town, the landscape gives way to rolling hills and valleys cut through by rustling rivers and dotted with lovely little hamlets, including the especially beautiful Vale of Avoca, favoured by song and busloads of tourists.

Rathdrum

POP 2123

The quiet village of Rathdrum at the foot of the

Walkers on the Lough Dan (p112) track, County Wicklow

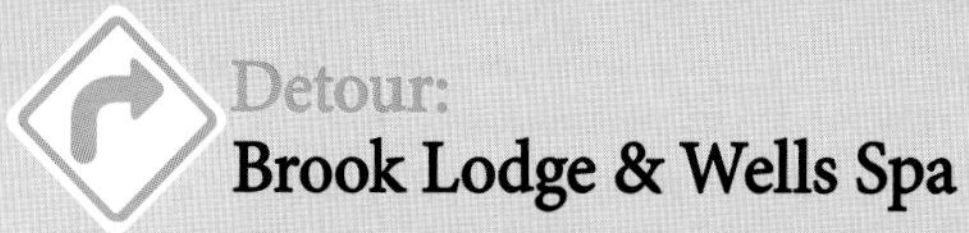

Detour: Brook Lodge & Wells Spa

One of Ireland's fanciest bolt-holes is the luxurious **Brook Lodge & Wells Spa** (0402-36444; www.brooklodge.com; Macreddin; r/ste from €260/330; P). It's a fine country house about 3km west of Rathdrum in the village of Macreddin. The 39 standard rooms set a pretty high tone, with four-poster and sleigh beds dressed in crisp Frette linen. But the suites sing an altogether more harmonious tune, each a minimalist marvel that wouldn't seem out of place in a New York boutique hotel – massive beds, flat-screen plasma TVs, top-of-the-range sound system and every other style sundry. The accommodation is pure luxury, but it's the outstanding spa that keeps guests coming back for more. Mud and flotation chambers, Finnish and aroma baths, *hammam* (Turkish bath) massages and a full range of Decléor and Carita treatments make this one of the top spas in the country. Your credit card will never have nestled in softer hands.

An **organic market** (10am-5pm Sun, Apr-Oct) is held in Macreddin on the first Sunday of each month during summer.

Vale of Clara comprises little more than a few old houses and shops, but in the late 19th century it had a healthy flannel industry and a poorhouse. It's not what's in the town that's of interest to visitors, however, but what's just outside it.

The small **tourist office** (0404-46262; 29 Main St; 9am-5.30pm Mon-Fri) has leaflets and information on the town and surrounding area, including the Wicklow Way.

Sights

AVONDALE HOUSE Historic Building
(0404-46111; adult/student & child €7/6.50; 11am-6pm May-Aug, Sat & Sun only Apr, by appointment only rest of year) This fine Palladian mansion surrounded by a marvellous 209-hectare estate was the birthplace and Irish headquarters of Charles Stewart Parnell (1846–91). Parnell was the 'uncrowned king of Ireland' and unquestionably one of the key figures in the Irish independence movement.

> Woe be to the man by whom the scandal cometh...It would be better for him that a millstone were tied about his neck and that he were cast into the depth of the sea rather than he should scandalise one of these, my least little ones.
>
> *James Joyce, A Portrait of the Artist as a Young Man*

Joyce's fictional dinner-table argument wasn't about a murderer or any such criminal but about Parnell.

Designed by James Wyatt in 1779, the house's many highlights include a stunning vermilion-hued library (Parnell's favourite room) and beautiful dining room.

From 1880 to 1890 Avondale was synonymous with the fight for Home Rule, which was brilliantly led by Parnell until 1890, when a member of his own Irish Parliamentary Party, Captain William O'Shea, sued his wife Kitty for divorce and named Parnell as co-respondent. Parnell's affair with Kitty O'Shea scandalised this 'priest-ridden' nation, and the ultraconservative clergy declared that Parnell was 'unfit to lead' – despite the fact that as soon as the divorce was granted the two lovers were quickly married. Parnell resigned as leader of the party and withdrew in despair to Avondale, where he died the following year.

unding the house are 200 s of forest and parkland, where . silvicultural experiments by h Forestry Service (Coillte) were ived, after the purchase of the house by the state in 1904. These plots, about half a hectare in size, are still visible today, flanking what many consider to be the best of Avondale's many walking trails, the Great Ride. You can visit the park during daylight hours year-round.

Sleeping

OLD PRESBYTERY HOSTEL Hostel **€**
(☎0404-46930; www.hostels-ireland.com; The Fairgreen, Rathdrum; dm/d €16/45; P) A modern, centrally located IHH hostel that looks more like campus accommodation. There is a mix of large, comfy dorms and well-appointed doubles with private bathrooms, as well as family rooms. A laundry and a TV room round off the facilities. You can also camp in the grounds.

Getting There & Away

Bus Éireann (☎01-836 6111; www.buseireann.ie) Service 133 goes to Rathdrum from Dublin (one way/return €7/9.70, 1¾ hours, 10 daily) on its way to Arklow.

Iarnród Éireann (☎01-836 6222) Serves Rathdrum from Dublin on the main Dublin to Rosslare Harbour line (one way/return €16.20/20.40, 1½ hours, five daily).

COUNTY KILDARE

Once a backwater from Dublin, the lush green pastures of County Kildare (Cill Dara) are prime suburbia, and charming towns like Maynooth and Kildare have become commuter bedrooms, a reality reflected in the ever-expanding motorway network that seeks to ease the traffic burden.

Still, the county has some of the best farmland in Ireland and is home to some of the country's most prestigious stud farms, many surrounding the sweeping grasslands of the Curragh. The northwest of the county is dominated by a vast swathe of bog. The county isn't especially stuffed with must-see attractions, but there are enough diversions to justify a day trip from the capital or a stop on your way out west.

Kildare horses

Maynooth

POP 10,715

Much of Maynooth's (Maigh Nuad) life comes from the university (National University of Ireland Maynooth; NUIM), which gives this tree-lined town with stone-fronted houses and shops a dynamism that belies its country-town appearance. It's within easy reach of Dublin by public transport, thanks as much to the university as to the legions of barristers and other swells who make the town their home.

Sights

ST PATRICK'S COLLEGE University
(01-628 5222; www.maynoothcollege.ie; Main St) Turning out Catholic priests since 1795, **St Patrick's College & Seminary** was founded to ensure that aspiring priests wouldn't skip off to seminary school in France and get infected with strains of republicanism and revolution. It became a Pontifical University in 1898 (granting control of the college's theological courses to the Holy See) but in 1910 it joined the newly established National University of Ireland (NUI), which governed the university's nontheological studies. Nevertheless, the student body remained exclusively clerical until 1966, when lay students were finally admitted.

The college buildings are impressive – Gothic architect Augustus Pugin had a hand in designing them – and well worth an hour's ramble. You enter the college via Georgian Stoyte House, where the **accommodation office** (01-708 3576; 8.30am-5.30pm & 8-11pm Mon-Fri, 8.30am-12.30pm & 1.30-11pm Sat & Sun) sells booklets (€5) for guiding yourself around. The college grounds contain a number of lofty Georgian and neo-Gothic buildings, gardens and squares, but the highlight of the tour has to be the **College Chapel**. Pull open the squeaky door and you enter the world's largest choir chapel, with stalls for more than 450 choristers and some magnificent ornamentation.

If You Like... Country Houses

If you like Brook Lodge (p121), you'll like these other fabulous country houses:

1 **BALLYKNOCKEN HOUSE & COOKERY SCHOOL**
(0404-69274; www.ballyknocken.com; Glenealy, Ashford; s/d €90/110, 3/4-course dinner €35/45;) Ivy-clad Victorian home with six beautifully appointed rooms and a renowned **cooking school** (www.thecookeryschool.ie; €110).

2 **TINAKILLY COUNTRY HOUSE & RESTAURANT**
(0404-69274; www.tinakilly.ie; Rathnew; r €115-200, dinner mains €22-29) Magnificent Victorian Italianate house with a superb restaurant.

3 **GHAN HOUSE**
(042-937 3682; www.ghanhouse.com; Main Rd, Carlingford; d from €105; P@) Eighteenth-century Georgian house with 12 exquisitely decorated guestrooms, a superb restaurant and a **cookery school** (cooking/wine-tasting courses from €95/35).

Activities

Golf

On the edge of town, **Carton House** (01-651 7720; www.cartonhousegolf.com; green fees €75 Mon-Thu, €85 Fri-Sun) is home to two outstanding 18-hole championship courses designed by Colin Montgomery and Mark O'Meara respectively.

Sleeping

CARTON HOUSE Hotel €€€
(01-505 2000; www.cartonhouse.com; r from €145; P@) It really doesn't get any grander than this vast, early 19th-century estate set on over 1000 acres of lavish grounds. The interiors belie the Palladian exterior and are stylishly minimalist. As

Detour: Castletown House

The magnificent **Castletown House** (01-628 8252; www.castletownhouse.ie; Celbridge; adult/child €4.50/3.50; 10am-4.45pm Tue-Sun Easter-Oct) is Ireland's largest and most imposing Georgian estate, and a testament to the vast wealth enjoyed by the Anglo-Irish gentry during the 18th century.

The house was built between the years 1722 and 1732 for William Conolly (1662–1729), speaker of the Irish House of Commons and, at the time, Ireland's richest man. The original design of the house was by the Italian architect Alessandro Galilei (1691–1737), who in 1718 designed the facade of the main block to resemble a 16th-century Italian palazzo. The project was then entrusted to Sir Edward Lovett Pearce (1699–1733). Inspired by the work of Andrea Palladio, Pearce enlarged the original design of the house and added the colonnades and the terminating pavilions.

The interior is as opulent as the exterior suggests, especially the Long Gallery, replete with family portraits and exquisite stucco work by the Francini brothers. (In the US, Thomas Jefferson became a Palladian acolyte and much of official Washington DC is in this style.)

Conolly didn't live to see the completion of his wonder-palace. His widow, Katherine, continued to live at the unfinished house after his death in 1729, instigating many improvements. Her main architectural contribution was the curious 42.6m **obelisk**, known locally as the Conolly Folly. Her other offering is the **Wonderful Barn**, six teetering storeys wrapped by an exterior spiral staircase, on private property just outside Leixlip.

Buses 120 and 123 run from Dublin to Celbridge (€3.50; 30 minutes; every half-hour Monday to Friday, hourly Saturday, six buses Sunday).

you'd expect, the beautiful rooms come equipped with all the latest high-tech gadgetry. To reach the hotel, follow the R148 east towards Leixlip along the Royal Canal.

Getting There & Away

Dublin Bus (873 4222; www.dublinbus.ie) Runs a service to Maynooth (€3.50, one hour) leaving several times an hour from Pearse St in Dublin.

Maynooth is on the main Dublin–Sligo line, with regular trains in each direction: to Dublin (€2.70, 35 minutes, one to four per hour); to Sligo (€35, two hours 40 minutes, four per day).

Straffan

POP 439

Teeny Straffan has a couple of small attractions including the **Steam Museum and Lodge Park Walled Garden** (www.steam-museum.com; adult/concession €7.50/5; 2-6pm Wed-Sun Jun-Aug) and the **Straffan Butterfly Farm** (www.straffanbutterflyfarm.com; Ovidstown; adult/child €7.50/5; noon-5.30pm Jun-Aug).

Two of Ireland's top golf courses can be found at the **K Club** (Kildare Hotel & Country Club; 601 7200; www.kclub.ie; Straffan; r from €200; P @), a Georgian estate and golfers' paradise. Inside there are 92 well-appointed rooms and lots of public spaces for having a drink and lying about your exploits outside. There are two golf courses: one, with Arnold Palmer's design imprimatur, is one of the best in Ireland. Green fees range from €85 to €295, depending on which course you play and at what time of year.

Bus Éireann (836 6111; www.buseireann.ie) runs buses from Dublin (one way/return €4/5.90, 30 minutes, every half hour, six buses Sunday).

COUNTY MEATH

Brú na Bóinne

The vast Neolithic necropolis known as Brú na Bóinne (the Boyne Palace) is one of the most extraordinary sites in Europe and shouldn't be missed. A thousand years older than Stonehenge, it's a powerful and evocative testament to the mind-boggling achievements of prehistoric humans.

The complex was built to house the remains of those who were at the top of the social heap and its tombs were the largest artificial structures in Ireland until the construction of the Anglo-Norman castles 4000 years later. The area consists of many different sites; the three principal ones are Newgrange, Knowth and Dowth.

Sights

NEWGRANGE Historic Site

(adult/child incl visitor centre €6/3) Even from afar, you know that Newgrange is something special. Its white round stone walls topped by a grass dome look otherworldly, and just the size is impressive: 80m in diameter and 13m high. But underneath it gets even better. Here lies the finest Stone Age passage tomb in Ireland, and one of the most remarkable prehistoric sites in Europe. It dates from around 3200 BC, predating the pyramids by some six centuries.

No one is quite sure of its original purpose. It could have been a burial place for kings or a centre for ritual – although the tomb's precise alignment with the sun at the time of the winter solstice also suggests it was designed to act as a calendar.

Over time, Newgrange, like Knowth and Dowth, deteriorated and at one stage was even used as a quarry. The site was extensively restored in 1962 and again in 1975.

You can walk down the narrow 19m passage, lined with 43 stone uprights (some of them engraved), which leads into the tomb chamber about one-third of the way into the colossal mound. The chamber has three recesses, and in these are large basin stones that held cremated human bones. As well as the remains, the basins would have held funeral offerings

Knowth ancient burial mounds (p126), Boyne Valley

Visiting Brú na Bóinne

In an effort to protect the tombs and preserve the mystical atmosphere around them, all visits to Brú na Bóinne start at the **Brú na Bóinne Visitor Centre** (041-988 0300; www.heritageireland.ie; Donore; adult/child visitor centre €3/2, visitor centre, Newgrange & Knowth €11/6; 9am-7pm Jun–mid-Sep, 9am-6.30pm May & mid-end Sep, 9.30am-5.30pm Oct & Feb, 9am-5pm Nov-Jan), from where a bus will take you to the tombs. Built in a spiral design echoing Newgrange, the centre houses an extraordinary series of interactive exhibits on prehistoric Ireland and its passage tombs, and has regional tourism info, an excellent cafe and a book/souvenir shop. Upstairs, a glassed-in observation mezzanine looks out over Newgrange.

Tours are primarily outdoors with no shelter – bring raingear, just in case.

The visitor centre is on the south side of the river. It's 2km west of Donore and 6km east of Slane, where bridges cross the river from the N51. (Ignore your GPS, which will normally direct you to the monuments rather than the visitor centre, and be sure to follow the signs for Newgrange and/or the Brú na Bóinne visitor centre, rather than Newgrange Farm.) For tours to Brú na Bóinne, see p127.

of beads and pendants, but these were stolen long before the archaeologists arrived.

Above, the massive stones support a 6m-high corbel-vaulted roof. A complex drainage system means that not a drop of water has penetrated the interior in 40 centuries.

KNOWTH Historic Site

(adult/child incl visitor centre €5/3, incl visitor centre & Newgrange €11/6; Easter-Oct) Northwest of Newgrange, the burial mound of Knowth was built around the same time and seems set to surpass its better-known neighbour in both its size and the importance of the discoveries made here. It has the greatest collection of passage-grave art ever uncovered in Western Europe, and has been under excavation since 1962.

The excavations soon cleared a passage leading to the central chamber, which at 34m is much longer than the one at Newgrange. In 1968 a 40m passage was unearthed on the opposite side of the mound. Although the chambers are separate, they're close enough for archaeologists to hear each other at work. Also in the mound are the remains of six early-Christian souterrains (underground chambers) built into the side. Some 300 carved slabs and 17 satellite graves surround the main mound.

Further excavations are likely to continue for the next decade at least, so you may see archaeologists at work when you visit.

DOWTH Historic Site

The circular mound at Dowth is similar in size to Newgrange – about 63m in diameter – but is slightly taller at 14m high. It has suffered badly at the hands of everyone from road builders and treasure hunters to amateur archaeologists, who scooped out the centre of the tumulus in the 19th century. For a time, Dowth even had a tearoom ignobly perched on its summit. Relatively untouched by modern archaeologists, Dowth shows what Newgrange and Knowth looked like for most of their history.

Because it's unsafe, Dowth is closed to visitors, though the mound can be viewed from the road between Newgrange and Drogheda. Excavations began in 1998 and will continue for years to come.

Tours

Brú na Bóinne is one of the most popular tourist attractions in Ireland, and there are oodles of organised tours. Most depart from Dublin.

MARY GIBBONS TOURS Historic Tour
(**283 9973; www.newgrangetours.com; tour €35)** Tours depart from numerous Dublin hotels, beginning at 9.30am Monday to Friday, 7.50am Saturday and Sunday, and take in the whole of the Boyne Valley including Newgrange and the Hill of Tara. The expert guides offer a fascinating insight into Celtic and pre-Celtic life in Ireland, and you'll get access to Newgrange even on days when all visiting slots are filled. Highly recommended. Pay cash on the bus (no credit cards).

OVER THE TOP TOURS Historic Tour
(**1800 424 252; www.overthetoptours.com; return ticket €17)** One or two trips daily from central Dublin.

Getting There & Away

Bus Éireann (041-983 5023; www.buseireann.ie) Has a service linking the Brú na Bóinne visitor centre with Drogheda's bus station (one way/return €3.40/6.20, 20 minutes, two daily Monday to Saturday), with connections to Dublin.

Battle of the Boyne Site

More than 60,000 soldiers of the armies of King James II and King William III fought on this patch of farmland on the border of counties Meath and Louth in 1690. In the end, William prevailed and James sailed off to France.

Today, the **battle site** (**www.battleoftheboyne.ie; adult/child €4/2; 10am-6pm May-Sep, 9.30am-5.30pm Mar & Apr, 9am-5pm Oct-Feb)** is part of the Oldbridge Estate farm. At the visitor centre you can watch a short show about the battle, see original and replica weaponry of the time and explore a laser battlefield model. Self-guided walks through the parkland and battle site allow ample time to ponder the events that saw Protestant interests remain in Ireland. Costumed re-enactments take place in summer.

The battle site is 3km north of Donore, signposted off the N51. From Drogheda, it's 3.5km west along Rathmullan Rd (follow the river).

Trim

POP 1375

Dominated by its mighty castle and atmospheric ruins, the quiet town of Trim was an important settlement in medieval times. Five city gates surrounded a busy jumble of streets, and as many as seven

Reenactment at the Battle of the Boyne site
PHOTOGRAPHER: © DAVID LYONS / ALAMY

monasteries were established in the immediate area.

It's hard to imagine nowadays, but a measure of Trim's importance was that Elizabeth I considered building Trinity College here. One student who did go to school here – at least for a short time – was Dublin-born Arthur Wellesley, the Duke of Wellington, who studied in Talbot Castle and St Mary's Abbey.

Today, Trim's history is everywhere, with ruins scattered about the town and streets still lined with tiny old workers' cottages.

Sights

TRIM CASTLE Castle

(King John's Castle; www.heritageireland.ie; adult/child €4/2; 10am-6pm Easter-Sep, 9.30am-5.30pm Oct, 9.30am-5.50pm Sat & Sun Feb-Easter, 9am-5pm Sat & Sun Nov-Jan) This remarkably preserved edifice was Ireland's largest Anglo-Norman fortification and is proof of Trim's medieval importance. Hugh de Lacy founded Trim Castle in 1173, but Rory O'Connor, said to have been the last high king of Ireland, destroyed this motte and bailey within a year. The building you see today was begun around 1200 and has hardly been modified since.

In 1996 the castle briefly returned to its former glory as a location for Mel Gibson's *Braveheart*, in which it served as a 'castle double' for the castle at York.

The castle's grassy 2-hectare enclosure is dominated by a massive stone keep, 25m tall and mounted on a Norman motte. Inside are three levels, the lowest divided by a central wall. Just outside the central keep are the remains of an earlier wall.

The principal outer-curtain wall, some 500m long and for the most part still standing, dates from around 1250 and includes eight towers and a gatehouse. It also has a number of sally gates from which defenders could exit to confront the enemy.

The finest stretch of the outer wall runs from the River Boyne through Dublin Gate to Castle St. Within the northern corner was a church and, facing the river, the Royal Mint, which produced Irish coinage (called 'Patricks' and 'Irelands') into the 15th century.

Medieval Trim Castle

Sleeping

You can easily cover Trim's sights as a day trip, but accommodation is plentiful.

TRIM CASTLE HOTEL Hotel **€€**
(**046-948 3000; www.trimcastlehotel.com; Castle St; d €65-130; P @) This stylish boutique hotel is part of a development that's doing its best to spiff up an area close to the castle. The 68 rooms here have a compact but comfortable modern design; facilities include jacuzzis in some rooms, as well as a carvery restaurant.

Eating & Drinking

AN TROMÁN Cafe **€**
(**http://artisanfoodstoretrim.webs.com; Market St; dishes €4.50-7; breakfast & lunch Mon-Sat)** Crammed with gourmet goodies, this fabulous deli is perfect for picking up the makings of a picnic. If it's not picnic weather, you can order daily specials like a bowl of soup and tuna and sweet corn sandwich, or chicken-and-mushroom pie and a meringue nest with fruit and fresh cream.

MARCY REGAN'S Pub
(**Lackanash Rd, Newtown; Thu-Tue)** This small, traditional pub beside St Peter's Bridge claims to be Ireland's second-oldest. It's a no-frills kind of place just steeped in old-world atmosphere. There's often a trad music session on Friday nights.

Getting There & Around

Bus Éireann runs a bus at least once an hour between Dublin and Trim (€9.27, 70 minutes). Buses stop on New Rd just beyond the bridge.

Tara

The **Hill of Tara** is Ireland's most sacred stretch of turf, an entrance to the underworld, occupying a place at the heart of Irish history, legend and folklore. It was the home of the mystical druids, the priest-rulers of ancient Ireland, who practised their particular form of Celtic paganism under the watchful gaze of the all-powerful goddess Maeve (Medbh). Later it was the ceremonial capital of the high kings – 142 of them in all – who ruled until the arrival of Christianity in the 6th century. It is also one of the most important ancient sites in Europe, with a Stone Age passage tomb and prehistoric burial mounds that date back up to 5000 years.

Although little remains other than humps and mounds of earth on the hill, its historic and folkloristic significance is immense. History and preservation have run headlong into the demands of sprawl and convenience in the Tara Valley, however. A battle between government and campaigners over contentious road construction has been raging for years, and work had to be halted on the first day of digging in 2007 when an ancient site that could rival Stonehenge was uncovered. Despite pleas from eminent historians and archaeologists around the world, the controversy is ongoing. For an update on the current situation, visit www.tarawatch.org.

History

The Celts believed that Tara was the sacred dwelling place of the gods and the gateway to the other world. The passage grave was thought to be the final resting place of the Tuatha dé Danann, the mythical fairy folk – they were real enough, but instead of pixies and brownies, they were earlier Stone Age arrivals on the island.

As the Celtic political landscape began to evolve, the druids' power was usurped by warlike chieftains who took kingly titles; there was no sense of a united Ireland, so at any given time there were countless *rí tuaithe* (regional kings) controlling many small areas. The king who ruled Tara, though, was generally considered the big shot, the high king, even though his direct rule didn't extend too far beyond the provincial border. The most lauded of all the high kings was Cormac MacArt, who ruled during the 3rd century.

If You Like... Pubs

If you like Marcy Regan's (p129), then you might want to venture into these classic traditional pubs:

1 **C NÍ CAIRBRE**
(Carberry's; North Strand, Drogheda) A national treasure, this tiny pub has been owned by the same family since 1880.

2 **CLARKE & SONS**
(Peter St, Drogheda) Wonderful old boozer with unrestored wooden interior right out of a time capsule.

3 **HARBOUR BAR**
(Seapoint Rd, Bray) A strong contender for Ireland's best pub, here you can enjoy an excellent pint of Guinness in a quiet atmosphere of conviviality.

4 **PJ O'HARES**
(www.pjoharescarlingford.com; Newry St, Carlingford; mains €9.50-19.50; lunch & dinner) Stone-floor classic with top-class beer garden, regular live music and a superb menu.

The most important event in Tara's calendar was the three-day harvest *feis* (festival) that took place at Samhain, a precursor to modern Halloween. During the festival, the high king pulled out all the stops: grievances would be heard, laws passed and disputes settled amid an orgy of eating, drinking and partying.

When the early Christians hit town in the 5th century, they targeted Tara straight away. Although the legend has it that Patrick lit the paschal fire on the Hill of Slane, some people believe it took place on Tara's sacred hump. The arrival of Christianity marked the beginning of the end for Celtic pagan civilisation, and the high kings began to desert Tara, though the kings of Leinster continued to be based here until the 11th century.

In August 1843, Tara saw one of the greatest crowds ever to gather in Ireland. Daniel O'Connell, the 'Liberator' and the leader of the opposition to union with Great Britain, held one of his monster rallies at Tara, and up to 750,000 people came to hear him speak.

RATH OF THE SYNODS Historic Site

The names applied to Tara's various humps and mounds were adopted from ancient texts, and mythology and religion intertwine with the historical facts. The Protestant church grounds and graveyard spill onto the remains of the Rath of the Synods, a triple-ringed fort where some of St Patrick's early synods (meetings) supposedly took place. Excavations of the enclosure suggest that it was used between AD 200 and 400 for burials, rituals and living quarters. Originally the ring fort would have contained wooden houses surrounded by timber palisades.

Excavations have uncovered Roman glass, shards of pottery and seals, showing links with the Roman Empire even though the Romans never extended their power into Ireland.

ROYAL ENCLOSURE Historic Site

To the south of the church, the Royal Enclosure is a large, oval Iron Age hill fort, 315m in diameter and surrounded by a bank and ditch cut through solid rock under the soil. Inside the Royal Enclosure are several smaller sites.

The **Mound of the Hostages**, a bump in the northern corner of the enclosure, is the most ancient known part of Tara and the most visible of its remains. Supposedly a prison cell for hostages of the 3rd-century king Cormac MacArt, it is in fact a small Stone Age passage grave dating from around 1800 BC that was later used by Bronze Age people. The passage contains some carved stonework, but is closed to the public.

The mound produced a treasure trove of artefacts, including some ancient Mediterranean beads of amber and faience (glazed pottery). More than 35 Bronze Age burials were found here, as well as a mass of cremated remains from the Stone Age.

Although two other earthworks inside the enclosure, **Cormac's House** and the **Royal Seat**, look similar, the Royal Seat is a ring fort with a house site in the centre, while Cormac's House is a barrow (burial mound) in the side of the circular bank. Cormac's House commands the best views of the surrounding lowlands of the Boyne and Blackwater Valleys.

Atop Cormac's House is the phallic **Stone of Destiny**, originally located near the Mound of the Hostages, which represents the joining of the gods of the earth and the heavens. It's said to be the inauguration stone of the high kings, although alternative sources suggest that the actual coronation stone was the Stone of Scone, which was removed to Edinburgh, Scotland, and used to crown British kings. The would-be king stood on top of the Stone of Destiny and, if the stone let out three roars, he was crowned. The mass grave of 37 men who died in a skirmish on Tara during the 1798 Rising is next to the stone.

ENCLOSURE OF KING LAOGHAIRE Historic Site

South of the Royal Enclosure is this large but worn ring fort where the king, a contemporary of St Patrick, is supposedly buried standing upright and dressed in his armour.

BANQUET HALL Historic Site

North of the churchyard is Tara's most unusual feature, a rectangular earthwork measuring 230m by 27m along a north–south axis. Tradition holds that it was built to cater for thousands of guests during feasts. Much of this information comes from the 12th-century *Book of Leinster* and the *Yellow Book of Lecan*, which even includes drawings of the hall.

Opinions vary as to the site's real purpose. Its orientation suggests that it was a sunken entrance to Tara, leading directly to the Royal Enclosure. More recent research, however, has uncovered graves within the compound, and it's possible that the banks are in fact the burial sites of some of the kings of Tara.

GRÁINNE'S FORT Historic Site

Gráinne was the daughter of King Cormac. Betrothed to Fionn McCumhaill (Finn McCool), she eloped with Diarmuid, one of the king's warriors, on her wedding night, becoming the subject of the epic *The Pursuit of Diarmuid and Gráinne*. Gráinne's Fort and the northern and southern **Sloping Trenches** off to the northwest are burial mounds.

Eating

McGuires Coffee Shop Cafe €

(dishes €4-6; breakfast & lunch;) If a walk on the hill has worked up an appetite, this cafe/souvenir shop at the base can restore you with snacks like apple and cinnamon pancakes or waffles with toffee sauce.

Information

Entrance to Tara is free and the site itself is always open. There are good explanatory panels by the entrance. Unfortunately, many people let their dogs roam free on the hill – watch your step!

Old Tara Book Shop (Tue, Thu, Sat & Sun) At the base of the hill, this tiny, jumbled secondhand bookshop is run by Michael Slavin, who has authored an informative little book about the site, *The Tara Walk* (€3).

Tara Visitor Centre (046-902 5903; www.heritageireland.ie; adult/child €3/1; 10am-6pm Jun-mid-Sep) A former Protestant church (with a window by artist Evie Hone) is home to Tara's visitor centre, screening a 20-minute audiovisual presentation about the site.

Getting There & Away

Tara is 10km southeast of Navan, just off the Dublin–Cavan Rd (N3). It's poorly signposted – count on asking for directions.

Bus Éireann (836 6111) Services linking Dublin and Navan pass within 1km of the site (€11.40, 40 minutes, hourly Monday to Saturday and four times on Sunday). Ask the driver to drop you off at the Tara Cross, where you take a left turn off the main road.

Loughcrew Cairns

With all the hoopla over Brú na Bóinne, the amazing Stone Age passage graves strewn about the Loughcrew Hills are often overlooked. There are 30-odd tombs here but they're hard to reach and relatively few people ever bother, which means you can enjoy this moody and evocative place in peace.

It's well worth making the effort to get to the three hills, Carnbane East (194m), Carnbane West (206m) and Patrickstown (279m) – although the last has been so ruined by 19th-century builders that there's little to see other than splendid views of the surrounding countryside.

Like Brú na Bóinne, the graves were all built around 3000 BC, but unlike their better-known and better-excavated peers, the Loughcrew tombs were used at least until 750 BC. As at Newgrange, larger stones in some of the graves are decorated with spiral patterns. Some of the graves look like large piles of stones, while others are less obvious, their cairn having been removed. Archaeologists have unearthed bone fragments and ashes, stone balls and beads.

The cairns are west of Kells, along the R154, near Oldcastle.

Tours

BEYOND THE BLARNEY Historic Tours (**087 151 1511; www.beyondtheblarney.ie**) Knowledgeable Oldcastle-based outfit offering day tours (from €60) and workshops on subjects such as Loughcrew Cairns art (from €40).

Carnbane East

Carnbane East has a cluster of sites. **Cairn T** (**049-854 1240; www.heritageireland.ie; admission free; 10am-6pm Jun-Aug; P**) is the biggest at about 35m in diameter, with numerous carved stones. One of its outlying kerbstones is called the Hag's Chair, and is covered in gouged holes, circles and other markings. You need the gate key to enter the passageway and a torch to see anything in detail.

It takes about half an hour to climb Carnbane East from the car park. In summer, access to Cairn T is controlled by **Heritage Ireland** (**www.heritageireland.ie**), which provides guides. But locals are passionate about the place and at any time of the year you can arrange for guides who will not only show you Cairn T but take you to some of the other cairns as well. Enquire at Kells' tourist office, or pick up the key from the cafe at Loughcrew Gardens.

The Stone Age passage tombs of Loughcrew Cairns

Carnbane West

From the car park, it takes about an hour to reach the summit of Carnbane West, where Cairn D and L, both some 60m in diameter, are located. They're in poor condition, though you can enter the passage and chamber of Cairn L, where there are numerous carved stones and a curved basin stone in which human ashes were placed.

Cairn L is administered by **Heritage Ireland** (**www.heritageireland.ie**), which only gives out the key to those with an authentic research interest.

Loughcrew Gardens are northwest of Kells, along the R154, near Oldcastle.

COUNTY LOUTH

Drogheda

POP 28,973

Just 48km north of Dublin, Drogheda is a historic fortified town straddling the River Boyne. A clutch of fine old buildings, a handsome cathedral and a riveting museum give it plenty of cultural interest, while its atmospheric old pubs, fine restaurants and good transport links make it an excellent base for exploring the world-class attractions that surround it.

Eating & Sleeping

D HOTEL Hotel **€€**

(**041-987 7700; www.thed.ie; Scotch Hall, Marsh Rd; d €69-109; P @) Slick, hip and unexpected, this is Drogheda's top dog when it comes to accommodation. Minimalist rooms are bathed in light and decked out with designer furniture and cool gadgets. There's a stylish bar and restaurant, a mini gym and fantastic views of the city. The hotel is popular with hen and stag parties, so beware of pounding music on weekends.

EASTERN SEABOARD BAR & GRILL Modern Irish **€€**

(**041-980 2570; www.easternseaboard.ie; 1 Bryanstown Centre, Dublin Rd; mains €10.50-33; lunch & dinner;**) Build it and they will come... Despite its unpromising location in a business park near the train station, this stylised, contemporary space has been packed since opening, with switched-on staff and quirky details like a backlit decanter collection and metallic fish sculptures. Stunning food like pig's cheek terrine with apple slaw, smoked mackerel pâté, and coffee jelly and vanilla ice cream is served continuously from lunchtime on, or just drop by for frothy German beers on tap.

Around Drogheda

A number of historic sites lie close to Drogheda, but you'll need your own transport.

Sights

BEAULIEU HOUSE, GARDENS & CAR MUSEUM Historic Site

(**041-983 8557; www.beaulieu.ie; admission house €8, garden €6, museum €6, combined ticket €20; 11am-5pm Mon-Fri May–mid-Sep, plus 1-5pm Sat & Sun Jul & Aug**) Before Andrea Palladio and the ubiquitous Georgian style that changed Irish architecture in the early decades of the 18th century, there was the Anglo-Dutch style, a simpler, less ornate look that is equally handsome. **Beaulieu House** is a particularly good example and – apparently – the first unfortified mansion to be built in Ireland. It was built between 1660 and 1666 on lands confiscated from Oliver Plunkett's family by Cromwell, and given to the marshal of the army in Ireland, Sir Henry Tichbourne. The red-brick mansion, with its distinctive steep roof and tall chimneys, has been owned by the same family ever since.

The interiors are stunning and house a superb art collection ranging from lesser Dutch masters to 20th-century Irish painters. There's also a wonderfully elegant garden and a classic car museum.

It's about 5km northeast of Drogheda on the Baltray road.

OLD MELLIFONT ABBEY Historic Site

(**041-982 6459; www.heritageireland.ie; Tullyallen; adult/child €3/1; visitor centre 10am-6pm**

Easter-Sep; **P**) In its Anglo-Norman prime, this abbey was the Cistercians' first and most magnificent centre in the country. Although the ruins are highly evocative and well worth exploring, they still don't do real justice to the site's former splendour.

In the mid-12th century, Irish monastic orders had grown a little too fond of the good life and were not averse to a bit of corruption. In 1142 Malachy, bishop of Down (later canonised for his troubles), was at the end of his tether; he invited a group of hard-core monks from Clairvaux in France to set up shop in a remote location, where they would act as a sobering influence on the local clergy. The Irish monks didn't quite get on with their French guests, and the latter soon left for home. Still, the construction of Mellifont – named for the Latin *mellifons* (honey fountain) – continued, and within 10 years, nine more Cistercian monasteries were established. Mellifont was eventually the mother house for 21 lesser monasteries; at one point as many as 400 monks lived here.

Mellifont not only brought fresh ideas to the Irish religious scene, it also heralded a new style of architecture. For the first time in Ireland, monasteries were built with the formal layout and structure that was being used on the Continent. Only fragments of the original settlement remain, but the plan of the extensive monastery can easily be traced.

Mellifont's most recognisable building, and one of the finest pieces of Cistercian architecture in Ireland, is the lavabo, an octagonal washing house for the monks. It was built in the early 13th century and used lead pipes to bring water from the river. A number of other buildings would have surrounded this main part of the abbey.

After the Dissolution of the Monasteries, a fortified Tudor manor house was built on the site in 1556 by Edward Moore, using materials scavenged from the demolition of many of the buildings.

In 1603, this house was the scene of a poignant and crucial turning point in Irish history. After the disastrous Battle of Kinsale, the vanquished Hugh O'Neill, last of the great Irish chieftains, was given shelter here by Sir Garret Moore until he surrendered to the English lord deputy Mountjoy. After his surrender, O'Neill was pardoned but, despairing of his position, fled to the Continent in 1607 with other

Ruins of Old Mellifont Abbey Cistercian monastery (p133)

EOIN CLARKE / LONELY PLANET IMAGES ©

old-Irish leaders in the Flight of the Earls. In 1727 the site was abandoned altogether.

The visitor centre describes monastic life in detail. The ruins themselves are always open and there's good picnicking next to the rushing stream. The abbey is about 1.5km off the main Drogheda–Collon Rd (R168). A back road connects Mellifont with Monasterboice.

MONASTERBOICE Historic Site

(admission free; sunrise-sunset; P) Crowing ravens lend an eerie atmosphere to Monasterboice, an intriguing monastic site containing a cemetery, two ancient church ruins, one of the finest and tallest round towers in Ireland, and two of the best high crosses.

Down a leafy lane in sweeping farmland, the original monastic settlement here is said to have been founded in the 5th or 6th century by St Buithe, a follower of St Patrick, although the site probably had pre-Christian significance. St Buithe's name somehow got converted to Boyne, and the river is named after him. An invading Viking force took over the settlement in 968, only to be comprehensively expelled by Donal, the Irish high king of Tara, who killed at least 300 of the Vikings in the process.

The high crosses of Monasterboice are superb examples of Celtic art. The crosses had an important didactic use, bringing the gospels alive for the uneducated, and they were probably brightly painted originally, although all traces of colour have long disappeared.

The cross near the entrance is known as **Muirdach's Cross**, named after a 10th-century abbot. The western face relates more to the New Testament, and from the bottom depicts the arrest of Christ, Doubting Thomas, Christ giving a key to St Peter, the Crucifixion, and Moses praying with Aaron and Hur. The cross is capped by a representation of a gabled-roof church.

The **West Cross** is near the round tower and stands 6.5m high, making it one of the tallest high crosses in Ireland. It's much more weathered, especially at the base, and only a dozen or so of its 50 panels are still legible. The more distinguishable ones on the eastern face include David killing a lion and a bear. The western face shows the Resurrection.

A third, simpler cross in the northeastern corner of the compound is believed to have been smashed by Cromwell's forces and has only a few straightforward carvings. This cross makes a great evening silhouette photo, with the round tower in the background.

The **round tower**, minus its cap, is over 30m tall, and stands in a corner of the complex. Records suggest the tower interior went up in flames in 1097, destroying many valuable manuscripts and other treasures. It's closed to the public.

Come early or late in the day to avoid crowds. It's off the M1 motorway, about 8km north of Drogheda. The site can be reached directly from Mellifont via a winding route along narrow country roads.

MATT THE MILLER'S

Kilkenny & the Southeast

Counties Wexford, Waterford and Kilkenny are (along with the southern chunk of Tipperary) collectively referred to as the 'sunny southeast'. This being Ireland the term is, of course, relative. But due to the moderating effect of the Gulf Stream, it *is* the country's warmest, driest region.

Wexford and Waterford are wreathed with wide, sandy beaches, along with thatched fishing villages, genteel seaside towns and remote, windswept peninsulas littered by wrecks – as well as a swashbuckling history of marauding Vikings, lighthouse-keeping monks and shadowy knights' sects.

Deeper inland, the gently meandering River Barrow borders along verdant County Kilkenny, whose namesake city is home to a mighty castle, a magnificent cathedral, narrow, winding medieval lanes and cracking pubs – not to mention the hip eateries, happening clubs and a host of festivals that give this spirited little city a worldly sophistication.

The River Nore, Kilkenny City (p148)

Kilkenny & the Southeast

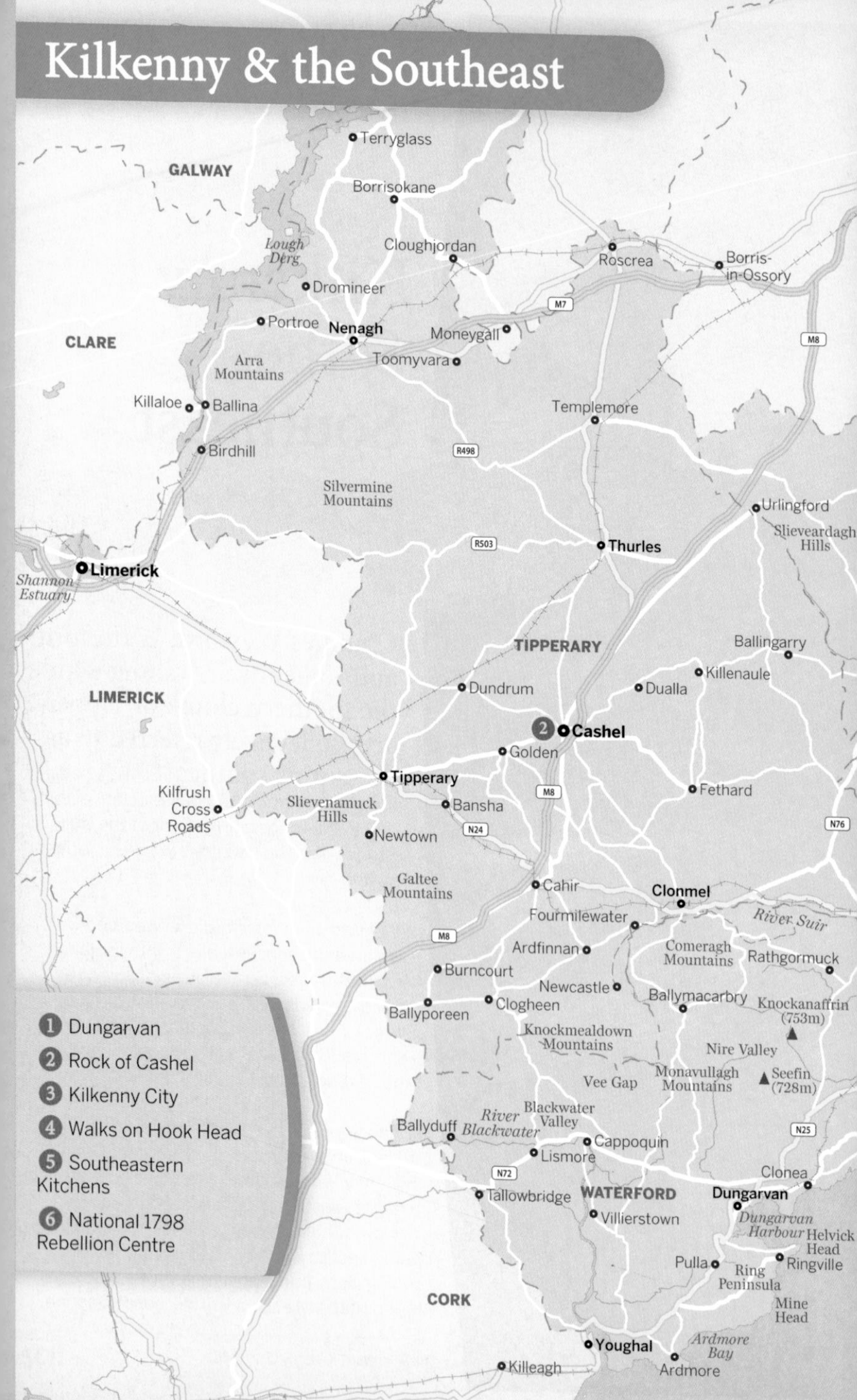

Terryglass
GALWAY
Borrisokane
Lough Derg
Cloughjordan
Roscrea
Borris-in-Ossory
Dromineer
M7
Portroe
Nenagh
Moneygall
M8
CLARE
Arra Mountains
Toomyvara
Killaloe
Ballina
Templemore
Birdhill
R498
Silvermine Mountains
Urlingford
Slieveardagh Hills
R503
Thurles
Limerick
Shannon Estuary
TIPPERARY
Ballingarry
Killenaule
LIMERICK
Dundrum
Dualla
2
Cashel
Golden
Tipperary
M8
Fethard
Kilfrush Cross Roads
Slievenamuck Hills
Bansha
N76
Newtown
N24
Galtee Mountains
Cahir
Clonmel
Fourmilewater
River Suir
M8
Ardfinnan
Comeragh Mountains
Rathgormuck
Burncourt
Newcastle
Ballymacarbry
Knockanaffrin (753m)
Ballyporeen
Clogheen
Knockmealdown Mountains
Nire Valley
Vee Gap
Monavullagh Mountains
Seefin (728m)
Blackwater Valley
Ballyduff
River Blackwater
N25
Cappoquin
Lismore
Clonea
N72
Tallowbridge
WATERFORD
Dungarvan
Villierstown
Dungarvan Harbour
Helvick Head
Pulla
Ring Peninsula
Ringville
CORK
Mine Head
Youghal
Ardmore Bay
Killeagh
Ardmore
1 Dungarvan
2 Rock of Cashel
3 Kilkenny City
4 Walks on Hook Head
5 Southeastern Kitchens
6 National 1798 Rebellion Centre

Kilpedder
Poulaphouca Reservoir
KILDARE
N78
Portlaoise
Ballitore
WICKLOW
LAOIS
M11
Baltinglass
M9
Abbeyleix
Rathvilly
Ballinakill
Hacketstown
N81
Carlow
Tinahely
Tullow
Arklow
Castlecomer
Ballyragget
River Dinin
CARLOW
Shillelagh
Ballon
Freshford
Leighlinbridge
Carnew
R693
Kildavin
Bagenalstown
Clonegal
Gorey
River Barrow
3 Kilkenny
Bunclody
Courtown
Mt Leinster (796m)
Gowran
N80
River Bann
Poulshone
Ferns
Blackstairs Mountains
Bennetsbridge
1 Dungarvan
Borris
Ballycarney
Cahore Point
Burnchurch
Tullaherin
Kiltealy
River Nore
Kilfane
Kells
Callan
Graiguenamanagh
6
Stonyford
Brandon Hill (516m)
Thomastown
Enniscorthy
Oulart
River Slaney
Ballyhale
St Mullins
Inistioge
WEXFORD
KILKENNY
Blackwater
Wexford Bay
R697
The Rower
Clonroche
M9
N30
Ballyhogue
Booley Hills
R704
New Ross
Castlebridge
Curracloe
Ferrycarrig
N25
Carrick-on-Suir
Piltown
Mullinavat
Dunganstown
Newbawn
Wexford
Wexford Harbour
Rosslare Point
5
Slieve Coillte (270m)
Foulksmills
Drinagh
R448
Campile
Murntown
Portlaw
N24
Arthurstown
Tintern Abbey
Wellington Bridge
Rosslare Harbour
Greenore Point
Waterford
Ballyhack
Bannow Bay
Tagoat
Passage East
Crooke
5
Duncannon
R733
Duncormick
Bridgetown
N25
Kilmacthomas
Waterford Airport
Fethard-on-Sea
Kilmore Quay
Carnsore Point
River Nire
Waterford Harbour
Templetown
Ballyteige Bay
Carne
Dunmore East
Hook Peninsula
Baginbun Head
Forlorn Point
Tramore
Tramore Bay
Annestown
4
Slade
Churchtown
Bunmahon
Great Newtown Head
Hook Head
Saltee Islands
St George's Channel
0
50 km
0
25 miles
ATLANTIC OCEAN

Kilkenny & the Southeast's Highlights

1

Dungarvan

Dungarvan has a blossoming reputation as a foodie hub that is more than well-deserved, but it's not putting it on for visitors or tourism. Dungarvan is a real town with lots going on – it just puts a high premium on good food. The Waterford Festival of Food, Dungarvan

Need to Know

Best Time to Visit Autumn often has the best weather and is quieter and cheaper than summer. **Advance Planning** Book cooking courses **For further coverage, see p162**.

Local Knowledge

Dungarvan Don't Miss List

BY PAUL FLYNN, HEAD CHEF AT TANNERY RESTAURANT & COOKERY SCHOOL

1 DUNGARVAN FARMERS MARKET

The Dungarvan Farmers Market (p163) helps engender a real sense of community as growers and customers come together to talk about produce, the weather and everything else! I love browsing the stalls – it is the best of what local growers have to offer.

2 WATERFORD FESTIVAL OF FOOD

The Waterford Festival of Food (p164) has a terrific food fair, a host of cooking workshops and demonstrations, and plenty of talks by local producers at their farms, which is about as close to the source as you can get. It takes place during the third weekend in April.

3 NUDE FOOD

Nude Food (p165) is the antithesis of what I call 'chefiness', which is all about drips, splodges and towers. Here you get big bowls of great food – impeccably sourced and put together in a wonderful way. As I often say to students, I spent 15 years trying to be a chef, and then the next 10 learning how to be a cook.

4 CLIFF HOUSE HOTEL

OK, so it's not technically in Dungarvan, but Ardmore isn't too far away and the Cliff House Hotel (p166) should be in any list of top picks for the southeast – it is a great restaurant in a wonderful and elegant boutique hotel that has managed to make the most of the views and location.

5 TANNERY RESTAURANT & COOKERY SCHOOL

The secret to my success is in my garden. Having the garden attached to the cooking school (p164) gives it soul. The economic downturn means that more people want to grow their own produce; we also help local special-needs schools set up gardens. A lot of people want to be celebrity chefs for the sake of it, but the ones I really admire, like Jamie Oliver and Rick Stein, are the ones who stand for something. I want to give something back.

Rock of Cashel

Surely a highlight of any trip to Ireland, the iconic and much-photographed Rock of Cashel (p169) is one of the country's most spectacular archaeological sites. For over a thousand years, the rock's sturdy walls have protected a fabulous castle, an atmospheric (if roofless) abbey, a perfectly preserved round tower and the country's finest example of a Romanesque chapel.

2

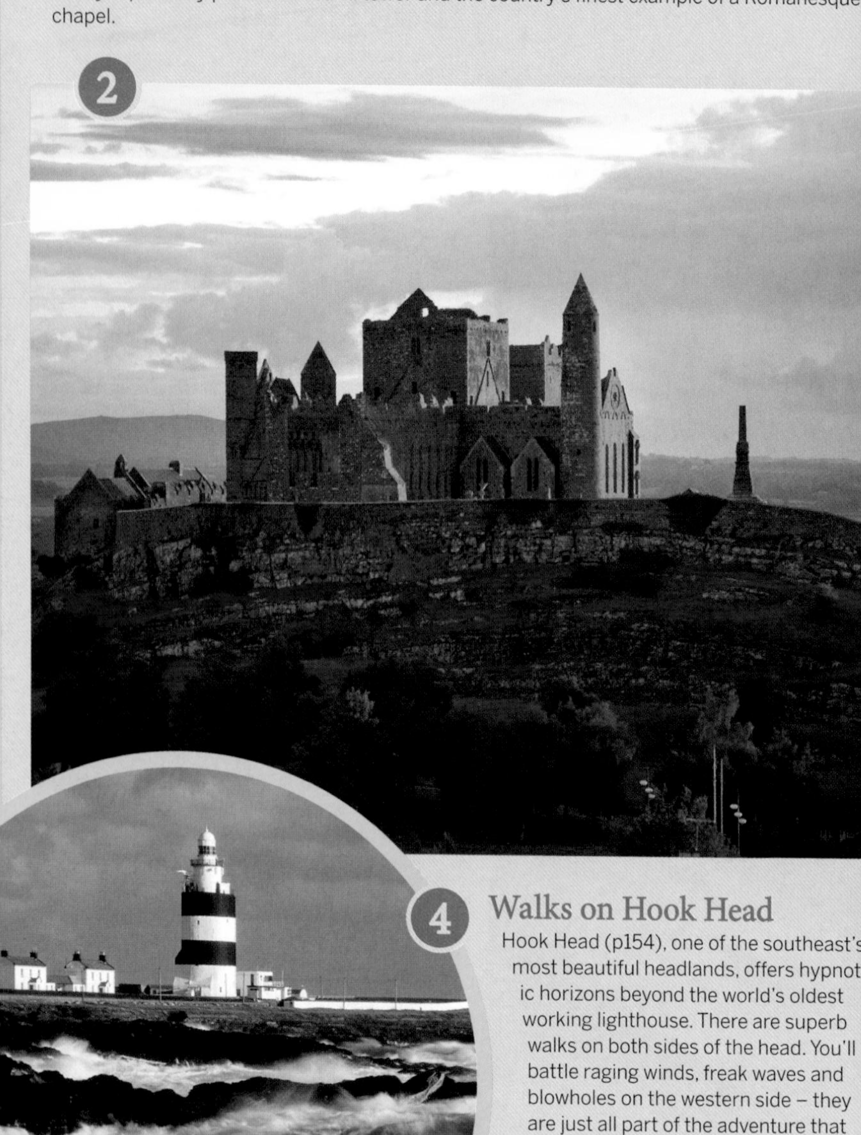

4

Walks on Hook Head

Hook Head (p154), one of the southeast's most beautiful headlands, offers hypnotic horizons beyond the world's oldest working lighthouse. There are superb walks on both sides of the head. You'll battle raging winds, freak waves and blowholes on the western side – they are just all part of the adventure that makes this area so special.

3 Kilkenny City

Forget Galway, ignore Cork and don't even bother with Dublin. Kilkenny (p148) can stake its claim as Ireland's best city because it combines a stunning medieval historical centre of winding streets and notable buildings with a rich heritage of arts and culture – best expressed in the myriad festivals it hosts – and a throbbing nightlife that draws them in from far afield. Parliament St, Kilkenny

5 Southeastern Kitchens

Although not quite as renowned as next-door County Cork, the southeast has been developing its own rep for gourmet excellence, thanks in part to pioneering chefs such as Paul Flynn in Dungarvan (p163) and Kevin Dundon in Arthurstown (p160), who have taken advantage of the southeast's fine local produce.

6 National 1798 Rebellion Centre

Ireland's history is rich in drama, struggle and tragedy, expressed poignantly in the National 1798 Rebellion Centre (p156), located in Enniscorthy, County Wexford. Near Vinegar Hill, site of the bloodiest battle of the 1798 Rebellion, this centre reconstructs the struggle for Irish independence in memorable, moving fashion.

Kilkenny & the Southeast's Best...

Beauty Spots

- **Kilmore Quay** (p152) Small fishing village that's all atmosphere.
- **Hook Head** (p152) Brave the winds for beauty.
- **Ardmore Cliffs** (p166) Stunning views from the clifftop.
- **Nire Valley** (p169) Beautiful stretch of north County Waterford.
- **Rock of Cashel** (p169) Best viewed from just north of town.

Festivals

- **Kilkenny Arts Festival** (p147) Second-largest festival of its kind in Ireland.
- **Kilkenny Rhythm & Roots** (p147) Ireland's biggest music festival.
- **Cat Laughs Comedy Festival** (p147) Acclaimed gathering of international comics.
- **Kilmore Seafood Festival** (p150) Traditional music, dancing and lots of seafood.
- **Waterford Festival of Food** (p164) The best of the region's produce.

Historic Notables

- **Kilkenny Castle** (p149) One of the country's most important heritage sites.
- **Dunbrody Heritage Ship** (p153) Full-scale replica of a 19th-century 'famine ship'.
- **Tintern Abbey** (p151) Evocative ruins of the 13th-century Cistercian abbey.
- **Jerpoint Abbey** (p155) Fine Cistercian ruin.
- **National 1798 Rebellion Centre & Vinegar Hill** (p156) A tale of rebellion and the hill it happened on.

Local Activities

- Try **sea angling** (p152) off the coast of Kilmore Quay.
- Walk **St Declan's Way** (p166), even as far as the Rock of Cashel.
- Try **fly fishing** (p169) in the Rivers Nire or Suir, County Waterford.
- Take a **cooking course** (p160) with either of the region's top chefs.

Left: Fishing boats, Kilmore Quay (p152); **Above:** Nire Valley, County Waterford (p167)

Need to Know

ADVANCE PLANNING

- **Five months before** Book hotels and tickets if you're attending any of the big festivals in Kilkenny or Wexford.
- **One month before** Book your hotel and make a reservation if you want to take a cooking course.
- **Two weeks before** Cram in a little bit of Irish history, especially about Ireland's monastic tradition and its long struggle against the English!

RESOURCES

- **Heritage Ireland** (www.heritageireland.ie) Info on Office of Public Works (OPW) sites.
- **Sailing Ireland** (www.sailingireland.ie) Details of sailing charters.
- **Kilmore Seafood Festival** (www.kilmorequayseafoodfestival.com) Details of a superb foodie fest in July.
- **Discover Ireland** (www.discoverireland.ie/southeast) Official tourist website.
- **Kilkenny Tourist** (www.kilkennytourist.com) What to see and do in Kilkenny and its environs.

GETTING AROUND

- **Bus** Good bus networks cover most of the area, but it's a slow way of exploring.
- **Train** The main towns are linked, but not necessarily to each other.
- **Car** The region's beauty is off the beaten path; you'll need a car to get there.

BE FOREWARNED

- **Crowds** Kilkenny gets slammed during the major festivals.
- **Weather** Statistically speaking, the southeast is the warmest region of Ireland, which doesn't necessarily mean it's warm. Come prepared.
- **Hurling** The sport of choice in the southeast, especially in Kilkenny, whose rivalry with Waterford and Wexford is passionate!

Kilkenny & the Southeast Itineraries

Medieval treasures, a rich monastic heritage and some of the finest coastline in Ireland await you as you explore the southeast. The following itineraries will give you ample opportunity to sample all of it and more.

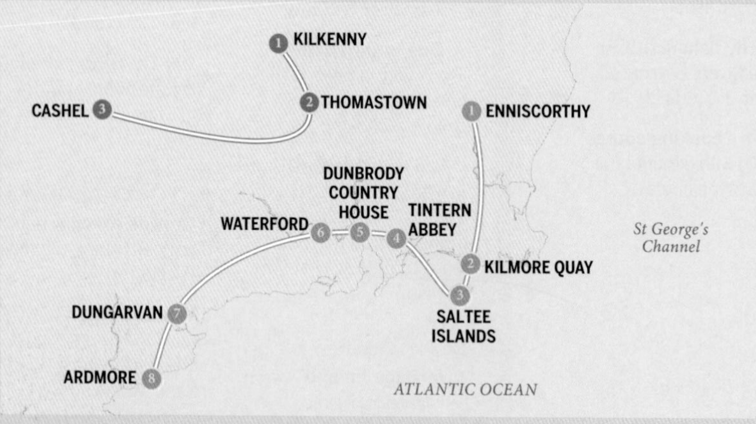

KILKENNY CITY TO CASHEL

Kilkenny Buzz

Between the city's imposing castle, the gorgeous medieval layout and its collection of world-class festivals, **(1) Kilkenny City** could keep you busy for months, never mind the three days you've allotted here. Still, to make the best of your time, make a beeline on day one to **Kilkenny Castle**, which has been central to the major developments of Irish history since its construction in 1192. The impressive **Long Gallery** is a good example of the kind of luxury the high and mighty afforded themselves. Be sure to look inside **St Canice's Cathedral** – which gave the city its name – and pay a visit to the **National Craft Gallery & Kilkenny Design Centre**, where you'll find some of the best-made Irish handicrafts and designs in the country. On day two, spread your wings and make for the antique shops of **(2) Thomastown** and the nearby ruins of **Jerpoint Abbey**. On day three, make the trek across the border into County Tipperary and feast your eyes on the rock-top stronghold of **(3) Cashel**. All the while, don't forget to sample Kilkenny's superb collection of great pubs!

WEXFORD TO WATERFORD
Southeastern Coastliner

In five days you can explore the best of the coastline counties of Wexford and Waterford. Start in the town of **(1) Enniscorthy,** visiting the **National 1798 Rebellion Centre** and historic **Vinegar Hill** before turning south, on day two, towards the coast and the traditional fishing village of **(2) Kilmore Quay**, from which you can visit the bird sanctuary on the **(3) Saltee Islands**. On day three, continue westward around the Hook Peninsula, where you should take a peak at the atmospheric ruins of **(4) Tintern Abbey** before stopping off to sample some of Kevin Dundon's excellent fare at **(5) Dunbrody Country House**; you could even try a half-day cooking course. Cross the border into County Waterford and visit **(6) Waterford City**, making sure not to miss the excellent **Waterford Museum of Treasures**. On day four, keep going west and make for **(7) Dungarvan** or **(8) Ardmore**, on the border with County Cork. Here you'll find some fine walks along the cliffs at the edge of town and the excellent Michelin-starred restaurant at the Cliff House Hotel.

Tintern Abbey (p153), Hook Peninsula

Discover Kilkenny & the Southeast

At a Glance

- **County Kilkenny** (p146) Dominated by a wonderful medieval city.
- **County Wexford** (p150) 'Sunny' southeast is a traditional holiday destination.
- **County Waterford** (p157) Less to explore, but just as beautiful as surrounding counties.
- **County Tipperary** (p170) Rolling hills, great farmland and lovely ruins.

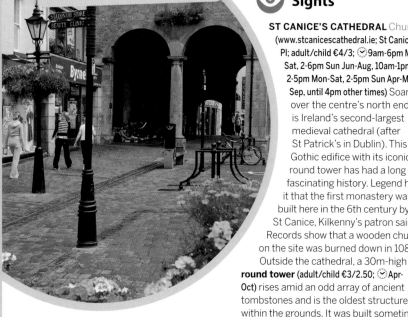

High St, Kilkenny City

PHOTOGRAPHER: CREDIT

COUNTY KILKENNY

POP 95,000

Kilkenny City

POP 8900

Kilkenny (Cill Chainnigh) is the Ireland of many visitors' imaginations. Its majestic riverside castle, tangle of 17th-century passageways, rows of colourful, old-fashioned shopfronts and centuries-old pubs with traditional live music all have a timeless appeal, as does its splendid medieval cathedral. But Kilkenny is also awash with contemporary eateries and is a hotbed of arts, crafts and cultural life.

Sights

ST CANICE'S CATHEDRAL Church (www.stcanicescathedral.ie; St Canice's Pl; adult/child €4/3; 9am-6pm Mon-Sat, 2-6pm Sun Jun-Aug, 10am-1pm & 2-5pm Mon-Sat, 2-5pm Sun Apr-May & Sep, until 4pm other times) Soaring over the centre's north end is Ireland's second-largest medieval cathedral (after St Patrick's in Dublin). This Gothic edifice with its iconic round tower has had a long and fascinating history. Legend has it that the first monastery was built here in the 6th century by St Canice, Kilkenny's patron saint. Records show that a wooden church on the site was burned down in 1087.

Outside the cathedral, a 30m-high **round tower** (adult/child €3/2.50; Apr-Oct) rises amid an odd array of ancient tombstones and is the oldest structure within the grounds. It was built sometime between AD 700 and 1000 on the site of an earlier Christian cemetery. Apart from missing its crown, the round tower is in

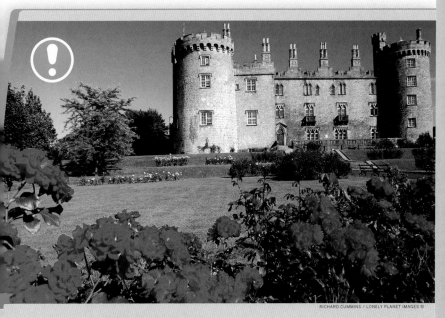

RICHARD CUMMINS / LONELY PLANET IMAGES ©

Don't Miss Kilkenny Castle

Rising above the Nore, Kilkenny Castle is one of Ireland's most visited heritage sites. The first structure on this strategic site was a wooden tower built in 1172 by Richard de Clare, the Anglo-Norman conqueror of Ireland better known as Strongbow. In 1192, Strongbow's son-in-law, William Marshall, erected a stone castle with four towers, three of which survive. Regular 40-minute guided tours focus on the **Long Gallery**, in the wing of the castle nearest the river. The gallery, which showcases stuffy portraits of the Butler family members over the centuries, is an impressive hall with high ceilings vividly painted with Celtic and Pre-Raphaelite motifs.

THINGS YOU NEED TO KNOW

www.kilkennycastle.ie; adult/child €6/2.50; 9am-5.30pm Mar-Sep, 9.30am-4.30pm Oct-Feb

excellent condition and those aged over 12 can admire a fine view from the top.

NATIONAL CRAFT GALLERY & KILKENNY DESIGN CENTRE Gallery
(www.ccoi.ie; Castle Yard; 10am-5.30pm Tue-Sat) Contemporary Irish crafts are showcased at this imaginative gallery in the former castle stables that also house the shops of the Kilkenny Design Centre. Ceramics dominate, but exhibits often feature furniture, jewellery and weaving.

Behind the complex, look for the walkway that extends into the beautiful **gardens** of Butler House, with an unusual water feature constructed from remnants of the British-built Nelson Column, blown up by nationalists in Dublin around a century ago.

Festivals & Events

Kilkenny Rhythm & Roots Music Festival
(www.kilkennyroots.com; early May) Over 30 pubs and other venues participate in hosting Ireland's biggest music festival, with an

Kilkenny

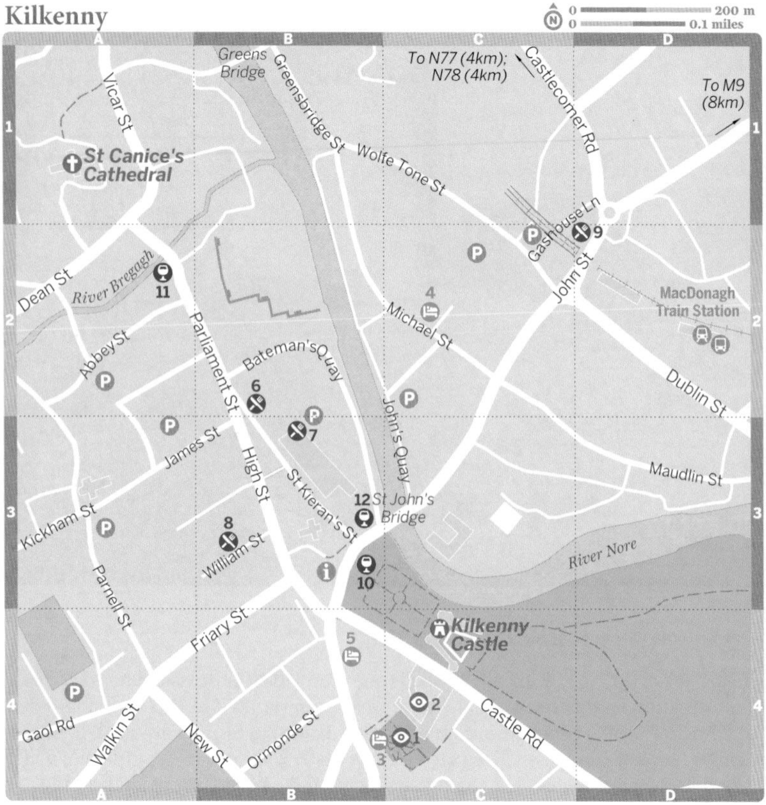

emphasis on country and 'old-timey' American roots music.

Cat Laughs Comedy Festival Comedy Festival
(www.thecatlaughs.com; late May-early Jun) Acclaimed gathering of world-class comedians in Kilkenny's hotels and pubs.

Kilkenny Arts Festival Arts Festival
(www.kilkennyarts.ie; mid-Aug) The city comes alive with theatre, cinema, music, literature, visual arts, children's events and street spectacles for 10 action-packed days.

Sleeping

BUTLER HOUSE Hotel €€
(056-772 2828; www.butler.ie; 16 Patrick St; s €60-120, d €100-180; P @) You can't stay in Kilkenny Castle, but this historic mansion is surely the next best thing. Once the home of the earls of Ormonde, who built the castle, these days it houses a boutique hotel with aristocratic trappings including sweeping staircases, marble fireplaces, an art collection and impeccably trimmed gardens. The 13 generously sized rooms are individually decorated.

PEMBROKE HOTEL Hotel €€€
(056-778 3500; www.pembrokekilkenny.com; Patrick St; r €120-200; P) Wake up to castle views (only from some of the 74 rooms) at this stylish, modern epicentral hotel. Deluxe rooms feature balconies, a rarity in Ireland (along with the air-con). There's a leather-sofa-filled bar on-site and use of swimming and leisure facilities are just around the corner.

Kilkenny

Top Sights

Kilkenny Castle C4
St Canice's Cathedral A1

Sights

1 Butler House Gardens C4
2 National Craft Gallery & Kilkenny Design Centre C4

Sleeping

3 Butler House B4
4 Celtic House C2
5 Pembroke Hotel B4

Eating

6 Blueberry Cafe B2
7 Blueberry Deli B3
8 Cafe Sol B3
9 Campagne D2

Drinking

10 Grapevine B3
11 John Cleere A2
12 Tynan's Bridge House B3

CELTIC HOUSE B&B **€€**
(**☎056-776 2249; www.celtic-house-bandb.com; 18 Michael St; r €70-90; P @**) Artist Angela Byrne extends one of Ireland's warmest welcomes at her spick-and-span B&B. Some of the bright rooms have sky-lit bathrooms, others have views of the castle, and Angela's landscapes adorn many of the walls. Book ahead.

Eating

CAMPAGNE Modern Irish **€€€**
(**☎056-777 2858; www.campagne.ie; The Arches, 5 Gashouse Lane; lunch 2-/3-course set menu €24/29, dinner mains €25-30; ⏰lunch Fri-Sun, dinner Tue-Sat**) Chef Garrett Byrne who gained fame and Michelin stars in Dublin is the genius behind this bold, stylish restaurant in his native Kilkenny. He's passionate about supporting local and artisan producers and he takes the goods and produces ever-changing, ever-memorable meals. There's a French accent to everything he does.

BLUEBERRY Cafe, Deli **€€**
(**www.blueberrykilkenny.com; Winston's, 8 Parliament St; dishes €7-9; ⏰9am-5pm Mon-Sat**) Deli (**2 Market Yard; ⏰8.30am-6pm Mon-Sat**) On the top floor of the posh Winston's department store there is a stunning cafe run by the long-running deli. Choose from coffees, juices and teas. Enjoy sandwiches, hot specials, cakes and more out on the spectacular rooftop terrace. The original deli is still the place for picnic supplies.

CAFE SOL Modern Irish **€€**
(**☎056-776 4987; William St; lunch mains €9-15, dinner mains €17-25; ⏰lunch & dinner**) Leisurely lunches stretch until 5pm at this much-loved restaurant. Local organic produce is featured in dishes that emphasise what's fresh each season. The flavours are frequently bold and have global influences. Service, albeit casual, is excellent.

Drinking

TYNAN'S BRIDGE HOUSE Pub
(**St John's Bridge**) Looking like it might fall down at any moment, this wonky Georgian pub is the best trad bar in town. To be sure, the 300-year-old building has settled a bit over the years, but then so have many of the customers.

JOHN CLEERE Pub
(**22 Parliament St**) One of Kilkenny's finest venues for live music, this long bar has blues, jazz and rock, as well as trad music sessions.

GRAPEVINE Bar
(**6 Rose Inn St**) If yet another pint in an atmospheric pub is just one too many, take refuge at this smart wine bar. There's also a stellar range of craft beers and a fine selection of tapas.

Entertainment

For information on local events, check out the weekly *Kilkenny People* newspaper (www.kilkennypeople.ie). Events are listed on the tourist office website, and on www.whazon.com.

Information

Tourist office (www.discoverireland.ie; Rose Inn St; ⏲9am-7pm Mon-Sat, 11am-5pm Sun Jul & Aug, 9.15am-1pm & 2-5pm Mon-Sat Sep-Jun) County Kilkenny's only tourist office, stocking excellent guides and walking maps, set in Shee Alms House, built in local stone in 1582 by local benefactor Sir Richard Shee to provide help for the poor.

Getting There & Away

Bus

Bus Éireann (www.buseireann.ie) Operates from a shelter about 200m east of John St adjacent to the train station. Patrick St in the centre of town is also a stop. Services Carlow (€9, 35 minutes, three daily), Cork (€18, three hours, two daily), Dublin (€12, 2¼ hours, five daily) and Waterford (€10, one hour, two daily).

JJ Kavanagh & Sons (www.jjkavanagh.ie; stop at Ormonde Rd) Dublin airport (€12, three hours, six daily).

Train

Trains (www.irishrail.ie) Eight times daily to/from Dublin's Heuston Station (from €10, 1¾ hours) and Waterford (from €10, 50 minutes). MacDonagh train station, on the eastern side of the shopping mall, has no lockers.

Central Kilkenny

Thomastown

POP 1800

This small market town has a serenity it hasn't known in decades now that the M9 has diverted Dublin traffic away. The centre makes for an interesting, short stroll. Named after Welsh mercenary Thomas de Cantwell, Thomastown has some fragments of a medieval wall and the partly ruined 13th-century **Church of St Mary**. Down by the bridge, **Mullin's Castle** is the sole survivor of the 14 castles once here. The Cistercian ruins of **Jerpoint Abbey** (see the boxed text on p154) lie 2.5km southwest of Thomastown.

Eating

BLACKBERRY CAFE Cafe €
(Market St; dishes €4.50-7.50, ⏲9.30am-5.30pm Mon-Fri, 10am-5.30pm Sat) Does superb thick-cut sandwiches and warming soups served with pumpkin-seed-speckled soda bread. Much is organic and the tarts and cakes are baked daily. Between noon and 2pm, great-value multicourse hot lunches see the place squeezed to bursting. It's right in town.

SOL BISTRO Modern Irish €€
(Low St; mains €12-25; ⏲lunch & dinner) Kilkenny's modern Irish cafe has a branch in Thomastown's centre. It's a small cafe in a tidy old storefront. The food combines the best local ingredients for Irish classics with a twist.

Getting There & Away

Trains on the Dublin to Waterford route via Kilkenny stop eight times daily in each direction in Thomastown. The station is 1km west of town.

COUNTY WEXFORD

Kilmore Quay

POP 400

Dotted with thatched cottages, Kilmore Quay is a small, working fishing village whose harbour is the jumping-off point for Ireland's largest bird sanctuary, the Saltee Islands, which are clearly visible out to sea. It is one of the busiest fishing ports in the southeast; the cry of gulls and smell of the sea provide atmosphere for fine fish and chips shops.

Mussel in on the four-day **Seafood Festival** (www.kilmorequayseafoodfestival.com) in July for music, dancing and, of course, tastings.

Getting There & Away

Wexford Bus (www.wexfordbus.com) Runs to/from Wexford up to four times daily (€6, 45 minutes).

Detour: Saltee Islands

Once the haunt of privateers, smugglers and 'dyvars pyrates', the **Saltee Islands** (www.salteeislands.info; open for visits 11.30am-4pm) now have a peaceful existence as one of Europe's most important bird sanctuaries. Over 375 recorded species make their home here, 4km offshore from Kilmore Quay, principally the gannet, guillemot, cormorant, kittiwake, puffin, aux and Manx shearwater. The best time to visit is the spring and early summer nesting season. The birds leave once the chicks can fly, and by early August it's eerily quiet.

Boats make the trip from Kilmore Quay harbour, but docking depends on the wind direction and is often impossible. Contact **Declan Bates** (053-912 9684, 087 252 9736; day trip €30); book in advance.

PRINCE OF THE SALTEES

The Saltees were bought in 1943 by Michael Neale, who immediately proclaimed himself 'Prince of the Saltees'. Something of a strange one, he erected a throne and obelisk in his own honour on Great Saltee, and had a full-blown coronation ceremony there in 1956. Although the College of Arms in London refuted Neale's claim to blue blood, he won a small victory when Wexford County Council began addressing letters to 'Prince Michael Neale'.

The prince broadcast his intention to turn Great Saltee into a second Monte Carlo, but was distracted by a war right on his doorstep. In an escalation of hostilities, he released two ferrets, then a dozen foxes, then 46 cats onto the island to kill the rabbits that he hated so. He died in 1998.

Hook Peninsula & Around

The road shadowing the long, tapering finger of the Hook Peninsula is signposted as the Ring of Hook coastal drive. Around every other bend is a quiet beach, a crumbling fortress, a stately abbey or a seafood restaurant, and the world's oldest working lighthouse is flung out at its tip.

Strongbow (Robert FitzGilbert de Clare, Earl of Pembroke) landed here on his way to capture Waterford in 1170, reputedly instructing his men to land 'by Hook or by Crooke', the latter referring to the nearby settlement of Crooke in County Waterford across the harbour.

Tintern Abbey

In better structural condition than its Welsh counterpart, from where its first monks hailed, Ireland's moody **Tintern Abbey** (Saltmills; adult/child €3/1; 10am-6pm mid-May–Sep) is secluded amid 40 hectares (100 acres) of woodland. William Marshal, Earl of Pembroke, founded the Cistercian abbey in the early 13th century after he nearly perished at sea and swore to establish a church if he made it ashore.

The abbey sits amid wooded trails, lakes and idyllic streams. The grounds are always open, and a walk here is worth the trip at any time.

Fethard-on-Sea

POP 325

Continuing south towards the Head, Fethard is the largest village in the area. It's home to the scant ruins of 9th-century church **St Mogue's** and the unstable ruins of a 15th-century **castle**, which belonged to the bishop of Ferns. The small **harbour** is worth a visit for its views.

Southeast Ireland has many good **dive sites**, especially around Hook Head. **Surfing** is hugely popular. **Scuba South East** (087 094 5771; www.scubasoutheast.ie;

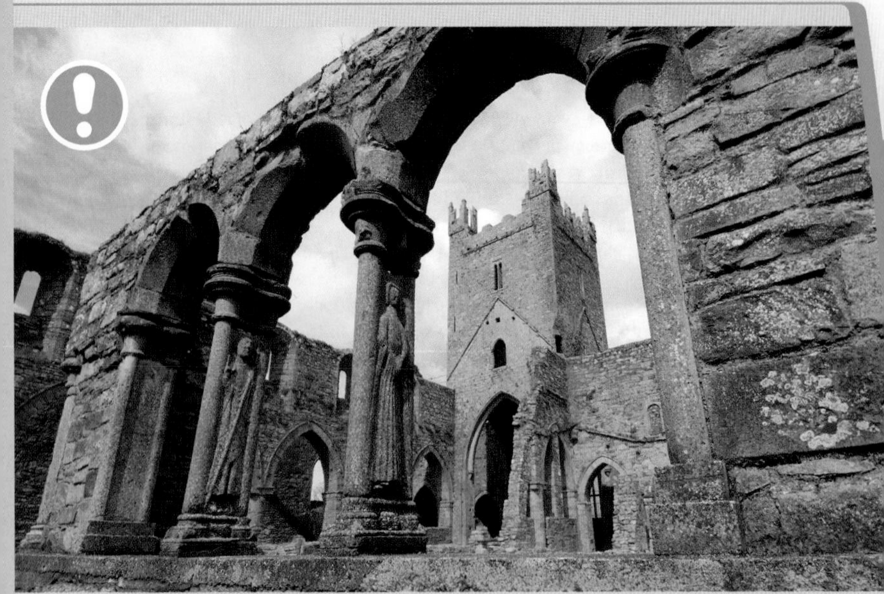

STEPHEN SAKS / LONELY PLANET IMAGES ©

Don't Miss Jerpoint Abbey

One of Ireland's finest Cistercian ruins, Jerpoint Abbey is about 2.5km southwest of Thomastown. It was established in the 12th century and has been partially restored. The tower and cloister are late 14th or early 15th century. Look for the series of often amusing figures carved on the cloister pillars, including a knight. There are also stone carvings on the church walls and in the tombs of members of the Butler and Walshe families. Faint traces of a 15th- or 16th-century painting remain on the northern wall of the church. This chancel area also contains a tomb thought to belong to hard-headed Felix O'Dulany, Jerpoint's first abbot and bishop of Ossory, who died in 1202. The excellent 45-minute tours run throughout the day. Set yourself apart in the remains of the cloisters and see if you can hear the faint echo of a chant. According to local legend, St Nicholas (or Santa Claus) is buried near the abbey, in the **Church of St Nicholas**.

THINGS YOU NEED TO KNOW

☎056-24623; www.heritageireland.ie; Hwy R448, Thomastown; adult/child €3/1; ⏲9am-5.30pm Mar-Oct, check hours Nov-Feb

Fethard-on-Sea) is an excellent resource, and surfing is hugely popular locally. **Monkey's Rock Surf Shop** (☎087 647 2068; Main St, Fethard-on-Sea) and **Freedom Surf School** (☎086 391 4908; www.freedomsurfschool.com) have surf gear and info.

The community-run **tourist office** (☎051-397 502; www.hooktourism.com; Wheelhouse Cafe, Main St; ⏲10am-6pm May-Sep) covers the region. The short main drag has cafes, pubs and there are B&Bs all around.

Hook Head & Around

The journey from Fethard to Hook Head takes in a hypnotic stretch of horizon, with few houses between the flat, open fields on the tapering peninsula. Views extend across Waterford Harbour and, on a clear day, as far as the Comeragh and Galtee Mountains.

Sights

HOOK HEAD LIGHTHOUSE Historic Site

(www.hookheritage.ie; adult/child €6/3.50; 9.30am-6pm Jun-Aug, 9.30am-5pm other times) On its southern tip, Hook Head is capped by the world's oldest working lighthouse. It's said that monks first lit a beacon on the head from the 5th century and that the first Viking invaders were so happy to have a guiding light that they left them alone. In the early 13th century William Marshal erected a more permanent structure, which is still standing today under its black and white exterior. Access is by half-hour guided tour, which includes a climb up the 115 steps for great views; the visitor centre has a simple cafe.

Activities

There are brilliant, blustery **walks** on both sides of Hook Head. Poke around the tide pools while watching for surprise showers from blowholes on the western side of the peninsula. The rocks around the shore are Carboniferous limestone, rich in **fossils**. Search carefully and you may find 350-million-year-old shells and tiny disc-like pieces of crinoids, a type of starfish. A good place to hunt is Patrick's Bay, on the southeast of the peninsula.

Eating

TEMPLARS INN Pub **€€**

(Templetown; mains €10-22; restaurant 12.30-8.30pm Mar-Oct, pub noon-late daily) This very inviting place opens to a panoramic outdoor terrace overlooking the ruins of the medieval church, fields and ocean beyond. Inside, the dark-timber interior looks like a wayfarers' tavern, but is a cosy place for a steak or seafood.

Getting There & Away

There's limited public transport as far as Fethard, but none to Hook Head.

Bus

Bus Éireann (www.buseireann.ie) Route 370 runs between Waterford, New Ross, Duncannon, Templetown and Fethard. The entire journey takes over two hours and there is only one bus in each direction each day Monday to Saturday.

Ferry

If you're travelling directly to Waterford city, the Ballyhack-Passage East car ferry (see p163) saves detouring via New Ross.

New Ross

POP 4600

The big attraction at New Ross (Rhos Mhic Triúin), 34km west of Wexford town, is the opportunity to board a 19th-century Famine ship. But New Ross' historical links stretch back much further – to the 12th century, when it developed as a Norman port on the River Barrow. A group of rebels tried to seize the town during the 1798 Rising. They were repelled by the defending garrison, leaving 3000 dead and much of the place in tatters.

Today its eastern bank retains some intriguing steep, narrow streets and the impressive ruins of a medieval abbey.

Sights & Activities

DUNBRODY FAMINE SHIP Museum

(051-425 239; www.dunbrody.com; The Quay; adult/child €7.50/4.50; 10am-6pm Apr-Sep, 10am-5pm Oct-Mar) Called 'coffin ships' due to the fatality rate of their passengers, the leaky, smelly boats that hauled a generation of Irish to America are recalled at this replica ship on the waterfront. The emigrants' sorrowful yet often inspiring stories (they paid an average of £7 for the voyage) are brought to life by docents during 30-minute tours. A 10-minute film gives you background on the original three-masted barque and the construction of the new one. Admission includes access to the on-site database of Irish emigration to America from 1845 to 1875, containing over two million records.

Sleeping & Eating

BRANDON HOUSE HOTEL Hotel €€
(☎051-421 703; www.brandonhousehotel.ie; New Ross; s/d from €105/140; P @ 🛜 ≈ 👪) This 1865-built red-brick manor certainly lives up to its reputation as family friendly, with kids happily bounding around the place. Winning elements include river views, open log fires, a library bar and large rooms, as well as a spa. It's up a steep driveway 2km south of New Ross.

CAFE NUTSHELL Irish €€
(8 South St; mains €10-16; ⌚9am-5.30pm Tue-Sat) It's a shame that Nutshell closes in the evening, as New Ross' town centre is short on places of this calibre. Scones, breads and buns are all baked on the premises, hot lunch specials utilise local produce and there's a great range of smoothies, juices and organic wines. Mains come with an array of fresh salads. The shop in the front, In a Nutshell, is the perfect place for picnic provisions.

Information

Tourist office (www.newrosstourism.com; The Quay; ⌚9am-6pm Apr-Sep, 9am-5pm Oct-Mar) In the flash new building that doubles as the ticket office for the Dunbrody Famine Ship.

Getting There & Away

Bus Éireann (www.buseireann.ie) Buses depart from Dunbrody Inn on the Quay and travel to Waterford (€6, 30 minutes, seven to 11 daily), Wexford (€7, 40 minutes, three to four daily) and Dublin (€14, three hours, four daily).

Enniscorthy

POP 3200

County Wexford's second-largest town, Enniscorthy (Inis Coirthaidh), has a warren of steep streets descending from Augustus Pugin's cathedral to the Norman castle and the River Slaney. Enniscorthy is inextricably linked to some of the fiercest fighting of the 1798 Rising, when rebels captured the town and set up camp at Vinegar Hill.

Sights

NATIONAL 1798 REBELLION CENTRE Museum
(www.1798centre.ie; Mill Park Rd; adult/child €6/3.50; ⌚same hours as tourist office) A visit here before climbing Vinegar Hill greatly enhances its impact. The centre's exhibits cover the French and American revolutions that sparked Wexford's abortive uprising against British rule in Ireland, before chronicling what was one of the most bloodthirsty battles of the 1798 Rebellion, and a turning point in the struggle. A month later, English troops attacked and forced the rebels to retreat, massacring hundreds of women and children in the 'follow-up' operation. Interactive displays include a chessboard with pieces representing key figures in the Rising, and a multiscreen re-creation of the finale atop a virtual Vinegar Hill. From Abbey Sq walk out of town along Mill Park Rd or south along the river.

VINEGAR HILL Historic Site
To visit the scene of the 1798 events, get a map from the tourist office and look for signs. It's a 2km drive or about a 45-minute walk from Templeshannon on the eastern side of the river. At the summit there's a memorial to the uprising, explanatory signs and views across the county.

Sleeping

The lush, rolling hills in this part of County Wexford shelter some lovely country houses.

WOODBROOK HOUSE Inn €€
(☎053-925 5114; www.woodbrookhouse.ie; Killanne; s/d from €95/150; ❄ @ 🛜 ≈) Damaged in the 1798 rebellion, this glorious country estate is now a three-room guesthouse. The entry features a gravity-defying spiral staircase that amazes

Detour: Wexford & the Kennedys

In 1848 Patrick Kennedy left the horrible conditions in County Wexford aboard a boat like the Famine ship in New Ross. Hoping to find something better in America, he succeeded beyond his wildest dreams (a US president, senators and rum-runners are just some of his progeny). You can recall the family's Irish roots at two sites near New Ross.

The birthplace of Patrick Kennedy, great-grandfather of John F Kennedy, **Kennedy Homestead** (☎051-388 264; www.kennedyhomestead.com; Dunganstown; adult/child €5/2.50; ⏰10am-5pm Jul & Aug, 11.30am-4.30pm Mon-Fri May, Jun & Sep, by appointment rest of year) is a farm that still looks – and smells – much as it must have 160 years ago. When JFK visited the farm in 1963 and hugged the current owner's grandmother, it was his first public display of affection, according to his sister Jean. The outbuildings have been turned into a recently expanded museum that examines the Irish-American dynasty's history on both sides of the Atlantic. It's about 7km south of New Ross along a very narrow but beautifully overgrown road.

On a sunny day, the **John F Kennedy Arboretum** (www.heritageireland.ie; New Ross; adult/child €3/1; ⏰10am-8pm May-Aug, 10am-6.30pm Apr & Sep, 10am-5pm Oct-Mar) is so nice for families that it could be called Camelot. The park, 2km southeast of the Kennedy Homestead, has a small visitor centre, tearooms and a picnic area; a miniature train tootles around in the summer months. It has 4500 species of trees and shrubs in 252 hectares of woodlands and gardens. **Slieve Coillte** (270m), opposite the park entrance, has a viewing point from where you can see the arboretum and six counties on a clear day.

now just as it did over 200 years ago. Green practices are used throughout and you can make arrangements for dinner (organic, of course). It is 13km west of Enniscorthy.

Information

Tourist office (☎053-923 4699; Mill Park Rd; ⏰9.30am-5pm Mon-Fri, noon-5pm Sat & Sun Apr-Sep, 9.30am-4pm Mon-Fri Oct-Mar) In the centre inside Enniscorthy castle.

Getting There & Away

Bus

Bus Éireann (www.buseireann.ie) stops on the Shannon Quay on the eastern bank of the river, outside the **Bus Stop Shop** (⏰9am-10pm) where you can buy tickets. There are nine daily buses to Dublin (€11, 2½ hours), and eight to Rosslare Harbour (€10, one hour) via Wexford (€6, 25 minutes).

Train

The **train station** (Templeshannon) is on the eastern bank of the river. Trains serve Dublin Connolly station (€24, 2¼ hours) and Wexford (€7, 25 minutes) three times daily.

COUNTY WATERFORD

POP 108,000

Waterford City

POP 45,000

Ireland's oldest city, Waterford (Port Láirge), is first and foremost a busy port. It lies on the tidal reach of the River Suir, 16km from the coast. Some parts of the city still feel almost medieval, though, with narrow alleyways leading off larger streets. An ongoing revitalisation campaign is polishing up one block after another. New and existing museums tell the story of Ireland's Middle Ages better than any other city in the country.

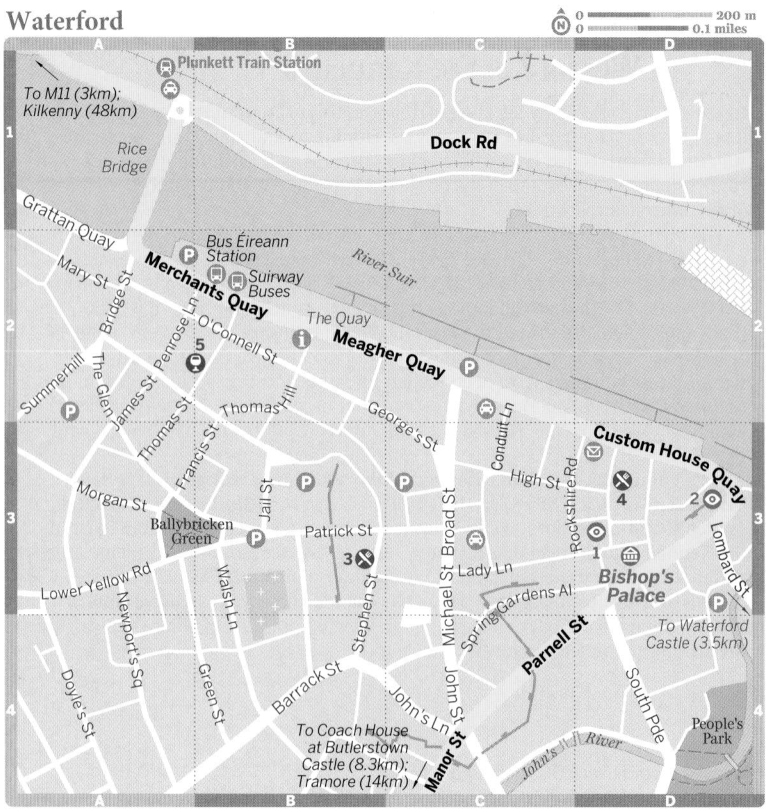

Sights & Activities

The ancient streets northwest of the Mall are getting a burnish with new museums and attractions that highlight the city's rich past.

WATERFORD MUSEUM OF TREASURES Museum

(Bishop's Palace, The Mall; adult/child €5/2; 9am-6pm Mon-Sat, from 11am Sun Jun-Aug, to 5pm Sep-May) This interactive museum detailing Waterford's long history is in the newly renovated **Bishop's Palace** (1741). It has dazzling displays covering Waterford's history from 1700 to 1970 and includes treasures from the city's collection, such as golden Viking brooches, jewel-encrusted Norman crosses and 18th-century church silver. The real star is the magnificent 1372 4m-long Great Charter Roll, which shows portraits of five medieval kings of England.

REGINALD'S TOWER Historic Building

(www.heritageireland.ie; The Quay; adult/child €3/1; 10am-5pm daily Easter-Oct, to 6pm

Waterford

Top Sights
Bishop's Palace D3

Sights
1 Raymond Chandler House D3
2 Reginald's Tower D3

Eating
3 Harlequin B3
4 L'Atmosphere D3

Drinking
5 Henry Downes Bar B2

Jun–mid-Sep, 10am-5pm Wed-Sun Oct-Easter) The oldest complete building in Ireland and the first to use mortar, 12th-century Reginald's Tower is an outstanding example of medieval defences and was the city's key fortification. The Normans built its 3m- to 4m-thick walls on the site of a Viking wooden tower. Over the years, the building served as an arsenal, a prison and a mint. The exhibits relating to the latter role are interesting: medieval silver coins, a wooden 'tally stick' with notches indicating the amount owed, a 12th-century piggy bank (smashed) and a coin balance used to determine weight and bullion value. Architectural oddities include the toilet that drained halfway up the building.

Sleeping

WATERFORD CASTLE Hotel €€€

(051-878 203; www.waterfordcastle.com; The Island, Ballinakill; s €90-150, d €120-240; P @) Getting away from it all is an understatement at this mid-19th-century turreted castle, which is located on its own 124-hectare (310-acre) island roamed by deer. A free, private car ferry signposted just east of the Waterford Regional Hospital provides round-the-clock access.

All 19 castle rooms have clawfoot baths, and some have poster beds. There are also 48 contemporary self-catering cottages on the island. Breakfast is available for €18 to €22, and both guests and nonguests can dine on organic fare in chef Michael Quinn's sublime oak-panelled restaurant (menus from €65), or play a round of golf.

COACH HOUSE AT BUTLERSTOWN CASTLE B&B €€

(051-384 656; www.butlerstowncastle.com; Butlerstown; r €80-150; P) A 10-minute drive from town, this 19th-century stone B&B is as appealing inside as it is out, with deep, studded leather armchairs to sink into, toasty open fires to warm up by, canopied beds to drift off in, and pancakes to wake up to. It has 17 rooms and is 5km west of town off the N25.

Eating

L'ATMOSPHERE French €€

(051-858 426; 19 Henrietta St; mains €12-25; lunch Mon-Fri, dinner daily;) Always crowded, this rollicking, casual bistro has an energy most places in Paris wish they could import. Classic French dishes with modern Irish flair (and Waterford produce) are served with élan. Perhaps hard to imagine, but you really will need to try to save room for dessert – they're superb.

HARLEQUIN Italian €€

(37 Stephen St; lunch mains €8-12, dinner mains €10-14; 8.30am-8.30pm Mon-Wed, 8.30am-10.30pm Thu & Fri, 9.30am-10.30pm Sat;) Run by young, charismatic Italian duo Simone and Alessandro, this authentic little trattoria morphs throughout the day from a coffee and pastry stop to a busy dining spot to a candlelit wine bar. House speciality antipasti platters are laden with cheeses, marinated vegetables and/or finely sliced cured meats.

Drinking

HENRY DOWNES BAR Pub

(Thomas St; from 5pm) For a change from stout, drop into Downes, which has been brewing its No 9 Irish whiskey for over two centuries. Have a dram in its series of character-filled rooms, or buy a bottle to take away.

Information

Waterford city tourist office (www.discoverwaterfordcity.ie; Merchants Quay; 9am-6pm Mon-Sat, 11am-5pm Sun Jul & Aug, shorter hr other times)

Getting There & Away

Air

Waterford Airport (www.flywaterford.com) The airport is 9km south of the city centre at Killowen. Primarily has flights to London Luton, Manchester and Birmingham.

Bus

Bus Éireann (**www.buseireann.ie; Merchant's Quay**) Frequent services to Tramore (€3, 30 minutes); Dublin (€13, three hours) via Enniscorthy or Carlow; Wexford (€8, one hour); Cork (€18, 2¼ hours); and Dungarvan (€11, 50 minutes).

Train

Plunkett train station (**051-873 401**) North of the river. Up to eight services to/from Dublin's Heuston Station (from €20, two to 2½ hours) and Kilkenny (from €10, 40 minutes).

Getting Around

There is no public transport to the airport. A **taxi** (**051-858 585, 051-77710**) costs around €15. There are taxi ranks at Plunkett train station, Dunnes Stores and Coal Quay.

Altitude (**051-870 356; www.altitude.ie; 22 Ballybricken; 9.30am-6pm Mon-Fri, 9.30am-5.30pm Sat**) Rents bicycles for €15 per day.

Southeast County Waterford

This hidden corner of the county makes an easy day trip from Waterford city or a lovely detour on an onward journey. The waters are tidal and have numerous personalities through the day.

Less than 14km east of Waterford is the estuary village of Passage East, from where car ferries yo-yo to Ballyhack in County Wexford. A pretty little fishing village, it's also lined with thatched cottages surrounding its neat harbour.

Although the main roads involve returning to Waterford, a little-travelled 11km-long **coast road** wiggles south between Passage East and Dunmore East. At times single-vehicle-width and steep, it offers mesmerising views of the ocean and undulating fields that you won't see from the main thoroughfares. On a bike it is a thrill.

Getting There & Away

Suirway (**www.suirway.com; adult/child €4/2**) buses connect Waterford with Passage East seven to eight times daily.

Dunmore East

POP 800

Some 19km southeast of Waterford, Dunmore East (Dún Mór) is strung out along a coastline of red sandstone cliffs full of screaming kittiwakes and concealed coves. In the 19th century, the town was a station for the steam packets that carried mail between England and the south of Ireland. Legacies left from the era include thatched cottages lining the main street and an unusual Doric **lighthouse** (1825) overlooking the working harbour.

HAVEN HOTEL Hotel **€€**
(**051-383 150; www.thehavenhotel.com; s/d from €60/100; restaurant dinner daily,**

Raymond Chandler & Waterford

Could Philip Marlowe have been spawned in the old medieval streets of Waterford? Author **Raymond Chandler** lived here for a time as a child with his mother and bachelor uncle after her marriage collapsed in the US in 1895. Look for blue markers on the side of an austere building on Peter St.

Near the end of his life Chandler said he had an idea for a story in which a vacationing Marlowe gets caught up in a Waterford murder. He never wrote it.

Waterford–Wexford Ferry

If you're going to travel between Counties Waterford and Wexford along the coast, you can cut out a long detour around Waterford Harbour and the River Barrow by taking the five-minute **car ferry** (www.passageferry.ie; 7am-10pm Mon-Sat, 9.30am-10pm Sun Apr-Sep, 7am-8pm Mon-Sat, 9.30am-8pm Oct-Mar) between Passage East and Ballyhack in County Wexford. Single/return tickets for pedestrians or cyclists cost €2/3 and for cars €8/12.

brunch Sun, hotel open Mar-Oct; P) Built in the 1860s as a summer house for the Malcolmson family, whose coat of arms can still be seen on the fireplaces, the Haven is now run by the Kelly family and remains an elegant retreat with wood-panelled bathrooms and, in two rooms, four-poster beds. Local produce underpins dishes in the casual restaurant (mains €12 to €20) and the low-lit crimson-toned bar.

Eating & Drinking

SPINNAKER BAR Seafood **€€**
(www.thespinnakerbar.com; mains €8-20; food noon-9pm) Eat at sidewalk tables watching beachgoers pass, inside amid nautical knickknacks or out back in the sheltered beer garden. Wherever you choose, you'll enjoy top-notch casual seafood fare. Chowders, fish and chips, salads and fresh specials are expertly prepared. There's live music on summer weekends.

LEMON TREE CAFE Modern Irish **€€**
(www.lemontreecatering.ie; mains €8-20; 10am-6pm Tue-Sun, dinner Fri & Sat Jun-Aug) Organic coffees and delectable baked goods hold the fort through much of the day. At lunch there's a long list of ever-changing sandwiches, soups and hot specials. It's pedal to the metal for summer dinners with a wide range of fresh and creative dishes.

Getting There & Away

Suirway (www.suirway.com; adult/child €4/2) buses connect Waterford with Dunmore East seven to eight times daily.

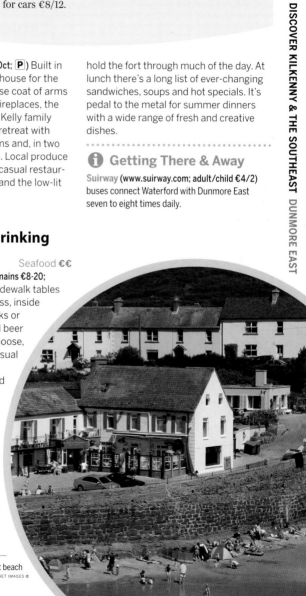

Dunmore East beach

Dungarvan

POP 7800

With its pastel-shaded buildings ringing the picturesque bay where the River Colligan meets the sea, beguiling Dungarvan (Dún Garbhán) resembles Galway in miniature. St Garvan founded a monastery here in the 7th century, but most of the centre dates from the early 19th century when the Duke of Devonshire rebuilt the streets around Grattan Sq. Overlooking the bay are a dramatic ruined castle and an Augustinian abbey, as well as lively pubs. Dungarvan is also renowned for its cuisine, with outstanding restaurants, a famous cooking school and the annual Waterford Festival of Food.

Sights

FREE DUNGARVAN CASTLE Historic Building

(www.heritageireland.ie; 10am-6pm Jun-Sep) Renovation is restoring this stone fortress to its former Norman glory. Once inhabited by King John's constable Thomas Fitz Anthony, the oldest part of the castle is the unusual 12th-century shell keep, built to defend the mouth of the river. The 18th-century British army barracks house a visitor centre with various exhibits. Admission is by guided tour only.

Activities

TANNERY COOKERY SCHOOL Cooking Course

(058-45420; www.tannery.ie; 10 Quay St; courses €50-200) Looking like a futuristic kitchen showroom, best-selling author and chef Paul Flynn's cookery school adjoins a fruit, vegetable and herb garden. Some courses include foraging for ingredients, while others cover market gardening. Other topics include seafood, advanced cooking and France. His books include the best-selling *The Tannery Cookbook: An Irish Adventure with Food*.

Festivals & Events

WATERFORD FESTIVAL OF FOOD Food Festival

(www.waterfordfestivaloffood.com; mid-Apr) The area's abundant fresh produce is celebrated at this hugely popular festival that features cooking workshops and demonstrations, talks by local producers at their farms, and a food fair. A new craft brew beer garden is an excellent addition.

FÉILE NA NDÉISE Music Festival

(www.feilenandeise.com; 1st May bank holiday weekend) Local pubs and hotels host a lively traditional music and

Dungarvan Castle gate

dance festival that attracts around 200 musicians.

Sleeping

POWERSFIELD HOUSE B&B €€
(058-45594; www.powersfield.com; Ballinamuck West; s/d from €60/90; P wi-fi) Energetic chef and Tannery cookery instructor Eunice Power lives in one half of this Georgian home with her family, and has opened six beautifully decorated rooms in the other for guests. Breakfast is a veritable feast of Eunice's baked goods, jams, chutneys and delicacies from her garden. It's a five-minute drive north of town on the road to Clonmel.

MOUNTAIN VIEW HOUSE Inn €€
(058-42588; www.mountainviewhse.com; O'Connell St; s/d from €45/70; P wi-fi) This beautiful Georgian house, built in 1815 and set in walled grounds, has great high-ceilinged rooms and views of the Comeragh Mountains. Rates drop if you forego breakfast (though with choices like porridge drizzled with warm honey on the menu, you may not want to). It's a five-minute walk down O'Connell St from Grattan Sq.

TANNERY TOWNHOUSE Inn €€
(058-45420; www.tannery.ie; Church St; s/d €65/110; Feb-Dec; P wi-fi) Just around the corner from the Tannery Restaurant is this boutique guesthouse, which spans two buildings in the town centre. Its 14 rooms are quite modern and stylish, and have fridges conveniently stacked with juices, fruit and muffins so you can enjoy a continental breakfast on your own schedule. An honour bar and snacks ease the transition from afternoon to evening.

If You Like... Fine Food

If you like the fine food County Waterford has to offer at the likes of the Tannery (p162) in Dungarvan and the Cliff House (p165) in Ardmore, County Wexford has a few gourmet offerings of its own:

1 **ALDRIDGE LODGE RESTAURANT & GUESTHOUSE**
(051-389 116; www.aldridgelodge.com; Duncannon; s/d from €55/100; dinner Tue-Sun; P) On windblown fields above Duncannon, Aldridge takes a bit of finding, but it's worth it for its elegant, contemporary guestrooms and fresh local seafood like Hook Head crab claws or Kilmore cod (dinner €39). Two caveats: book in advance, and kids under seven aren't allowed.

2 **DUNBRODY COUNTRY HOUSE HOTEL, RESTAURANT & COOKERY SCHOOL**
(051-389 600; www.dunbrodyhouse.com; Arthurstown; multicourse meals from €60; P wi-fi) Chef Kevin Dundon is a familiar face on Irish TV, and the author of cookbooks *Full On Irish* and *Great Family Food*. His spa hotel (single/double room from €140/225), in a period-decorated 1830s Georgian manor on 300-acre grounds, is the stuff of foodies' fantasies, with a gourmet restaurant and cookery school (one-day courses from €175).

3 **LOBSTER POT**
(Carne; lunch mains €8-12, dinner mains €20-35; restaurant dinner Tue-Sun, bar food noon-7.30pm Tue-Sun, closed Jan) Packs in locals and visitors in summer (at which time it doesn't take bookings), but it's worth the squeeze to get at the fab fresh seafood. The chowder – brimming with cockles, mussels, prawns, salmon, crab and cod – is among the best anywhere. Sunny tables outside are the pick, although the woody interior has its charms.

Eating

TANNERY Modern Irish €€€
(058-45420; www.tannery.ie; 10 Quay St; mains €18-29; 12.30-2.30pm Fri & Sun, 6-9.30pm Tue-Sat, also Sun Jul & Aug) An old leather tannery houses this innovative

and much-lauded restaurant, where Paul Flynn creates seasonally changing dishes that focus on just a few flavours and celebrate them through preparations that are at once comforting yet surprising. There's intimate seating downstairs or tables in the buzzing, loft-like room upstairs. Service is excellent. Book so you don't miss out.

NUDE FOOD Modern Irish **€€**
(www.nudefood.ie; 86 O'Connell St; mains €8-16; 9am-6pm Mon-Wed, 9am-9.30pm Thu-Sat) The only thing bare here is the plates after diners finish. From carefully crafted coffees to a beautiful selection of deli items, this cafe stands out. But save yourself for the lunch and dinner menus which feature top Waterford ingredients in sandwiches, salads, starters and hot mains that are hearty, honest and flavourful.

Information

Dungarvan has a handful of ATMs but by Sunday they may be as empty inside as the wallets of the weekend partiers who drained them.

Tourist office **(www.dungarvantourism.com; Courthouse Bldg, TF Meagher St; 9.30am-5pm Mon-Fri year-round, plus 10am-5pm Sat May-Sep)**

Getting There & Away

Bus Éireann **(www.buseireann.ie)** buses pick up and drop off on Davitt's Quay on the way to and from Waterford (€12, one hour, 12 daily) and Cork (€16, 1½ hours, 12 daily).

Ring Peninsula

POP 390

Just 15 minutes' drive from Dungarvan, the Ring Peninsula (An Rinn, meaning 'the headland') is one of Ireland's best-known Gaeltacht areas. En route, views of the Comeragh Mountains, Dungarvan Bay and the Copper Coast drift away to the northeast. At the peninsula's tip, the small working harbour in Helvick Head has a stoic **monument** to the crew of *Erin's Hope*. The crew brought guns from New York in 1867, intending to start a Fenian uprising, but were arrested when they landed here. Follow signs to An Rinn then Cé Heilbhic, passing Baíle na nGall ('village of strangers'; it was founded by fishermen from elsewhere).

You can easily spend a day exploring quiet country lanes here, with the promise of a hidden beach or fine old trad pub around the next bend in the road.

Ex-Waterford Crystal worker Eamonn Terry returned home to the peninsula to set up his own workshop, **Criostal na Rinne (058-46174; www.criostal.com; by appointment)**, where you can buy deep-prismatic-cut, full-lead crystal vases, bowls, clocks, jewellery and even chandeliers.

Getting There & Around

Pubs, accommodation and shops are scattered along the peninsula; you really need a car or bicycle to get around.

Bus Éireann **(www.buseireann.ie)** Stops in Ring en route between Ardmore (30 minutes) and Waterford (1¼ hours) via Dungarvan. But frequency is seldom: once daily in summer, much less often other times.

Ardmore

POP 410

The enticing seaside village of Ardmore may look quiet these days, but it's claimed that St Declan set up shop here between 350 and 420. This brought Christianity to southeast Ireland long before St Patrick arrived from Britain. Today's visitors come for its beautiful strand, watersports, ancient buildings and good places to eat and/or sleep. A winning combination!

Sights & Activities

Plan on spending a day on rambles about the town, ancient sites, coast and countryside.

ST DECLAN'S CHURCH Historic Site
In a striking position on a hill above town, the ruins of St Declan's Church stand on the site of St Declan's original monastery alongside an impressive cone-roofed, 29m-high, 12th-century **round tower**, one of the best examples of these structures in Ireland.

ST DECLAN'S WELL Historic Site

Pilgrims once washed in these waters, which are located in front of the ruins of Dysert Church, behind the hotel development above Ardmore Pottery.

BALLYQUIN BEACH Beach

Tide pools, fascinating rocks and sheltered sand are just some of the appeals of this beautiful beach. It's 1km off the R673 4km northeast of Ardmore. Look for the small sign.

ARDMORE POTTERY Pottery

(www.ardmorepottery.com; ⌚10am-6pm Mon-Sat, 2-6pm Sun May-Oct) Near the start of the cliff walk, this cosy little house sells beautiful pottery, many in lovely shades of blue and cream. Other locally produced goods include warm hand-knitted socks. This is a good source of tourist info for the area.

WALKS Walking

A 5km, cobweb-banishing **cliff walk** leads from St Declan's Well. On the one-hour round trip you'll pass the wreck of a crane ship that was blown ashore in 1987 on its way from Liverpool to Malta. The 94km **St Declan's Way** mostly traces an old pilgrimage route from Ardmore to the Rock of Cashel (County Tipperary) via Lismore. Catholic pilgrims walk along it on St Declan's Day (24 July).

Sleeping & Eating

CLIFF HOUSE HOTEL Hotel €€€

(☎024-87800; www.thecliffhousehotel.com; r €225-450; P @ 🛜 🏊) Built into the cliff-face, all guest rooms at this cutting-edge edifice overlook the bay, and most have balconies or terraces. Some suites even have two-person floor-to-ceiling glass showers (strategically frosted in places) so you don't miss those sea views. There are also sea views from the indoor swimming pool, outdoor jacuzzi and spa, the bar and the much-lauded modern Irish restaurant (menu from €60). Service is discreet but anticipatory.

WHITE HORSES Irish €€

(☎024-94040; Main St; lunch mains €8-13, dinner mains €13-24; ⌚11am-late Tue-Sun May-Sep, Fri-Sun other times) Energetically run by three sisters, this tasty bistro serves nourishing fare like fresh seafood chowder or locally caught seafood on plates

Wall carvings on St Declan's Church

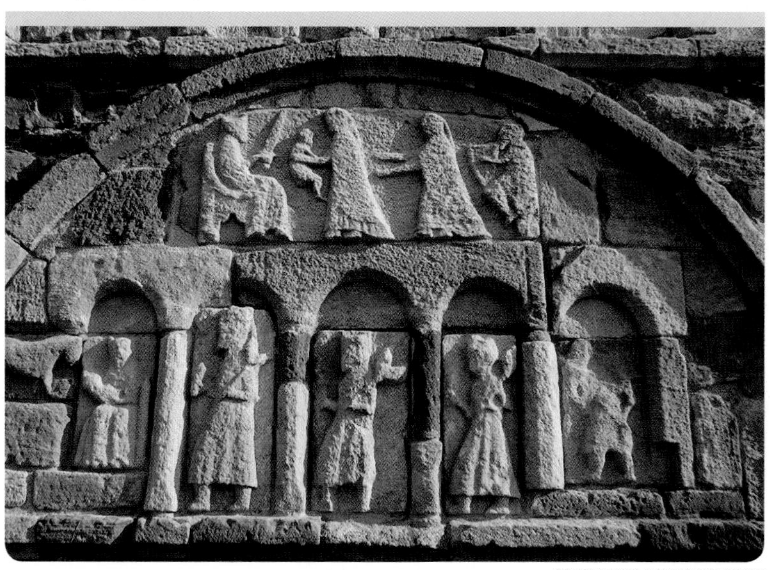

RICHARD CUMMINS / LONELY PLANET IMAGES ©

Waterford Farmstays

If you're beguiled by the beautiful Waterford countryside, why not bed down in the middle of it, with only the sound of a distant snoring cow to break the silence? **Waterford Farm Accommodation** (www.waterfordfarms.com) arranges stays on local farms near towns such as Dungarvan, Ardmore and Ring. Don't expect to sleep in a hayloft, however – accommodation is in rooms done up to a high B&B standard with private bathrooms and averages €40 to €45 per person per night.

handmade in the village. Enjoy a drink on the bench out front or a meal at a sunny lawn table out back.

Getting There & Away

Bus Éireann (www.buseireann.ie) operates one to three buses daily west to Cork (€15, 1¾ hours); connections east to Dungarvan and beyond range from one daily in summer to seldom other times.

Lismore

POP 750

Today, Lismore's enormous 19th-century castle seems out of proportion to this quiet, elegant town on the River Blackwater. Most of its existing buildings date from the early 19th century, but Lismore once had over 20 churches – many of which were destroyed during 9th- and 10th-century Viking raids.

Over the centuries, statesmen and luminaries have streamed through Lismore, the location of a great monastic university founded by St Carthage in the 7th century. King Alfred of Wessex attended the university, Henry II visited the papal legate Bishop Christian O'Conarchy (Gilla Crist Ua Connairche) here in 1171, and even Fred Astaire dropped by when his sister Adele married into the Cavendish family, who own the castle.

Sights

LISMORE CASTLE Historic Site

(www.lismorecastlearts.ie, www.lismorecastle.com; gardens adult/child €8/4; 11am-4.45pm mid-Mar–Sep) From the Cappoquin road there are stunning glimpses of the riverside 'castle', which has lots of windows that would undercut any efforts at defence. While you can't get inside the four impressive walls of the main, crenulated building (unless you're looking to rent it for a group event), you can visit the 3 hectares of ornate and manicured **gardens**. Thought to be the oldest in Ireland, they are divided into the walled Jacobean upper garden and less formal lower garden. There are brilliant herbaceous borders, magnolias and camellias, and a splendid yew walk where Edmund Spenser is said to have written *The Faerie Queen*.

ST CARTHAGE'S CATHEDRAL Church

'One of the neatest and prettiest edifices I have seen', commented William Thackeray in 1842 about the striking 1679 cathedral. And that was before the addition of the Edward Burne-Jones **stained-glass window**, which features all the Pre-Raphaelite hallmarks: an effeminate knight and a pensive maiden against a sensuous background of deep-blue velvet and intertwining flowers. Justice, with sword and scales, and Humility, holding a lamb, honour Francis Currey, who helped to relieve the suffering of the poor during the Famine. Among the cathedral's wonders and oddities are some noteworthy **tombs**, including the elaborately carved MacGrath family crypt dating from 1557 and fossils in the pulpit.

Sleeping & Eating

GLENCAIRN INN & PASTIS BISTRO B&B €€

(☎058-56232; www.glencairninn.com; Glencairn, Lismore; s/d from €60/95; ⊙restaurant dinner Thu-Sat, lunch Sun, inn & restaurant closed mid-Nov–mid-Jan; P 📶) Painted the colour of churned butter, this south-of-France-style country inn has four rooms with brass beds, classic French cuisine (mains €20 to €30), and a quintessentially Provençal *pétanque* pitch. Follow the signposts 4km west of town.

O'BRIEN CHOPHOUSE Modern Irish €€

(☎058-53810; www.obrienchophouse.ie; Main St; mains €14-28; ⊙lunch & dinner Wed-Sun; 📶) Up here in Waterford's hills the sea seems distant which makes the menu of steaks and chops all the more appropriate at this bastion of traditional cooking. But there's modern flair in the kitchen and always a surprise or two on the specials board. The Victorian decor of this old pub has been beautifully restored.

Information

Tourist office (www.discoverlismore.com; Main St; ⊙9.30am-5.30pm Mon-Fri, 10am-5.30pm Sat, noon-5.30pm Sun mid-Mar–Christmas) Inside the Lismore Heritage Centre; pick up the info-packed *Lismore Walking Tour Guide* (€3).

Getting There & Around

Bus Éireann (www.buseireann.ie) serves Cappoquin (€3) and Dungarvan (€5, 20 minutes) on Monday, Thursday and Saturday. Buses to Waterford and Cork run once or twice a week.

Lismore Cycling Holidays (☎087 935 6610; www.cyclingholidays.ie; rentals per day from €23) Hires out bikes and delivers them throughout the region.

Northern County Waterford

Some of the most scenic parts of County Waterford are in the north around Ballymacarbry and in the Nire Valley, which runs between the Comeragh and Monavullagh Mountains. While not as rugged as the west of Ireland, this mountain scenery has a stark beauty and doesn't attract much tourist traffic. It's a place of long walks and country stays.

Sights & Activities

Rolling hills and woodland stuffed with megalithic remains make the county's north a superb area for walkers. The

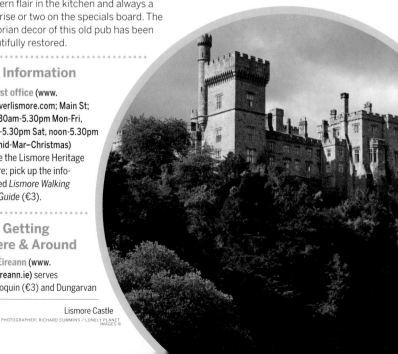

Lismore Castle

PHOTOGRAPHER: RICHARD CUMMINS / LONELY PLANET IMAGES ©

Comeragh Mountains, where there are ridges to trace and loughs to circle, are named after their many *coums* (valleys, often of glacial origin). Coumshingaun and Coum Iarthair – next to Crotty's Lough, and named after an outlaw who lay low in a cave there – are some of Ireland's finest.

Stop for a pint and panini in **Melody's Nire View** (Ballymacarbry), where the genial folk have info on local walks and activities.

Otherwise make sure you're around for the **Nire Valley Walking Festival** (www.nirevalley.com), which takes place on the second weekend in October, with guided walks and traditional music in the pubs.

The **East Munster Way** walking trail covers some 70km between Carrick-on-Suir in County Tipperary and the northern slopes of the Knockmealdown Mountains. Access is at Fourmilewater, about 10km northwest of Ballymacarbry.

Sleeping

HANORA'S COTTAGE B&B **€€**

(052-36134; www.hanorascottage.com; Nire Valley, Ballymacarbry; s/d from €80/150; restaurant dinner Mon-Sat; P) This 19th-century ancestral home next to Nire Church houses one of the country's best (and kid-free) B&Bs. All 10 posh rooms have jacuzzis (try for one overlooking the River Nire). Everything in the gourmet restaurant is made on the premises (dinner €40 to €50); they'll even pack you a walking lunch. Take the road east from Ballymacarbry, opposite Melody's; it's signposted 5km further on.

Getting There & Away

Bus service is very limited; this region is best done by car, bike or foot.

COUNTY TIPPERARY

Cashel

POP 2500

It's no wonder that Cashel (Caiseal Mumhan) is popular with visitors (the Queen included it on her historic visit in 2011). The iconic Rock of Cashel and the clutch of historical religious buildings that crown its breezy summit seem like a magical extension of the rocky landscape itself, and although tourism has been

Waterfall, Comeragh Mountains (p172)

hard-hit by the economic crisis, Cashel maintains a certain charm as a smallish market town.

Sights

ROCK OF CASHEL

(www.heritageireland.com; adult/child €6/2; ⌚9am-6.15pm Jun-Sep, to 4.45pm Oct-May) The Rock of Cashel is one of Ireland's most spectacular archaeological sites. The 'Rock' is a prominent green hill, banded with limestone outcrops. It rises from a grassy plain on the edge of the town and bristles with ancient fortifications – the word 'cashel' is an anglicised version of the Irish word *caiseal,* meaning 'fortress'. Sturdy walls circle an enclosure that contains a complete round tower, a 13th-century Gothic cathedral and the finest 12th-century Romanesque chapel in Ireland. For more than 1000 years the Rock of Cashel was a symbol of power and the seat of kings and churchmen who ruled over the region.

It's a five-minute stroll from the town centre to the Rock and you can take some very pretty paths including the Bishop's Walk.

The Rock is a major draw for coach parties for most of the year and is extremely busy during July and August.

HISTORY

In the 4th century the Rock of Cashel was chosen as a base by the Eóghanachta clan from Wales, who went on to conquer much of Munster and become kings of the region. For some 400 years it rivalled Tara (p129) as a centre of power in Ireland. The clan was associated with St Patrick, hence the Rock's alternative name of St Patrick's Rock.

In the 10th century, the Eóghanachta lost possession of the rock to the O'Brien (or Dál gCais) tribe under Brian Ború's leadership. In 1101, King Muircheartach O'Brien presented the Rock to the Church, a move designed to curry favour with the powerful bishops and to end secular rivalry over possession of the Rock with the Eóghanachta, by now known as the MacCarthys. Numerous buildings must have occupied the Rock over the years, but it is the ecclesiastical relics that have survived even the depredations of the Cromwellian army in 1647.

HALL OF THE VICARS CHORAL

The entrance to the Rock of Cashel is through this 15th-century building, once home to the male choristers who sang in the cathedral. It houses the ticket office. The exhibits in the adjoining undercroft include some very rare silverware, Bronze Age axes and St Patrick's Cross – an impressive, although eroded, 12th-century crutched cross with a crucifixion scene on one face and animals on the other. A replica stands outside in the castle courtyard.

The kitchen and dining hall upstairs contain some period furniture, tapestries and paintings beneath a fine carved-oak roof and gallery.

A 20-minute audiovisual presentation on the Rock's history runs every half hour. Showings are in English, French, German and Italian.

CATHEDRAL

This 13th-century Gothic structure overshadows the other ruins. Entry is through a small porch facing the Hall of the Vicars Choral. The cathedral's western location is formed by the **Archbishop's Residence**, a 15th-century, four-storey castle that had its great hall built over the nave. Soaring above the centre of the cathedral is a huge square tower with a turret on the southwestern corner.

Scattered throughout are monuments, panels from 16th-century altar tombs and coats of arms. If you have binoculars, look for the numerous stone heads on capitals and corbels high above the ground.

ROUND TOWER

On the northeastern corner of the cathedral is an 11th- or 12th-century round tower, the earliest building on the Rock of Cashel. It's 28m tall and the doorway is 3.5m above the ground – perhaps for structural rather than defensive reasons.

CORMAC'S CHAPEL

If the Rock of Cashel boasted only Cormac's Chapel, it would still be an outstanding place. This compelling building dates from 1127 and the medieval integrity of its trans-European architecture survives. It was probably the first Romanesque church in Ireland. The style of the square towers that flank it to either side may reflect Germanic influences, but there are haunting similarities in its steep stone roof to the 'boat-hull' shape of older Irish buildings, such as the Gallarus Oratory in County Kerry and the beehive huts of the Dingle Peninsula.

The true Romanesque splendour is in the detail of the exquisite doorway arches, the grand chancel arch and ribbed barrel vault, and the outstanding carved vignettes that include a trefoil-tailed grotesque and a Norman-helmeted centaur firing an arrow at a rampaging lion.

The chapel's interior is tantalisingly dark, but linger for a while and your eyes will adjust. Inside the main door, on the left, is the sarcophagus said to house King Cormac, dating from between 1125 and 1150. Frescoes once covered the walls, but only vestiges of these survive. The southern tower leads to a stone-roofed vault and a croft above the nave (no access).

Sleeping

CASHEL PALACE HOTEL Hotel **€€€**
(062-62707; www.cashel-palace.ie; Main St; s/d from €95/176; P @) Built in 1732 for a Protestant archbishop, this handsome red-brick, late–Queen Anne house is a local landmark. Fully restored, it has 23 antique-furnished rooms in the gracious main building or quaint mews, with luxuries like trouser presses (as if you wouldn't have someone else attend to that). Some rooms have soaking tubs you'll leave only after you're totally prunified.

The **bar** (bar food €10-16; lunch & dinner) is the place to talk about your upcoming hunt before dining at the vaulted-

Left: Rock of Cashel cross and Cormac's Chapel; **Below:** Rock of Cashel Hall of the Vicar's Choral (p169)

PHOTOGRAPHER: (LEFT) STEPHEN SAKS / LONELY PLANET IMAGES ©; (BELOW) JOHN ELK III / LONELY PLANET IMAGES ©

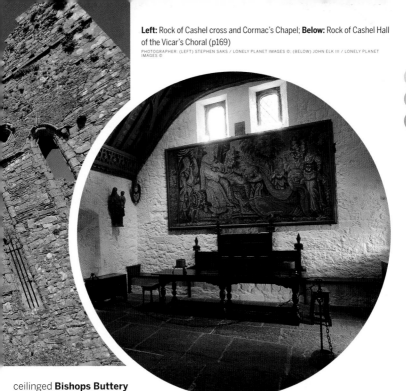

ceilinged **Bishops Buttery Restaurant** (2-/3-course menus from €22/25; lunch & dinner).

Eating

CAFE HANS Cafe €€

(062-63660; Dominic St; mains €13-19; noon-5pm Tue-Sat;) Competition for the 32 seats is fierce at this gourmet cafe run by the same family as Chez Hans next door. There's a fantastic selection of salads (the Caesar is always a winner), open sandwiches (including succulent prawns with tangy rose marie sauce) and filling fish, shellfish, lamb and vegetarian dishes, with a discerning wine selection and mouth-watering desserts like homemade caramel ice cream with butterscotch sauce.

Arrive before or after the lunchtime rush or plan on queuing.

Drinking

Davern's Pub

(20 Main St) Old, old pub popular for a good chat.

Ryan's Pub

(Ladyswell St) Congenial place with a large beer garden that really is a garden.

Mikey Ryan's Pub

(76 Main St) Local gathering spot.

Information

Banks and ATMs are in the centre.

Tourist office (062-62511; www.cashel.ie; Town Hall, Main St; 9.30am-5.30pm mid-Mar–Oct, closed Sat & Sun Nov–mid-Mar) Helpful office with reams of info on the area.

If You Like… Exploring on Foot

If you like exploring the southeast on foot on designated trails like the East Munster Way, then you'll enjoy these other walking routes:

1 **WEXFORD COASTAL WALK**
Signposted 221km-walk along Wexford's wreck-littered coastline.

2 **MT LEINSTER**
Views of five counties from the 796m summit of Wexford's highest peak, in the heart of the Blackstairs Mountains.

3 **ST DECLAN'S WAY**
Pilgrim route (94km) via Lismore Castle that also goes through Ardmore, County Waterford.

4 **COMERAGH MOUNTAINS**
Glacial moraine and Stone Age remains, not to mention stunning views, in a range that stretches across County Waterford.

Getting There & Away

Bus Éireann (www.buseireann.ie) runs eight buses daily between Cashel and Cork (€11.70, 1½ hours) via Cahir (€4.50, 20 minutes, six to eight daily). The bus stop for Cork is outside the Bake House on Main St. The Dublin stop (€11.70, three hours, six daily) is opposite.

Around Cashel

The atmospheric – and, at dusk, delightfully creepy – ruins of **Athassel Priory** sit in the shallow and verdant River Suir Valley, 7km southwest of Cashel. The original buildings date from 1205, and Athassel was once one of the richest and most important monasteries in Ireland. What survives is substantial: the gatehouse and portcullis gateway, the cloister and stretches of walled enclosure, as well as some medieval tomb effigies. To get here, take the N74 to the village of **Golden**, then head 2km south along the narrow road signed Athassel Abbey. Roadside parking is limited and very tight. The Priory is reached across often-muddy fields. The welter of back lanes is good for cycling.

Cahir

POP 2850

At the eastern tip of the Galtee Mountains 15km south of Cashel, Cahir (An Cathair; pronounced 'care') is a compact and attractive town that encircles its namesake castle, which does a good job of looking like every castle you ever tried building at the beach, with towers, a moat and battlements. Walking paths follow the banks of the River Suir – you can easily spend a couple of hours wandering about.

CAHIR CASTLE Historic Site
(www.heritageireland.ie; Castle St; adult/child €3/1; 9am-6.30pm mid-Jun–Aug, 9.30am-5.30pm mid-Mar–mid-Jun & Sep–mid-Oct, 9.30am-4.30pm mid-Oct–mid-Mar) Cahir's awesome castle is feudal fantasy in a big way. A river-island site with moat, rocky foundations, massive walls, turrets and towers, defences and dungeons are all there. This castle is one of Ireland's largest. Founded by Conor O'Brien in 1142, it was passed to the Butler family in 1375. In 1599 it lost the arms race of its day when the Earl of Essex used cannons to shatter the walls, an event explained with a huge model.

The castle was surrendered to Cromwell in 1650 without a struggle; its future usefulness may have discouraged the usual Cromwellian 'deconstruction' – it is largely intact and still formidable. It was restored in the 1840s and again in the 1960s when it came under state ownership.

A 15-minute audiovisual presentation puts Cahir in context with other Irish castles. The buildings within the castle are sparsely furnished, although there are good displays. The real rewards come from simply wandering through this remarkable survivor of Ireland's medieval past. There are frequent guided tours; several good printed guides are for sale at the entrance.

SWISS COTTAGE Historic Building
(www.heritageireland.ie; Cahir Park; adult/child €3/1; 10am-6pm Apr-late Oct) A pleasant riverside path from behind the town car park meanders 2km south to Cahir Park and the thatched Swiss Cottage, surrounded by roses, lavender and honeysuckle. Built in 1810 as a retreat for Richard Butler, 12th Baron Caher, and his wife, it was designed by London architect John Nash, creator of the Royal Pavilion at Brighton and London's Regent's Park. The cottage-orné style emerged during the late 18th and early 19th centuries in England in response to the prevailing taste for the picturesque. Thatched roofs, natural wood and carved weatherboarding were characteristics and most examples were built as ornamental features on estates.

The cottage is a lavish example of Regency Picturesque. It's more of a sizeable house and has extensive facilities. The 30-minute (compulsory) guided tours are thoroughly enjoyable, although you may have to wait for one in the busier summer months.

Sleeping

TINSLEY HOUSE B&B €
(052-744 1947; www.tinsleyhouse.com; The Square; d from €55; Apr-Sep;) This mannered house has a great location, four period-furnished rooms and a roof garden. The owner, Liam Roche, is an expert on local history and can recommend walks and other activities.

CAHIR HOUSE HOTEL Hotel €€
(052-744 3000; www.cahirhousehotel.ie; The Square; s €60, d €90-100; @) On a prominent corner of the central Square, this landmark hotel has elegant rooms, a beauty salon offering treatments from reflexology and massages through to fake tans, and a long menu of **bar food** (mains €9-13; lunch & dinner).

Information

AIB Bank (Castle St) Has an ATM and bureau de change.

Tourist office (052-744 1453; www.discoverireland.ie/tipperary; Main St; 9.30am-5pm Mon-Sat Easter-Oct)

Getting There & Away

Cahir is a hub for several Bus Éireann routes, including Dublin–Cork, Limerick–Waterford, Galway–Waterford, Kilkenny–Cork and Cork–Athlone. There are eight buses per day from Monday to Saturday (six buses on Sunday) to Cashel (€4.50, 20 minutes). Buses stop in the car park beside the tourist office.

Cork & the Ring of Kerry

The southwest corner of Ireland – encompassing the counties of Cork and Kerry – epitomises romantic, rustic and rural Ireland. While it may groan under the weight of tourist numbers, the southwest never fails to astonish and beguile those who drive, cycle, walk and amble through the twists, turns and inlets of the eroded coasts and the endless fields of green criss-crossed by stone walls and ancient monuments.

Yet the southwest is not just about amazing views and wondrous rambles. It's about food – Cork City and the surrounding county have deservedly earned a reputation as the gourmet heart of Ireland. It's about history – from the monuments of the Beara Peninsula to the monastic ruins on unforgiving Skellig Michael and the extraordinary collection of Celtic runes and stones around Dingle. If you were forced to visit only one corner of the Emerald Isle, the southwest would leave you feeling like you didn't miss a thing.

Ring Fort along the Ring of Kerry (p204)

Cork & the Ring of Kerry

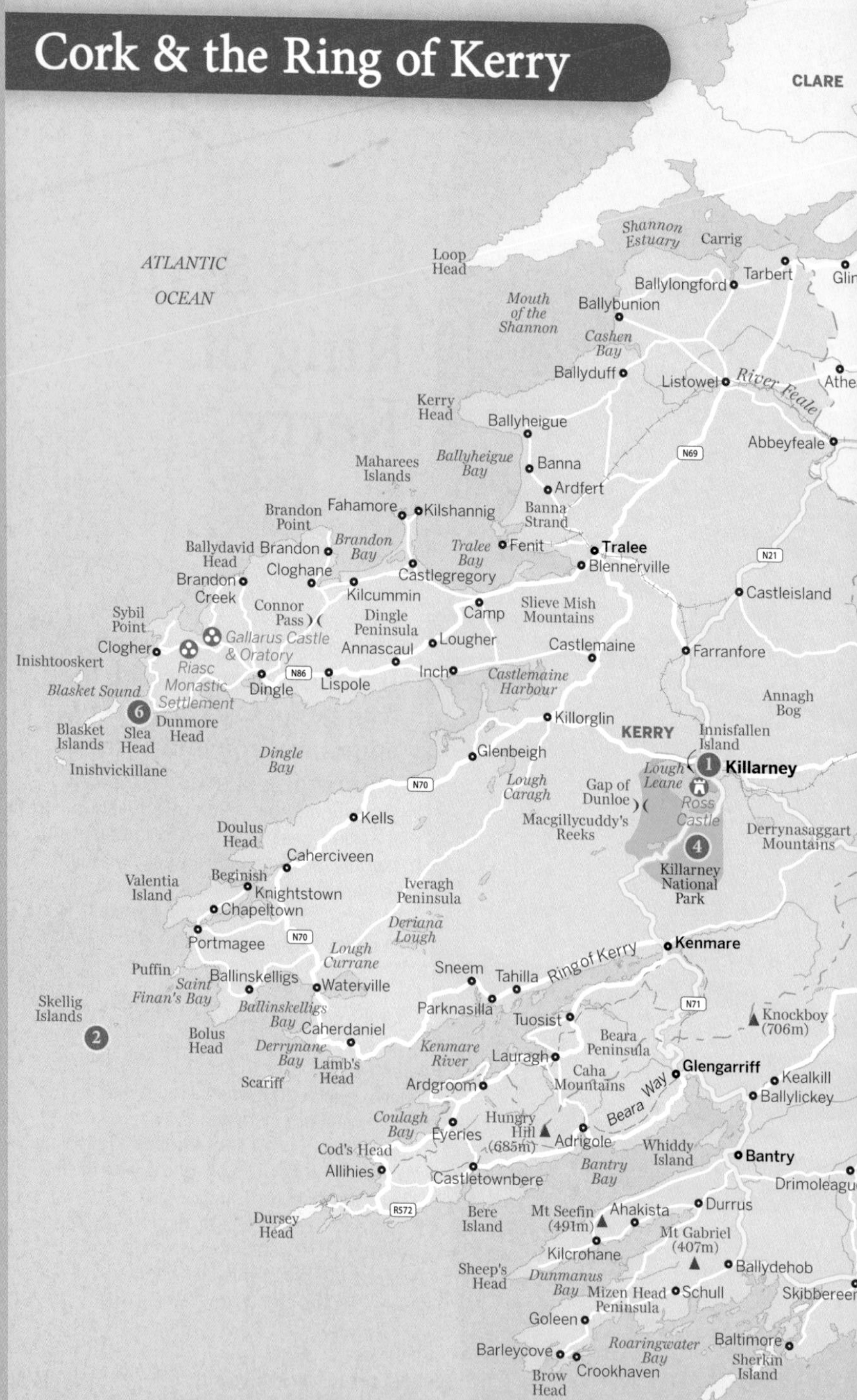

CLARE
ATLANTIC OCEAN
Loop Head
Shannon Estuary
Carrig
Tarbert
Glin
Ballylongford
Mouth of the Shannon
Ballybunion
Cashen Bay
Ballyduff
Listowel
River Feale
Athea
Kerry Head
Ballyheigue
Abbeyfeale
N69
Maharees Islands
Ballyheigue Bay
Banna
Ardfert
Brandon Point
Fahamore
Kilshannig
Banna Strand
Ballydavid Head
Brandon
Brandon Bay
Tralee Bay
Fenit
Tralee
N21
Brandon Creek
Cloghane
Castlegregory
Blennerville
Kilcummin
Castleisland
Sybil Point
Connor Pass
Dingle Peninsula
Camp
Slieve Mish Mountains
Clogher
Gallarus Castle & Oratory
Lougher
Castlemaine
Farranfore
Inishtooskert
Riasc Monastic Settlement
Annascaul
Inch
N86
Dingle
Lispole
Castlemaine Harbour
Annagh Bog
Blasket Sound
6
Slea Head
Dunmore Head
Killorglin
KERRY
Innisfallen Island
Blasket Islands
Inishvickillane
Dingle Bay
Glenbeigh
1
Killarney
Lough Leane
Lough Caragh
Gap of Dunloe
Ross Castle
N70
Macgillycuddy's Reeks
Kells
Derrynasaggart Mountains
4
Doulus Head
Killarney National Park
Caherciveen
Valentia Island
Beginish
Knightstown
Iveragh Peninsula
Chapeltown
Deriana Lough
Portmagee
N70
Kenmare
Lough Currane
Ring of Kerry
Puffin
Sneem
Tahilla
Skellig Islands
Saint Finan's Bay
Ballinskelligs
Waterville
2
Ballinskelligs Bay
Parknasilla
N71
Tuosist
Knockboy (706m)
Bolus Head
Caherdaniel
Beara Peninsula
Derrynane Bay
Kenmare River
Lauragh
Scariff
Lamb's Head
Caha Mountains
Glengarriff
Kealkill
Ardgroom
Beara Way
Ballylickey
Coulagh Bay
Eyeries
Hungry Hill (685m)
Adrigole
Cod's Head
Whiddy Island
Bantry
Allihies
Castletownbere
Bantry Bay
Drimoleague
R572
Dursey Head
Bere Island
Mt Seefin (491m)
Ahakista
Durrus
Mt Gabriel (407m)
Kilcrohane
Ballydehob
Sheep's Head
Dunmanus Bay
Mizen Head Peninsula
Schull
Skibbereen
Goleen
Roaringwater Bay
Baltimore
Barleycove
Crookhaven
Sherkin Island
Brow Head

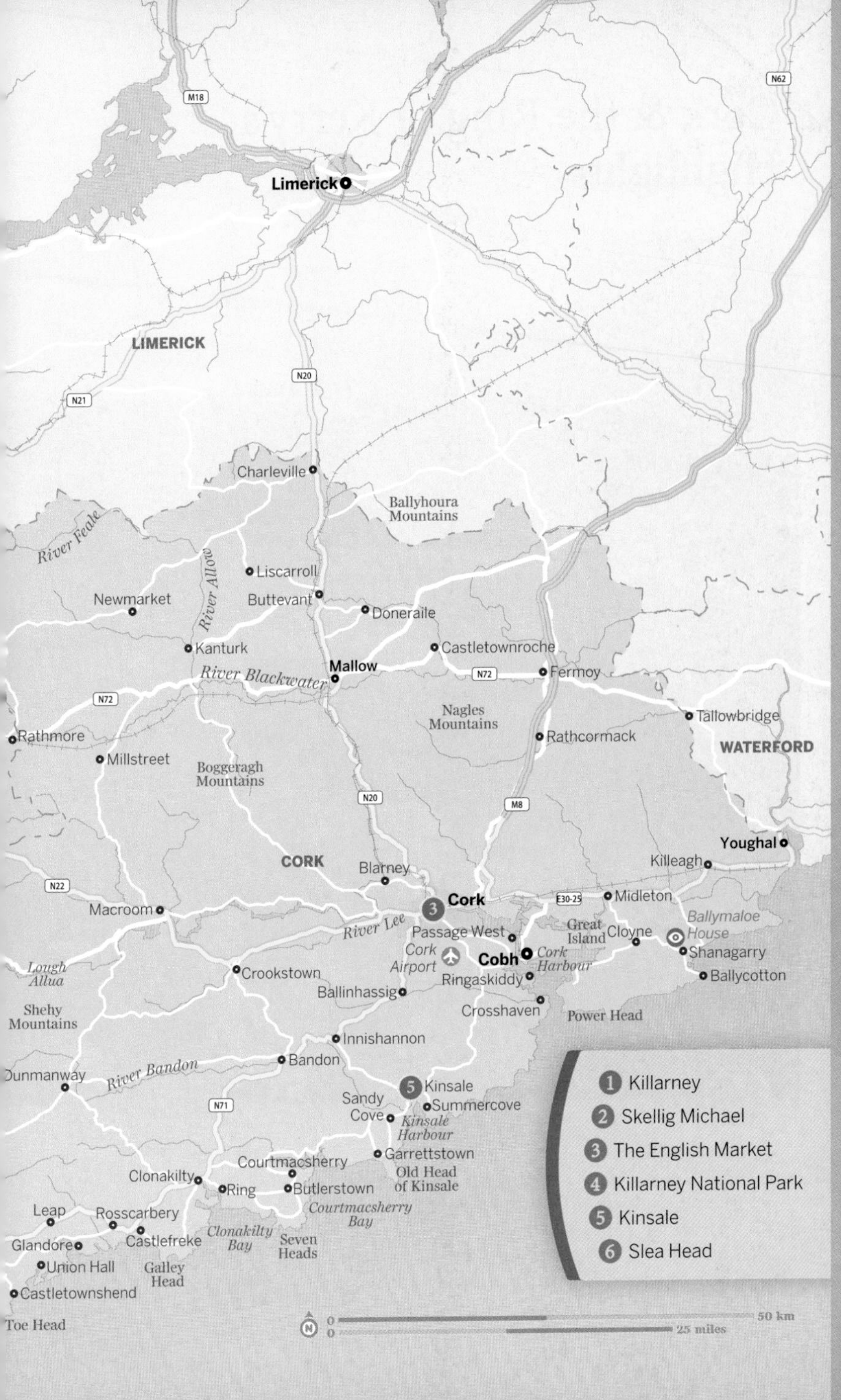

Limerick
LIMERICK
M18
N62
N20
N21
Charleville
Ballyhoura Mountains
River Feale
River Allow
Liscarroll
Newmarket
Buttevant
Doneraile
Kanturk
Castletownroche
Mallow
River Blackwater
N72
Fermoy
Tallowbridge
Rathmore
Millstreet
Boggeragh Mountains
Nagles Mountains
Rathcormack
WATERFORD
N20
M8
Youghal
Killeagh
CORK
Blarney
N22
Cork
Macroom
E30-25
Midleton
River Lee
Passage West
Great Island
Cloyne
Ballymaloe House
Cork Airport
Cobh
Cork Harbour
Shanagarry
Lough Allua
Crookstown
Ringaskiddy
Ballycotton
Ballinhassig
Shehy Mountains
Crosshaven
Power Head
Innishannon
Bandon
Dunmanway
River Bandon
Kinsale
Sandy Cove
Summercove
N71
Kinsale Harbour
Garrettstown
Courtmacsherry
Old Head of Kinsale
Clonakilty
Ring
Butlerstown
Courtmacsherry Bay
Leap
Rosscarbery
Clonakilty Bay
Glandore
Castlefreke
Seven Heads
Union Hall
Galley Head
Castletownshend
Toe Head
1 Killarney
2 Skellig Michael
3 The English Market
4 Killarney National Park
5 Kinsale
6 Slea Head
0 50 km
0 25 miles

Cork & the Ring of Kerry's Highlights

1

Killarney

'I was born and raised in Killarney', Weeshie says proudly. 'When people ask me where I'm from, I say, "I'm from beauty's home." "Where's that?" they ask. "Heaven's Reflect," I tell them, and it's true: there's no more beautiful place on earth than Killarney and its surrounds.' Rhododendrons in Killarney National Park

Need to Know

Best Time to Visit Autumn lacks the summer crush and still has great weather. **Advance Planning** Book your accommodation well in advance. **For further coverage, see p196.**

Local Knowledge

Killarney's Don't Miss List

BY ALOYSIUS 'WEESHIE' FOGARTY, RADIO PRESENTER AND EX-KERRY FOOTBALLER

1 KILLARNEY TOWN

Killarney (p196) is one of the top tourist attractions in the world, absolutely buzzing in summer and very cosmopolitan too: it's so busy that every time you step off the sidewalk, you're likely to meet a person from anywhere in the world.

2 KILLARNEY NATIONAL PARK

There's nowhere more special to me than **Killarney National Park** (p200), which is part of Killarney Town but in a world of its own. The lakes, mountains and stunning views are as beautiful as any I've seen in all my years of travelling. Thank God they're on my doorstep!

3 JIMMY O'BRIEN'S

It is said that the secret to Ireland is to go into a pub and meet a local. Killarney's pubs are fine pubs indeed, but the best of them is unquestionably Jimmy O'Brien's. It's old, unique and full of wonderful characters: no matter when you're in there's always someone two stools away who knows twice as much as yourself!

4 THE RING OF KERRY

Killarney is the doorway to the **Ring of Kerry** (p204), a circular drive of such stunning beauty that you'd have to travel to **Slea Head** (p211) at the tip of the Dingle Peninsula to see its equal. You haven't seen Ireland until you've seen the Ring.

5 THE CHANGING SEASONS

Killarney is a year-round destination and each season is special. There's the green haze of summer, the rich bloom of spring and the bare frost of winter, when the whole place might be enveloped in snow. But my favourite is the brown of the autumn, when the Deenagh River ripples through the park into the lakes.

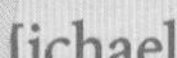

[M]ichael

[…]e, storm-lashed rocky outcrop off the Kerry coast was the ideal spot for a group [of] monks to set up shop in ancient times, and today the Unesco World Heritage site [Skellig M]ichael (p209) reminds us not just of the extraordinary efforts they went to for a [solitu]de but of how magnificent untrammelled nature can truly be.

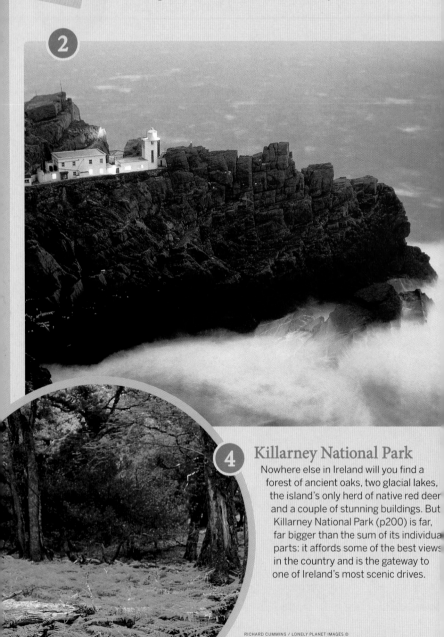

2

4

Killarney National Park

Nowhere else in Ireland will you find a forest of ancient oaks, two glacial lakes, the island's only herd of native red deer and a couple of stunning buildings. But Killarney National Park (p200) is far, far bigger than the sum of its individual parts: it affords some of the best views in the country and is the gateway to one of Ireland's most scenic drives.

© HEMIS / ALAMY

3 The English Market

County Cork, renowned as the gourmet food basket of Ireland, has no better example of its commitment to good, locally sourced produce than Cork City's English Market (p190), where scores of vendors sell all kinds of meats, cheeses, veg and other goodies. It is also home to the excellent Farmgate Café (p190), one of the region's best eateries.

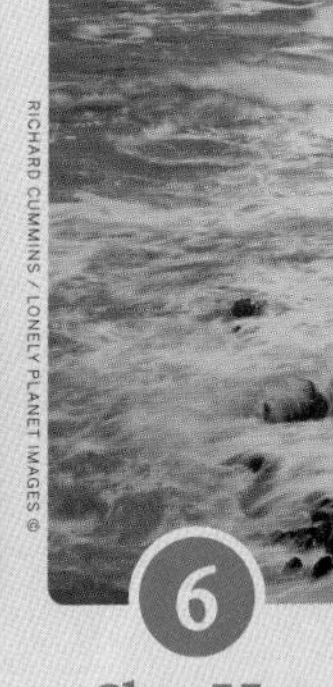

RICHARD CUMMINS / LONELY PLANET IMAGES ©

5 Kinsale

History, scenery and great food conspire to make Kinsale (p191) one of Ireland's top destinations, a picture-postcard idyll at the head of a sheltered bay. After walking around the bay to explore the vast Charles Fort (p191), recharge your batteries with a memorable seafood platter at the Fishy Fishy Café (p192). Charles Fort, Kinsale

6 Slea Head

One of Europe's great scenic circular routes is Slea Head (p211), at the western tip of the Dingle Peninsula. It is one of the country's most dynamic Gaeltacht (Irish-language) areas and is peppered with ancient sites: spread about the 50km route are beehive huts, forts, church sites and inscribed stones from Ireland's ancien

Cork & the Ring of Kerry's Best...

Beauty Spots

- **Kinsale** (p191) The perfect southern town.
- **Ladies' View** (p203) Queen Victoria and her ladies loved the scenery.
- **Gap of Dunloe** (p200) Awe-inspiring mountain pass.
- **Connor Pass** (p215) Ireland's highest pass has stunning views.
- **Bantry Bay** (p195) Watery perfection.

Local Activities

- Taking in a game of **Gaelic football** (p199) in Killarney.
- Trout or salmon **fishing** (p196) in the rivers around Killarney.
- **Bird-watching** (p206) on the Skellig Islands.
- Improving your **cooking** (p193) at Ballymaloe House.

Historic Notables

- **Skellig Michael** (p209) One of the most impressive monastic sites in the world.
- **Lisnagun** (p206) Ring fort perfectly reconstructed on its original site.
- **Kerry Bog Village Museum** (p205) A typical 19th-century bog village.
- **Slea Head** (p211) Packed with Stone Age monuments.
- **Charles Fort** (p191) Best-preserved 17th-century fort.

Memorable Drives

- The **Ring of Kerry** (p204), especially the stretch between Kenmare and Killarney.
- The R575 coastal road between Allihies and Lauragh on the north side of the **Beara Peninsula** (p194).
- The **Healy Pass** (p194), between Cork and Kerry.
- The scenic detour off the N71 to **Brandon's Cottage** (p200) along the R568.

eft: Cycling the Gap of Dunloe (p200), Killarney; **Above:** Kittiwakes, Skellig Islands (p206)

Need to Know

ADVANCE PLANNING

- **Two months before** Book hotels, especially in popular areas such as Killarney, the Dingle Peninsula and West Cork.
- **One month before** Book now if you want a place in a cooking course at the likes of Ballymaloe.
- **Two weeks before** Make a list of sweater sizes for friends and family *not* travelling with you.

RESOURCES

- **People's Republic of Cork** (www.peoplesrepublicofcork.com) Picking up on the popular nickname for this liberal-leaning city, this indie website has excellent info.
- **Discover Ireland** (www.discoverireland.ie/southwest) Official tourist website.
- **Killarney** (www.killarney.ie) The official site for the town, with lots of tourism links.
- **GAA** (www.gaa.ie) For all things related to Gaelic sports.

GETTING AROUND

- **Bus** Good bus networks cover most of the area, but it's a slow way of exploring.
- **Train** The main towns are linked, but not necessarily to each other.
- **Car** The region's beauty is off the beaten path; you'll need a car to get there.

BE FOREWARNED

- **Crowds** Summer crowds and traffic jams – especially on the Ring of Kerry – are a mainstay of the peak tourist season.
- **Weather** The southwest has a microclimate, which allows for warm summers and the growth of palm trees (!) but, like the rest of the island, the weather can be very unpredictable.
- **Gaelic football** It's a *religion* in Kerry, which makes sense as they're the best county at it by far; Cork are very good at both football and hurling.

Cork & the Ring of Kerry Itineraries

If you don't have a month or more to spend in the southwest, these itineraries will allow you to explore stunning landscapes and dip into the region's outstanding culinary reputation in a limited amount of time.

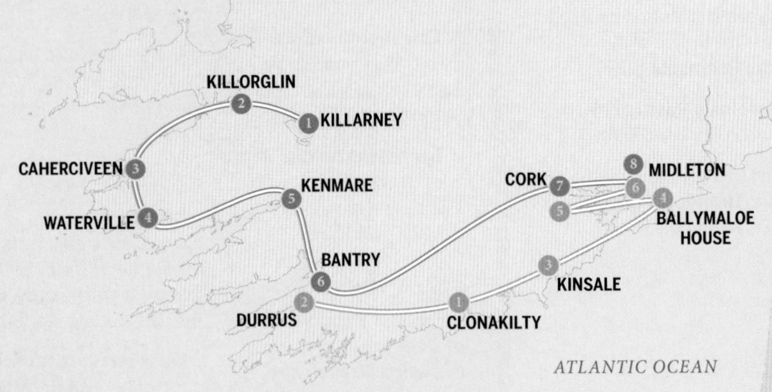

3 DAYS

KILLARNEY TO MIDLETON

Southwest Blitz

Having only three days to visit such an extraordinary region is a real tragedy, but here's more than a decent flavour of the southwest's delights. Start in the region's most popular tourist town, **(1) Killarney**, visiting magnificent **Killarney National Park** – Muckross House is well worth the visit – before embarking on the perenially popular **Ring of Kerry**, taking in towns like **(2) Killorglin**, **(3) Caherciveen**, **(4) Waterville**, where you can play some fabulous golf, and **(5) Kenmare**. This is an ideal stopover town as it has some fine B&Bs, welcoming pubs and excellent restaurants. On day two, cross over to historic **(6) Bantry** before heading east to **(7) Cork City**. Spend the day discovering the city, visiting the excellent **Crawford Municipal Gallery** and the unmissable **English Market**, where you can sample some of the finest produce from the region – this is unquestionably Ireland's best covered market. With the taste of Cork's gourmet genius now firmly on the palate, head east to **(8) Midleton**, visit the distillery museum (and purchase some fine Irish whiskey) and wrap up your lightning tour with a meal in the sublime **Farmgate Restaurant**.

CLONAKILTY TO MIDLETON

The Southern Pantry

County Cork has earned itself a justifiable reputation as the gourmet capital of Ireland. Start in West Cork, where gourmet cuisine is taken for granted. If you're looking for the best black pudding, head to **(1) Clonakilty** (the town is famous for it) and try **Edward Twomey**, which has followed the same recipe for over a century. Not far away is **(2) Durrus**, where you should make a pit stop at the superb **Good Things Café**. Further east, **(3) Kinsale** is just full of top nosh, including the **Fishy Fishy Café** and John Edwards – although it looks like an ordinary pub, it's anything but. Over the weekend, enrol in a cooking course at the world-famous **(4) Ballymaloe House**, south of Cork City. Back in **(5) Cork City**, stock up at the daily **English Market**, which wowed Queen Elizabeth during her 2011 visit. Baskets full, head east to **(6) Midleton** for the **Farmgate Restaurant**, one of Ireland's very best – make a visit to the classic **Old Jameson Distillery** while you're in town. Midleton's weekly **farmers' market** is better than the one in Cork City, but it's only a weekly affair.

Copper still at the Jameson Experience (p191), Midleton

PHOTOGRAPHER: © GEORGE MUNDAY / ALAMY

Discover Cork & the Ring of Kerry

At a Glance

- **County Cork** (p186) Ireland's second city is surrounded by beautiful landscapes and gourmet heaven.
- **County Kerry** (p196) When you think of breathtaking Irish scenery, you're thinking of County Kerry.

Crawford Municipal Art Gallery, Cork City
PHOTOGRAPHER: RICHARD CUMMINS / LONELY PLANET IMAGES ©

COUNTY CORK

Cork City

POP 120,000

Ireland's second city is first in every important respect, at least according to the locals, who cheerfully refer to it as the 'real capital of Ireland'. The compact city centre is surrounded by interesting waterways and is chock full of great restaurants fed by arguably the best foodie scene in the country. Its location is also something of a blessing, on the doorstep of the scenic mecca that is the southwest but also within easy reach of lesser-known idylls in East Cork and West Waterford.

Sights

FREE CRAWFORD MUNICIPAL ART GALLERY Art Gallery
(**☎021-490 7855; www.crawfordartgallery.ie; Emmet Pl; admission free; ⏰10am-5pm Mon-Sat, to 8pm Thu**) Cork's public gallery houses a small but excellent permanent collection covering the 17th century to the modern day.

ST FIN BARRE'S CATHEDRAL Cathedral
(**☎021-496 3387; www.cathedral.cork.anglican.org; Bishop St; adult/child €4/2; ⏰9.30am-5.30pm Mon-Sat & 12.30-5pm Sun**) Spiky spires, gurning gargoyles and rich sculpture make up the exterior of Cork's Protestant cathedral, an attention-grabbing mixture of French Gothic and medieval whimsy. Local legend says that the golden angel on the eastern side will blow its horn when the Apocalypse is due to start... Yikes!

The cathedral sits about 500m south of the centre, on the spot where Cork's patron saint, Finbarre, founded his monastery in the 7th century.

Sleeping

City Centre

IMPERIAL HOTEL Hotel **€€**

(☎021-427 4040; www.flynnhotels.com; South Mall; r €90-220; P @ ᯤ) Fast approaching her bicentenary, the Imperial knows how to age gracefully. Public spaces resonate with opulent period detail such as marble floors, elaborate floral bouquets and more. The 130 rooms are of four-star hotel standard and include writing desks, restrained decor and modern touches, like a digital music library. A posh Aveda spa is a recent addition – something unheard of when Charles Dickens stayed here.

EMERSON HOUSE B&B **€€**

(☎021-450 3647; www.emersonhousecork.com; 2 Clarence Tce, North Summer Hill; s/d from €60/80; P ᯤ) Near the top of busy Summer Hill is this gay and lesbian B&B tucked away on a quiet terrace. The accommodation, in a Georgian house retaining many original features, is comfortably elegant, and host Cyril is a mine of information on the area.

Western Rd & Around

GARNISH HOUSE B&B **€€**

(☎021-427 5111; www.garnish.ie; Western Rd; s/d €75/80; P ᯤ) Every attention is lavished upon guests at this award-winning B&B. The legendary breakfast menu (30 choices!) includes fresh fish, French toast, omelettes and a whole lot more. Typical of the touches here is the freshly cooked porridge, which comes with creamed honey and your choice of whiskey or Baileys. Enjoy it out on the garden terrace. The 14 rooms are very comfortable; reception is open 24 hours.

HAYFIELD MANOR Hotel **€€€**

(☎021-484 9500; www.hayfieldmanor.ie; Perrott Ave, College Rd; r €180-350; P @ ᯤ) Roll out the red carpet and pour yourself a sherry for *you have arrived*. A kilometre and a half (one mile) from the city centre but with all the ambience of a country house, Hayfield combines the luxury and facilities of a big hotel with the informality and welcome of a small one. The 88 beautiful bedrooms (choose from traditional or contemporary styling) enjoy 24-hour room service, although you may want to idle the hours away in the library.

Eating

MARKET LANE International **€€**

(☎021-427 4710; www.marketlane.ie; 5 Oliver Plunkett St; mains €10-26; ⊙noon-late Mon-Sat, 1-9pm Sun) It's always hopping at this bright corner bistro with an open kitchen. Service is quick and attentive, but you may want to pause at the long wooden bar anyway. The menu is broad and changes often to reflect what's fresh: how about braised ox-cheek stew to challenge the palate? Steaks come with awesome aioli. The €10 lunch menu, with half a sandwich, soup and tea or coffee, is a steal. Lots of wines by the glass.

CAFE PARADISO Vegetarian **€€€**

(☎021-427 7939; www.cafeparadiso.ie; 16 Lancaster Quay; mains €23-25; ⊙noon-3pm & 6-10.30pm Tue-Sat) A contender for best eatery in town, this down-to-earth vegetarian restaurant serves a superb range of dishes, including vegan fare: how about sweet-chilli-glazed panfried tofu with asian greens in a coconut and lemongrass broth, soba noodles and a gingered adzuki bean wonton; or spring cabbage dolma of roast squash, caramelised onion and hazelnut with cardamom yoghurt, harissa sauce, broad beans and saffron-crushed potatoes? Reservations are essential.

Drinking

AN SPAILPÍN FÁNAC Pub

(South Main St) 'The Wandering Labourer' really hangs on to its character, with exposed brickwork, stone-flagged floors,

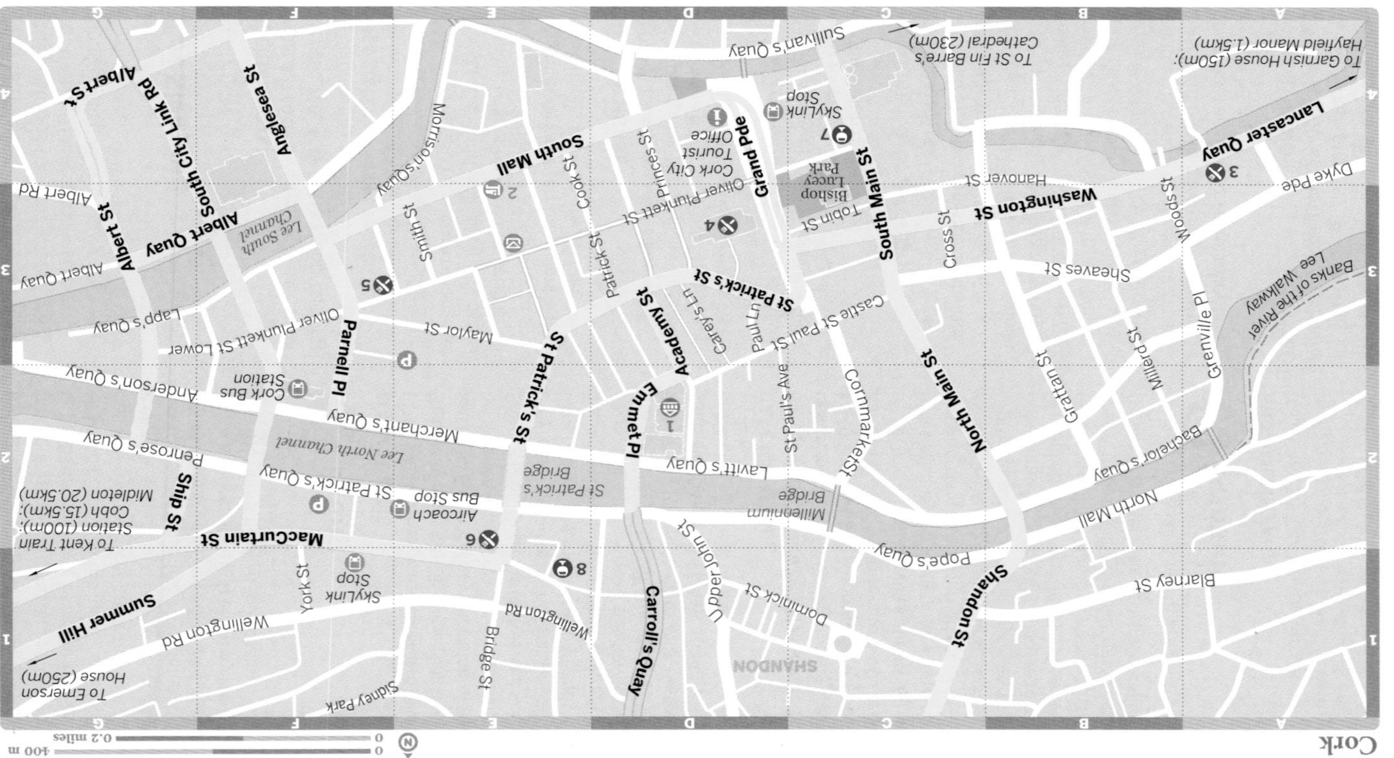
Cork
400 m
0.2 miles
To Emerson House (250m)
Summer Hill
Wellington Rd
To Kent Train Station (100m); Cobh (15.5km); Midleton (20.5km)
Ship St
MacCurtain St
York St
SkyLink Stop
Sidney Park
Penrose's Quay
St Patrick's Quay
Aircoach Bus Stop
Anderson's Quay
Merchant's Quay
Lee North Channel
Cork Bus Station
Lapp's Quay
Oliver Plunkett St Lower
Parnell Pl
Maylor St
Albert Quay
Albert St
Albert Rd
South City Link Rd
Anglesea St
Lee South Channel
Morrison's Quay
Smith St
South Mall
Cook St
Patrick St
St Patrick's St
St Patrick's Bridge
Bridge St
Wellington Rd
Carroll's Quay
Emmet Pl
Academy St
Lavitt's Quay
Princes St
Oliver Plunkett St
Cork City Tourist Office
Grand Pde
Carey's Ln
Paul Ln
Upper John St
Dominick St
SHANDON
Millennium Bridge
St Paul's Ave
Castle St
Paul St
Cornmarket St
Tobin St
Bishop Lucey Park
SkyLink Stop
Sullivan's Quay
South Main St
North Main St
Pope's Quay
Shandon St
Cross St
Washington St
Hanover St
To St Fin Barre's Cathedral (230m)
Grattan St
Sheaves St
North Mall
Blarney St
Bachelor's Quay
Millerd St
Woods St
Grenville Pl
Banks of the River Lee Walkway
Dyke Pde
Lancaster Quay
To Garnish House (150m); Hayfield Manor (1.5km)
A
B
C
D
E
F
G
1
2
3
4
5
6
7
8

Cork

Sights

Sleeping

Eating

Drinking

snug corners and open fires. There are good trad sessions most nights.

SIN É Pub

(Coburg St) You could easily while away an entire day at this great old place, which is everything a craic-filled pub should be. There are no frills or fuss here – just a comfy, sociable pub, long on atmosphere and short on pretension. There's music most nights, much of it traditional, but with the odd surprise.

Information

Cork City Tourist Office (**021-425 5100; www.cometocork.com; Grand Pde; 9am-6pm Mon-Sat, 10am-5pm Sun Jul & Aug, 9.15am-5pm Mon-Fri & 9.30am-4.30pm Sat Sep-Jun)** has a souvenir shop and information desk with plenty of brochures and books about the city and county, as well as Ordnance Survey maps. **Stena Line (see p379)** ferries has a desk here.

Getting There & Away

Air

Cork Airport (**ORT; 021-431 3131; www.cork-airport.com)** is 8km south of the city on the N27. Facilities include ATMs and car-hire desks for all the main companies. Airlines servicing the airport include Aer Lingus, BMI, Ryanair and Wizz. There are flights to Dublin, London Heathrow and a few cities in Europe.

Boat

Brittany Ferries (**021-427 7801; www.brittanyferries.ie; 42 Grand Pde)** sails to Roscoff (France) weekly from the end of March to October. The crossing takes 15 hours and fares are widely variable. The ferry terminal is at Ringaskiddy.

Bus

Aircoach (**01-844 7118; www.aircoach.ie)** serves Dublin Airport and Dublin city centre from St Patrick's Quay (€18; 4¼ hours; every two hours 7am to 7pm).

Bus Éireann (**021-450 8188; www.buseireann.ie)** operates from the bus station on the corner of Merchant's Quay and Parnell Pl. You can get to most places in Ireland from Cork, including Dublin (€11.70, 3 hours, six daily), Killarney (€15.30, 1¾ hours, 14 daily), Kilkenny (€16.65, two hours, three daily) and Waterford (€17.10, 2¾ hours, 14 daily).

Citylink (**1890 280 808; www.citylink.ie)** operates services to Galway (3¼ hours) and Limerick (2¼ hours). Buses are frequent and fares are as low as €10.

Train

Kent Train Station (**021-450 4777)** is north of the River Lee on Lower Glanmire Rd. Bus 5 runs into the centre (€1.80) and a taxi costs from €9 to €10.

The train line goes through Mallow, where you can change for the line to Tralee, and Limerick Junction, for the line to Ennis (and the new extension to Galway), then on to Dublin (€38, three hours, 16 daily).

Getting Around

To/From the Airport

SkyLink (**021-432 1020; www.skylinkcork.com; adult/child €5/2.50; hourly)** buses pick up around central Cork and take up to 30 minutes.

A taxi to/from town costs €15 to €20.

To/From the Ferry Terminal

The ferry terminal is at Ringaskiddy, 15 minutes by car southeast of the city centre along the N28.

© CHRIS ROUT / ALAMY

Don't Miss The English Market

It could just as easily be called the Victorian Market for its ornate vaulted ceilings and columns, but the **English Market** (Princes St; 9am-5.30pm Mon-Sat) is a true gem, no matter what you name it. Scores of vendors sell some of the very best local produce, meats, cheeses and takeaway food in the region. On decent days, take your lunch to nearby Bishop Lucey Park, a popular alfresco eating spot. A few favourites:

- **Joup** (021-422 6017) Has a range of soups and Med-flavoured salads, plus sandwiches on a variety of homemade breads.
- **On the Pig's Back** (021-427 0232) Boasts house-made sausages and incredible cheeses, many ready to munch.
- **Sandwich Stall** Has a drool-worthy display of remarkable and creative sandwiches.

On a mezzanine overlooking part of the market is one of Cork's best eateries. **Farmgate Café** (021-427 8134; English Market; lunch €4-13, dinner €18-30; 8.30am-10pm Mon-Sat) is an unmissable experience. Like its sister restaurant in Midleton (see p191), this cafe has mastered the magic art of producing delicious meals without fuss or faddism. The food, from rock oysters to the lamb for an Irish stew, is sourced from the market below. There are tables but the best seats are at the balcony counter, where you can ponder the passing parade of shoppers. We still have memories of the seafood chowder and the raspberry crumble.

Taxis cost €28 to €35. Bus Éireann runs a service from the bus station to link up with departures (bus 223; adult/child €5.30/3.20, 50 minutes). Confirm times. There's also a service to Rosslare Harbour (bus 40, adult/child €23.70/16.70, four to five hours).

Around Cork City

Blarney Castle

If you need proof of the power of a good yarn, then join the queue to get into this

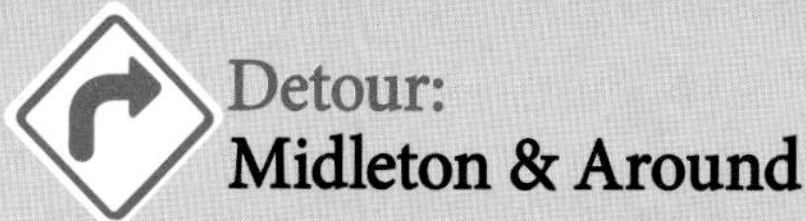

Detour: Midleton & Around

Aficionados of a particularly fine Irish whiskey will recognise the name, and the main reason to linger in this bustling market town is to visit the **Jameson Experience** (021-461 3594; www.jamesonwhiskey.com; Old Distillery Walk; tours adult/student/child €13.50/11/8; shop 9am-6.30pm, tour times vary). Coachloads pour in to tour the restored 200-year-old building and purchase bottles from the gift shop. Exhibits and tours explain the process of taking barley and creating whiskey (Jameson is today made in a modern factory in Cork).

Highly recommended is the **Farmgate Restaurant** (021-463 2771; www.farmgate.ie; The Coolbawn; restaurant mains around €18; coffee & snacks 9am-5.30pm, lunch noon-3.30pm Mon-Sat, dinner 6.30-9.30pm Thu-Sat), original and sister establishment to Cork's Farmgate Café. Here you'll find the same superb blend of traditional and modern Irish in its approach to cooking. In the front is a shop selling amazing baked goods and local produce, including organic fruit and vegetables, cheeses and preserves.

Midleton is 20km east of Cork. There are buses every 30 minutes from Monday to Saturday (hourly on Sunday) from Cork bus station (€6.40, 25 minutes). There are no buses between Cobh and Midleton, and you'll need a car to explore the surrounding area.

15th-century **castle** (021-438 5252; www.blarneycastle.ie; Blarney; adult/student/child €10/8/3.50; 9am-7pm Mon-Sat & 9am-5.30pm Sun Jun-Aug, 9am-6.30pm Mon-Sat & 9.30am-5.30pm Sun May & Sep, 9am-sundown Sun Oct-Apr), one of Ireland's most inexplicably popular tourist attractions.

They're here, of course, to plant their lips on the **Blarney Stone**, a cliché that has entered every lexicon and tour route. The object of their affections is perched at the top of a steep climb up slippery spiral staircases. On the battlements, you bend backwards over a long, long drop (with safety grill and attendant to prevent tragedy) to kiss the stone; as your shirt rides up, coachloads of onlookers stare up your nose.

Once you're upright, don't forget to admire the stunning views before descending. Try not to think of the local lore about all the fluids that drench the stone *other* than saliva.

Blarney is 8km northwest of Cork and buses run frequently from Cork bus station (adult/child €3.30/2, 30 minutes).

Western Cork

Kinsale

POP 4100

Narrow winding streets lined with artsy little shops and a handsome harbour full of bobbing fishing boats and pleasure yachts make Kinsale (Cionn tSáile) one of Ireland's favourite mid-sized towns; its superb foodie reputation is just another reason to visit. Its sheltered bay is guarded by a huge and engrossing fort, just outside the town at Summercove.

Most of Kinsale's hotels and restaurants are situated near the harbour and within easy walking distance of the town centre; Scilly, a peninsula to the southeast, is barely a 10-minute walk away. A path continues from there to Summercove and Charles Fort.

CHARLES FORT Historic Site
(021-477 2263; www.heritageireland.ie; adult/child €4/2; 10am-6pm mid-Mar–Oct) One of the best-preserved 17th-century star-shaped forts in Europe, this fortress

would be worth a visit for its spectacular views alone. But there's much more here: ruins inside the vast site date from the 18th and 19th centuries and make for some fascinating wandering. Displays explain the typically tough lives led by the soldiers who served here and the comparatively comfortable lives of the officers. Built in the 1670s to guard Kinsale Harbour, the fort was in use until 1921, when much of it was destroyed as the British withdrew. The best way to get here is to walk – follow the signs on the lovely walk around the bay from Scilly to Summercove, 3km east of Kinsale.

Sleeping

PIER HOUSE B&B **€€**
**(021-477 4475; www.pierhousekinsale.com; Pier Rd; r €80-140; P) This superb guesthouse, set back from the road in a sheltered garden, is a lovely place to rest your head. Pristine rooms, decorated with shell-and-driftwood sculptures, have black-granite bathrooms with power showers and underfloor heating. Four of the rooms also have balconies and views of the milling mobs outside.

Eating

FISHY FISHY CAFE Seafood **€€**
(021-470 0415; www.fishyfishy.ie; Crowley's Quay; mains €13-34; noon-4pm Mon-Fri, noon-4.30pm Sat & Sun) Arguably the best seafood restaurant in the country has a wonderful setting, with stark white walls splashed with bright artwork and a terrific decked terrace at the front. All the fish is caught locally; have the cold seafood platter, a tasty spectacle that's a concert of what's fresh. Scallops are dollops of goodness. Front-of-house staff are charmers, but waitstaff can look as tired as week-old haddock. The Fishy Fishy empire also includes a superb fish 'n' chip shop.

JIM EDWARDS Seafood **€€**
(021-477 2541; www.jimedwardskinsale.com; Market Quay; bar meals €7-20, restaurant meals €15-30; bar 12.30-10pm, restaurant 6-10pm) If Fishy Fishy has a serious rival, it's 200m away in this unassuming pub, where the bar food is way above standard and the restaurant exceptional. A very traditional ambience belies the high quality of the

Kinsale

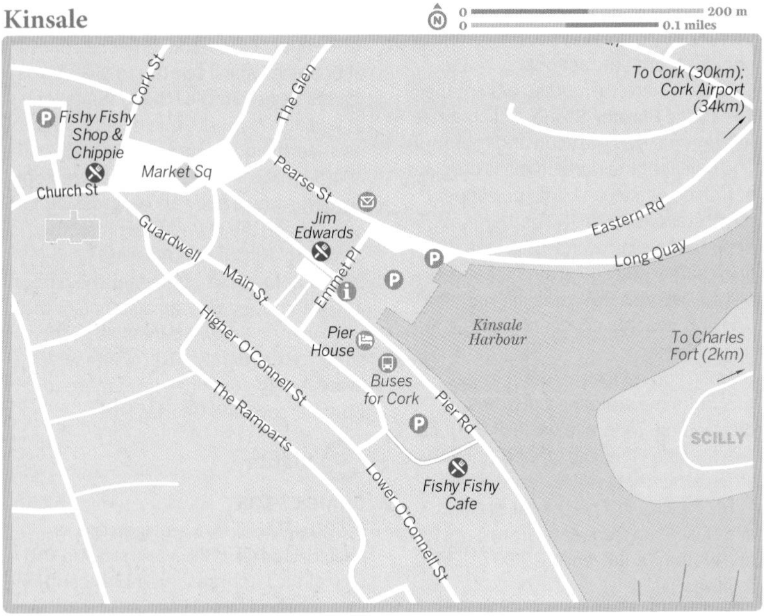

Detour: The Gourmet Heartland of Ballymaloe

Drawing up at wisteria-clad **Ballymaloe House** (021-465 2531; www.ballymaloe.ie; Shanagarry; s/d from €130/260;), you know you've arrived somewhere special. The Allen family has been running this superb hotel and restaurant in the old family home for more than 40 years now; Myrtle is a living legend, acclaimed internationally for her near single-handed creation of fine Irish cooking. The rooms have been individually decorated with period furnishings and are a pleasing mass of different shapes and sizes. Guests enjoy beautiful grounds and amenities, which include a tennis court, a swimming pool, a shop, minigolf and public rooms. And don't forget the celebrated **restaurant**, whose menu is drawn up daily to reflect the availability of produce from Ballymaloe's extensive farms and other local sources. The hotel also runs wine and gardening weekends; check the website for details.

A few kilometres down the road on the R628, TV personality Darina Allen runs a famous **cookery school** (021-464 6785; www.cookingisfun.ie). Lessons, from half-day sessions (€75 to €115) to 12-week certificate courses (€10,295), are often booked well in advance. There are pretty cottages amid the 100 acres of grounds for overnight students.

menu, which doffs a cap to meat-eaters but specialises mostly in all kinds of locally caught fish.

Information

The tourist office (021-477 2234; www.kinsale.ie; cnr Pier Rd & Emmet Pl; 9.15am-5pm Tue-Sat Nov-Mar, Mon Apr-Jun, Sep & Oct, 10am-5pm Sun Jul & Aug) has a good map detailing walks in and around Kinsale.

Getting There & Away

Bus Éireann (021-450 8188) services connect Kinsale with Cork (€7, 50 minutes, 14 daily Monday to Friday, 11 Saturday and five Sunday) via Cork airport. The bus stops on Pier Rd, near the tourist office.

Clonakilty

POP 4200

Cheerful, brightly coloured Clonakilty is a bustling market town that serves as a hub for the score of beguiling little coastal towns that surround it. Here you'll find smart B&Bs, top restaurants and cosy pubs alive with music. Little waterways coursing through add a drop of charm.

Clonakilty is famous for two things: it's the birthplace of Michael Collins, embodied in a large **statue** on the corner of Emmet Sq; and it's home of the most famous black pudding in the country.

Sights

LISNAGUN Historic Site

(Lios na gCon; 023-883 2565; www.liosnagcon.com; adult/child €5/3; tours noon-4pm summer) Of the more than 30,000 ring forts scattered across Ireland, Lisnagun is the only one that's been reconstructed on its original site. Complete with souterrain and central thatched hut, it gives a vivid impression of life in a 10th-century farmstead. To get there, take the turn signposted to Bay View House B&B at the roundabout at the end of Strand Rd. Follow the road uphill to the T-junction, turn right, then continue for about 800m before turning right again (signposted).

Sleeping

EMMET HOTEL Hotel €€

(023-883 3394; www.emmethotel.com; Emmet Sq; r €65-120;) This lovely Georgian

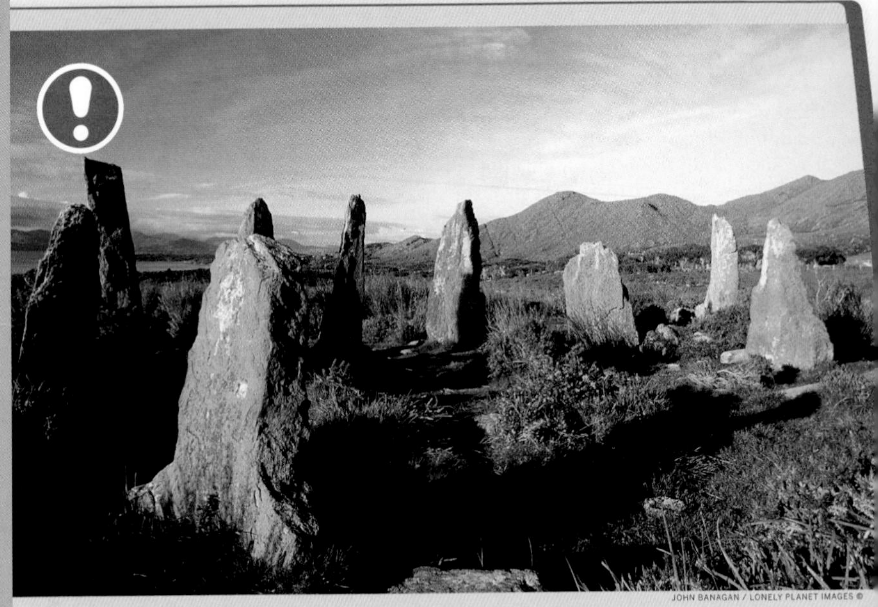

JOHN BANAGAN / LONELY PLANET IMAGES ©

Don't Miss Eyeries to Lauragh

Heading north and east from Allihies, the beautiful coastal road (R575), with hedges of fuchsias and rhododendrons, twists and turns for about 12km to **Eyeries**. The cluster of brightly coloured houses overlooking Coulagh Bay is often used as a film set. The town is also home to **Milleens cheese** (027-74079; www.milleenscheese.com), from pioneering producer Veronica Steele. She welcomes visitors to her farm; phone ahead.

From Eyeries, forsake the R571 for the even smaller coast roads (lanes really) to the north and east. This is the Beara at its most spectacular – and intimate. Tiny coves are like pearls in a sea of rocks, the views of the Ring of Kerry to the north sublime.

Rejoin the R571 at the crossroads of **Ardgroom** (Ard Dhór). As you head east towards Lauragh, look for signs pointing to the Ardgroom **stone circle** (pictured above), an unusual Bronze Age monument with nine tall, thin uprights. There's muddy parking at the end of a 500m-long narrow approach lane. The circle is visible about 200m away and a path leads to it across bogland. A crude sign says simply 'money' and a US dollar under a rock gives a hint.

Lauragh (Laith Reach), situated northeast of Ardgroom, is in County Kerry. It's home to the **Derreen Gardens** (064-83103; adult/child €6/3; 10am-6pm Apr-Oct), planted by the fifth Lord Lansdowne around the turn of the 20th century. Mossy paths weave through an abundance of interesting plants, including spectacular New Zealand tree ferns and red cedars, and you may see seals on the shore. There are walking opportunities in the area but gaining access can be problematic; ask locally for advice.

From Lauragh, a serpentine road travels 11km south across the other-worldly **Healy Pass** and down to Adrigole, offering spectacular views of the rocky inland scenery. About 1km west of Lauragh, along the R571, is a road to **Glanmore Lake**, with the remains of an old hermitage on a tiny island in the middle.

The Best Black Pudding

Clonakilty's most treasured export is its black pudding, the blood sausage that features on most local restaurant menus. The best place to buy it is **Edward Twomey** (023-883 3733; www.clonakiltyblackpudding.ie; 16 Pearse St; puddings from €2.75), where you can buy different varieties based on the original recipe, formulated in the 1880s.

accommodation option on the elegant square happily mixes period charm and old-world service with the perks of a modern hotel. The 20 rooms are large and plush; O'Keeffe's restaurant on site serves up tasty Irish food made from organic and local ingredients.

Eating

AN SÚGÁN Modern Irish **€€€**
(023-883 3719; www.ansugan.com; 41 Wolfe Tone St; bar menu €5-25, dinner mains €14-28; noon-10pm) A traditional bar with a national reputation for excellent seafood. You dine in a room crammed with knick-knacks – jugs dangle from the ceiling, patrons' business cards are stuffed beneath the rafters, and lanterns and even ancient fire extinguishers dot the walls. But there's nothing idiosyncratic about the food – the seafood chowder is great for a light meal, the crab cakes are memorable and there's a choice of around 10 different kinds of fish, depending on the daily catch.

Entertainment

DE BARRA'S Pub
(www.debarra.ie; 55 Pearse St) A marvellous atmosphere, walls splattered with photos, press cuttings, masks and musical instruments, plus the cream of live music every night of the week (starting around 9.30pm) make this a busy pub.

Information

Tourist office (023-883 3226; www.clonakilty.ie; Ashe St; 9.30am-5.30pm Mon-Sat Sep-Jun, 9am-7pm Mon-Sat & 10am-5pm Sun Jul & Aug) Has a good, free map.

Getting There & Away

There are eight daily buses Monday to Saturday and seven Sunday to Cork (€11.50, 65 minutes) and Skibbereen (€8, 40 minutes). Buses stop across from Harte's Spar shop on the bypass going to Cork.

Mizen Head Peninsula

Bantry

POP 3300

Framed by the craggy Caha Mountains, vast, magnificent Bantry Bay is one of the country's most attractive inlets and a worthwhile stop on any West Cork itinerary. Pride of place goes to Bantry House, the former home of one Richard White, who earned his place in history when in 1798 he warned authorities of the imminent landing of patriot Wolfe Tone and his French fleet in their effort to join the countrywide rebellion of the United Irishmen (see p335).

Sights

BANTRY HOUSE Notable Building
(027-50047; www.bantryhouse.com; Bantry Bay; adult/child €10/3; 10am-6pm mid-Mar–Oct) With its melancholic air of faded gentility, 18th-century Bantry House makes for an intriguing visit. Experienced pianists are invited to tinkle the ivories of the ancient piano in the library. It's possible to stay the night in the wings. It is 1km southwest of the town centre on the N71.

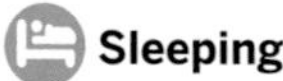

Sleeping

BALLYLICKEY HOUSE B&B **€€**
(027-50071; www.ballylickeymanorhouse.com; Ballylickey; r €90-180; Mar-Nov;) Possessing a name that rolls off the tongue, Ballylickey is a beautiful manor house with manicured lawns overlooking the bay. There are two choices for the night:

If You Like... Restaurants

If you like restaurants like the Fishy Fishy Café (p192) and Jim Edwards (p192) in Kinsale, then you'll salivate over these other fine eateries in County Cork:

1 **GOOD THINGS CAFÉ**
(027-61426; www.thegoodthingscafe.com; Ahakista Rd, Durrus; lunch mains €10-20, dinner mains €21-38; 12.30-3pm & 7-9pm Thu-Mon mid-Jun–Dec) Great contemporary dishes made with organic, locally sourced ingredients.

2 **HACKETT'S**
(Main St, Schull; lunch daily year-round, dinner Wed-Thu Jul-Aug, Fri & Sat year-round; bar meals €4-9, dinner €15-20) Hackett's rises above the norm with a creative pub menu of organic dishes prepared from scratch.

3 **STAR ANISE**
(021-455 1635; 4 Bridge St, Cork City; mains €19-27; lunch & dinner Mon-Sat) Fresh and creative cooking at this narrow little shopfront bistro. Three-course dinner specials are a fine deal at €29.

rooms in the house or cute cottages set round a swimming pool. All are spacious and comfortably furnished.

Eating

Wolfe Tone Sq takes on a heady mix of aromas for the **Friday Market**, which draws in the masses – both vendors and shoppers – from a wide area.

FISH KITCHEN Modern Irish €€
(027-56651; New St; mains €8-20; noon-9pm Tue-Sat) This outstanding little restaurant above a fish shop does seafood to perfection, from the local oysters (served with lemon and tabasco sauce) to a particularly fine dish of pan-seared scallops. But if for some reason you don't fancy sea fare, it does a juicy steak too. Friendly, unfussy and absolutely delicious.

Getting There & Away

Bus Éireann (www.buseireann.ie) has eight buses daily Monday to Saturday (four on Sunday) between Bantry and Cork (€15.50, two hours). There's one or two daily to Glengarriff. Heading north to the Ring of Beara, Kenmare and Killarney requires backtracking through Cork.

Beara Peninsula (Ring of Beara)

The Beara Peninsula is the third major 'ring' (circular road around a peninsula) in the west. Dingle and Kerry are comfortably in the number one and two spots respectively, leaving Beara in third place, which is just about right.

Northside of the Beara

The entire north side is the scenic highlight of the Beara Peninsula.

COUNTY KERRY

Killarney

POP 16,900

In a town that's been practising the tourism game for over 250 years, Killarney is a well-oiled machine in the middle of the sublime scenery of its namesake national park. Beyond the obvious proximity to lakes, waterfalls, woodland and moors dwarfed by 1000m-plus peaks, it has many charms of its own. Competition keeps standards high, and no matter your budget, you can expect to find good restaurants, fine pubs and plenty of accommodation. Mobbed in summer, Killarney is perhaps at its best in late spring and early autumn.

Sights & Activities

Killarney's biggest attraction, in every sense, is Killarney National Park – see p200. The town itself can easily be explored on foot in an hour or two.

Killarney

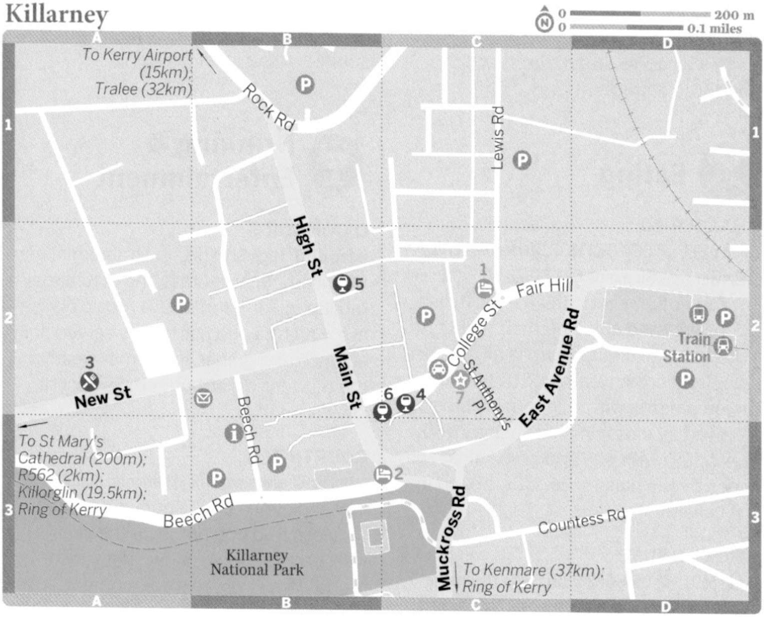

To Kerry Airport (15km); Tralee (32km)
Rock Rd
Lewis Rd
High St
Main St
College St
Fair Hill
East Avenue Rd
St Anthony's Pl
New St
Beech Rd
Train Station
To St Mary's Cathedral (200m); R562 (2km); Killorglin (19.5km); Ring of Kerry
Killarney National Park
Muckross Rd
Countess Rd
To Kenmare (37km); Ring of Kerry

Killarney

Sleeping
- 1 Fairview C2
- 2 Killarney Plaza Hotel C3

Eating
- 3 Chapter 40 .... A2
- Smoke House .... (see 5)

Drinking
- 4 Courtney's C2
- 5 O'Connor's B2
- 6 Tatler Jack's C2

Entertainment
- 7 McSorley's C2

Sleeping

CRYSTAL SPRINGS B&B €€

(Map p202; ☎064-663 3272; www.crystalspringsbb.com; Ballycasheen; d €80-110; P Wi-Fi family) You can cast a line from the timber deck of this wonderfully relaxing riverside B&B or just laze about on the adjacent lawn. Rooms are richly furnished with patterned wallpapers and walnut timber; private bathrooms (most with spa baths) are larger than many Irish hotel rooms. The glass-enclosed breakfast room also overlooks the fast-flowing River Flesk. It's about a 15-minute stroll to town.

FAIRVIEW Inn €€

(Map p197; ☎064-663 4164; www.fairviewkillarney.com; College St; d from €110; P Wi-Fi) Done out in beautiful timbers, the individually decorated rooms (some with classical printed wallpaper, some with contemporary sofas and glass) at this boutique guesthouse offer better bang for your buck than bigger, less personal places around town. A veritable feast is laid on at breakfast; the elegant on-site restaurant is a winner come evening.

KILLARNEY PLAZA HOTEL Hotel €€€

(Map p197; ☎064-662 1100; www.killarneyplaza.com; Kenmare Pl; s/d from €115/238; P @ pool Wi-Fi family) Dominating the view of the south end of Main St, on the edge of Killarney National Park, this large, 198-room hotel is built in a brilliant white traditional style. Classically furnished guestrooms and public facilities are in keeping with its class; besides the marble lobby and lavishly tiled indoor pool, there's a sauna, steam room and spa, and three restaurants.

Eating

CHAPTER 40 Modern Irish **€€**

(Map p197; ☎064-667 1833; www.chapter40.ie; Lower New St; mains €22.50-28.50; ⏰dinner Tue-Sat) Popular with Killarney's stylish bounders (and chefs on their nights off), this beautiful dining room is all polished wood and cream leather. Starters like grilled polenta with wild mushrooms are followed by classy mains such as pork Wellington with pea and crab salsa. The wines by the glass show a deft hand in the cellar.

SMOKE HOUSE Bistro **€€**

(Map p197; ☎064-662 0801; www.thesmokehouse.ie; High St; mains €13-34; ⏰breakfast, lunch & dinner) One of Killarney's newest and busiest ventures, this tiled bistro is the first establishment in Ireland to cook with a Josper (Spanish charcoal oven). Stylish salads include Norwegian king crab; its Kerry surf 'n' turf burger – with gambas tails and house-made barbecue sauce – has a local following.

Drinking & Entertainment

O'CONNOR'S Pub

(Map p197; High St) This tiny traditional pub with lead-glass doors is one of Killarney's most popular haunts. Live music plays every night; good bar food is served daily at lunch and dinner. In warmer weather, the crowds spill out onto the adjacent laneway.

COURTNEY'S Pub

(Map p197; www.courtneysbar.com; Plunkett St) Inconspicuous on the outside, inside this timeless trad pub bursts at the seams with trad sessions many nights year-round. This is where locals come to see their old mates perform and to kick off a night on the town.

MCSORLEY'S Bar, Nightclub

(Map p197; www.mcsorleyskillarney.com; College St) A local favourite for its big beer garden

Pub front in Killarney

EOIN CLARKE / LONELY PLANET IMAGES ©

Football Fever

Gaelic football clubs are as common in Ireland as green fields and pub signs bearing the 'G' word. However, among Kerrymen, the obsession with the sport reaches fever pitch.

Run by the GAA (Gaelic Athletic Association), the 15-a-side game is played with a heavy leather ball on a rectangular grass pitch with H-shaped, net-backed goals. Teams score through a confusing combination of kicking, carrying, hand-passing and soloing (dropping and toe-kicking the ball into the hands). See p367 for an explanation of the rules. The game, which closely resembles Australian Rules football, dates back to the 16th century, but took its current form in the 19th century.

If you'd like to watch Gaelic football and you're in town during the season (February to September), head to the **Fossa GAA Ground** in Fossa (map p202). To learn about the game from some lifelong pub commentators, have a drink at GAA bars such as **Tatler Jack's**.

and nightclub with a decently sized dance floor. Trad sessions take place from early evening to 10pm, with live bands from 11.30pm. Admission to the main bar is free.

Information

Tourist office (**064-663 1633; www.corkkerry.ie; Beech Rd; 9am-8pm Jun-Aug, 9.15am-5pm Sep-May**) Can handle almost any query, especially dealing with transport intricacies.

Getting There & Away

Air

Kerry Airport (**KIR; www.kerryairport.com;**) is at Farranfore, about 15km north of Killarney along the N22, then a further 1.5km along the N23. **Ryanair** (**www.ryanair.com**) rules the roost with daily flights to Dublin and London's Luton and Stansted airports, and less frequent services to Hahn, Germany, Faro, Portugal and Alicante, Spain. **Aer Arann** (www.aerarann.com) has four flights a week to Manchester.

Bus

Bus Éireann (**064-663 0011; www.buseireann.ie**) operates from the east end of the Killarney Outlet Centre, offering regular links to destinations including Cork (€17, two hours, 15 daily); Dublin (€25.50, six hours, six daily); Galway (€23.50, seven hours, seven daily) via Limerick (€18, 2¼ hours); Tralee (€8.70, 40 minutes, hourly); and Waterford (€23.50, 4½ hours, hourly).

Train

Killarney's train station is behind the Malton Hotel, just east of the centre. **Irish Rail** (**064-6631067; www.irishrail.ie**) has up to three direct trains a day to Cork (€20, 1½ hours) and nine to Tralee (€9.50, 45 minutes). There are some direct trains to Dublin (from €26.40, 3½ hours), but you usually have to change at Mallow.

Getting Around

To/From the Airport

Bus Éireann has six to seven services daily between Killarney and Kerry Airport (€4.50, 20 minutes).

A taxi to Killarney costs about €35.

Bicycle

Bicycles are ideal for exploring the scattered sights of the Killarney area, many of which are accessible only by bike or on foot.

O'Sullivan's Bike Hire (**www.killarneyrentabike.com; per day €15**) has branches on New St, opposite the cathedral, and on Beech Rd, opposite the tourist office.

Car

The centre of Killarney can be thick with traffic at times. **Budget** (☎064-663 4341; Kenmare Pl) is the only car-hire outfit with an office in town. Otherwise contact the companies at the airport.

There is a sizeable, free car park next to St Mary's Cathedral.

Jaunting Car

The horse-drawn **jaunting car** (☎064-663 3358; www.killarneyjauntingcars.com), also known as a trap, comes with a driver known as a jarvey. The pick-up point, nicknamed 'the Ha Ha' or 'the Block', is on Kenmare Pl. Trips cost €30 to €70, depending on distance; traps officially carry four people. Jaunting cars also congregate in the N71 car park for Muckross House and Abbey, and at the Gap of Dunloe.

Taxi

The town taxi rank is on College St. Taxi companies include **Killarney Taxi & Tours** (☎086 389 5144; www.killarneytaxi.com).

Around Killarney

Killarney National Park

You can escape Killarney for the surrounding wilderness surprisingly quickly. Buses rumble up to Ross Castle and Muckross House, but it's possible to find your own refuge in the 102 sq km of **Killarney National Park** (www.killarneynationalpark.ie) among Ireland's only wild herd of native red deer, the country's largest area of ancient oak woods and views of most of its major mountains.

The glacial Lough Leane (the Lower Lake or 'Lake of Learning'), Muckross Lake and the Upper Lake make up about a quarter of the park. Their peaty waters are as rich in wildlife as the surrounding soil: cormorants skim across the surface, deer swim out to graze on the islands, and salmon, trout and perch prosper in a pike-free environment.

Designated a Unesco Biosphere Reserve in 1982, the park extends to the southwest of town. There are pedestrian entrances opposite St Mary's Cathedral in Killarney, with other entrances for drivers off the N71.

Ross Castle

Restored by Dúchas, **Ross Castle** (Map p202; ☎064-663 5851; www.heritageireland.ie; Ross Rd; adult/child €6/2; ⏰9am-5.45pm Apr-Sep, 9.30am-5.45pm Oct & mid-late Mar) dates back to the 15th century, when it was a residence of the O'Donoghues. It was the last place in Munster to succumb to Cromwell's forces, thanks partly to its cunning spiral staircase, every step of which is a different height in order to break an attacker's stride.

The castle is a lovely 3km walk from the St Mary's Cathedral pedestrian park entrance; you may well see deer. If you're driving from Killarney, turn right opposite the petrol station at the start of Muckross Rd. Access is by guided tour only.

Inisfallen Island

The first monastery on Inisfallen Island (at 22 acres, the largest of the national park's 26 islands) is said to have been founded by St Finian the Leper in the 7th century. The island's fame dates from the early 13th century when the Annals of Inisfallen were written here. Now in the Bodleian Library at Oxford, they remain a vital source of information on early Munster history. On Inisfallen are the ruins of a 12th-century **oratory** with a carved Romanesque doorway and a **monastery** on the site of St Finian's original.

You can hire boats (around €5) from Ross Castle to row to the island.

Gap of Dunloe

Geographically, the Gap of Dunloe is outside the Killarney National Park, but most people include it in their visit to the park. The land is ruggedly beautiful, and fast-changing weather conditions add drama.

In the winter, it's an awe-inspiring mountain pass, overshadowed by Purple Mountain and Macgillycuddy's Reeks. In high summer, though, it's a bottleneck for the tourist trade, with buses ferrying countless visitors for horse-and-trap rides.

In the south, surrounded by lush, green pastures, **Brandon's Cottage** (Map p202; dishes €3-6; ⏰breakfast & lunch Apr-Oct) is a simple old 19th-century hunting lodge with an open-air cafe and a dock for boats

RICHARD CUMMINS / LONELY PLANET IMAGES ©

Don't Miss Muckross Estate

The core of Killarney National Park is the Muckross Estate, donated to the state by Arthur Bourn Vincent in 1932. **Muckross House** (Map p202; ☎064-667 0144; www.muckross-house.ie; adult/child €7/3, combined ticket with farms €12/6; ⏰9am-7pm Jul & Aug, to 5.30pm Sep-Jun) is a 19th-century mansion (pictured above), restored to its former glory and packed with contemporaneous fittings. Entrance is by guided tour.

The beautiful gardens slope down, and a block behind the house contains a restaurant, craft shop and studios where you can see potters, weavers and bookbinders at work. Jaunting cars wait to run you though deer parks and woodland to Torc Waterfall and Muckross Abbey (about €20 each return; haggling can reap discounts). The visitor centre has an excellent cafe.

Immediately east of Muckross House are the **Muckross Traditional Farms** (☎064-663 1440; adult/child €7.50/4, combined ticket with Muckross House €12/6; ⏰10am-6pm Jun-Aug, 1-6pm May & Sep, 1-6pm Sat, Sun & public holidays Apr & Oct). These reproductions of 1930s Kerry farms, complete with chickens, pigs, cattle and horses, show farming and living conditions when people had to live off the land.

Muckross House is 5km south of town, signposted from the N71. If you're walking or cycling, there's a cycle track alongside the Kenmare road for most of the first 2km. A path then turns right into Killarney National Park. Following this path, after 1km you'll come to **Muckross Abbey**, which was founded in 1448 and burned by Cromwell's troops in 1652. William Thackeray called it 'the prettiest little bijou of a ruined abbey ever seen'. Muckross House is another 1.5km from the abbey ruins.

Cycling around Muckross Lake (Middle Lake) is easier and more scenic in an anticlockwise direction.

Around Killarney

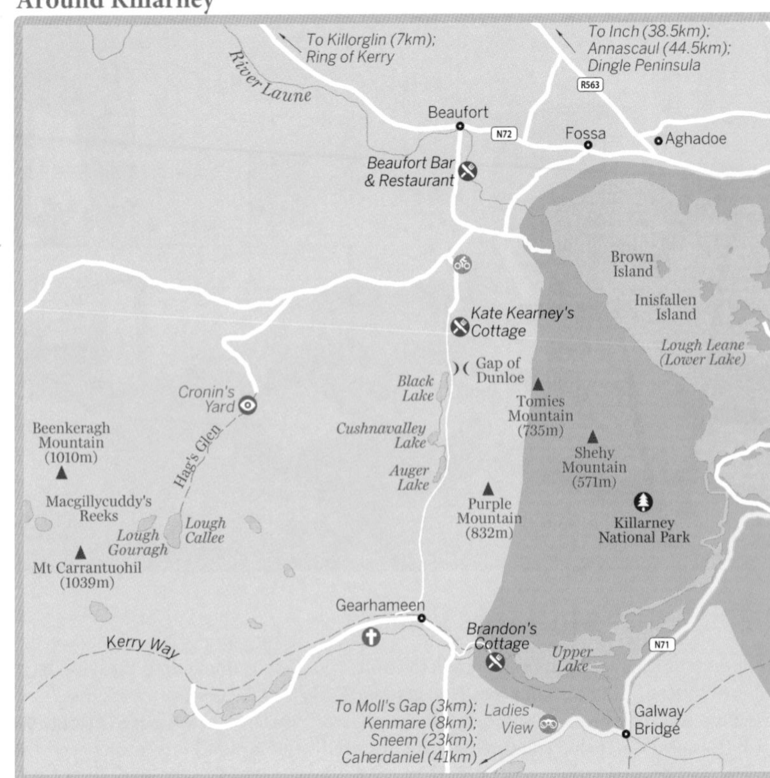

crossing the Upper Lake. From here a narrow road weaves up the hill to the Gap. Heading down towards the north the scenery is a fantasy of rocky bridges over clear mountain streams and lakes.

Eventually you reach the 19th-century pub **Kate Kearney's Cottage** (Map p202; 064-664 4146; www.katekearneyscottage.com; mains €8.50-19.50; lunch & dinner), where many drivers park in order to walk up to the Gap. You can also rent ponies and jaunting cars here (bring cash).

Beaufort Bar & Restaurant (Map p202; 064-664 4032; www.beaufortbar.com; Beaufort; mains €16-22; lunch Sun, dinner Fri & Sat) Continuing north to the N72, you'll reach this charming 1851 stone pub. Upstairs, its exceptional restaurant utilises local produce in starters such as Aghadoe black pudding and mains based on Kerry lamb. The gleaming timber dining room is refined, intimate and relaxed.

The best way to see the Gap is to hire a bike in Killarney and cycle to Ross Castle. Arrive before 11am to catch a boat up the lakes to Brandon's Cottage, then cycle through the Gap and back to town via the N72 and a path through the golf course (bike hire and boat trip about €30).

On land, walking, pony or four-person trap can be substituted for cycling. The Gap pony men charge €50 per hour or €80 for the two-hour trip between Brandon's Cottage and Kate Kearney's Cottage. Note that it's hard to do the Gap as part of a walking loop. You can get as far as Kate Kearney's, from where your best bet would be to call a cab, as it's a long slog back to Killarney on busy roads.

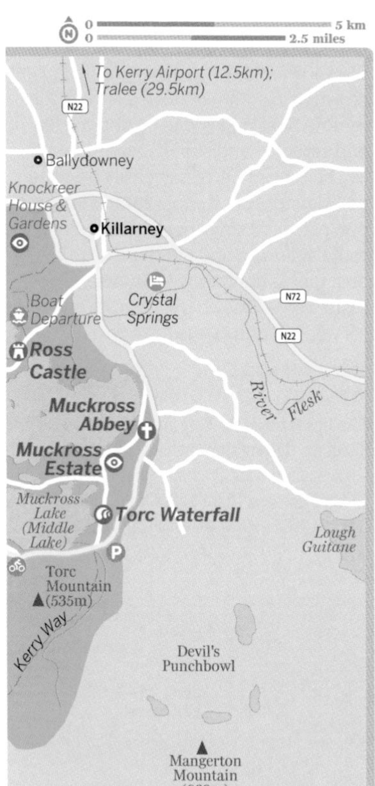

You can also drive this route, but really only outside summer and even then walkers and cyclists have the right of way, and the blind hairpin bends are nerve testing. To reach Brandon's Cottage by car you have to drive a long, scenic detour on the N71 to the R568 and then come back down a gorgeous rugged valley. It takes about 45 minutes.

Macgillycuddy's Reeks

Ascending **Macgillycuddy's Reeks** and their neighbours (Purple, Tomies and Shehy mountains, between the Gap of Dunloe and Lough Leane, and Torc and Mangerton mountains, southeast of Muckross Lake) should never be attempted without a map and compass (and knowing how to use them). Weatherproof and waterproof footwear and clothing are essential at all times of the year. Seek advice locally before attempting mountain walks.

There are several ways up **Carrantuohil**, the country's highest peak, in the Macgillycuddy's Reeks range. Some require reasonable hill-walking ability, others are serious scrambling or rock-climbing routes. Get a taste of the Reeks at close quarters by walking up Hag's Glen, the beautiful approach valley that leads to the Callee and Gouragh lakes below the north face of Carrantuohil.

The popular but hair-raising way to summit Carrantuohil from the lakes is via Devil's Ladder, a gruelling trudge up a badly eroded gully path, southwest of the lakes. The ground is loose in places, and in wet conditions the way becomes muddy. It takes six hours return from Cronin's Yard.

Tours

KILLARNEY GUIDED WALKS Walks
(**☎087 639 4362; www.killarneyguidedwalks.com; adult/child €9/5**) Guided two-hour national park walks leave at 11am daily from opposite St Mary's Cathedral at the western end of New St. Tours meander through Knockreer gardens, then to spots where Charles de Gaulle holidayed, David Lean filmed *Ryan's Daughter* and Brother Cudda slept for 200 years. Trips are available at other times on request.

ROSS CASTLE OPEN BOATS Boat
(**☎087 689 9241**) The open boats you can charter at Ross Castle offer more appealing trips with boatmen who define 'character'. It normally costs €10 from Ross Castle to the Muckross (Middle) Lake and back; €15 for a tour of all three lakes.

Killarney to Kenmare

The vista-crazy N71 to Kenmare (32km) winds between rock and lake, with plenty of lay-bys to stop and admire the views (and recover from the switchback bends). Watch out for the buses squeezing along the road.

About 2km south of the entrance to Muckross House, a path leads 200m to the pretty **Torc Waterfall**. After another

8km on the N71 you come to **Ladies' View**, where the fine views along Upper Lake were much enjoyed by Queen Victoria's ladies-in-waiting. A further 5km on **Moll's Gap** is worth a stop for great views and food – and not necessarily in that order.

Avoca Cafe (www.avoca.ie; Moll's Gap; mains €9-13; lunch) has jaw-dropping panoramas and delicious fare like smoked salmon salad, pistachio-studded pork terrine and decadent cakes.

Ring of Kerry

The Ring of Kerry is the longest and the most diverse of Ireland's big circle drives, combining jaw-dropping coastal scenery with emerald pastures and villages.

The 179km circuit winds past pristine beaches, the island-dotted Atlantic, medieval ruins, mountains and loughs (lakes). The coastline is at its most rugged between Waterville and Caherdaniel in the southwest of the peninsula. It can get crowded in summer, but even then, the remote Skellig Ring can be uncrowded and serene – and starkly beautiful.

The Ring of Kerry can easily be done as a day trip, but if you want to stretch it out, places to stay are scattered along the route. Killorglin and Kenmare have the best dining options, with some excellent restaurants; elsewhere, basic (sometimes very basic) pub fare is the norm.

Getting Around

Tour buses travel the Ring in an anticlockwise direction. Getting stuck behind one is tedious, so consider driving clockwise; just watch out on blind corners. There's little traffic on the **BALLAGHBEAMA GAP**, which cuts across

Ring of Kerry

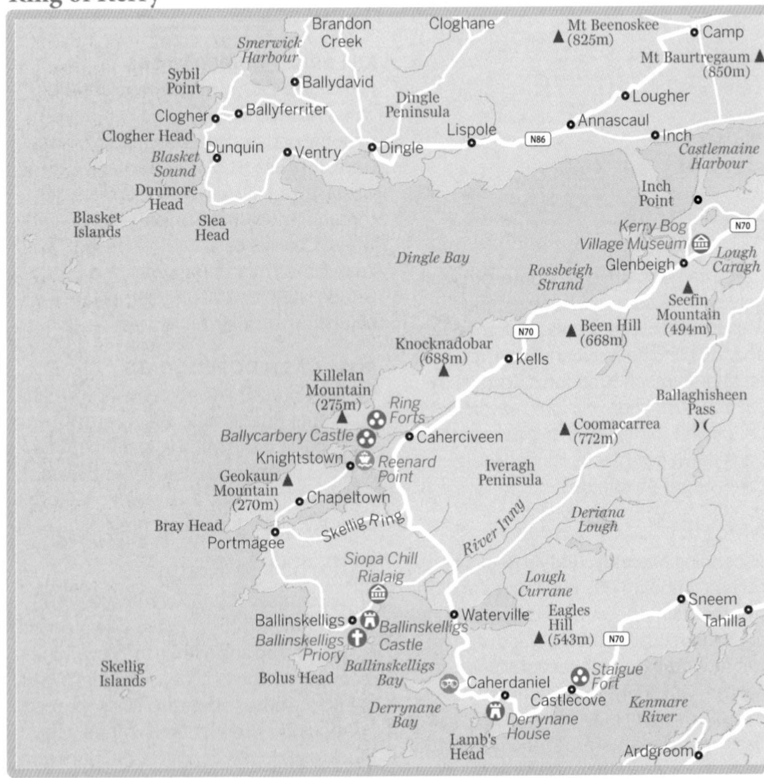

the peninsula's central highlands with some spectacular views: it's perfect for a long cycle, as is the longer **BALLAGHISHEEN PASS** to Waterville.

Between mid-June and mid-September, **Bus Éireann** (064-663 0011; www.buseireann.ie) circumnavigates the Ring of Kerry daily (Killarney to Killarney €25.50, seven hours). Stops include Killorglin, Glenbeigh, Caherciveen, Waterville (stopping for one hour) and Caherdaniel. Outside summer, transport on the Ring is not good.

Killorglin

POP 3900

Travelling anticlockwise from Killarney, the first town on the Ring is Killorglin (Cill Orglan), 23km northwest. The town is quieter than the waters of the River Laune that lap against the eight-arched bridge, built in 1885. In August, there's an explosion of time-honoured ceremonies at the famous

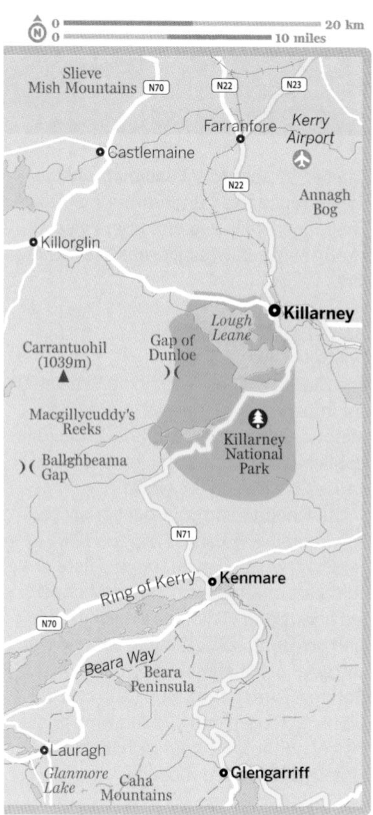

pagan festival, the Puck Fair. A statue of King Puck (a goat) peers out from the Killarney side of the river. Author Blake Morrison documents his mother's childhood here in *Things My Mother Never Told Me*.

Festivals

PUCK FAIR FESTIVAL Historic
(Aonach an Phuic; www.puckfair.ie; mid-Aug) First recorded in 1603, with hazy origins, this lively festival is based around the custom of installing a billy goat (a poc, or puck), the symbol of mountainous Kerry, on a pedestal in the town, its horns festooned with ribbons. Other entertainment ranges from a horse fair and bonny baby competition to street theatre, concerts and fireworks; the pubs stay open until 3am.

Sleeping & Eating

BIANCONI Inn €€
(066-976 1146; www.bianconi.ie; Bridge St; s/d €60/90, mains €12.50-25; restaurant lunch & dinner Mon-Sat) Bang in the centre of town, this low-lit inn has a classy ambience and cooked-to-perfection Modern Irish fare like sage-stuffed roast chicken with cranberry sauce. Its spectacular salads, such as Cashel blue cheese, apple, toasted almonds and chorizo, are a meal in themselves. Guestrooms were undergoing refurbishment at the time of writing – check for updates.

Kerry Bog Village Museum

On the N70 between Killorglin and Glenbeigh, the **Kerry Bog Village Museum** (Map p204; www.kerrybogvillage.ie; admission €5; 8.30am-6pm) re-creates a 19th-century bog village, typical of the small communities that carved out a precarious living in the harsh environment of Ireland's ubiquitous peat bogs. You'll see the thatched homes of the turfcutter, blacksmith, thatcher and labourer, as well as a dairy, and meet rare Kerry Bog ponies.

Caherciveen

POP 1300

Caherciveen's population, over 30,000 in 1841, was decimated by the Great Famine and emigration to the New World. A sleepy outpost remains, overshadowed by the 688m peak of Knocknadobar. It looks rather dour compared with the peninsula's other settlements, but in many ways this village does more to recall the tough 1930s in Ireland than any other you'll see in Kerry.

Sights

BALLYCARBERY CASTLE & RING FORTS Castle, Forts

The best attraction locally is the ruins of 16th-century Ballycarbery Castle, 2.4km along the road to White Strand Beach from the barracks. The atmospheric remains are surrounded by green pastures inhabited by cows who like to get in the pictures.

Along the same road are two stone ring forts. **Cahergall**, the larger one, dates from the 10th century and has stairways on the inside walls, a *clochán* (beehive hut), and the remains of a house. The smaller, 9th-century **Leacanabuile** has the entrance to an underground passage. Their inner walls and chambers give a strong sense of what life was like in a ring fort.

Skellig Islands

GANNET POP 45,000

The Skellig Islands (Oileáin na Scealaga) are impervious to the ever-pounding Atlantic. George Bernard Shaw said Skellig Michael was 'the most fantastic and impossible rock in the world'.

You'll need to do your best grisly seadog impression ('argh!') on the 12km crossing, which can be rough. There are no toilets or shelter on Skellig Michael, the only island visitors are permitted to land on. Bring something to eat and drink and wear stout shoes and weatherproof clothing. Due to the steep (and often slippery) terrain and sudden wind gusts, it's not suitable for young children or people with limited mobility.

Left: Puffins, Skellig Michael (p209); **Below:** Hikers climb Skellig Michael (p209)
PHOTOGRAPHERS: (LEFT) © IMAGEBROKER / ALAMY; (BELOW) GARETH MCCORMACK / LONELY PLANET IMAGES ©

Activities

The Skelligs are a **birdwatching** paradise. During the boat trip you may spot diminutive storm petrels (also known as Mother Carey's chickens) darting above the water like swallows. Gannets are unmistakable with their savage beaks, imperious eyes, yellow caps and 100cm-plus wing spans. Kittiwakes – small, dainty seabirds with black-tipped wings – are easy to see and hear around Skellig Michael's covered walkway as you step off the boat. They winter at sea then land in their thousands to breed between March and August.

Further up the rock you'll see stubby-winged fulmars, with distinctive bony 'nostrils' from which they eject an evil-smelling green liquid if you get too close. In May, puffins come ashore to lay a solitary egg at the far end of a burrow, and parent birds can be seen guarding their nests. Puffins stay only until the first weeks of August.

Small Skellig

While Skellig Michael looks like two triangles linked by a spur, Small Skellig is longer, lower and much craggier. From a distance it looks as if someone battered it with a feather pillow that burst. Close up you realise you're looking at a colony of over 20,000 pairs of breeding gannets, the second-largest breeding colony in the world. Most boats circle the island so you can see the gannets and you may see basking seals as well. Small Skellig is a bird sanctuary; no landing is permitted.

Getting There & Away

Skellig Michael's fragility places limits on the number of daily visitors. The 15 boats are licensed to carry no more than 12 passengers each, for a maximum of 180 people at any one time. It's wise to book ahead in July and August, bearing in mind that if the weather's bad the boats may not sail (about two days out of seven). Trips usually run

If You Like... Festivals

If high-octane festivals like Puck Fair (p205) are your thing, then you should consider some other of Kerry's celebrations:

1 **LISTOWEL WRITERS' WEEK** (www.writersweek.ie; ⏲Jun) Bibliophiles flock to Listowel for readings, poetry, music, drama, seminars, storytelling and many other events held at various places around town.

2 **LUGHNASA** (⏲late Jul) The north side of the Dingle Peninsula celebrates the ancient Celtic harvest festival of Lughnasa with events – especially bonfires – both in the village of Cloghane and atop Mt Brandon.

3 **ROSE OF TRALEE** (www.roseoftralee.ie; ⏲Aug) In Ireland and beyond, Tralee is synonymous with the Rose of Tralee, a beauty pageant open to Irish women and women of Irish descent from around the world (the 'roses').

from Easter until September, depending, again, on weather.

Boats leave around 10am and return at 3pm, and cost about €45 per person. You can depart from Portmagee, Ballinskelligs or Derrynane. Boat owners generally restrict you to two hours on the island, which is the bare minimum to see the monastery, look at the birds and have a picnic. The crossing takes about 1½ hours from Portmagee, 35 minutes to one hour from Ballinskelligs and 1¾ hours from Derrynane.

Local pubs and B&Bs will point you in the direction of boat operators, including the following:

Casey's (☎066-947 2437; www.skelligislands.com; Portmagee)

John O'Shea (☎087 689 8431; www.skelligtours.com; Derrynane)

Seanie Murphy (☎066-947 6214; www.skelligsrock.com; Reenard Point, Valentia Island)

Waterville

POP 550

Waterville, a line of colourful houses strung on the N72 between Lough Currane and Ballinskelligs Bay, is charm-challenged in the way of many such mass-consumption beach resorts. A statue of its most famous guest, Charlie Chaplin, beams out from the seafront. The **Charlie Chaplin Comedy Film Festival** (charliechaplincomedyfilmfestival.com) takes place in late August.

Caherdaniel

POP 350

Hiding between Derrynane Bay and the foothills of Eagles Hill, Caherdaniel barely qualifies as a tiny hamlet. Businesses are scattered about the undergrowth like smugglers, fitting since this was once a haven for same.

This is the ancestral home of Daniel O'Connell, 'the Liberator' (see p335), whose family made money smuggling from their base by the dunes. The area boasts a blue flag beach, plenty of activities, good hikes and some pubs where you may be tempted to break into pirate talk. Lines of wind-gnarled trees add to the wild air.

Sights

DERRYNANE NATIONAL HISTORIC PARK Historic Site

(☎066-947 5113; www.heritageireland.ie; Derrynane; adult/child €3/1; ⏲10.30am-6pm Apr-Sep, 10.30am-5pm Wed-Sun Oct-late Nov) **Derrynane House** is the family home of Daniel O'Connell, the campaigner for Catholic emancipation. His ancestors bought the house and surrounding parkland, having grown rich on smuggling with France and Spain. It's largely furnished with O'Connell memorabilia, including the restored triumphal chariot in which he lapped Dublin after his release from prison in 1844.

The gardens, warmed by the Gulf Stream, hold palms, 4m-high tree ferns, gunnera ('giant rhubarb') and other South American species. A walking track through them leads to wetlands,

RICHARD MILLS / LONELY PLANET IMAGES ©

Don't Miss Skellig Michael

The jagged, 217m-high rock of **Skellig Michael** (Archangel Michael's Rock; like St Michael's Mount in Cornwall and Mont Saint Michel in Normandy) is the larger of the two islands and a Unesco World Heritage site. It looks like the last place on earth where anyone would try to land, let alone establish a community, yet early Christian monks survived here from the 6th until the 12th or 13th century.

The **monastic buildings** perch on a saddle in the rock, some 150m above sea level, reached by 600 steep steps cut into the rock face. The astounding 6th-century oratories and beehive cells vary in size; the largest cell has a floor space of 4.5m by 3.6m. You can see the monks' south-facing vegetable garden and their cistern for collecting rainwater. The most impressive structural achievements are the settlement's foundations – platforms built on the steep slope using nothing more than earth and drystone walls.

Not much is known about the life of the monastery, but there are records of Viking raids in AD 812 and 823. Monks were kidnapped or killed, but the community recovered and carried on. In the 11th century a rectangular oratory was added to the site, but although it was expanded in the 12th century, the monks abandoned the rock around this time.

After the introduction of the Gregorian calendar in 1582, Skellig Michael became a popular spot for weddings. Marriages were forbidden during Lent, but since Skellig used the old Julian calendar, a trip to the islands allowed those unable to wait for Easter to tie the knot.

In the 1820s two lighthouses were built on Skellig Michael, together with the road that runs around the base.

There are no toilets on the island.

beaches and clifftops. You can spot wild pheasants and other birds, whose musical calls add a note of contrast to the dull roar of the surf. The **chapel**, which O'Connell added to Derrynane House in 1844, is a copy of the ruined one on **Abbey Island**, which can usually be reached on foot across the sand.

Look out for the **Ogham stone** on the left of the road to the house. With its carved notches representing the simple Ogham alphabet of the ancient Irish, the stone has several missing letters, but is thought to represent the name of a local chieftain.

Sneem

Halfway between Caherdaniel and Kenmare, Sneem (An tSnaidhm) is a good place to pause for something restorative, especially if you're travelling anticlockwise, as for the remaining 27km to Kenmare the N70 drifts away from the water and coasts along under a soothing canopy of trees.

The area is home to one of the finest castle hotels in the country.

Parknasilla Resort & Spa (☎064-667 5600; www.parknasillahotel.ie; Sneem; d from €180; P @ ≋ ᯤ) has been wowing guests (including one George Bernard Shaw) since 1895 with its 500 acres of pristine resort on the edge of the village of Sneem with the broad expanse of the Kenmare River separating it from the Beara Peninsula to the south (oh, the views!). From the modern, luxuriously appointed bedrooms to the top-grade spa (which includes a lap pool) and the elegant restaurant serving superb modern Irish cuisine, everything here is done just right: the service is friendly and professional without ever becoming fussy or overly obsequious. Irish hospitality at its very best.

Kenmare

POP 2500

The copper-covered limestone spire of Holy Cross Church, drawing the eye to the wooded hills above town, may make you forget for a split second that Kenmare is a seaside town. But with rivers named Finnihy, Roughty and Sheen emptying into Kenmare Bay, you couldn't be anywhere other than southwest Ireland.

In the 18th century, Kenmare was laid out on an X-plan, with a triangular market square in the centre. Today the inverted V to the south is the focus. Kenmare Bay stretches out to the southwest, and there are glorious views of the mountains.

Sleeping

VIRGINIA'S GUESTHOUSE B&B **€€**

(☎064-664 1021; www.virginias-kenmare.com; Henry St; s/d €60/80; ᯤ 👪) You can't get more central than this award-winning B&B, whose creative breakfasts celebrate organic local produce (rhubarb and blueberries in season, for example, as well as fresh-squeezed OJ and porridge with whiskey). Its eight rooms are super comfy without being fussy. Outstanding value.

Kenmare Bay

SHEEN FALLS LODGE Boutique Hotel €€€
(064-664 1600; www.sheenfallslodge.ie; d €115-230; Feb-Dec; P @) The Marquis of Landsdowne's former summer residence still feels like an aristocrats' playground, with a spa and 66 rooms with DVD players and Italian marble bathrooms, and views of the falls and across Kenmare Bay to Carrantuohil. Amenities are many (fancy clay-pigeon shooting, anyone?).

Eating

HORSESHOE Pub €€
(064-664 1553; www.thehorseshoekenmare.com; 3 Main St; mains €14.50-26.50; lunch & dinner) Ivy frames the entrance to this gastropub, which has a short but excellent menu that runs from Kenmare Bay mussels in creamy apple cider sauce to local lamb on mustard mash and Kerry's best burgers. Vegetarian specials appear daily.

Getting There & Away

The twisting, 32km-long drive on the N71 fr Killarney is surprisingly dramatic with tunne stark mountain vistas.

Twice-daily buses serve Killarney (€8.82, 50 minutes), with additional services in summer. Buses stop outside Roughty Bar (Main St).

Finnegan's Coach & Cab (064-664 1491; www.kenmarecoachandcab.com) Runs a variety of tours including the Ring of Kerry.

Dingle Peninsula

Unlike the Ring of Kerry, where the cliffs tend to dominate the ocean, it's the ocean that dominates the smaller Dingle Peninsula. The opal-blue waters surrounding the promontory's multihued landscape of green hills and golden sands give rise to aquatic adventures and to fishing fleets that haul in impossibly fresh seafood that appears on the menus of some of the county's finest restaurants.

Centred on charming Dingle town, there's an alternative way of life here, lived by artisans and idiosyncratic characters and found at trad sessions

Blasket Islands

The Blasket Islands (Na Blascaodaí), 5km out into the Atlantic, are the most westerly in Ireland. All of the Blaskets were inhabited at one time or another; there is evidence of Great Blasket being inhabited during the Iron Age and early Christian times. The last islanders left for the mainland in 1953 after they and the government agreed that it was no longer feasible to live in such isolated and harsh conditions, although today a few people make their home out here for part of the year.

Boats trips generally run from Easter to September, but even then weather can cause boat cancellations – call for seasonal sailing times.

Blasket Island Ferries (066-915 1344, 066-915 6422; www.blasketisland.com; adult/child €20/10) Boats depart from Dunquin Harbour and take 20 minutes; add €15 for an ecotour of the island.

Blasket Islands Eco Marine Tours (066-915 4864, 087 231 6131; www.marinetours.ie; morning/afternoon/day tour €25/35/40) Eco-oriented tours departing from Ventry Harbour.

Dingle Marine & Leisure (066-915 1344, 087 672 6100; www.dinglebaycharters.com; ferry adult/child return €30/15, 3hr island tour €40/15) Ferries take 45 minutes from Dingle town's marina.

and folkloric festivals across Dingle's tiny settlements.

The classic loop drive around Slea Head from Dingle town is 50km, but allow a day to take it all in – longer if you have time to stay overnight in Dingle town. The main road to Dingle town is the N86 via Tralee, but the coast road is far more beautiful and shouldn't be missed.

Tours

A number of Killarney companies run daily day trips by bus around the Dingle Peninsula (see p203). Alternatively, Dingle-based companies operate guided minibus tours of the peninsula daily from May to September.

O'CONNOR'S SLEA HEAD TOURS
Historic

(☎087 248 0008; www.dingletourskerry.com; €10 per person, per hr; 🕑11am & 2pm daily) Mainly covers the coast, with a focus on forts and other ancient sites. Tours last approximately three to four hours, departing from Dingle town's tourist office.

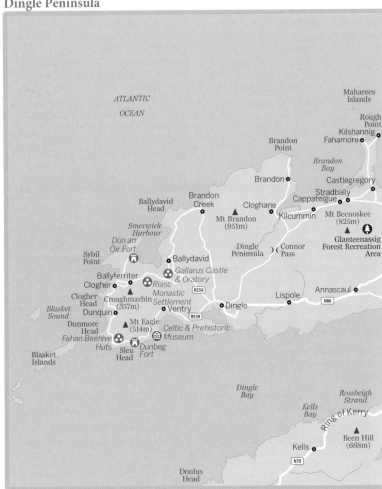

Dingle Peninsula

Dingle Town

POP 1800

Framed by its fishing port, the peninsula's charming little 'capital' is quaint without even trying. Dingle is one of Ireland's largest Gaeltacht towns; many pubs double as shops, so you can enjoy Guinness and a singalong among screws and nails, wellies and horseshoes. In summer its hilly streets can be clogged with visitors; there's no way around it. In other seasons its authentic charms are yours for the savouring.

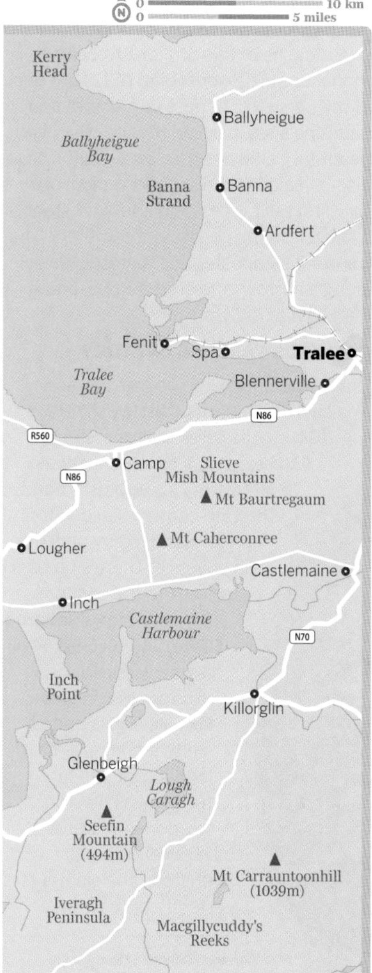

Sights

FUNGIE THE DOLPHIN

(**066-915 2626; www.dingledo... Pier; adult/child €16/8**) Boats run by ... gle Boatmen's Association cooperative leave the pier daily for one-hour dolphin-spotting trips of Dingle's most famous resident, Fungie. It's free if Fungie doesn't show, but he usually does.

In the warmer months, the association also runs a daily two-hour boat trip when you can **swim with Fungie** (**066-915 1146; per person €25, plus wetsuit hire €20; 8am or 9am Apr–mid-Sep**). Advance bookings are essential.

Sleeping

PAX HOUSE B&B €€

(**066-915 1518; www.pax-house.com; Upper John St; s/d from €90/120;**) From its highly individual decor (including contemporary paintings) to the outstanding views over the estuary from room balconies and the terrace, Pax House is a treat. Choose from cheaper hill-facing rooms, rooms that overlook the estuary, and two-room family suites opening to the terrace. Wi-fi is available in the lounge. It's 1km from the town centre.

Eating

OUT OF THE BLUE Seafood €€€

(**066-915 0811; The Wood; lunch €10-20, mains €15-30; dinner daily, lunch Sun**) 'No chips', the menu of this funky blue-and-yellow, fishing-shack-style restaurant on the waterfront reads. Despite its rustic surrounds, this is Dingle's best restaurant, with an intense devotion to fresh local seafood; if they don't like the catch, they don't open. Creative dishes change nightly, but might include steamed crab claws in garlic butter or pan-seared scallops flambéed in Calvados. Who needs chips?

Drinking & Entertainment

JOHN BENNY'S Pub

(**www.johnbennyspub.com; Strand St**) A toasty cast-iron woodstove, stone-slab floor, memorabilia on the walls, great staff and no intrusive TV make this one of Dingle's most enjoyable traditional pubs. An influx of local musos pours in most nights for rockin' trad sessions. The **bar menu (mains €10-19; lunch & dinner)**, including creamy seafood chowder, is hands-down the best in town.

Getting There & Away

Bus Éireann (www.buseireann.ie) buses stop outside the car park behind the supermarket. Up to six buses a day serve Killarney (€12.87, 80 minutes) via Tralee (€10.53, 45 minutes), where you can connect across Ireland or hop on the train.

West of Dingle

At the tip of the peninsula is the Slea Head drive along the R559. It has the greatest concentration of ancient sites in Kerry, if not the whole of Ireland.

The landscape is dramatic, especially in shifting mist, although full-on sea fog obliterates everything. For the best views, follow the Slea Head drive in a clockwise direction. Although a mere 50km in length, doing this drive justice requires a full day, at least.

SLEA HEAD & DUNMORE HEAD

Overlooking the mouth of Dingle Bay, Mt Eagle and the Blasket Islands, Slea Head has fine beaches, good walks and superbly preserved structures from Dingle's ancient past including beehive huts, forts, inscribed stones and church sites. Dunmore Head is the westernmost point on the Irish mainland and the site of the wreckage in 1588 of two Spanish Armada ships.

RIASC MONASTIC SETTLEMENT

The remains of this 5th- or 6th-century monastic settlement (Map p212) are one of the peninsula's more impressive and haunting sites, particularly the pillar with beautiful Celtic designs. Excavations have also revealed the foundations of an oratory first built with wood and later stone, a kiln for drying corn and a cemetery. The ruins are signposted as 'Mainistir Riaisc' along a narrow lane off the R559, about 2km east of Ballyferriter.

GALLARUS CASTLE & ORATORY

One of the Dingle Peninsula's few surviving castles, **Gallarus Castle (087 249 7034; www.heritageireland.ie; adult/child €3/free; 10am-6pm Jun-Aug)** was built by the FitzGeralds around the 15th century. Guided tours can be arranged by phoning in advance. There's no parking next to the castle.

The dry-stone **Gallarus Oratory (066-915 6444; www.heritageireland.ie; admission free; 10am-6pm Jun-Aug)** is quite a sight, standing in its lonely spot beneath the brown hills as it has done for some 1200 years. It has withstood the elements perfectly, apart from a

View from Dunmore Head, Dingle Peninsula

PHOTOGRAPHER: TRISH PUNCH / LONELY PLANET IMAGES ©

slight sagging in the roof. Traces of mortar suggest that the interior and exterior walls may have been plastered. Shaped like an upturned boat, it has a doorway on the western side and a round-headed window on the eastern side. Inside the doorway are two projecting stones with holes that once supported the door.

The castle and oratory are signposted off the R559, about 2km further on from the Riasc Monastic Settlement turn-off.

Connor Pass

At 456m, the Connor (or Conor) Pass is Ireland's highest mountain pass. On a foggy day you'll see nothing but the road just in front of you, but in fine weather it offers phenomenal views of Dingle Harbour to the south and Mt Brandon to the north. The road is in good shape, despite being very narrow and *very* steep (large signs portend doom for buses and trucks).

The summit car park yields views down to two lakes in the rock-strewn valley below plus the remains of walls and huts where people once lived impossibly hard lives. When visibility is good, the 10-minute climb to the summit is well worthwhile for the kind of vistas that inspire mountain-climbers.

If you're cycling, the pass is best approached from the northeast heading southwest, as you'll get the narrowest and steepest section over with early in the ride and can coast down the (relatively) gentler gradient and wider road towards Dingle town.

Galway, Clare & the West

In the heart of the west, Galway city is a swirl of enticing old pubs that hum with trad music sessions throughout the year. To the north, the Connemara Peninsula matches the beauty of the other Atlantic outcrops to the south: tiny roads wander along a coastline studded with islands, surprisingly white beaches and intriguing old villages with views over it all. This is the place to don the hiking boots and take to the well-marked network of trails that wander through lonely valleys and past hidden lakes before ending at sprays of surf at the Atlantic. Beyond it, the rugged beauty stretches in County Mayo, home to Ireland's most sacred pilgrimage site, Croagh Patrick, which rewards the penitent with stunning views of the surrounding countryside.

South of Galway, Clare combines the stunning natural beauty of its long and meandering coastline with unique windswept landscapes and a year's worth of dollops of Irish culture.

Kilronan pier, Inishmór (p235), Aran Islands

Galway, Clare & the West

Belderrig
Ballycastle
Mullet Peninsula
Bangor Erris
River Owenmore
Blacksod Bay
Aghleam
Blacksod Point
Ballycroy National Park
N59
Castlehill
Dugort
Ballycroy
Nephin Beg (628m)
Mt Nephin (806m)
Achill Head
Achill Island
Keel
Achill Sound
MAYO
Curraun Peninsula
Mulranny
Newport
ATLANTIC OCEAN
Clare Island
Clew Bay
Westport
Roonagh Quay
Louisburgh
Murrisk
Croagh Patrick (765m)
Doolough Valley
Inishturk
Killadoon
Cregganbaun
Sheeffry Hills
Delphi
Inishshark
Partry Mountains
Lough Mask
Renvyle
Tully
Killary Harbour
Leenane
Cleggan
Letterfrack
Joyce's Country
Claddaghduff
Kingston
Twelve Bens
Clonbur
Omey Island
Clifden
Connemara
Maumturk Mountains
Recess
Ballinaboy
Maam Cross
Ballyconneely
Toombeola
Cashel
Oughterard
Roundstone
Gortmore
Screeb
Moyrus
Glinsk
Rosmuc
Iar Connaught
Carna
Kilkieran Bay
Costello
Gorumna Island
Rossaveal
Carraroe
R336
Inverin

North Sound
Kilronan
Galway Bay
Inishmór
Aran Islands
Inishmaan
Inisheer
Doolin Point
Doolin
Cliffs of Moher
Hag's Head
Liscannor
Lahinch
Liscannor Bay
Miltown Malbay
Mutton Island
Quilty
Doonbeg Bay
Doonbeg
Donegal Point
Kilkee
Moyasta
Kilrush
Loop Head
Carrigaholt
Shannon Estuary
Killimer
Kilbaha
KERRY

1 Trad Sessions in Clare
2 Connemara
3 Galway
4 Music Festivals
5 Cliffs of Moher
6 Clonmacnoise
7 Aran Islands

0 50 km
0 25 miles

Kilcummin
Killala Bay
Killala
Dromore West
Sligo
Ballysadare
N16
FERMANAGH
Ballina
Lough Conn
SLIGO
Tubbercurry
N3
CAVAN
Foxford
Pontoon
Swinford
Charlestown
Straide
Boyle
LEITRIM
Turlough
Kilkelly
Castlebar
N5
Balla
ROSCOMMON
Tulsk
Ballyhaunis
Longford
Claremorris
N61
Partry
Ballymoe
Ballinrobe
Roscommon
LONGFORD
N4
Dunmore
N83
Lough Ree
Athleague
Cong
WESTMEATH
Tuam
River Clare
Headford
Mount Bellew
N63
River Suck
Lough Corrib
Athlone
Moate
Horseleap
M6
Kilbeggan
N59
Moycullen
GALWAY
Ballinahown
Clara
Ballinasloe
Carnmore
Galway
Athenry
Aughrim
Barna
Salthill
Oranmore
Bullaun
M6
Shannonbridge
Rahan
Tullamore
Clarinbridge
Laurencetown
Cloghan
OFFALY
Kilcolgan
Loughrea
River Shannon
Banagher
Frankford
Finavarra Point
Kinvara Bay
N66
Killimor
Fanore
Burren Village
Kinvara
LAOIS
Ballyvaughan
Slieve Aughty Mountains
Portumna
Birr
Kinnitty
Oughtmama Valley
The Burren
Gort
Lisdoonvarna
Carron
Kilfenora
R461
Flagmount
Kilnaboy
Whitegate
Roscrea
N7
Clare Lakelands
Feakle
Ennistymon
Corofin
Cloughjordan
Scarriff
Lough Derg
R460
CLARE
Inagh
Ennis
Tulla
Bodyke
Nenagh
Ogonnelloe
Quin
Broadford
M7
Clarecastle
Killaloe
Ballina
Templemore
Slieve Bernagh Hills
Birdhill
Fergus Bay
Kilmurry
O'Briensbridge
N68
TIPPERARY
Shannon
Knockalough
Cratloe
Bunratty
M8
Limerick
Labasheeda
LIMERICK

Galway, Clare & the West's Highlights

1 Trad Sessions in Clare

Other counties have their distinctive musical styles, but County Clare is the heartland of traditional music: nowhere else will you find such a concentration of talented musicians, singers and dancers.

Need to Know

Best Time to Visit Summers are best for festivals, but off-season *seisúns* are more atmospheric. **Public Transport** Your own transport is best. **For further coverage, see p247.**

Local Knowledge

Trad Sessions in Clare Don't Miss List

BY DICK O'CONNELL, SET DANCE INSTRUCTOR AT THE LIBRARY BAR, ENNIS

1 SET DANCING

I may be a little biased, but there's nowhere better to see the finest set dancing in the country – and to learn the basic steps – than at the **Cois na hAbhna** (p246), where some of the finest talents in Ireland gather on a regular basis to show off their best moves.

2 DOOLIN

Of all of Clare's musical towns and villages, none is more justifiably famous than **Doolin** (p254), which is known throughout the world. Many of the country's top musicians have gone to live there to perfect their craft and enjoy the *blas*, or flavour, of the place, which is all about music and a bit of craic.

3 FESTIVALS

It seems that not a week goes by without there being some kind of traditional music festival. Most are small and relatively informal, but there are a few show-stoppers not to miss. Ennis has the **Fleadh Nua** (p254) and the **Ennis Trad Festival** (p254), and don't forget the **Willie Clancy Irish Music Festival** (p254) in Miltown Malbay.

4 SEISÚNS

From Kinvara to Ennis, the beating heart of traditional music is the informal *seisún* – literally a 'session' where musicians gather for an organised or impromptu gig in a 'music house' (more often than not a pub). Besides the festivals, this is where you'll hear the best music in Ireland. There are also regular ones in Corofin, Ennistymon, Kilrush and Killaloe.

5 KILFENORA CÉILI BAND

Ireland's most recognised *céili* band are the Kilfenora Céili Band, founded in 1909 with a view towards raising money for charity. They've come a long way since then – and you can see many of them playing regularly in **Linnane's** (☎065-708 8157; Main St, Kilfenora).

Connemara

Connemara is the 'real Ireland' and one of the few places where you'll hear Irish spoken in the local pubs. Peat bogs are still being cut and dried by farmers and local fishermen can be seen using *currachs* (rowing boats) on the Killary Fjord.

Need to Know

Best Time to Visit May to July. **Advance Planning** Public transport is patchy; you're better off with your own wheels. **Fitness Levels** There are activities for all fitness levels. **For further coverage, see p237.**

2

Connemara Don't Miss List

BY STEVE WHITFIELD, OUTDOOR INSTRUCTOR, KILLARY ADVENTURE CENTRE

1 KAYAKING THE KILLARY FJORD

As you paddle your way through this mountainous region, often with seals, dolphins and sea otters for company, you can follow the old famine track used during the Great Famine of 1845–9, along the shoreline, all the way to the Atlantic.

2 HIKE THE TWELVE BENS

Although dedicated fell runners have been known to race up all 12 peaks in a single day, just climbing one is an unforgettable experience – the views from the top are spectacular, whether you're looking out on to the coastline or inland to the brooding expanse of Connemara itself.

3 KYLEMORE ABBEY

Kylemore Abbey (pictured above) looks like a fairytale castle shimmering in the lake. It was a castle, but then in 1920, it was handed over to the Benedictines; today it's a girls' school. And while you might just photograph it and move on, you should spend a couple of hours wandering about the castle or the gorgeous gardens.

4 ROUNDSTONE

The road into Roundstone is one of the most spectacular coastal drives in the country, and the village itself is just as beautiful. The lovely coloured terraces are home to some great seafood restaurants and craft shops; the beach is always busy with lobster trawlers and *currachs* (rowing boats); and there are some fine beaches nearby.

5 KILLARY ADVENTURE CENTRE

If you want to get your blood pumping or crave an action-packed adventure while enjoying the surrounds of Connemara, this is the place for you. There's such a huge range of activities – from rock climbing and gorge walking to kayaking and bungee jumps, speed boating and sailing, and lots more.

Galway

The 'City of the Tribes' is one of Ireland's loveliest burgs, a thriving centre that has retained much of its easygoing charm. The real treat is enjoying its wonderful pubs, not least Séhán Ua Neáchtain (p233), a contender for finest watering hole in Ireland, and Tig Cóilí (p233), where Galway's famed traditional musicians take a break from playing for everyone else.

Spanish Arch district, Galway

3

5

Cliffs of Moher

Rising to a height of 203m from the constantly churning Atlantic, the Cliffs of Moher (p251) are one of Ireland's most visited natural attractions. Yet, unlike so many hugely popular wonders, the hype is spot on, especially if you wend your way past the open-mouthed crowds and venture south beyond the viewing areas to observe the entirely vertical cliffs as nature intended them.

4 Music Festivals

Traditional music comes to life in the peat-warmed pubs of Ennistymon, Killaloe, Doolin, Kilfenora and Kinvara, and is also celebrated in festivals throughout the year. Don't miss the Fleadh na gCuach or Cuckoo Festival (p254), which takes place in the scenic village of Kinvara in County Galway over four days in late April/early May. This well-established festival attracts hundreds of musicians from all over the country.

6 Clonmacnoise

Ireland's most important ecclesiastical site, Clonmacnoise (p242) is one of the main reasons Ireland was known as the 'land of saints and scholars'. Scholars and monks from all over Europe came to what was then a thriving city to study, and while it's quieter these days, the ruined temples and cathedral, as well as the superb collection of high crosses, is still very impressive. Cross of the Scriptures, Clonmacnoise

7 Aran Islands

These islands are the embodiment of a traditional, almost mystical Ireland. From the breathtaking stone fort of Dún Aengus (p237) on Inishmór to the jagged, rocky coastlines and sparse population of Inishmaan (p234), they're a powerful reminder of a world that has long since disappeared almost everywhere else – but where you can still get an internet connection and a decent coffee. Inishmaan Island, Aran Islands

Galway, Clare & the West's Best...

Music Houses

- **Tig Cóilí** (p233) Where Galway's musicians go to hear music.
- **Cíaran's Bar** (p245) A nightly trad session.
- **Matt Molloy's** (p259) Owner Matt Molloy plays fife in The Chieftains.
- **O'Friel's Bar** (p250) In the traditional heartland.
- **MacDiarmada's** (p255) The definition of great craic.

Beauty Spots

- **Oughterard** (p239) William Thackeray's idea of heaven.
- **Roundstone** (p239) Stunning harbour village.
- **Croagh Patrick** (p257) The perfect summit.
- **Inishmaan** (p234) Traditional island living.
- **Cliffs of Moher** (p251) Hardly a surprise, but always capable of springing one.

Scenic Drives

- **Sky Road** (p239) A spectacular loop from Clifden to Kingston.
- **Lough Inagh Valley** (p241) Cut through Connemara in the shadow of the brooding Twelve Bens.
- **Killary Harbour** (p241) A drive along Ireland's only fjord.
- **The Burren** (p252) Cut through this bizarre landscape from Ballyvaughan to Ennistymon.
- **Clare Coast** (p244) Scenic coastal route from the Cliffs of Moher to Ballyvaughan.

Unlikely Activities

- **Patrician Pilgrimage** (p257) You don't have to be a believer to be struck by the spirituality of the climb.
- **Get Adventurous** (p241) Try kayaking, rock climbing or spelunking...
- **Go Underground** (p256) Explore the ancient Aillwee Caves.
- **Clonmacnoise Cruise** (p242) Travel the Shannon to the monastic site.
- **Walk the Burren** (p252) A beautiful but bizarre landscape that makes for excellent walks.

Left: Trad session in Matt Molloy's pub (p259), Westport; **Above:** Roundstone (p239), Connemara

Need to Know

ADVANCE PLANNING

- **Two months before** Book hotels, especially in popular areas such as Galway City, Connemara and the music towns of County Clare if there's a festival on.
- **One month before** Book your flight to the Aran Islands if you don't fancy a stormy crossing.
- **Two weeks before** Check out the weather forecast for the likes of an Aran Island crossing. Then ignore it – weather changes every 20 minutes.

RESOURCES

- **Discover Ireland** (www.discoverireland.ie/west)
- **Galway.Net** (www.galway.net) Unofficial tourist site.
- **Visit Mayo** (www.mayo.ie) Attractions, restaurants, pubs and clubs.
- **Surf Mayo** (www.surfmayo.com) Beaches, breaks and other surf info.
- **Visit Clare** (www.visitclare.net) Official East Clare Tourism Authority.

GETTING AROUND

- **Bus** Good bus networks cover most of the region, but it's a slow way of exploring.
- **Train** Only the major towns are served by train – Galway, Ennis and Westport.
- **Car** You'll need your own car to really explore the Burren and Connemara.
- **Boat** The most straightforward way of getting to the Aran Islands.

BE FOREWARNED

- **Crowds** Summer festival season sees throngs flooding into Clare.
- **Weather** The Aran Islands can be weather-bound, making crossings impossible.
- **Reek Sunday** 20,000-plus people will climb Croagh Patrick on the third Sunday in July. You've been warned!

Galway, Clare & the West Itineraries

Follow these itineraries to experience the west's three distinct but interwoven characters – the exciting urban feel of Galway, the rich musical heritage of County Clare and the jaw-dropping beauty of the landscape.

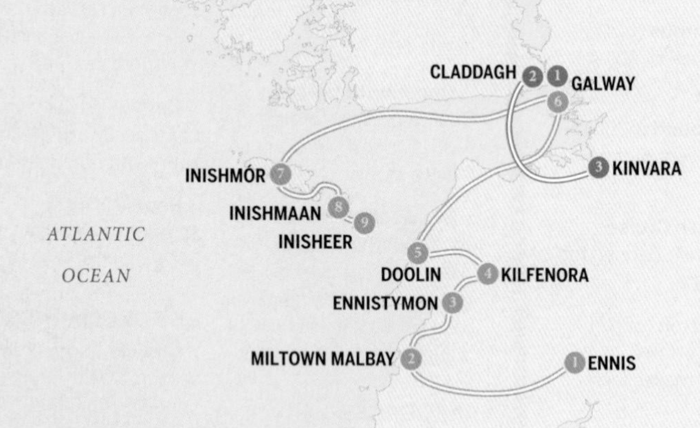

3 DAYS

GALWAY CITY TO KINVARA

Galway & Around

You could spend a week in **(1) Galway City** and not get bored, such is the variety of things to enjoy in the west's largest city. Explore the old city, including the **Spanish Arch** and **medieval walls**, and if you're in town between May and June, make your way up to the **salmon weir** to see the fish pass down on their final descent to the sea. Visit the **house** where James Joyce courted the love of his life, Nora Barnacle. Then indulge the local culture with a pint (or more) in one of Ireland's great bars, **Séhán Ua Neáchtain** – there's a good chance you'll have musical accompaniment of the traditional kind as you quench your thirst. The other great pub in town is **Tig Cóilí**, where musicians go to be entertained by other musicians. If you can tear yourself away, get out of town and visit the small fishing village of **(2) Claddagh** before heading to pretty **(3) Kinvara**, which is the doorway to the Burren and County Clare.

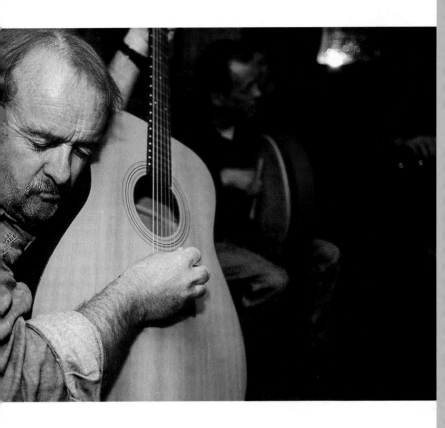

ENNIS TO THE ARAN ISLANDS

A Musical Landscape

This five-day route takes in the traditional charms of the region, both musical and otherwise. Begin in central Clare in **(1) Ennis**, from which you can reach any part of the county in under two hours. Head west to **(2) Miltown Malbay** and begin your exploration of the area's rich musical heritage by attending a formal (or informal) pub 'session' – unless you're a player with any kind of pedigree, you won't be encouraged to join in with more than a toe-tap or hand-clap! Continue your explorations in **(3) Ennistymon** and **(4) Kilfenora** before crossing the heart of the Burren, making a pitstop in **(5) Doolin** before heading towards **(6) Galway City**. From here, take the boat (or plane from Minna, about 35km west of the city) and make the short hop across the choppy waters to **(7) Inishmór** and get to grips with a traditional life that has changed little for centuries. You could easily spend a couple of days here, or use the time to visit the other two islands, **(8) Inishmaan** and **(9) Inisheer**, where life really is untroubled by the demands of the modern age.

Irish musicians, O'Connor's pub (p255), Doolin

Discover Galway, Clare & the West

At a Glance

- **Galway City** (p230) The west's hippest city.
- **Connemara** (p237) Filigreed coastline and stunning interiors.
- **Aran Islands** (p234) Wild, beguiling and very ancient.
- **County Clare** (p244) Beautiful music to match the unique landscape.
- **County Mayo** (p256) In the shadow of Ireland's holiest mountain.

Houses along Galway Bay

PHOTOGRAPHER: JOHN ELK III / LONELY PLANET IMAGES ©

COUNTY GALWAY

Galway City

POP 75,000

Arty, bohemian Galway (Gaillimh) is renowned for its pleasures. Brightly painted pubs heave with live music, while cafes offer front-row seats for observing street performers, weekend hen parties run amok, lovers entwined and more.

Steeped in history, the city nonetheless has a contemporary vibe. Students make up a quarter of its population, and remnants of the medieval town walls lie between shops selling Aran sweaters, handcrafted Claddagh rings, and stacks of secondhand and new books. Bridges arc over the salmon-filled River Corrib, and a long promenade leads to the seaside suburb of Salthill, on Galway Bay, the source of the area's famous oysters.

Sights & Activities

COLLEGIATE CHURCH OF ST NICHOLAS OF MYRA Church

(Market St; admission by donation; 9am-5.45pm Mon-Sat, 1-5pm Sun Apr-Sep, 10am-4pm Mon-Sat, 1-5pm Sun Oct-Mar) Crowned by a pyramidal spire, the Collegiate Church of St Nicholas of Myra is Ireland's largest medieval parish church still in use. Dating from 1320, the church has been rebuilt and enlarged over the centuries, though much of the original form has been retained.

Christopher Columbus reputedly worshipped here in 1477. One theory suggests that the story of Columbus' visit to Galway arose from tales of

St Brendan's 6th-century voyage to America. Seafaring has long been associated with the church – St Nicholas, for whom it's named, is the patron saint of sailors.

HALL OF THE RED EARL Archaeological Site

(www.galwaycivictrust.ie; Druid Lane; admission free; 9.30am-4.45pm Mon-Fri) Back in the 13th century when the de Burgo family ran the show in Galway, Richard – the Red Earl – had a large hall built as a seat of power. Here locals could come looking for favours or to do a little grovelling as a sign of future fealty. After the 14 tribes took over, the hall fell into ruin and was lost. Lost, that is, until 1997 when expansion of the city's Custom House uncovered its foundations. Now after 10 years of archaeological research, the site is open for exploration. The Custom House is built on stilts overhead, leaving the old foundations open. Artefacts and a plethora of fascinating displays give a sense of Galway life 900 years ago.

SPANISH ARCH & MEDIEVAL WALLS Historic Building

Framing the river east of Wolfe Tone Bridge, the Spanish Arch (1584) is thought to be an extension of Galway's medieval walls. The arch appears to have been designed as a passageway through which ships entered the city to unload goods, such as wine and brandy from Spain.

Today it reverberates to the beat of bongo drums, and the lawns and riverside form a gathering place for locals and visitors on any sunny day. Many watch kayakers manoeuvre over the minor rapids of the River Corrib.

SALMON WEIR Landmark

Upstream from Salmon Weir Bridge, which crosses the River Corrib just east of Galway Cathedral, the river cascades down the great weir, one of its final descents before reaching Galway Bay. The weir controls the water levels above it, and when the salmon are running you can often see shoals of them waiting in the clear waters before rushing upriver to spawn.

The salmon and sea-trout seasons usually span February to September, but most fish pass through the weir during May and June.

Sleeping

HOUSE HOTEL Hotel €€€

(091-538 900; www.thehousehotel.ie; Spanish Pde; r €100-200; P) It's a design odyssey at this boutique hotel. Public spaces contrast modern art with trad details and bold accents. The 40 rooms are plush, with beds having elaborately padded headboards (so you don't bonk your, er, well…) and a range of colour schemes. Bathrooms are commodious and ooze comfort.

ST MARTINS B&B B&B €€

(091-568 286; 2 Nun's Island Rd; s/d from €50/80; @) This beautifully kept, renovated older house right on the canal has a flower-filled garden overlooking the William O'Brien Bridge and the River Corrib. The four rooms have all the comforts and the breakfast is a few cuts above the norm (fresh-squeezed OJ!). Owner Mary Sexton wins raves.

SKEFFINGTON ARMS HOTEL Hotel €€

(091-563 173; www.skeffington.ie; Eyre Sq; r €65-160; @) Rooms at the Skeff, overlooking Eyre Sq, eschew the frilly cliché. In fact the only lace you may find in any of the 24 rooms is on your underwear. Pass through the arched traditional entrance into a minimalist haven. Air-con allows early risers to cut out noise from the frolicsome masses roaming the streets on long summer nights.

Eating

CAVA Spanish €€

(www.cavarestaurant.ie; 51 Lower Dominick St; meals €10-25; noon-10pm, later Fri & Sat) The best tapas in Ireland? Possibly yes. Now that no one can afford a trip to Iberia the next best thing is a meal at this superb West Side storefront. From typical fare

Galway

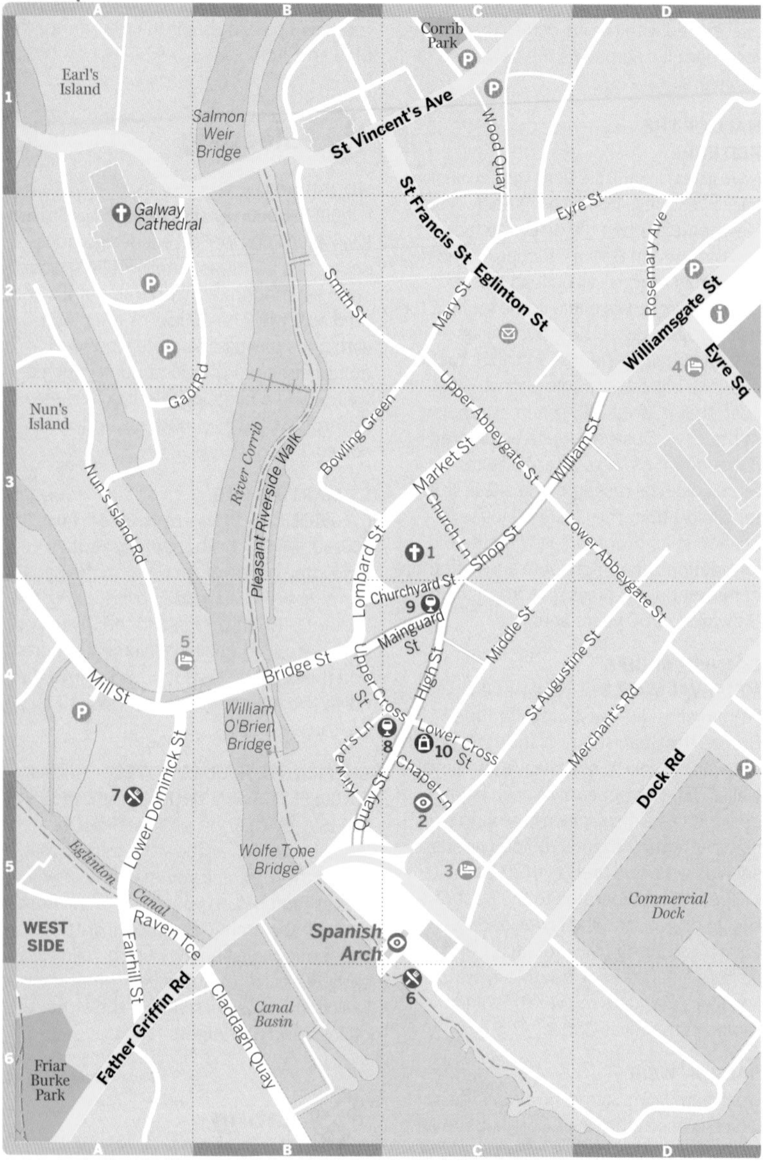

A B C D
1 2 3 4 5 6
Corrib Park
Earl's Island
Salmon Weir Bridge
St Vincent's Ave
Wood Quay
Galway Cathedral
St Francis St
Eyre St
Rosemary Ave
Smith St
Mary St
Eglinton St
Williamsgate St
Eyre Sq
Gaol Rd
Nun's Island
Bowling Green
Upper Abbeygate St
River Corrib
Pleasant Riverside Walk
Market St
William St
Nun's Island Rd
Church Ln
Lombard St
Shop St
Lower Abbeygate St
Churchyard St
Mainguard St
Bridge St
Upper Cross St
High St
Middle St
St Augustine St
Mill St
William O'Brien Bridge
Kirwan's Ln
Lower Cross St
Merchant's Rd
Lower Dominick St
Chapel Ln
Quay St
Dock Rd
Wolfe Tone Bridge
Eglinton Canal
Raven Tce
Commercial Dock
WEST SIDE
Fairhill St
Spanish Arch
Father Griffin Rd
Claddagh Quay
Canal Basin
Friar Burke Park

like roasted potatoes with aioli to more fanciful dishes such as free-range quail with dried figs, the kitchen's efforts never fail to astound.

ARD BIA AT NIMMO'S Modern Irish €€

(www.ardbia.com; Spanish Arch; cafe dishes €6-12, lunch mains €10-14, dinner mains €16-30; cafe noon-3pm Wed-Sun, restaurant 6.30-

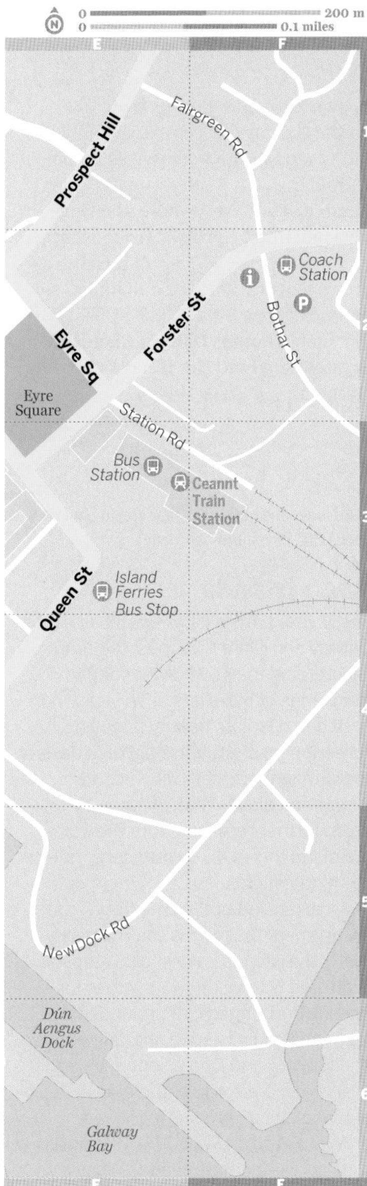

10.30pm Wed-Sat) In Irish, Ard Bia means 'High Food', and that's somewhat apt, given its location in the 18th-century customs house near the Spanish Arch. Local seafood and organic produce feature on the seasonal menu in a setting that

Galway

Top Sights

Spanish Arch C5

Sights

1 Collegiate Church of St Nicholas of Myra C3
2 Hall of the Red Earl C5

Sleeping

3 House Hotel C5
4 Skeffington Arms Hotel D2
5 St Martin's B&B A4

Eating

6 Ard Bia at Nimmo's C6
7 Cava A5

Drinking

8 Séhán Ua Neáchtain C4
9 Tig Cóilí C4

Shopping

10 Thomas Dillon's Claddagh Gold C4

defines funky chic. The cafe is a perfect place for a coffee and carrot cake.

Drinking

SÉHÁN UA NEÁCHTAIN Pub

(17 Upper Cross St) Painted a bright cornflower blue, this 19th-century pub, known simply as Neáchtain's (*nock*-tans) or Naughtons, has a wrap-around string of tables outside, many shaded by a large tree. It's a place where a polyglot mix of locals plop down and let the world pass them by – or stop and join them for a pint.

TIG CÓILÍ Pub

(Mainguard St) Two live *céilidh* a day draw the crowds to this authentic fire-engine-red pub, just off High St. It's where musicians go to get drunk or drunks go to become musicians...or something like that. A gem.

Information

Tourist Information

Ireland Tourism (www.discoverireland.ie; Forster St; 9am-5.45pm daily Easter-Sep, 9am-5.45pm

Claddagh Rings

The fishing village of Claddagh once had its own king as well as its own customs and traditions. Now subsumed into the Galway city centre, virtually all remnants of the original village are gone, but Claddagh rings survive as both a timeless reminder and a timeless source of profits.

Popular with people of real or imagined Irish descent everywhere, the rings depict a heart (symbolising love) between two outstretched hands (friendship), topped by a crown (loyalty). Rings are handcrafted at jewellers around Galway, and start from about €20 for a silver band to well over €1000 for a diamond-set blinged-up version worthy of Tony O'Soprano.

Jewellers include Ireland's oldest jewellery shop, **Thomas Dillon's Claddagh Gold** (www.claddaghring.ie; 1 Quay St), which was established in 1750. It has some vintage examples in its small back-room 'museum'.

Mon-Sat Oct-Easter) Large, efficient regional information centre that can help arrange local accommodation, and bus tours and ferry trips.

Getting There & Away

Bus

Bus Éireann (www.buseireann.ie) has services to all major cities in the Republic and the North from the **bus station** (091-562 000) just off Eyre Sq, near the train station. The one-way fare to Dublin (three to 3¾ hours, hourly) is €15. Other services fan out across the region, including buses to County Clare and Sligo.

Several private bus companies are based at the glossy **coach station** (Bothar St), which is located near the tourist office. They include the following:

Citylink (www.citylink.ie) Offers service to Dublin (2½ to 3¼ hours, hourly), Dublin Airport, Cork, Limerick and Connemara. Departures are frequent and fares are as low as €10.

gobus.ie (www.gobus.ie) Frequent service to Dublin (2½ hours) and Dublin Airport (three hours). Buses have wi-fi.

Train

From the **train station** (091-564 222; www.irishrail.ie), just off Eyre Sq, there are up to eight fast, comfortable trains daily to/from Dublin's Heuston Station (one-way from €25, 2¾ hours). Connections with other train routes can be made at Athlone (one hour). The new line to Ennis is open (€12, 75 minutes, six daily).

Aran Islands

Easily visible from large swaths of coastal Galway and Clare Counties, the Aran Islands sing their own siren song to thousands of travellers each year who find their desolate beauty beguiling. Day-trippers shuttle through in a daze of rocky magnificence, while those who stay longer find places that, in many ways, seem further removed from the Irish mainland than a 40-minute ferry ride or 10-minute flight.

An extension of the limestone escarpment that forms the Burren in Clare, the islands have shallow topsoil scattered with wildflowers, grass for grazing and jagged cliffs pounded by surf. Ancient forts such as Dún Aengus on Inishmór and Dún Chonchúir on Inishmaan are some of the oldest archaeological remains in Ireland.

A web of stone walls (1600km in all) runs across all three islands. They also have a smattering of early *clochán*s (drystone beehive huts from the early Christian period), resembling stone igloos.

Although quite close in appearance as well as proximity, the three Arans have distinct personalities:

Inishmór (Árainn in Irish, meaning 'Big Island') The largest Aran and the most easily accessible from Galway. It is home to one of Ireland's most important and impressive archaeological sites, as well as some lively pubs and restaurants, particularly in the only town, Kilronan. Gets over a thousand or more day-trippers in summer.

Inishmaan (Inis Meáin, 'Middle Island') Often bypassed by the majority of tourist traffic, preserving its age-old traditions and evoking a sense of timelessness. It is a place of great solitude with isolated B&Bs and stark rocky vistas.

Inisheer (Inis Oírr, 'Eastern Island') The smallest island is easily reached from Galway year-round and from Doolin in the summer months. It offers a good combination of ancient sites, interesting walks, trad culture and a bit of life at night.

Hardy travellers find that low season showcases the islands at their wild, wind-swept best.

Getting There & Away

AIR

All three islands have landing strips. The mainland departure point is Connemara regional airport at Minna, near Inverin (Indreabhán), about 35km west of Galway. Aer Arann Islands (☎091-593 034; www.aerarannislands.ie) offers return flights to each of the islands several times daily (hourly in summer) for adult/child/student €45/25/37; the flights take about 10 minutes, and groups of four or more can get group rates.

BOAT

Island Ferries (☎091-568 903; www.aranislandferries.com; 37-39 Forster St, Galway; adult/child/student €25/13/20) Serves all three islands and also links Inishmaan and Inisheer. Schedules peak in July and August, with several boats a day. The crossing can take up to one hour and is subject to cancellation in high seas. Boats leave from Rossaveal, 40km west of Galway City on the R336. Buses from Galway (€6 return) connect with the sailings; ask when you book.

Ferries to the Arans (primarily Inisheer) also operate from Doolin (p255).

Festivals of Fun

Galway's packed calendar of festivals turns the city and surrounding communities into what feels like one nonstop party – streets overflow with revellers, and pubs and restaurants often extend their opening hours.

Highlights include the following:

Cúirt International Festival of Literature (www.galwayartscentre.ie/cuirt) Top-name authors converge on Galway in April for one of Ireland's premier literary festivals, featuring poetry slams, theatrical performances and readings.

Galway Arts Festival (www.galwayartsfestival.ie) A two-week extravaganza of theatre, music, art and comedy in mid-July.

Galway Film Fleadh (www.galwayfilmfleadh.com) One of Ireland's biggest film festivals, held in July around the same time as the arts festival.

Galway Race Week (www.galwayraces.com) Horse races in Ballybrit, 3km east of the city, are the centrepiece of Galway's biggest, most boisterous festival of all. Thursday is a real knees-up: by night the swells have muddy knees on their tuxes and are missing random high heels. The week occurs in late July or early August.

Galway International Oyster Festival (www.galwayoysterfest.com) Oysters are washed down with plenty of pints in the last week in September.

Island-Hopping the Arans

It's possible to bounce between the three Aran Islands, allowing you to start at one and return to the mainland from another. However, schedules are geared to return trips to a single island. In order to find ferries between the islands, you'll need to consult with Island Ferries as well as the boats operating from Doolin. There will be at least one connection a day between any two islands; just be prepared for ad hoc schedules. Fares should run from €5 to €10.

Inishmór

POP 850

Most visitors who venture out to the islands don't make it beyond Inishmór (Árainn) and its main attraction, Dún Aengus, the stunning stone fort perched perilously on the island's towering cliffs. The arid landscape west of Kilronan (Cill Rónáin), Inishmór's main settlement, is dominated by stone walls, boulders, scattered buildings and the odd patch of deep-green grass and potato plants.

Sleeping

KILMURVEY HOUSE B&B **€€**

(099-61218; www.kilmurveyhouse.com; Kilmurvey; s/d from €65/110; Apr-Sep) On the path leading to Dún Aengus is this grand 18th-century stone mansion. It's a beautiful setting, and the 12 rooms are well maintained. Hearty meals (dinner €30) incorporate vegetables from the garden, and local fish and meats. You can swim at a pretty beach that's a short walk from the house.

Eating & Drinking

JOE WATTY'S BAR Pub

(Kilronan) This is the best pub in Kilronan, with traditional sessions most nights and rather posh pub food (noon to 8pm) from June to August. Turf fires warm the air on the 50 weeks a year when this is needed.

TÍ JOE MAC'S Pub

(Kilronan) Informal music sessions, turf fires and a broad terrace with harbour views make Tí Joe Mac's a local favourite. Food is limited to a few sandwiches slapped together between pints.

Shopping

Glossy shops in Kilronan sell Aran-style sweaters that come with gaudy labels that obfuscate their origins (never the islands, often not Ireland at all).

MARY O'FLAHERTY Crafts

(099-61117; Oat Quarter) For an authentic hand-knitted version, visit Mary O'Flaherty. Chances are you'll see Mary knitting when you call in. Expect to pay around €100 for the genuine article.

Information

Tourist office (099-61263; Kilronan; 10am-5.45pm May-Sep, 11am-5pm Oct-May) Useful office on the waterfront west of the ferry pier in Kilronan. This is the place for local books and maps – especially the highly recommended *The Aran Islands* by JM Synge.

Getting Around

The airstrip is 2km southeast of town; a shuttle to Kilronan costs €5 return.

You can bring your own bicycle on the ferry for free. Most places to stay have bicycles for use or rent (universally €10 per day).

Burke Bicycle Hire (087 280 8273) Patrick Burke is an expert on local cycling and can advise on routes that avoid crowds and reach seldom-visited ends of the island.

Inishmaan

POP 150

The least-visited of the islands, with the smallest population, Inishmaan (Inis Meáin) is a rocky respite. Inishmaan's scenery is breathtaking, with a jagged coastline of startling cliffs, empty beaches,

© KEN WELSH / ALAMY

Don't Miss Dún Aengus

Three spectacular forts stand guard over Inishmór, each believed to be around 2000 years old. Chief among them is Dún Aengus, which has three nonconcentric walls that run right up to sheer drops to the ocean below. It is protected by remarkable *chevaux de frise,* fearsome and densely packed defensive stone spikes that surely helped deter ancient armies from invading the site.

Powerful swells pound the 60m-high cliff face. A complete lack of rails or other modern additions that would spoil this amazing ancient site means that you can not only go right up to the cliff's edge but also potentially fall to your doom below quite easily. When it's uncrowded, you can't help but feel the extraordinary energy that must have been harnessed to build this vast site.

THINGS YOU NEED TO KNOW

Dún Aonghasa; www.heritageireland.ie; adult/child €3/1; ⌚10am-6pm

and fields where the main crop seems to be stone.

Inisheer

POP 200

Inisheer (Inis Oírr), the smallest of the Aran Islands, has a palpable sense of enchantment, enhanced by the island's deep-rooted mythology, its devotion to traditional culture and ethereal landscapes.

Connemara

Think of the best crumble you've ever had, one with a craggy crust that accumulates hollows of perfect flavour. Similarly, the filigreed coast of the Connemara Peninsula is endlessly pleasing, with pockets of sheer delight awaiting discovery.

Connemara

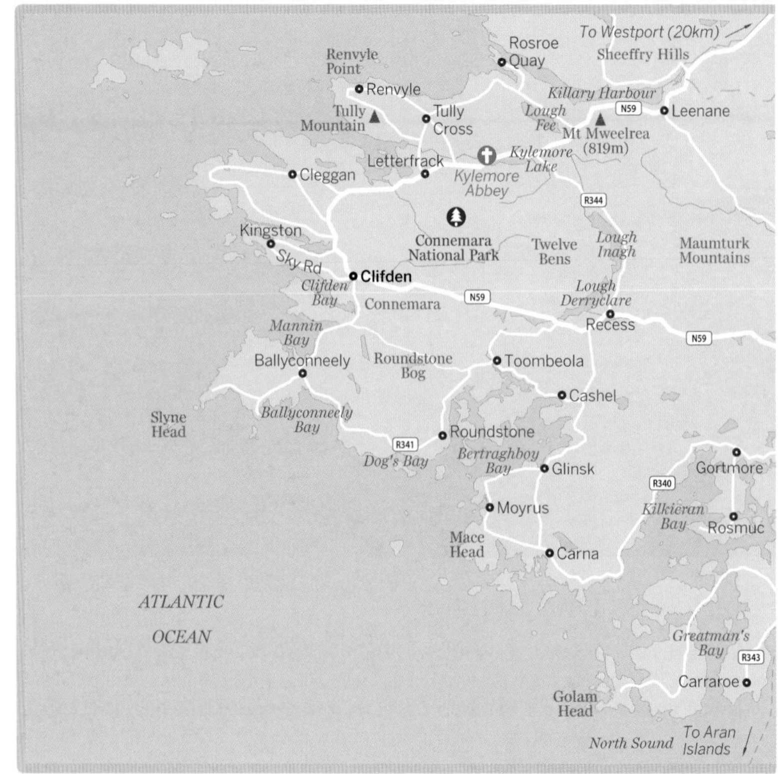

Information

Galway's tourist office (p233) has a wealth of information on the area. Online, **Connemara Tourism** (www.connemara.ie) and **Go Connemara** (www.goconnemara.com) have region-wide info and links.

Getting There & Around

BUS

Organised tours from Galway (p233) are plentiful and offer a good overview of the region, though ideally you'll want more than one day to absorb the area's charms, plus you'll want the freedom to make your own discoveries.

Bus Éireann (091-562 000; www.buseireann.ie) Serves most of Connemara. Services can be sporadic, and many buses operate May to September only, or July and August only. Some drivers will stop in between towns.

Citylink (www.citylink.ie) Has several buses a day linking Galway city with Clifden, with stops in Moycullen, Oughterard, Maam Cross and Recess, and on to Cleggan and Letterfrack. If you're going somewhere between towns, you might be able to arrange a drop-off with the driver.

CAR

Your own wheels are the best way to get off this scenic region's beaten track – though watch out for the narrow roads' stone walls, just waiting to scrape the sides of your car.

Keep an eye out, too, for meandering Connemara sheep – characterised by thick creamy fleece and coal-black faces and legs – which frequently wander onto the road. Even Connemara's flattest stretches of road tend to be bumpy due to the uneven bog beneath the tarmac.

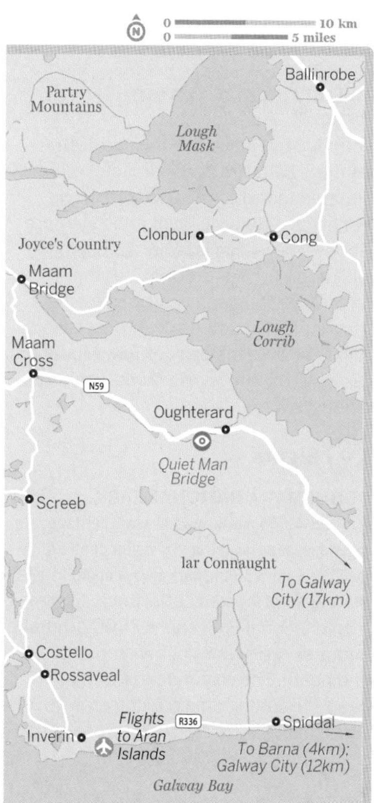

Oughterard & Around

POP 2400

The writer William Makepeace Thackeray sang the praises of the small town of Oughterard (Uachtar Árd), saying, 'A more beautiful village can scarcely be seen'. Even if those charms have faded over the years, it still makes a good gateway to Connemara. And it is one of Ireland's principal angling centres.

Getting There & Away

Bus Éireann (www.buseireann.ie) and **Citylink** (www.citylink.ie) have regular buses from Galway to Oughterard.

Roundstone

POP 400

Clustered around a boat-filled harbour, Roundstone (Cloch na Rón) is one of Connemara's gems. Colourful terrace houses and inviting pubs overlook the dark recess of Bertraghboy Bay, which is home to lobster trawlers and traditional *currachs* with tarred canvas bottoms stretched over wicker frames.

Sleeping & Eating

ROUNDSTONE HOUSE Hotel **€€**

(091-35864; www.roundstonehousehotel.com; Main St; s/d from €50/90; Apr-Oct) A dignified presence lining Main St, this sprawling inn has 13 restful rooms with tea kettles and other creature comforts, plus views across the bay. The pub, Vaughan's, has trad sessions some nights in summer, and you can enjoy pints and local seafood out on the terrace.

O'DOWD'S Seafood **€€**

(091-35809; Main St; mains €15-22; restaurant noon-10pm Apr-Sep, noon-3pm & 6-9.30pm Oct-Mar) This well-worn, comfortable old pub hasn't lost any of its authenticity since it starred in the 1997 Hollywood flick *The Matchmaker*. Specialities at its adjoining restaurant include seafood sourced off the old stone dock right across the street.

Clifden

POP 1800

Connemara's 'capital', Clifden (An Clochán), is an appealing Victorian-era country town with an amoeba-shaped oval of streets offering evocative strolls. It presides over the head of the narrow bay where the River Owenglin tumbles into the sea. The surrounding countryside beckons you to walk through woods and above the shoreline.

Sights & Activities

SKY ROAD Scenic Route

This 12km route traces a spectacular loop out to the township of Kingston and back to Clifden, taking in some rugged, stunningly beautiful coastal scenery en route. The round trip of about 12km can be easily walked or cycled, but, if you're short on time, you can also drive. Head directly west from Clifden's Market Sq.

Sleeping

LPHIN BEACH B&B €€
(095-21204; www.dolphinbeachhouse.com; Lower Sky Rd; r €80-180; P) It's hard to find the bones of the 19th-century manor house that forms the basis for this posh B&B set amid some of Connemara's best coastal scenery. Clean lines abound in the bright common areas and in the plush yet relaxed rooms. It's 5km west of Clifden.

Eating & Drinking

MITCHELL'S Seafood €€
(095-21867; Market St; mains €15-25; noon-10pm Mar-Oct) Seafood takes centre stage at this elegant spot. From a velvety chowder right through a long list of ever-changing specials, the produce of the surrounding waters is honoured. The wine list does the food justice. Book for dinner. (Lunch specials include sandwiches and casual fare.)

MULLARKY'S PUB Pub
(Main St) Another Foyle family production, this rollicking pub is a riot of local merriment, with live music many nights. Join the fun and you may need to stay in Clifden longer than you thought.

Letterfrack & Around

POP 200

Founded by Quakers in the mid-19th century, Letterfrack (Leitir Fraic) is ideally situated for exploring Connemara National Park, Renvyle Point and Kylemore Abbey. The village is really a crossroads with a few pubs and B&Bs, but the forested setting and nearby coast are a magnet for outdoors adventure seekers. A 4km walk to the peak of Tully Mountain takes 40 minutes and affords wonderful ocean views.

Sights

CONNEMARA NATIONAL PARK Park
(095-41054; www.npws.ie, www.heritageireland.ie; admission free; visitor centre & facilities 9am-5.30pm, park always open) Immediately southeast of Letterfrack, Connemara National Park spans 2000 dramatic hectares (20 sq km) of bog, mountain and heath. The visitor centre is in a beautiful setting off a parking area 300m south of the Letterfrack crossroads.

Bridging the Quiet Man

Whenever an American cable TV station needs a ratings boost (and they've already just shown *Gone With the Wind*), they trot out the iconic 1952 film *The Quiet Man*. Starring John Wayne and filmed in lavish colour to capture the crimson locks of his co-star Maureen O'Hara, the film regularly makes the top-10 lists of aging romantic-comedy lovers for its high-energy portrayal of rural Irish life, replete with drinking and fighting, fighting and drinking etc.

Director John Ford returned to his Irish roots and filmed the movie almost entirely on location in Connemara and the little village of Cong, just over the border in County Mayo. One of the most photogenic spots from the film, the eponymous **Quiet Man Bridge**, is just 3km west of Oughterard off the N59. Looking much as it did in the film, the picture-perfect little arched span (whose original name was Leam Bridge) would be a lovely spot even if it hadn't achieved screen immortality. Purists will note, however, that the scene based here had close-ups done on a cheesy set back in Hollywood. That's showbiz.

Hard-core fans will want to buy the superb *The Complete Guide to The Quiet Man* by Des MacHale. It is sold in most tourist offices in the area.

© VINCENT LOWE / ALAMY

Don't Miss Lough Inagh Valley

Magnificent desolation. If Buzz Aldrin hadn't said it on the moon, we'd say it here. Okay, we will anyway. This stark brown landscape beguiles by its very simplicity. Cloud shadows throw patterns on the jutting peaks; pause and let the ceaseless winds tousle your hair.

The R344 enters the valley from the south, just west of playfully named Recess. The moody waters of Loughs Derryclare and Inagh reflect the colours of the moment. On the western side is the brooding **Twelve Bens** mountain range. At the north end of the valley, the R344 meets the N59, which loops around Connemara to Leenane (p241).

Towards the northern end of the valley, a track leads west off the road up a blind valley, which is well worth exploring.

KYLEMORE ABBEY Historic Building

(www.kylemoreabbey.com; adult/child €12/free; 9am-7pm summer, 10am-4.30pm winter) A few kilometres east of Letterfrack stands Kylemore Abbey. Magnificently situated on the shores of a lake, this crenulated 19th-century neo-Gothic fantasy was built for a wealthy English businessman, Mitchell Henry, who spent his honeymoon in Connemara.

Getting There & Away

Bus Éireann (www.buseireann.ie) and **Citylink** (www.citylink.ie) buses continue to Letterfrack several times daily from Clifden, 15km southwest on the N59.

Leenane & Killary Harbour

The small village of Leenane (also spelled Leenaun) drowses on the shore of dramatic Killary Harbour. Dotted with mussel rafts, the long, narrow harbour is Ireland's only fjord – maybe. Slicing 16km inland and more than 45m deep in the centre, it certainly looks like a fjord, although some scientific studies suggest it may not actually have been glaciated. Mt Mweelrea (819m) towers to its north.

Activities

ILLARY CRUISES Boat Cruises
(**www.killarycruises.com; adult/child €21/10; Apr-Oct**) From Nancy's Point, about 2km west of Leenane, Killary Cruises offers 1½-hour cruises of Killary Harbour. Dolphins leap around the boat, which passes by a mussel farm and stops at a salmon farm, where you'll see the fish being fed. There are four cruises daily in summer.

KILLARY ADVENTURE CENTRE
Adventure Activities
(**095-43411; www.killaryadventure.com; 10am-5pm**) Canoeing, sea kayaking, sailing, rock climbing, windsurfing and day hikes are but a few of the activities on offer at this adventure centre approximately 3km west of Leenane on the N59. Rates begin at adult/child €48/32.

Sleeping & Eating

DELPHI LODGE Inn €€€
(**095-42222; www.delphilodge.ie; s/d from €130/200; P @ **) You'll wish the dreamy views at this gorgeous country estate could follow you into your dreams. Set among truly stunning mountain and lake vistas, this isolated country house has 12 posh bedrooms and a bevy of common areas including a library and billiards room. The cooking is modern Irish, sourced locally. Meals are taken at a vast communal table. Walks, fishing and much more await outside.

South of Galway City

Kinvara

POP 400

The small stone harbour of Kinvara (sometimes spelt Kinvarra) sits smugly at the southeastern corner of Galway Bay, which accounts for its Irish name, Cinn Mhara (Head of the Sea). It's a posh little village, the kind of place where all the jeans have creases in them. It makes a good pit stop between Galway and Clare.

Eating & Drinking

KEOUGH'S Pub €€
(**Main St, Kinvara; mains €8-25; kitchen 9am-10pm**) This friendly local, where you'll often hear Irish spoken, serves up a fresh battered cod; specials are more ambitious and allow the kitchen to show off its considerable talents. Traditional music sessions take place on Mondays and Thursdays, while Saturday nights swing with old-time dancing.

CLONMACNOISE

Gloriously placed overlooking the River Shannon, **Clonmacnoise** (**Clonmacnoise; www.heritageireland.ie; adult/child €6/2; 9am-7pm mid-May–mid-Sep, 10am-5.30pm mid-Sep–mid-May, last admission 45min before**

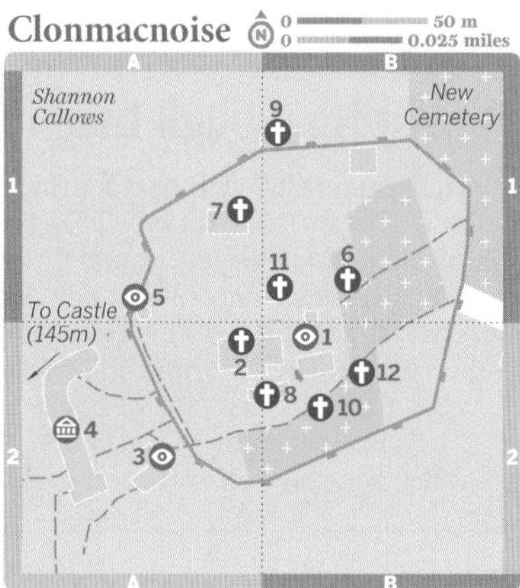

Clonmacnoise

Sights

1 Bullaun B2
2 Cathedral A2
3 Entrance A2
4 Museum A2
5 O'Rourke's Tower A1
6 Temple Ciarán B1
7 Temple Connor A1
8 Temple Doolin B2
9 Temple Finghin & Tower B1
10 Temple Hurpan B2
11 Temple Kelly B1
12 Temple Melaghlin B2

closing; P) is one of Ireland's most important ancient monastic cities. The site is enclosed in a walled field and contains numerous early churches, high crosses, round towers and graves in astonishingly good condition. The surrounding marshy area is know as the **Shannon Callows**.

History

Roughly translated, Clonmacnoise (Cluain Mhic Nóis) means 'Meadow of the Sons of Nós'. The marshy land in the area would have been impassable for early traders, who instead chose to travel by water or on eskers (raised ridges formed by glaciers). When St Ciarán founded a monastery here in AD 548, it was the most important crossroads in the country, the intersection of the north–south River Shannon, and the east–west Esker Riada (Highway of the Kings).

The giant ecclesiastical city had a humble beginning and Ciarán died just seven months after building his first church. Over the years, however, Clonmacnoise grew to become an unrivalled bastion of Irish religion, literature and art and attracted a large lay population. Between the 7th and 12th centuries, monks from all over Europe came to study and pray here, helping to earn Ireland the title of the 'land of saints and scholars'. Even the high kings of Connaught and Tara were brought here for burial.

Sights

MUSEUM

Three connected conical huts near the entrance, housing the museum, echo the design of early monastic dwellings. The centre's 20-minute audiovisual show is an excel introduction to the site.

The exhibition area contair original high crosses (replicas put in their former locations ou and various artefacts uncoverec excavation, including silver pins, glass and an Ogham stone. It also contains the largest collection of early Christian grave slabs in Europe. Many are in remarkable condition, with inscriptions clearly visible, often starting with *oroit do or ar* (a prayer for).

CATHEDRAL

The biggest building at Clonmacnoise, the cathedral was originally built in AD 909, but was significantly altered and remodelled over the centuries. Its most interesting feature is the intricate 15th-century Gothic doorway with carvings of Sts Francis, Patrick and Dominic. A whisper carries from one side of the door to the other, and this feature was supposedly used by lepers to confess their sins without infecting the priests.

Clomnacnoise cross

TEMF
Th

ES

e small churches are called temples, a derivation of the Irish word *teampall*. The little roofed church is **Temple Connor**, still used by Church of Ireland parishioners on the last Sunday of the summer months. Walking towards the cathedral, you'll pass the scant foundations of **Temple Kelly** (1167) before reaching tiny **Temple Ciarán**, reputed to be the burial place of St Ciarán, the site's founder.

Near the temple's southwestern corner is a *bullaun* (ancient grinding stone), supposedly used for making medicines for the monastery's hospital. Today the rainwater that collects in it is said to cure warts.

Continuing round the compound you come to the 12th-century **Temple Melaghlin**, with its attractive windows, and the twin structures of **Temple Hurpan** and **Temple Doolin**.

ROUND TOWERS

Overlooking the River Shannon is the 20m-high **O'Rourke's Tower**. Lightning blasted the top off the tower in 1135, but the remaining structure was used for another 400 years.

Temple Finghin and its round tower are on the northern boundary of the site, also overlooking the Shannon. The building dates from around 1160 and has some fine Romanesque carvings. The herringbone-patterned tower roof is the only one in Ireland that has never been altered. Most round towers became shelters when the monasteries were attacked, but this one was probably just used as a bell tower since the doorway is at ground level.

Getting There & Away

Clonmacnoise is 7km northeast of Shannonbridge on the R444 and about 24km south of Athlone in County Westmeath.

BOAT **Silver Line** (www.silverlinecruisers.com; adult/child €12/8; 2pm Wed & Sun Jul & Aug) Runs boat trips from Shannonbridge to Clonmacnoise.

There are also river and bus tours to Clonmacnoise from Athlone in County Westmeath.

TAXI A taxi from Athlone will cost roughly €50 to €70 round trip, including an hour's wait.

COUNTY CLARE

Ennis

POP 19,000

Ennis (Inis) is the busy commercial centre of Clare. It lies on the banks of the smallish River Fergus, which runs east, then south into the Shannon Estuary.

It's the place to stay if you want a bit of urban flair; from Ennis, you can reach any part of Clare in under two hours. Short on sights, the town's strengths are its food, lodging and

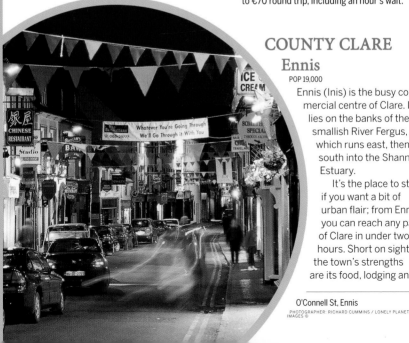

O'Connell St, Ennis

PHOTOGRAPHER: RICHARD CUMMINS / LONELY PLANET IMAGES ©

Ennis

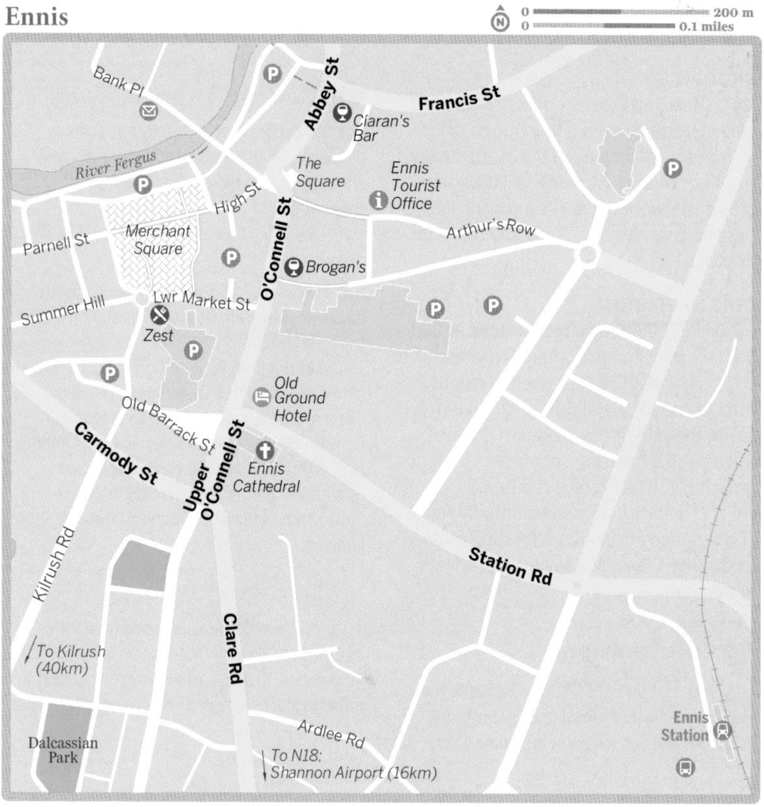

traditional entertainment. The town centre, with its narrow, pedestrian-friendly streets, is good for shopping.

Sleeping

OLD GROUND HOTEL Hotel €€

(**065-682 8127; www.flynnhotels.com; O'Connell St; s/d from €90/140; P @ **) The lobby at this local institution is always a scene: old friends sprawl on the sofas, deals are cut at the tables and ladies from the neighbouring church's altar society exchange gossip over tea. Parts of this rambling landmark date back to the 1800s.

The 83 rooms vary greatly in size and decor – don't hesitate to inspect a few. On balmy days, retire to tables on the lawn.

Eating

ZEST Food Hall €

(**Market Pl; meals €5-10; 8am-6pm Mon-Sat**) A much-welcomed addition to Ennis' fresh food scene, Zest combines a deli, bakery, shop and cafe. Excellent prepared foods from the region are offered along with salads, soups and much more. It's ideal for a coffee or lunch.

Drinking & Entertainment

CÍARAN'S BAR Pub

(**Francis St**) Slip into this small place by day and you can be just another geezer pondering a pint. At night there's usually trad music. We bet you wish you had a copy of the Guinness mural out front!

BROGAN'S Pub

(24 O'Connell St) On the corner of Cooke's Lane, Brogan's sees a fine bunch of musicians rattling even the stone floors from about 9pm Monday to Thursday, plus even more nights in summer. It's a big pub that rambles from one room to another.

COIS NA HABHNA Live Music

(065-682 0996; www.coisnahabhna.ie; Gort Rd) This pilgrimage point for traditional music and culture is housed in a custom-built pentagonal hall 1.5km north of town along the N18. It has frequent performances and a full range of classes in dance and music. The archive is a resource centre and a library of Irish traditional music, song, dance and folklore relating mainly to County Clare; books and recordings are on sale.

Information

Ennis Tourist Office (065-682 8366; www.visitennis.ie; Arthur's Row; 9.30am-1pm & 2-5.30pm Tue-Sat, longer hr in summer) Very helpful and efficient. Can book accommodation for a €4 fee; lots of shamrock-embellished gifts.

Getting There & Away

The N18 bypass east of the city lets traffic between Limerick and Galway whiz right past, although trips to the coast still take you through the centre.

Bus

Bus Éireann (065-682 4177; www.buseireann.ie) Services operate from the bus station beside the train station.

Buses run from Ennis to Cork (€15, three hours, nine daily); Doolin (€12, 1½ hours, two daily) via Corofin, Ennistymon, Lahinch and Liscannor; Galway (€9, 1½ hours, hourly) via Gort; Limerick (€9, 40 minutes, hourly) via Bunratty; and Shannon Airport (€7, 50 minutes, hourly).

To reach Dublin (€19), connect through Limerick.

Train

Irish Rail (www.irishrail.ie) trains from **Ennis station (065-684 0444)** serve Limerick (€9, 40 minutes, 10 daily), where you can connect to trains to places further afield like Dublin. The line

Bunratty Castle (p247), County Clare

RICHARD CUMMINS / LONELY PLANET IMAGES ©

Finding Traditional Music in County Clare

From atmospheric small pubs in tiny villages where non-instrument-playing patrons are a minority to rollicking urban boozers in Ennis, Clare is one of Ireland's best counties for traditional music. Eschewing any modern influences from rock or even polkas (as is heard elsewhere), Clare's musicians stick resolutely to the jigs and reels of old, often with little vocal accompaniment.

Although you can find pubs with trad sessions at least one night a week in almost every town and village, the following are our picks for where to start.

- **Doolin** A much-hyped collection of pubs with nightly trad music sessions. However, tourist crowds can erase any sense of intimacy or even enjoyment.
- **Ennis** You can bounce from one music-filled pub to another on most nights, especially in the summer. Musicians from around the county come here to show off and there are good venues for serious trad pursuits.
- **Ennistymon** A low-key farming village inland from Doolin with a couple of ancient pubs that attract superb local talent.
- **Kilfenora** Small village with a big musical heritage, which you'll also find at the great local pub Vaughan's.
- **Miltown Malbay** This tiny village hosts the annual Willie Clancy Irish Music Festival, one of Ireland's best music festivals. The talented locals can be heard performing through the year in several old pubs.

to Galway (€12, 75 minutes, six daily) is now open and features good Burren scenery.

Bunratty

Conveniently located beside the N18 motorway and with plenty of bus-sized parking, Bunratty (Bun Raite) – home to government schemes for hawking tourism hard – draws more tourists than any other place in the region. The namesake castle has stood over the area for centuries. In recent decades it's been spiffed up and surrounded by attractions. A theme park re-creates a clichéd Irish village of old (where's the horseshit, lash and disease, we ask?) and each year more and more shops crowd the access roads – many selling authentic Irish goods just out of the container from China. There are some rather pricey dining options.

Groups lay siege to Bunratty from April to October. With all the hoopla, it's easy to overlook the actual village, which is at the back of the theme park. It is a pretty place and has numerous leafy spots to stay and eat. It's good if you want something close to Shannon Airport, only 5km west.

Sights & Activities

There's a joint-entry-fee ticket to the **castle & folk park** (www.shannonheritage.com; adult/child €16/9). You can get separate entrance tickets to the park when the castle is closed; all prices are slightly reduced in the low season.

BUNRATTY CASTLE Castle

Square and hulking Bunratty Castle (9am-4pm) is only the latest of several constructions to occupy its location beside the River Ratty. Vikings founded a settlement here in the 10th century, and other occupants included the Norman Thomas de Clare in the 1270s. The present structure was put up in the early 1400s by the energetic MacNamara family, falling shortly thereafter to the O'Briens, kings of Thomond, in whose possession it remained until the 17th century. A complete restoration was carried out more recently, and today the castle is full of fine 14th- to 17th-century furniture, paintings and wall hangings.

BUNRATTY FOLK PARK Folk Park

The **folk park** (**⏲9am-6pm Jun-Aug, 9am-5.30pm Sep-May, last admission 45min before closing**) adjoins the castle. It is a reconstructed traditional Irish village with cottages, a forge and working blacksmith, weavers, post office, pub and small cafe.

There's a pervading theme-park artificiality (without the rides); you'll find far more surviving authenticity of rural village Ireland in a place like Ennistymon than you will here.

A TRADITIONAL IRISH NIGHT Traditional Event

(**☎061-360 788; adult/child €40/24; ⏲7-9.30pm Apr-Oct**) This is held in a corn barn in the folk park. Lots of red-haired (real or fake, it's clearly a big help in securing employment) servers dish up trad music, dancing, Irish stew, apple pie and soda bread. There's nontraditional wine as well, which may put you in the mood for the singalong. Book online or by phone.

MEDIEVAL BANQUET Banquet

(**☎061-360 788; adult/child €50/24; ⏲5.30pm & 8.45pm**) If you skip the high-jinks in the corn barn, you may opt for a medieval banquet, replete with harp-playing maidens, court jesters and food with a medieval motif (lots of meaty items, but somehow we think the real stuff would empty the place right out). It's all washed down with mead – a kind of honey wine. The banquets are very popular with groups, so it's advisable for independent travellers to book well ahead.

Kilkee

POP 1300

Kilkee's wide beach has the kind of white, powdery sand that's made the Caribbean, well, the Caribbean. Granted the waters

Surfing

Like swells after a storm, Clare's surfing scene keeps getting bigger. Lahinch is the centre for a roiling surf scene: on weekends the breaks in front of the town fill with hundreds of surfers. Thick wetsuits dry on railings and scores of people watch the action from the town's beach and pubs.

Conditions are excellent for much of the year, with the bay's cliffs funnelling regular and reliable sets. And as the waters fill in Lahinch, the action is moving to other spots along the coast, like Doonbeg and Fanore.

Surf shops are proliferating. You can rent gear and get lessons from about €40 per two-hour session; board and wetsuit rentals are about €15 per day. Outfits in Lahinch include the following:

Ben's Surf Clinic (**☎086 844 8622; www.benssurfclinic.com**) Offers lessons plus rents out boards and wetsuits (essential!).

Lahinch Surf School (**☎087 960 9667; www.lahinchsurfschool.com; Main St**) Champion surfer John McCarthy offers lessons and various multiday packages.

Lahinch Surf Shop (**☎065-708 1108; www.lahinchsurfshop.com; Old Promenade**) Sells gear from a dramatic surfside location.

Ocean Scene Surf School (**☎065-708 1108; www.oceanscene.ie; Church St**) Gives lessons plus has a good live surf-cam on the website.

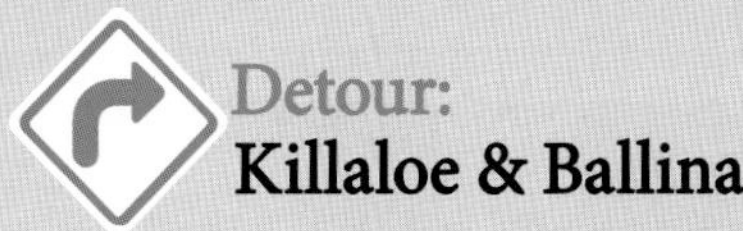

Detour: Killaloe & Ballina

Facing each other across a narrow channel, Killaloe and Ballina are really one destination, even if they have different personalities (and counties). A fine 1770 13-arch one-lane bridge spans the river, linking the pair. You can walk it in five minutes or drive it in about 20 (a Byzantine system of lights controls traffic).

Killaloe (Cill Da Lúa) is picturesque Clare at its finest. It lies on the western banks of lower Loch Deirgeirt, the southern extension of Lough Derg, where the lough narrows at one of the principal crossings of the River Shannon. The village lies snugly against the Slieve Bernagh Hills that rise abruptly to the west. The Arra Mountains create a fine balance to the east and all of Lough Derg is at hand. The village is also on the 180km East Clare Way.

Not as quaint as Killaloe, Ballina is in County Tipperary and has some of the better pubs and restaurants. It lies at the end of a scenic drive from Nenagh along Lough Derg on the R494.

are chilly and the winds often brisk, but in summer the strand is thronged with day-trippers and holidaymakers. The sweeping semicircular bay has high cliffs on the north end and weathered rocks to the south. The waters are very tidal, with wide open sandy expanses replaced by pounding waves in just a few hours.

Kilkee to Lahinch

Doonbeg

POP 600

Doonbeg (An Dún Beag) is a tiny seaside village about halfway between Kilkee and Quilty. Another Spanish Armada ship, the *San Esteban,* was wrecked on 20 September 1588 near the mouth of the River Doonbeg. The survivors were later executed at Spanish Point. Note the surviving wee little 16th-century **castle tower** next to the graceful seven-arch stone bridge over the river.

Doonbeg also has some decent **surfing** for those who want to get away from the crowds in Lahinch. For **golf**, the economic collapse means that the **Doonbeg Golf Club** (www.doonbeglodge.com; greens fees from €140) has lost a load of its previous snoot. The championship course is laid out amid the bare, rolling dunes.

Sleeping & Eating

MORRISSEY'S Inn €€
(065-905 5304; www.morrisseysdoonbeg.com; Main St; s/d €70/100; Mar-Oct; @) Under its fourth-generation owner, this old pub has been transformed into a stylish coastal haven. The six rooms feature king-size beds, flat-screen TVs and large soaking tubs.

The pub's restaurant is renowned for its casual but enticing seafood (mains €12 to €22), from fish and chips to succulent local crab claws. Outside there's a terrace overlooking the river, while inside colours reminiscent of a box of good bonbons mingle with stark white walls.

LODGE AT DOONBEG Hotel €€€
(065-905 5600; www.doonbeglodge.com; r from €200; P) Built in the style of a vaguely British manor house of indeterminate vintage, this golf resort is actually quite modern and has a range of luxurious rooms, suites and cottages. It sits in grand isolation amid the links and right behind the dunes backing White Strand, one of Clare's finest beaches. Service is unstuffy and public spaces feel intimate.

Don't Miss Clare's Best Music Festival

Half the population of Miltown Malbay seems to be part of the annual **Willie Clancy Irish Music Festival**, a tribute to a native son and one of Ireland's greatest pipers. The eight-day festival usually begins in the first or second week in July, when impromptu sessions occur day and night, the pubs are packed and Guinness is consumed by the barrel. Workshops and classes underpin the event; don't be surprised to attend a recital with 40 noted fiddlers. Asked how such a huge affair has happened for almost four decades, a local who teaches fiddle said: 'No one knows, it just does.'

THINGS YOU NEED TO KNOW

065-708 4148; www.oac.ie

Miltown Malbay

POP 1600

A classically friendly place in the chatty Irish way, Miltown Malbay has a thriving music scene. Every year it hosts the Willie Clancy Irish Music Festival (see the boxed text, p250), one of Ireland's great trad music events.

Sleeping & Eating

AN GLEANN B&B B&B **€€**

(065-708 4281; www.angleann.net; Ennis Rd; s/d from €35/70; P) Possibly the friendliest welcome in town is at this B&B off the R474 about 1km from the centre. The five rooms are basic and comfy and owner Mary Hughes is a delight. Caters for cyclists.

OLD BAKE HOUSE Seafood **€**

(Main St; meals €6-15; noon-9pm) In a region of great seafood chowder, some of the best is at the Old Bake House, which serves Irish classics in humble surrounds.

BAKER'S CAFÉ Bakery **€**

(Main St; meals €4; 7am-7pm Mon-Sat) Close to the Old Bake House, this cafe has excellent baked goods and creates enormous sandwiches – perfect for seaside picnics.

O'FRIEL'S BAR Pub
(Lynch's; ☎065-708 4275; The Square) A genuine old-style place with occasional trad sessions.

Lahinch

POP 650

Surf's up, dude! This scruffy old holiday town is now one of the centres of Ireland's hot surfing scene. Schools and stores dedicated to riding the waves cluster here, like surfers waiting for the perfect set.

Lahinch (Leacht Uí Chonchubhair) has always owed its living to beach-seeking tourists. The town sits on protected Liscannor Bay and has a fine beach. Free-spending mobs descend in summer, many wielding golf clubs for play at the famous, traditional links-style **Lahinch Golf Club** (**☎065-708 1003; www.lahinchgolf.com; greens fees from €100**).

 Sleeping & Eating

WEST COAST LODGE Inn **€**
(**☎065-708 2000; www.lahinchaccommodation.com; Station Rd; dm from €18, r from €50; P @ 📶**) Flashpackers will cheer this stylish and downright plush hostel and inn in the heart of Lahinch. Power showers, fine cotton sheets and down duvets are just some of the touches found throughout the seven- to 12-bed dorms and private rooms. Check out the surf from the roof deck; rent a bike to go exploring.

BARRTRA SEAFOOD RESTAURANT Seafood **€€**
(**☎065-708 1280; www.barrtra.com; Miltown Malbay Rd; mains €16-28; ⏲Apr-Sep**) The 'Seafood Symphony' menu item says it all at this rural repose 3.5km south of Lahinch. Enjoy views over pastures to the sea from this lovely country cottage, surrounded by lovely kitchen gardens. The cooking eschews flash and lets the inherent tastiness of the food shine.

Cliffs of Moher

Star of a million tourist brochures, the Cliffs of Moher (Aillte an Mothair, or Ailltreacha Mothair) are one of the most popular sights in Ireland. But like many an ageing star, you have to look beyond the famous facade to appreciate the inherent attributes behind the postcard image.

The entirely vertical cliffs rise to a height of 203m, their edge falling away abruptly into the constantly churning sea. A series of heads, the dark limestone seems to march in a rigid formation that amazes, no matter how many times you look.

Such appeal comes at a price: mobs. This is check-off tourism big time and busloads come and go constantly in summer. A vast visitor centre handles the hordes. Set back into the side of a hill, it's impressively unimpressive – it blends right in. As part of the development, however, the main walkways and viewing areas along the cliffs have been surrounded by a 1.5m-high wall. It's lovely stone, but it's also way too high and set too far back from the edge. The entire reason for coming here (the view – unless you're a bus-spotter) is obscured.

But, like so many overpopular natural wonders, there's relief and joy if you're willing to walk for 10 minutes. Past the end of the 'Moher Wall' south, there's still a **trail** along the cliffs to Hag's Head – few venture this far. There's also a path heading north, but you're discouraged from it, so use your common sense.

With binoculars you can spot the more than 30 species of **birds** – including darling little puffins – that make their homes among the fissure-filled cliff faces. On a clear day you'll channel Barbra Streisand as you can see forever; the Aran Islands stand etched on the waters of Galway Bay, and beyond lie the hills of Connemara in western Galway.

The roads leading to the cliffs pass through refreshingly undeveloped lands, the rolling hills giving no hint of the dramatic vistas just over the edge.

For uncommon views of the cliffs and wildlife you might consider a **cruise**. The boat operators in Doolin (p255) offer popular tours of the cliffs.

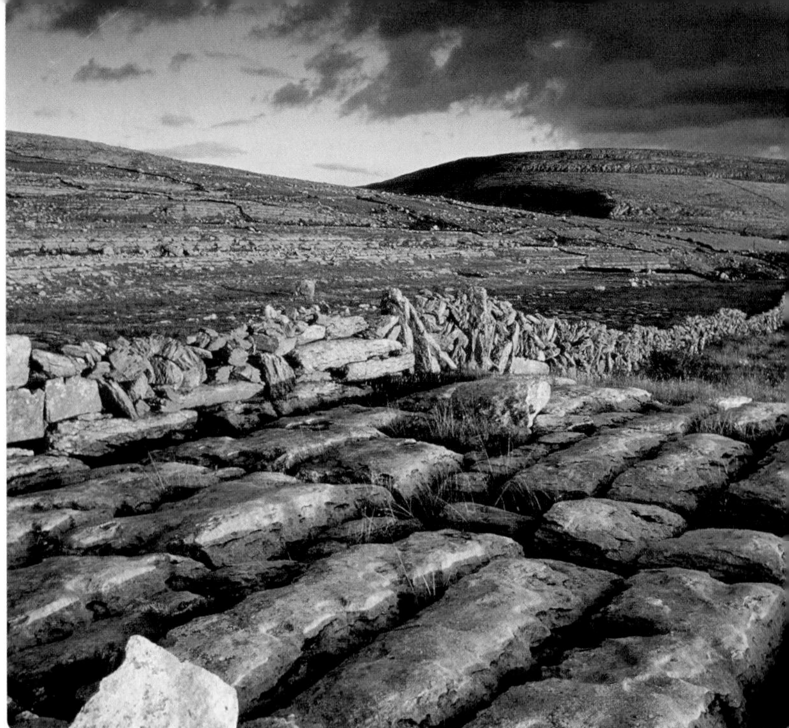

Information

Visitor centre (www.cliffsofmoher.ie; admission to site adult/child €6/free; 9am-9.30pm Jul & Aug, 9am-7pm May, Jun & Sep, 9am-6pm Mar, Apr & Oct, 9.15am-5pm Nov-Feb) Actually, revealingly, it's called the 'Cliffs of Moher Visitor Experience', and has glitzy exhibitions about the cliffs and the environment called the 'Atlantic Edge'. Staff lead tours outside and answer questions.

Vendors of 'authentic' sweaters and other tat have stalls near the large free parking area. The basement cafe seems designed to urge you up to the views at the pricier restaurant.

Getting There & Away

Bus Éireann runs one to three buses daily past the cliffs on the Doolin-Ennis/Galway routes. Waits between buses may exceed your ability to enjoy the spectacle so you might combine a bus with a walk. Numerous private tour operators run tours to the cliffs from Galway and the region.

The Burren

The Burren region is rocky and windswept, an apt metaphor for the hardscrabble lives of those who've eked out an existence here. Stretching across northern Clare, from the Atlantic coast to Kinvara in County Galway, it's a unique striated limestone landscape that was shaped beneath ancient seas, then forced high and dry by a great geological cataclysm. In the Burren, land and sea seem to merge into one vast, moody, rocky and at times fearsome space beneath huge skies, and are accented with ancient burial chambers and medieval ruins.

This is not the green Ireland of postcards. But there are wildflowers in spring, giving the Burren brilliant, if ephemeral, colour amid the arid beauty. There are also intriguing villages to enjoy. These include the music hub of Doolin on the west coast, Kilfenora inland and Ballyvaughan in the north, on the shores of Galway Bay.

Left: The Burren's limestone landscape
Below: Walkers on a riverside path, Ashford Castle (p257)
PHOTOGRAPHER: (LEFT) GARETH McCORMACK / LONELY PLANET IMAGES ©; (BELOW) EOIN CLARKE / LONELY PLANET IMAGES ©

Walking

The Burren is a walkers' paradise. The bizarre, beautiful landscape, numerous trails and many ancient sites are best explored on foot. 'Green roads' are the old highways of the Burren, crossing hills and valleys to some of the remotest corners of the region. Many of these unpaved ways were built during the Famine as part of relief work, while some date back possibly thousands of years. They're now used mostly by hikers and the occasional farmer. Some are signposted.

The **Burren Way** is a 123km network of marked hiking routes throughout the region.

Guided nature, history, archaeology and wilderness walks are great ways to appreciate the Burren. Typically the cost of the walks averages €15 and there are many options, including individual trips. Recommended guides (call to confirm times, walk locations and to book):

Burren Guided Walks & Hikes (☎065-707 6100, 087 244 6807; www.burrenguidedwalks.com) Long-time guide Mary Howard leads groups on a variety of itineraries.

Burren Hill Walks (☎065-707 7168) 'Gentle' walks visit historic sites while enjoying geologic and floral oddities.

Burren Wild Tours (☎087 877 9565; www.burrenwalks.com) John Connolly offers a broad range of walks and packages.

Heart of Burren Walks (☎065-682 7707; www.heartofburrenwalks.com) Local Burren author Tony Kirby leads walks and archaeology hikes.

Getting There & Away

A few Bus Éireann (www.buseireann.ie) buses pass through the Burren. The main routes include one from Limerick and Ennis to Corofin, Ennistymon, Lahinch, Liscannor, the Cliffs of Moher, Doolin and Lisdoonvarna; another connects Galway with Ballyvaughan,

If You Like... Trad Music Festivals

If you like the **Willie Clancy Irish Music Festival** (p250), you'll like these other great trad festivals:

1 **FLEADH NUA**
(☎065-682 4276; www.fleadhnua.com) A lively traditional music festival held in Ennis in late May, with singing, dancing and workshops.

2 **ENNIS TRAD FESTIVAL**
(www.ennistradfestival.com) Traditional music in venues across town for one week in early November.

3 **FLEADH NA GCUACH**
(www.kinvara.com) Over 100 traditional musicians descend on Kinvara in late May for the 'Cuckoo Festival' that involves over 50 organised sessions.

4 **CRAICEANN INIS OÍRR INTERNATIONAL BODHRÁN SUMMER SCHOOL**
(☎099-75067; www.craiceann.com) Weeklong festival in late June on Inisheer that keeps the focus strictly on the bodhrán, includes masterclasses and workshops as well as great music.

Lisdoonvarna and Doolin. Usually there are one to three buses daily, with the most in summer.

Doolin

POP 250

Doolin gets plenty of press and lots of other chatter as a centre of Irish traditional music, owing to a trio of pubs that have sessions through the year. It's also known for its setting – 6km north of the Cliffs of Moher and down near the ever-unsettled sea, the land is windblown, with huge rocks exposed by the long-vanished topsoil.

Given all its attributes, you might be surprised when you realise that Doolin as it's known barely exists. Rather, when you arrive you might be forgiven for exclaiming, 'There's no there here!' For what's called Doolin is really three infinitesimally small neighbouring villages. **Fisherstreet** is right on the water, **Doolin** itself is about 1km east on the little River Aille and **Roadford** is another 1km east. None has more than a handful of buildings, which results in a scattered appearance, without a centre. Still, the area is hugely popular. It's also a place to get boats to the Aran Islands offshore.

Sleeping

CULLINAN'S GUESTHOUSE Inn €€
(☎065-707 4183; www.cullinansdoolin.com; Doolin; s €40-60, d €60-90; P 📶) The eight rooms here are all of a high standard, with power showers and comfortable fittings. Right on the Aille (two rooms have balconies), it has a lovely back terrace for enjoying the views. The restaurant is one of the village's best. The owner is well-known local musician James Cullinan.

SEA VIEW HOUSE Inn €€
(☎065-707 4826; www.ireland-doolin.com; Fisherstreet; r €60-120; P 📶) On high ground right above Fisherstreet village, this big house and its terrace have sweeping ocean views. The common lounge has a telescope for enjoying the vantage point. The rooms have solid mahogany furnishings and DVD players (there's a library).

Drinking & Entertainment

Doolin's rep is largely based on music. A lot of musicians live in the area, and they have a symbiotic relationship with the tourists: each desires the other and each year things grow a little larger.

MCGANN'S Pub
(Roadford) McGann's has all the classic touches of a full-on Irish music pub; the action often spills out onto the street. The food here is the best of the trio. Inside you'll find locals playing darts in its war-

ren of small rooms, some with turf fires. There's a small outside covered area.

O'CONNOR'S Pub

(Fisherstreet) Right on the water, this sprawling favourite packs them in and has a rollicking atmosphere when the music and drinking are in full swing. It easily gets the most crowded and has the highest tourist quotient; on some summer nights you won't squeeze inside and trying to eat is like playing the fiddle for the first time.

MACDIARMADA'S Pub

(Roadford) Also known as McDermott's, this simple red-and-white old pub can be the rowdy favourite of locals. When the fiddles get going, it can seem like a scene out of a John Ford movie. The inside is pretty basic, as is the menu of sandwiches and roasts. McGann's is a one-minute walk.

Getting There & Away

BOAT

Doolin is one of two ferry departure points to the Aran Islands (p255) from April to October. Various ferry companies offer numerous departures in season. It takes around 30 minutes to cover the 8km to Inisheer, the closest of the three islands and the best choice for a day trip from Doolin.

Cliffs of Moher Cruises (065-707 5949; www.mohercruises.com; Doolin Pier; Apr-Oct) Offers combined Aran Islands trips with Cliffs of Moher cruises on the *Jack B*.

Doolin Ferries (065-707 4455, 065-707 4466; www.doolinferries.com; Doolin Pier) Offers sailings to the islands and the cliffs on the *Happy Hooker*.

O'Brien Line (065-707 5555; www.obrienline.com) Usually has the most sailings to the Arans; also offers cliff cruises and combo tickets.

BUS

Bus Éireann runs one to two buses daily to Doolin from Ennis (€12, 1½ hours) and Limerick (€15, 2½ hours) via Corofin, Lahinch and the Cliffs of Moher. Buses also go to Galway (€14, 1½ hours, one or two daily) via Ballyvaughan.

In the summer, various backpacker shuttles often serve Doolin from Galway and other points in Clare. These are amply marketed in hostels.

Ballyvaughan & Around

POP 220

Something of a hub for the otherwise dispersed charms of the Burren, Ballyvaughan (Baile Uí Bheacháin) sits between the hard land of the hills and a quiet leafy

Village pub in Ballyvaughan

...er of Galway Bay. It makes an excel-...ase for visiting the northern reaches ... Burren.

Sights & Activities

AILLWEE CAVES Caves

(www.aillweecave.ie; combined ticket adult/child €17/10; 10am-5.30pm, to 6.30pm Jul & Aug) Send the kids underground. The main cave here penetrates 600m into the mountain, widening into larger caverns, one with its own waterfall. The caves were carved out by water some two million years ago. Near the entrance are the remains of a brown bear, extinct in Ireland for more than 10,000 years. Often crowded in summer, there's a cafe, and a large raptor exhibit has captive hawks, owls and more. A shop sells locally produced Burren Gold cheese, which is excellent.

Sleeping & Entertainment

GREGAN'S CASTLE HOTEL Hotel **€€€**

(065-707 7005; www.gregans.ie; s/d from €150/200; P) This hidden Clare gem is housed in a grand estate dating to the 19th century. The 20 rooms and suites, however, have a plush, stylish feel with just enough modern touches to keep you from feeling you've bedded down in a waxworks.

The restaurant specialises in inventive fresh fare sourced locally while the bar is the kind of place to sip something brown and let hours roll away in genteel comfort.

The grounds are a fantasy of gardens and, when you're not walking in the Burren, there's croquet. The estate is some 6km south of Ballyvaughan on the N67 at Corkscrew Hill.

ÓLÓLAINN Pub

(Main St) A tiny family-run place on the left as you head out to the pier, Ólólainn (o-*loch*-lain) is the place for a timeless moment or two in old-fashioned snugs. Look for the old whiskey bottles in the window, but save all your energy for the amazing selection of rare whiskeys within.

COUNTY MAYO

Cong

POP 150

Sitting on a sliver-thin isthmus between Lough Corrib and Lough Mask, Cong complies with romantic notions of a traditional Irish village. Time appears to have stood still ever since the evergreen classic *The Quiet Man* was filmed here in 1951. As such, the arrival of the morning's first tour bus instantly doubles the number of people strolling the town's tiny streets, but the wooded trails between the lovely old abbey and stately Ashford Castle offer genuine quietude. There are no banks or ATMS, but you can change money at the post office on Main St or at the museum.

Croagh Patrick pilgrims (p257)

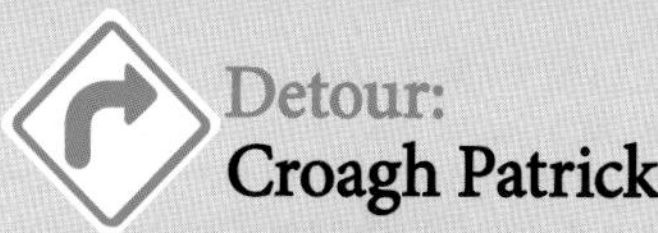

Detour: Croagh Patrick

Just 8km southwest of Westport, St Patrick couldn't have picked a better spot for a pilgrimage than this conical mountain (also known as 'the Reek'). On a clear day the tough two-hour climb rewards with stunning views over Clew Bay and its sandy islets.

It was on Croagh Patrick that Ireland's patron saint fasted for 40 days and nights, and where he reputedly banished venomous snakes. Climbing the 765m holy mountain is an act of penance for thousands of pilgrims on the last Sunday of July (Reek Sunday). The truly contrite take the original 40km route from Ballintubber Abbey, Tóchar Phádraig (Patrick's Causeway), and ascend the mountain barefoot.

The trail taken by less contrite folk begins in the village of Murrisk. Opposite the car park is the **National Famine Memorial**, a spine-chilling sculpture of a three-masted ghost ship wreathed in swirling skeletons, commemorating the lives lost on so-called 'coffin ships' employed to help people escape the Famine. The path down past the memorial leads to the scant remains of **Murrisk Abbey**, founded by the O'Malleys in 1547.

For warming turf fires, good food and a convivial atmosphere head for the raspberry-pink-painted pub, the **Tavern** (www.tavernmurrisk.com; Murrisk; mains €9-27), which serves great seafood.

Sights

FREE **CONG ABBEY** Historic Site

(dawn-dusk) An evocative reminder of ecclesiastical times past, the weathered shell of Cong's 12th-century Augustinian abbey is scored by wizened lines from centuries of exposure to the elements. Nevertheless, several finely sculpted features have survived, including a carved doorway, windows and lovely medieval arches (touched up in the 19th century).

ASHFORD CASTLE Historic Building

(094-954 6003; www.ashford.ie; grounds admission €5; 9am-dusk) Just beyond Cong Abbey, the village abruptly ends and the woodlands surrounding Ashford Castle begin. First built in 1228 as the seat of the de Burgo family, owners over the years included the Guinness family (of stout fame). Arthur Guinness turned the castle into a regal hunting and fishing lodge, which it remains today.

QUIET MAN MUSEUM Museum

(Circular Rd; admission €5; 10am-4pm Mar-Oct) Modelled on Sean Thornton's White O' Mornin' Cottage from the film, the Quiet Man Museum also squeezes in a fascinating regional archaeological and historical exhibition of items from 7000 BC to the 19th century. Film fanatics (or those with a postmodern fascination for the way reality and fiction blur) can take a 75-minute **location tour** (€15; 11am Apr-Sep), which includes museum entry.

Sleeping

LISLOUGHREY LODGE Hotel €€€

(094-954 5400; www.lisloughreylodgehotel.ie; The Quay; r from €160; P @) The lodge, built in the 1820s by Ashford Castle's owners, has been stunningly renovated in bold, contemporary cranberry and blueberry tones, with 50 guest rooms named for wine regions and champagne houses. Kick back in the bar, billiards room, or beanbag-strewn Wii room. Nab a room original house for the old-world cter.

ORD CASTLE Hotel **€€€**
(4-954 6003; www.ashford.ie; r €350-850; P @) Old-world elegance, exquisite rooms and faultless service are on tap at Ashford Castle, but if you can't afford to stay you can come for dinner (from €70) at the George V restaurant. Do dress the part, though (that's a jacket and tie, guys), as it's rather posh around here.

Getting There & Away

BUS There are three buses to Galway (€10.30, one hour) Monday to Saturday and four to Westport (€9.30, one hour). The bus stops on Main St.

Westport

POP 5163

Bright and vibrant even in the depths of winter, Westport is a photogenic Georgian town with tree-lined streets, a riverside mall and a great vibe. With an excellent choice of accommodation, restaurants and pubs renowned for their music, it's an extremely popular spot yet has never sold its soul to tourism. A couple of kilometres west on Clew Bay, the town's harbour, Westport Quay, is a picturesque spot for a sundowner. Westport's central location makes it a convenient base for exploring the county.

Sights

WESTPORT HOUSE Historic Building
(098-27766; www.westporthouse.ie; Quay Rd; house & gardens adult/child €12/6.50, house, gardens & Pirate Adventure Park adult/child €24/16.50; house & gardens 10am-6pm mid-Apr–Aug, to 4pm Mar & Sep) Built in 1730 on the ruins of Grace O'Malley's 16th-century castle, this charming Georgian mansion retains much of its original contents and has some stunning period-styled rooms. The house is set in glorious gardens, but the overall effect is marred by its commercial overhaul of recent years. Children will love it, however, and the **Pirate Adventure Park**, complete with a swinging pirate ship, a 'pirate's playground' and a roller-coaster-style flume ride through a water channel, are big hits.

Westport

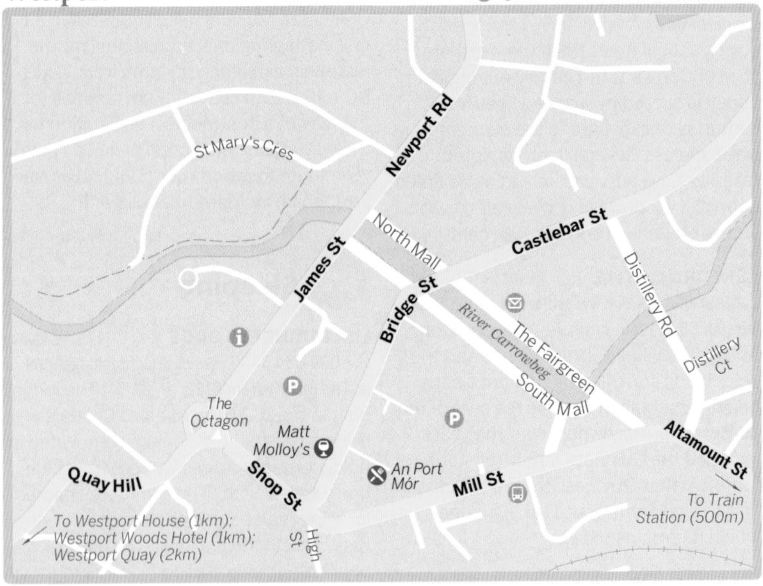

0 200 m
0 0.1 miles

St Mary's Cres
Newport Rd
North Mall
Castlebar St
James St
Bridge St
Distillery Rd
River Carrowbeg
The Fairgreen
South Mall
Distillery Ct
The Octagon
Matt Molloy's
Quay Hill
Shop St
An Port Mór
Mill St
Altamount St
To Train Station (500m)
To Westport House (1km); Westport Woods Hotel (1km); Westport Quay (2km)
High St

To reach Westport House, turn right just before Westport Quay.

Sleeping

WESTPORT WOODS HOTEL Hotel €€

(098-25811; www.westportwoodshotel.com; Quay Rd; s/d from €75/110; P @) Hidden behind the stone wall of Westport House, this place prides itself on its green credentials. Rooms are large and spacious but lacking a little soul, while service is professional but impressively personalised, too, for a hotel its size. There's an excellent free children's club, bicycles to borrow, a zip wire, high rope course, a climbing wall and free pick up from the local train station.

Eating

AN PORT MÓR Seafood €€

(098-26730; www.anportmore.com; 1 Brewery Pl; mains €15-24; 6-10pm Tue-Sun) Hidden down a lane off Bridge St, this wonderful little restaurant packs quite a punch. It's an intimate kind of place with a series of long narrow rooms and a menu that's understandably strong on seafood. Dishes such as Inishturk crab linguine and pan-fried organic Achill sea trout are deceptively simple but just packed with flavour. Book ahead.

Drinking & Entertainment

Westport is thronged with pubs, many of them with live music nightly.

MATT MOLLOY'S Pub

(Bridge St) Matt Malloy, the fife player from the Chieftains, opened this old-school pub years ago and the good times haven't let up. Head to the back room around 9pm and you'll catch live *céilidh* (traditional music and dancing). Or perhaps an old man will simply slide into a chair and croon a few classics.

Getting There & Away

BUS Services run to Dublin (€17.10, 4½ hours, two daily), Galway (€14.40, two hours, five daily), Sligo (€17, 2½ hours, four Monday to Saturday, two Sunday) and Achill (€12.50, 30 minutes, two daily). Buses depart from Mill St.

TRAIN There are three daily connections to Dublin (€35, 3½ hours).

Counties Sligo & Donegal

Packing poetry, myth and folklore into their broody, dramatic landscapes, the northwestern counties of Sligo and Donegal match any other part of the country for sheer beauty, but have no equal when it comes to wildness.

County Sligo is Yeats country, as in William Butler (1865–1939) and Jack Butler (1871–1957), who helped cement its pastoral reputation through verse and paintbrush, respectively.

County Donegal is the wild child of the Irish family. Its rugged landscapes, relative isolation and impetuous weather have all served to forge the county's distinctly stubborn character. It has plenty to offer the visitor, including magnificent coastlines, great surfing and its wonderfully photogenic interior.

Fanad Head (p287), County Donegal

Rosses Point (p273), County Sligo
RICHARD CUMMINS / LONELY PLANET IMAGES ©

Counties Sligo & Donegal

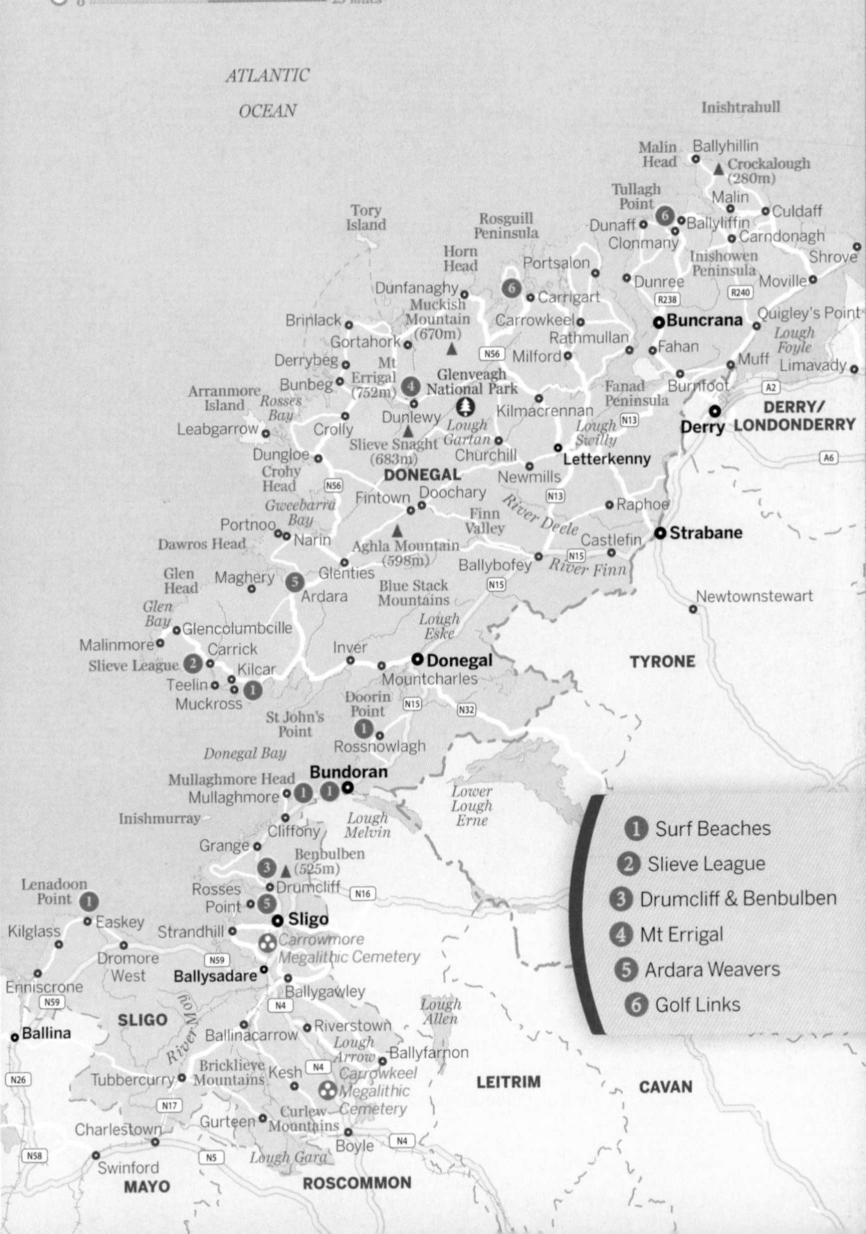

Counties Sligo & Donegal's Highlights

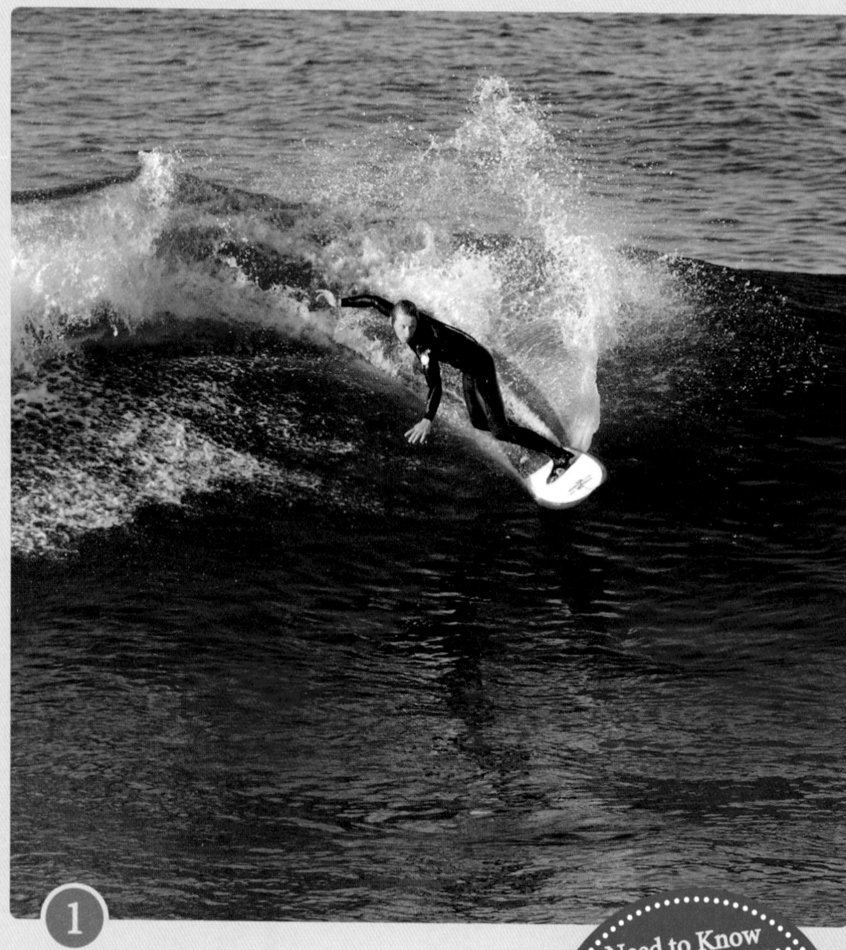

1

Surf Beaches

Northwest Ireland's location and the particular geology of large stretches of coastline mean this is a surfer's paradise. There are beaches ideal for the beginner, high-performance breaks for the competent surfer or massive wave spots for the truly adventurous. Surfing at Easkey, County Sligo

Need to Know

Best Time to Visit September to Christmas. **Advance Planning** Best to do two to three days ahead to get the best conditions. **For further coverage, see p276.**

Surf Beaches Don't Miss List

BY NEIL BRITTON, PRO TOUR SURF JUDGE AND OWNER OF FIN MCCOOL SURF SCHOOL, ROSSNOWLAGH

1 BUNDORAN, COUNTY DONEGAL

This traditional seaside town (p280) is home to four surf schools and has turned itself into an Irish surf city. If you wait until low tide and look out straight to sea, you will see 'the Peak', one of the best surf breaks in Europe, which has already hosted two European Surfing Championships.

2 EASKEY, COUNTY SLIGO

For a really authentic Irish surfing experience, you don't need to go any further than Easkey (p275) in County Sligo. There are two intermediate surf breaks right under the iconic ruins of Easky Castle, and images of this distinctive landmark have been in surfing magazines throughout the world.

3 MULLAGHMORE, COUNTY SLIGO

The sleepy fishing village of Mullaghmore (p276) is a big-wave surfer's mecca. The wave itself – which is only for experienced professionals – is about 500m past the harbour and is easily accessible on a nice seaside walk; you'll often spot pro surfers being towed into the 40ft waves by jet ski.

4 ROSSNOWLAGH, COUNTY DONEGAL

This 2km-long sandy beach (p279) is the safest and easiest spot on which to learn how to surf. The views are stunning and it's home to the Surfer's Bar, full of memorabilia stretching back to the earliest days of Irish surfing in the 1960s.

5 MUCKROSS, COUNTY DONEGAL

Heading west out of Killybegs, look out for a road off to the left past the Blue Haven Hotel. This lovely scenic road leads down to the sheltered beach of Muckross, which is a great area to get away from the crowds.

Slieve League

The Cliffs of Moher might draw greater numbers, but that's the only concession Slieve League (p282) makes to its southern rival. Plunging some 600 vertical metres into an often wild and raging sea, these sea cliffs are the tallest and most spectacular in Europe, and with viewing locations like the aptly named One Man's Pass, they can be quite treacherous, too.

2

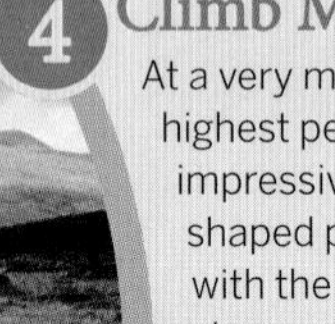

4

Climb Mt Errigal

At a very manageable 752m, Donegal's highest peak (p283) might not seem that impressive, but this stunning pyramid-shaped peak will leave you breathless... with the sheer beauty of its summit views, which take in most of the coastline and the offshore islands. Otherwise, it's a relatively easy climb up either of two routes, unless of course it's misty or raining, and then the climb is far more challenging.

GARETH McCORMACK / LONELY PLANET IMAGES ©

Drumcliff & Benbulben

3

Ireland's greatest poet, WB Yeats, lies buried in the graveyard of the small Protestant church in Drumcliff (p276), County Sligo. His final resting place lies in the shadow of the magnificent Benbulben, as beautiful a bit of raised earth as you'll see anywhere on your Irish travels. Limestone plateau of Benbulben

5

Ardara Weavers

Sure, you can buy an Irish-made woollen or tweed pretty much anywhere in the world these days, but how often do you get the chance to see it hand-woven at the source? The pretty Donegal town of Ardara (p281) is the heart of Donegal's traditional knitwear and hand-woven tweed, and virtually all of the town's manufacturers will gladly let you observe the process…before gently inviting you to purchase the fruit of their looms!

6

Golf Links

If Scotland is the home of golf, then Ireland is where golf goes on holidays, particularly to the Northwest, which is dotted with some of the best golf links in the world. There's the world-famous County Sligo Golf Course (p273) at Rosses Point, in the shadow of Benbulben, as well as the less renowned but equally beautiful links at Ballyliffin (p289) and Rosapenna (p287). Golfing in Ballyliffin, Donegal

Counties Sligo & Donegal's Best...

Beauty Spots

- **Glen Gesh Pass** (p284) A touch of the Alps in southwestern Donegal.
- **Poisoned Glen** (p283) Stunning ice-carved rock face overshadowing the glen.
- **Horn Head** (p284) A towering headland with superb views.
- **Benbulben** (p276) A mountain so beautiful that Yeats wanted to be buried in its shadow.
- **Rosguill Peninsula** (p287) Its rugged splendour is best appreciated by car.

Walking Beaches

- **Portsalon** (p287) Ireland's most beautiful beach.
- **Enniscrone** (p275) The 5km Hollow is probably Sligo's most beautiful beach.
- **Mullaghmore** (p276) Sligo's only Blue Flag beach has safe shallow waters lapping up to its sweeping arc of golden sand.
- **Tramore** (p285) This stunning beach was recently voted the second-best walking beach in Ireland.
- **Trá na Rossan** (p287) A gorgeous, secluded beach just by the village of Carrigart.

Historical Sites

- **Glencolumbcille** (p280) Ruins of a 6th-century monastic settlement.
- **Carrowkeel Megalithic Cemetery** (p275) Cairns, dolmens and graves from the late Stone Age.
- **Carrowmore Megalithic Cemetery** (p274) Ireland's largest Stone Age cemetery.
- **Glenveagh National Park** (p286) Where the pain of Irish history still resonates.
- **Grianáin of Aileách** (p289) A pre-Celtic site with an amphitheatre-shaped stone fort.

Restaurants

- **Olde Glen Bar** (p287) Low ceilings, slate floor, great beer...perfect.
- **Kitty Kelly's** (p280) Live rock and folk on summer weekends.
- **Mill Restaurant & Guesthouse** (p284) Old converted flax mill, now a superb restaurant.
- **Beach House** (p289) Cafe that takes surf-and-turf to a whole new level of goodness.

Left: Glen Gesh Pass (p284), County Donegal; **Above:** Poisoned Glen (p283), County Donegal.

Need to Know

ADVANCE PLANNING

- **Two months before** Learn some basic Irish words to impress in Donegal's Gaeltacht.
- **One month before** Book a surf lesson.
- **Two weeks before** Check out the weather forecast. Then ignore it.
- **Upon arrival** Realise that Donegal Irish sounds nothing like what you heard on those tapes.

RESOURCES

- **Donegal Tourism** (www.donegaldirect.ie) Donegal Tourism's official website.
- **Failte Ireland** (www.discoverireland.ie) The national tourism authority.
- **John McGinley Bus** (www.johnmcginley.com) Bus operator serving northwestern Donegal from Dublin.

GETTING AROUND

- **Bus** There are excellent national services to main towns. You'll have to rely on private operators for transport between smaller towns.
- **Train** Good for Sligo, but service in Donegal is nonexistent.
- **Car** The best way of getting around; watch out for sheep and boy racers!

BE FOREWARNED

- **Roads** Tortuously winding narrow roads can make travel in the northwest quite slow; it's a good thing there's plenty of scenery to keep you occupied!
- **Seasonal tourism** Many hotels and restaurants shut down between December and Easter.
- **Weather** Warm, sunny summers and ferocious winters make the northwest a place of extremes.

Counties Sligo & Donegal Itineraries

Two neighbouring counties, two distinct personalities: the first itinerary explores the artistically inspiring Sligo, the other gives you the best of awe-inspiring Donegal, so wild in parts that art just can't imitate nature.

3 DAYS

DONEGAL TOWN TO BUNCRANA

Delights of Donegal

Five days is barely enough time to make a dent in what Donegal has to offer, but the following itinerary should whet your appetite for a longer visit. Start in the southwest, perhaps basing yourself in **(1) Donegal Town** for visits to the beach at **(2) Rossnowlagh** – a surfing mecca for beginners and advanced surfers alike – and the sea cliffs at **(3) Slieve League**, best appreciated from below aboard a tour boat. On day three, move in a northwesterly arc around the county, checking out the monastic ruins at **(4) Glencolumbcille** before heading toward **(5) Dunfanaghy**, which is a fine base from which to explore the county's northern coasts. Your remaining two days could include **(6) Glenveagh National Park** and the **(7) Rosguill Peninsula's** superbly scenic Atlantic Drive. Finally, the remote beauty of the Inishowen Peninsula will leave you in Ireland's northernmost point; the seaside resort of **(8) Buncrana** is very popular with summer visitors from Derry, but in the off-season it is a quiet resort.

Top Left: Donegal Town (p277); **Top Right:** WB Yeats monument by Rowan Gillespie, Sligo Town (p272)

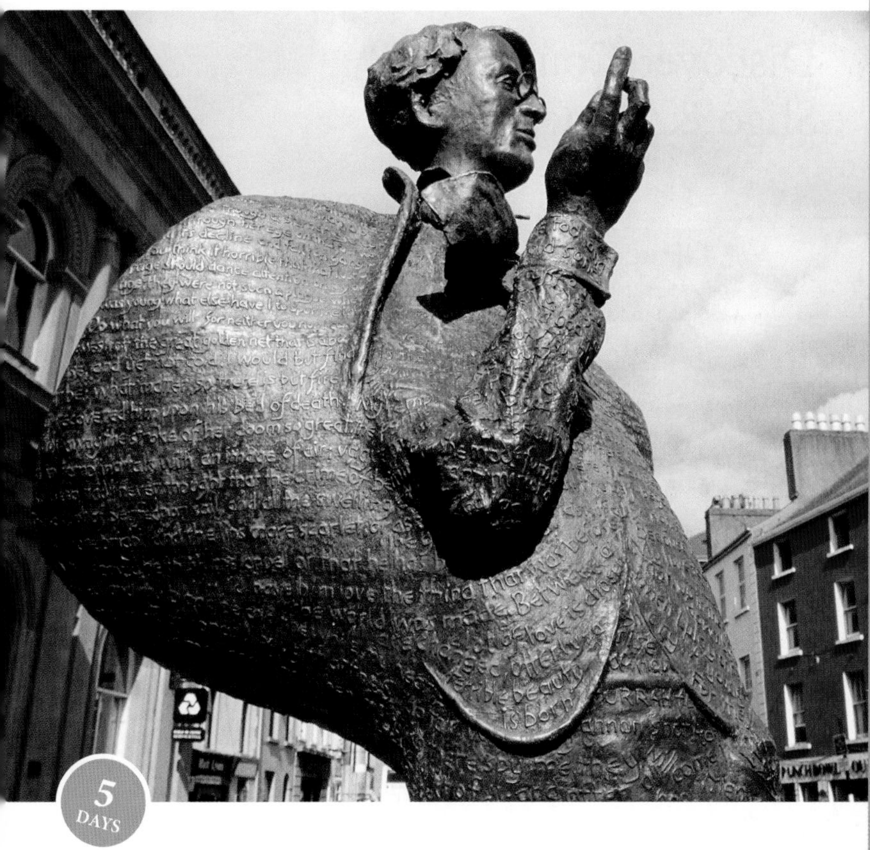

5 DAYS

SLIGO TOWN & AROUND

Sligo Surrounds

The Northwest's most dynamic town is unquestionably **(1) Sligo Town**, a pleasant spot on the River Garavogue that has its own distractions but is also a fine base from which to explore the surrounding area. The Yeats connection is everywhere, from the room devoted to the two brothers, poet and dramatist William Butler and painter Jack Butler, in the **Sligo County Museum**, to WB Yeats' final resting place in **(2) Drumcliff**, under the shadow of the memorable Benbulben, carefully chosen by Yeats so as to forever reside in the shadow of the distinctive peak. You can appreciate the majesty of the mountain and spoil a good walk by playing the stunning **(3) County Sligo Golf Course**, designed in such a way that almost every hole is in view of the peak. Unwind by immersing yourself in a traditional seaweed bath in **(4) Strandhill** before returning to Sligo Town, but don't forget the county's prehistoric heritage, at **(5) Carrowkeel** and **(6) Carrowmore**.

Discover Counties Sligo & Donegal

At a Glance

- **County Sligo** (p272) Ancient ruins and poetry-inspiring landscapes.
- **County Donegal** (p276) Wild, savage beauty that cannot be tamed.

Sligo Town, on the River Garavogue

PHOTOGRAPHER: GARETH MCCORMACK / LONELY PLANET IMAGES ©

COUNTY SLIGO

Sligo Town

POP 19,402

Sligo town is in no hurry to shed its cultural traditions, nor does it sell them out. Pedestrian streets with inviting shop fronts, stone bridges spanning the River Garavogue, and *céilidh* (traditional music) pub sessions contrast with genre-bending contemporary art and glass towers rising from prominent corners of the town.

Sights

FREE **SLIGO COUNTY MUSEUM** Museum

(Stephen St; 9.30am-12.30pm & 2-4.45pm Tue-Sat May-Sep, 9.30am-12.30pm Tue-Sat Oct-Apr) The major draw here is the Yeats room, featuring photographs, letters and newspaper cuttings connected with the poet WB Yeats, as well as drawings by his brother Jack B Yeats, one of Ireland's most important modern artists.

Festivals & Events

YEATS INTERNATIONAL FESTIVAL Poetry, Culture

(www.yeats-sligo.com) In late July to mid-August Irish poetry, music and culture are celebrated with three weeks of performances and events.

Sleeping

GLASS HOUSE Hotel €€

(071-919 4300; www.theglasshouse.ie; Swan Point; r from €109; P @) You can't miss this futuristic-looking hotel in the centre of town, its sharp glass facade pointing skyward. Inside things are a little more retro with a lurid swirly carpet in the foyer and bedrooms in a choice of psychedelic orange or lime green. It's fun and funky but perhaps trying a little too hard to be cool.

PEARSE LODGE B&B €€
(☎071-916 1090; www.pearselodge.com; Pearse Rd; s/d €50/74; P @ 📶) Welcoming owners Mary and Kieron not only impeccably maintain the six stylish guest rooms at their cosy B&B but are also up on what's happening in town. Mary's breakfast menu includes smoked salmon, French toast with bananas and homemade muesli (and Illy coffee!). A sunny sitting room opens to a beautifully landscaped garden.

Eating

SOURCE Irish €€
(☎071-914 7605; www.sourcesligo.ie; 1 John St; mains €15-20; ⏰9.30am-5pm Mon, 9.30am-9.30pm Tue-Sun) Three stories of sparkling glass announce Sligo's newest, and most ambitious, culinary project. Source is all about traceability in the food chain and the project champions local suppliers and foodstuffs. Large, arty photos of its favourite fishermen, farmers and cheese producers grace the walls of the ground-floor restaurant with its open kitchen and buzzy atmosphere, while upstairs in the **wine bar** (dishes €4-9; ⏰3-11pm Tue-Sun) things are more sedate with wine from the owners' vineyard in France and plates of Irish-style tapas on offer. The top floor, with its glorious views of Benbulben, is a **cookery school** offering everything from classes on organic growing to boning and butchery.

Getting There & Away

Bus

Bus Éireann (☎071-916 0066) leaves from the bus station, situated below the train station on Lord Edward St. Destinations include Ballina (€13, 1½ hours, three daily), Westport (€17, two hours, twice daily) and Dublin (€17, four hours, four daily), as well as Galway and Donegal town. Services are less frequent on Sunday.

Feda O'Donnell (☎074-954 8114; www.feda.ie) operates a service between Crolly (County Donegal) and Galway twice daily (four times on Sunday). Call to confirm departure points.

Train

Trains leave the station (☎071-916 9888) for Dublin (€32, four hours, eight daily) via Boyle, Carrick-on-Shannon and Mullingar.

If You Like... Festivals

If you like the Yeats International Festival, you might enjoy these other festivals in town:

1 **SÓ SLIGO**
(www.sosligo.com; ⏰mid-Mar) A five-day celebration of fine food and artisan produce along with cooking competitions, live music and street parties.

2 **TEMPLE HOUSE FESTIVAL**
(www.templehousefestival.com; ⏰early Jun) Three-day festival featuring an eclectic line up of music, arts, workshops and woodland crafts.

3 **SLIGO JAZZ FESTIVAL**
(www.sligojazzproject.com; ⏰mid-Jul) Sligo swings during this three-day festival.

4 **SLIGO LIVE**
(www.sligolive.ie; ⏰Oct) Sligo's biggest cultural event is this live music festival.

Around Sligo Town

Rosses Point

POP 872

Rosses Point is a picturesque seaside resort with grassy dunes rolling down to the golden strand. Benbulben, Sligo's most recognisable landmark, arches skywards in the distance. Offshore, the odd **Metal Man** beacon dates from 1821.

Sligo Town

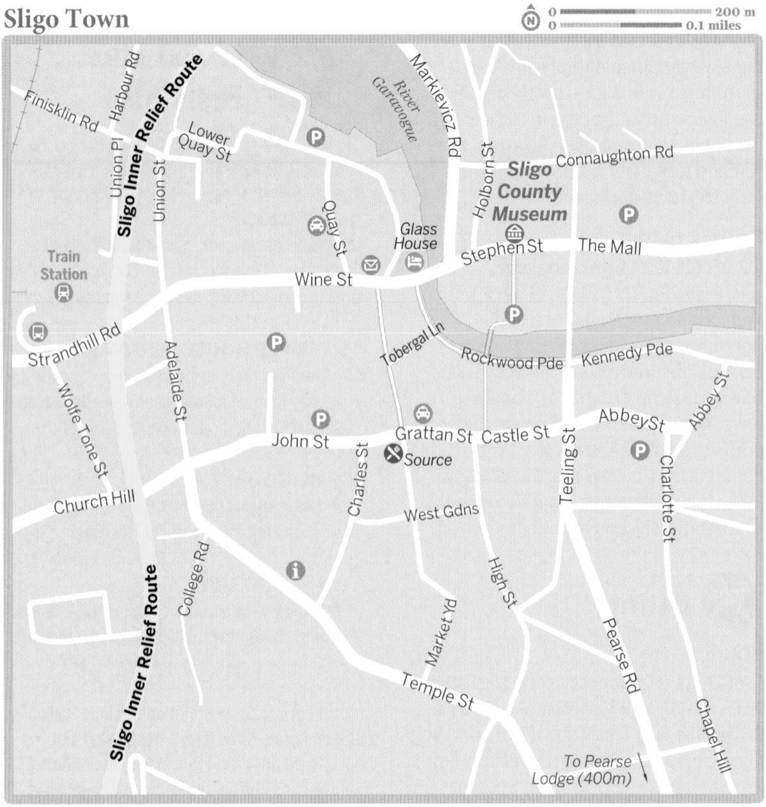

Finisklin Rd
Harbour Rd
Sligo Inner Relief Route
Lower Quay St
River Garavogue
Markievicz Rd
Union Pl
Union St
Quay St
Holborn St
Sligo County Museum
Connaughton Rd
Glass House
Stephen St
The Mall
Train Station
Wine St
Strandhill Rd
Tobergal Ln
Rockwood Pde
Kennedy Pde
Adelaide St
Wolfe Tone St
John St
Grattan St
Castle St
Abbey St
Source
Charles St
Teeling St
Charlotte St
Church Hill
West Gdns
College Rd
High St
Market Yd
Pearse Rd
Temple St
Chapel Hill
To Pearse Lodge (400m)

Rosses Point has two wonderful **beaches** and also boasts one of Ireland's most challenging and renowned golf links, **County Sligo Golf Course** (www.countysligogolfclub.ie), which attracts golfers from all over Europe.

Rosses Point is 8km northwest of Sligo on the R291. There are regular buses from Sligo.

Carrowmore Megalithic Cemetery

Despite its impressive scale and international importance, **Carrowmore** (www.heritageireland.ie; adult/child €3/1; ⏲10am-6pm mid-Apr–mid-Oct, final admission 5pm; P), one of the largest Stone Age cemeteries in Europe, is little visited and largely undervalued. Some 60 monuments including stone circles, passage tombs and dolmens adorn the rolling hills of this haunting site, which is thought to predate Newgrange in County Meath by 700 years. Over the centuries, many of the stones have been destroyed, and several remaining stones are on private land.

The delicately balanced dolmens were originally covered with stones and earth, so it requires a bit of mental effort to picture what this 2.5km-wide area might once have looked like. A large central cairn has been reconstructed to give visitors some insight into the materials and methods used at this time, while an exhibit in the roadside **visitor centre** gives the full low-down on this fascinating site.

To get here, follow the N4 south from Sligo for 5km and follow the signposts.

Strandhill

POP 1413

The great Atlantic rollers that sweep the shorefront of Strandhill make this long, red-gold **beach** unsafe for swimming. They have, however, made it a surfing mecca. Its handy 24-hour **surfcam** (www.strandhillsurf.eu) brings surfers scurrying whenever the surf's up. Gear hire and lessons can be arranged through **Perfect Day Surf Shop** (www.perfectdaysurfing.com; Shore Rd) and **Strandhill Surf School** (www.strandhillsurf.eu; Beach Front).

Sleeping

OCEAN WAVE LODGE B&B **€€**

(071-916 8115; www.oceanwavelodge.com; Top Rd; dm/s/d €20/35/50; P) This large modern house has excellent value, newly decorated rooms. Pale walls and linens contrast with dark wood furniture, cushions and throws in what are fairly minimalist but comfortable rooms. Breakfast is included, but there's also a self-catering kitchen and large lounge area for guest use.

Eating & Drinking

TRÁ BÁN Seafood **€€**

(071-912 8402; www.trabansligo.ie; Shore Rd; mains €17-27; closed Mon) This justly popular spot serves a menu strong on seafood but with a good selection of steak and pasta dishes thrown in. It has a lovely relaxed atmosphere that belies the quality of the food and the chic decor. It's a very popular local haunt so you'd be well advised to book in advance.

Getting There & Away

Strandhill is situated 8km due west of Sligo off the R292 airport road. Buses run from Sligo regularly.

South of Sligo Town

Carrowkeel Megalithic Cemetery

With a God's-eye view of the county from high in the Bricklieve Mountains, it's little wonder this hilltop site was sacred in prehistoric times. The windswept location is simultaneously eerie and uplifting, it's undeveloped nature and spectacular setting giving it an instantly momentous atmosphere. Dotted with around 14 cairns, dolmens and the scattered remnants of other graves, the site dates from the late Stone Age (3000 to 2000 BC).

West off the N4 road, Carrowkeel is closer to Boyle than Sligo town. From the latter, turn right in Castlebaldwin, then left at the fork; it's 2km uphill from the gate. Or take an Athlone bus from Sligo and ask to be dropped off at Castlebaldwin.

Easkey & Enniscrone

The town of Easkey seems blissfully unaware that it's one of Europe's best year-round surfing destinations. Pub

Carrowmore Megalithic Cemetery

PHOTOGRAPHER:GARETH McCORMACK / LONELY PLANET IMAGES ©

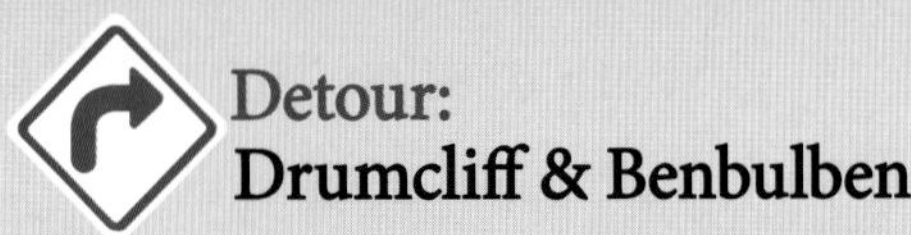

Detour: Drumcliff & Benbulben

Visible right along Sligo's northern coast, Benbulben (525m), often written Ben Bulben, resembles a table covered by a pleated cloth: its limestone plateau is uncommonly flat, and its near-vertical sides are scored by earthen ribs. Walking here can be dangerous for the uninitiated – the **Sligo Mountaineering Club** (www.sligomountaineeringclub.org) has advice.

Benbulben's beauty was not lost on WB Yeats. Before the poet died in Menton, France, in 1939, he had requested: 'If I die here, bury me up there on the mountain, and then after a year or so, dig me up and bring me privately to Sligo'. His wishes weren't honoured until 1948, when his body was interred in the churchyard at Drumcliff, where his great-grandfather had been rector.

Yeats' grave is next to the doorway of the Protestant church, and his youthful bride Georgie Hyde-Lee is buried alongside. Almost three decades her senior, Yeats was 52 when they married. The poet's epitaph is from his poem *Under Ben Bulben:*

Cast a cold eye
On life, on death.
Horseman, pass by!

Visiting the grave is somewhat disturbed by traffic noise along the N15 that no doubt has Yeats rolling over.

conversations revolve around hurling and Gaelic football, and the road to the beach isn't even signposted (turn off next to the childcare centre). Facilities are few; most surfers camp (free) around the castle ruins by the sea. If you want to hit the waves, information and advice are available from **Easkey Surfing & Information Centre** (Irish Surfing Association; ☎096-49428; www.isasurf.ie), **Longboard Ireland** (www.longboardireland.com) and **Irish Surfer** (www.irishsurfer.com).

Some 14km south at Enniscrone, a stunning beach known as the Hollow stretches for 5km. Surf lessons and board hire are available from Enniscrone-based **Seventh Wave Surf School** (☎087 971 6389; www.surfsligo.com).

Buses run four times daily (once on Sunday) from Sligo to Easkey (€10.20, one hour) and Enniscrone (€11.50, 1½ hours), from where they continue on to Ballina.

North of Sligo Town

Mullaghmore

The sweeping arc of dark-golden sand and the safe shallow waters make the pretty fishing village of Mullaghmore a popular family destination.

Mullaghmore Head is becoming known as one of Ireland's premier **big wave surf** spots with swells of up to 17m allowing for Hawaiian-style adventure. The country's first big wave tow-in surfing competition was held off Mullaghmore Head in 2011.

COUNTY DONEGAL

Getting There & Away

Donegal Airport (www.donegalairport.ie) has flights to/from Dublin (50 minutes, two daily) and to Glasgow Prestwick (50 minutes, three per week). It's in the townland (an ancient unit of local government) of Carrick Finn (Charraig Fhion), about 3km northwest of Annagry along the northwestern coast. There's no public transport to the airport, but there are car-rental desks in the terminal.

The City of Derry Airport (www.cityofderryairport.com) is just beyond the county's eastern border, in Northern Ireland.

Donegal Town

POP 2339

Pretty Donegal town occupies a strategic spot at the mouth of Donegal Bay. With a backdrop of the Blue Stack Mountains, a handsome and well-preserved castle, friendly locals and a good choice of places to eat and stay, it makes an excellent base for exploring the wild coastline nearby.

Sights & Activities

DONEGAL CASTLE Historic Building
(www.heritageireland.ie; Castle St; adult/child €4/2; 10am-6pm Easter–mid-Sep, 9.30am-4.30pm Thu-Mon mid-Sep–Easter) Guarding a picturesque bend of the River Eske, Donegal Castle remains an imperious monument to both Irish and English might. Built by the O'Donnells in 1474, it served as the seat of their formidable power until 1607, when the English decided to be rid of pesky Irish chieftains once and for all. Rory O'Donnell was no pushover, though, torching his own castle before fleeing to France in the infamous Flight of the Earls. Their defeat paved the way for the Plantation of Ulster by thousands of newly arrived Scots and English Protestants, creating the divisions that still afflict the island to this day.

DONEGAL BAY WATERBUS Boat Trips
(www.donegalbaywaterbus.com; Donegal Pier; adult/child €15/5; Easter-Oct) The most enjoyable way to explore the highlights of Donegal Bay is to take a 1¼-hour boat tour taking in everything from historic sites to seal-inhabited coves, admiring an island manor and a ruined castle

Donegal

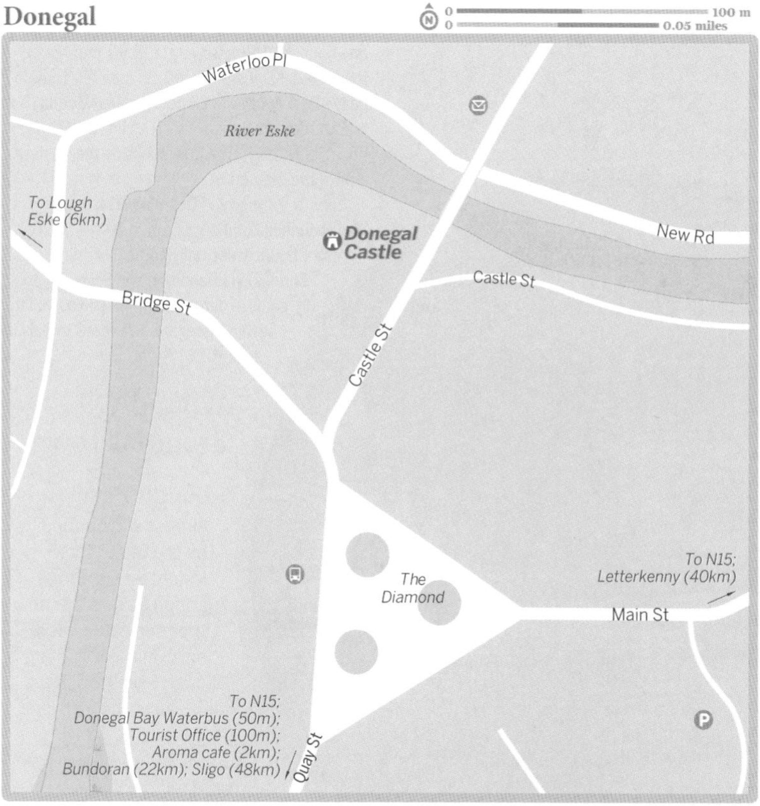

0 100 m
0 0.05 miles
Waterloo Pl
River Eske
To Lough Eske (6km)
Donegal Castle
New Rd
Castle St
Bridge St
Castle St
The Diamond
To N15; Letterkenny (40km)
Main St
To N15; Donegal Bay Waterbus (50m); Tourist Office (100m); Aroma cafe (2km); Bundoran (22km); Sligo (48km)
Quay St

along the way. The tour runs up to three times daily.

Sleeping & Eating

Good B&Bs and mediocre hotels are plentiful around Donegal town; for high-end luxury head out to nearby Lough Eske.

ARD NA BREATHA B&B **€€**

(074-972 2288; www.ardnabreatha.com; Drumrooske Middle; s/d from €70/110; Feb-Oct; P) In an elevated setting 1.5km north of town, this boutique guesthouse on a working farm has tasteful rooms with pine furniture and wrought-iron beds. It's an incredibly warm and welcoming place, with a full bar and restaurant (three-course dinner €38). Food is organic and from the farm or its neighbours where possible. Dinner is available at least Friday to Sunday by reservation.

AROMA Cafe **€**

(Donegal Craft Village; dishes €5-13; 9.30am-5.30pm Mon-Sat) Hidden in the far corner of Donegal's craft village, this small cafe has a big reputation for fine food. Along with the excellent coffee and luscious cakes, the blackboard specials feature seasonal local produce whipped up into tantalising soups, salads and wholesome hot dishes. There's seating outside for extra space on fine days.

Information

Tourist office (074-972 1148; donegal@failteireland.ie; Quay St; 9am-6pm Mon-Sat, noon-4pm Sun Jul-Aug, 9am-1pm & 2-5pm Mon-Sat Sep-Jun) In the 'Discover Ireland' building by the waterfront.

Getting There & Away

Bus Éireann (074-913 1008; www.buseireann.ie) services connect Donegal with Sligo (€12.50, one hour, six daily), Galway (€18.90, four hours, four daily), Killybegs (€6.90, 35 minutes, three daily), Derry (€14.30, 1½ hours, seven Monday to Saturday, six Sunday) and Dublin (€17.60, 4½ hours, nine daily). The bus stop is on the western side of the Diamond.

Feda O'Donnell (074-954 8114; www.fedaodonnell.com) buses run to Galway (€20, four hours, twice daily, three on Friday and Sunday) via Bundoran and Sligo. Call to confirm departure point. Minimum fare within Donegal is €7; buses to Galway cost €20.

Around Donegal Town

Lough Eske

Almost surrounded by the Blue Stack Mountains, tranquil Lough Eske is a scenic spot perfect for walking, cycling or fishing. Lough Eske translates as 'Lake of the Fish' and

Blue Stack Mountains reflected in Lough Eske

Mermaid Dreams

Ireland's only native spa therapy is the stuff of mermaid (or merman) fantasies. Part of Irish homeopathy for centuries, steaming your pores open then submerging yourself in a seaweed bath is said to help rheumatism and arthritis, thyroid imbalances, even hangovers. Certainly it leaves your skin feeling baby-soft: seaweed's silky oils contain a massive concentration of iodine, a key presence in most moisturising creams.

Seaweed baths are prevalent along the west coast but two places stand out. **Kilcullen's Seaweed Baths** (☎091-36238; www.kilcullenseaweedbaths.com; Enniscrone; s/tw bath €25/40; ⏰10am-8pm Jun-Sep, noon-8pm Mon-Fri & 10am-8pm Sat & Sun Oct-May) is the most traditional and has buckets of character. Set within a grand Edwardian structure, it seems perfectly fitting to sit with your head exposed and your body ensconced in an individual cedar steam cabinet before plunging into one of the original gigantic porcelain baths filled with amber water and cavorting seaweed.

For an altogether more modern setting, try **Voya Seaweed Baths** (☎071-916 8686; www.celticseaweedbaths.com; Shore Rd, Strandhill; s/tw bath €25/50; ⏰noon-8pm Mon & Tue, 11am-8pm Wed-Fri, 10am-8pm Sat & Sun), which has a beachfront location but somehow just isn't quite as much fun.

If too much relaxation is barely enough, both establishments also offer the chance to indulge in various other seaweed treatments, including body wraps and massages.

is a popular angling centre. The season runs from May to September, and there's a purpose-built angling centre on the shore where you can buy permits and hire boats.

There is no public transport to the lake.

Sleeping & Eating

LOUGH ESKE CASTLE Hotel €€€
(☎074-972 5100; www.solislougheskecastle.com; d €185-410; ⏰closed Sun-Wed Nov-Mar; P @ ᯤ ≈) Set in vast grounds, this imposing 19th-century castle was all but razed by fire in 1939 but has been painstakingly rebuilt and restored and is now the epitome of elegant country living. Most of the complex including the minimalist rooms, decadent spa and smart restaurant (mains €19 to €36) is spanking new but exudes a sense of classic sophistication mixed with impeccable contemporary style.

Rossnowlagh

POP 50

Rossnowlagh's spectacular 3km-long Blue Flag beach is a wide, sandy stretch of heaven that attracts families, surfers, kite-surfers and walkers throughout the year. The gentle rollers are great for learning to surf or honing your skills, and Ireland's largest and longest-running surfing competition, the **Rossnowlagh Intercounty Surf Contest**, is held here in late October. It's popularly known as the most sociable event in Ireland's surfing calendar.

Sights & Activities

FIN MCCOOL SURF SCHOOL Surfing
(☎071-985 9020; www.finmccoolsurfschool.com; gear rental per 3hr €29, 2hr lesson incl gear rental €35; ⏰10am-7pm Easter-Oct, 10am-7pm Sat & Sun mid-Mar–Easter & Nov-Christmas) Tuition, gear rental and accommodation are

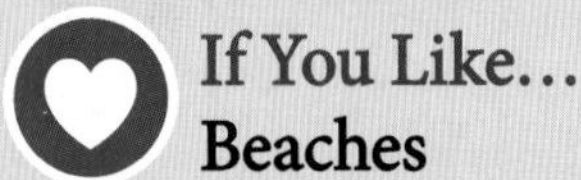

If You Like... Beaches

If you like the beach at Rossnowlagh (p279), you should explore some other beaches along Donegal's wild and rugged coastline:

1 TRAMORE Hike through the dunes from Dunfanaghy and you'll be rewarded with pristine sands on this secluded stretch of coast.

2 CARRICK FINN A gorgeous sweep of undeveloped sand near Donegal Airport.

3 PORTNOO A wishbone-shaped sheltered cove backed by undulating hills on the Loughrea Peninsula.

4 PORTSALON An idyllic stretch of sand lapped by turquoise water.

5 CULDAFF A long stretch of golden sand on the Inishowen Peninsula, popular with families.

available at this friendly surf lodge run by Pro Tour surf judge Neil Britton with the help of his extended family, most of whom have competed on the international circuit. The three- and four-bed dorms cost €20 per night, doubles €50.

Sleeping & Eating

SMUGGLERS CREEK B&B **€€**
(☎071-985 2367; www.smugglerscreekinn.com; s/d €45/80; daily Apr-Sep, Thu-Sun Oct-Mar; P) This combined pub/restaurant/guesthouse perches on the hillside above the bay. It's justifiably popular for its excellent food (mains €13 to €25) and sweeping views (room 4 has the best vantage point and a balcony into the bargain). There's live music on summer weekends.

Getting There & Away

Rossnowlagh is 17km southwest of Donegal town, and isn't served by public transport.

Bundoran

POP 1964

Blinking amusement arcades, hurdy-gurdy fairground rides and fast-food diners are Bundoran's stock-in-trade. But Donegal's best-known seaside resort also has superb surf, and attracts a mixed crowd of young families, OAPs and beach dudes. Outside summer, the carnival atmosphere abates and the town can be quite desolate.

Southwestern Donegal

Kilcar, Carrick & Around

POP 260

Kilcar (Cill Chártha) and its more attractive neighbour Carrick (An Charraig) make good bases for exploring the breathtaking coastline of southwestern Donegal, especially the stunning sea cliffs at Slieve League (see the boxed text on p282).

Glencolumbcille & Around

POP 255

'There's nothing feckin' here!', endearingly blunt locals forewarn visitors to Glencolumbcille (Gleann Cholm Cille). But, with some stunning walks fanning out from the three-pub village, scalloped beaches, an excellent Irish language and culture centre, and a fine little folk museum, chances are you'll disagree.

Approaching Glencolumbcille via the Glen Gesh Pass reinforces just how cut off this starkly beautiful coastal haven is from the rest of the world. You drive past miles of hills and bogs before the ocean appears, followed by a narrow, green valley and the small Gaeltacht village within it. This spot has been inhabited since 3000 BC and you'll find plenty of Stone Age remains.

GARETH McCORMACK / LONELY PLANET IMAGES ©

Don't Miss Surf Spots

Bundoran has two main surf spots: 'the Peak', an imposing reef break directly in front of the town, which should only be attempted by experienced surfers, and the less formidable beach break at Tullan Strand, just north of the town centre. In spring Bundoran hosts the annual **Bundoran Surfing Championships** (www.isasurf.ie).

The town has three surf schools, each of which rents gear and has its own basic hostel-style accommodation. A three-hour lesson costs about €35, gear rental €20 per day and accommodation €20 for a dorm room or €50 for a double. All offer deals on surf and accommodation packages.

THINGS YOU NEED TO KNOW

Bundoran Surf Co (☎071-984 1968; www.bundoransurfco.com; Main St)

Donegal Adventure Centre (☎071-984 2418; www.donegaladventurecentre.net; Bayview Ave) Youth-oriented place that also offers kayaking and gorge walking.

Turf n Surf (☎071-984 1091; www.turfnsurf.ie; Bayview Tce) Also runs hill-walking tours and sea-kayaking trips.

Ardara

POP 564

The heart of Donegal's traditional knitwear and tweed industry, the heritage town of Ardara is a pretty gateway to the switchbacks of Glen Gesh Pass. You can visit the weavers at work and see the region's most traditional crafts in action.

Sights

ARDARA HERITAGE CENTRE Museum

(☎074-954 1704; Main St; adult/child €3/1.20; 10am-6pm Mon-Sat, 2-6pm Sun Easter-Sep)

Set in the old town courthouse, this centre traces the story of Donegal tweed from sheep shearing to dye production and

GARETH McCORMACK / LONELY PLANET IMAGES ©

Don't Miss Slieve League

The Cliffs of Moher get more publicity, but the sea cliffs at Slieve League are higher. In fact, these spectacular polychrome cliffs are thought to be the highest in Europe, plunging some 600m to the sea. Looking down, you'll see two rocks nicknamed the school desk and chair by locals for reasons that are immediately obvious. From the lower car park, there's a path skirting up around the near-vertical rock face to the aptly named **One Man's Pass**. You can now also drive all the way to the top, where there's a car park. Be aware that mist and rain can roll in unexpectedly and rapidly, making conditions treacherous. The cliffs are particularly scenic at sunset when the waves crash dramatically far below and the ocean reflects the last rays of the day.

The cliffs are, if possible, even more impressive when viewed from the ocean below. Sightseeing boat trips along the Slieve League cliffs can be arranged by contacting **Nuala Star Teelin**. Prices are €20 to €25 per person, depending on numbers, with reductions for children. The 12-seater boat departs from the Teelin pier approximately every two hours (weather permitting). Sea angling and diving trips can also be arranged.

THINGS YOU NEED TO KNOW

Inishduff House (☎074-973 8542; www.inishduffhouse.com; Largy; s/d €50/85; P ☎) On the main road between Killybegs and Kilcar, this modern B&B has large, comfortable rooms, an incredibly warm welcome and wonderful sea views.

Kitty Kelly's (☎074-973 1925; Kilcar Rd; 3-course dinner €40; ⏱dinner May-Sep) Dining at this restaurant in a 200-year-old farmhouse feels more like attending an intimate dinner party. The menu is a gourmet take on traditional Irish favourites like rich stew and creamy trifle. It's on the coast road, 5km west of Killybegs. Opening hours vary annually; bookings are essential.

Nuala Star Teelin (☎074-973 9365; www.sliabhleagueboattrips.com; ⏱Apr-Oct)

weaving. A weaver demonstrates how a loom works and explains the stitches used in traditional garments.

Sleeping & Eating

GORT NA MÓNA
B&B **€€**
(📞074-953 7777; www.gortnamonabandb.com; Donegal Rd, Cronkeerin; s/d €50/70; P 📶) Huge but cosy and colourful rooms with orthopaedic mattresses, knotty pine furniture and silky throws. There are excellent home baking and preserves for breakfast, mountain views and a pristine beach on the doorstep. Gort na Móna is 2km south of town on the N56.

Shopping

Signs in the town centre point you to the town's knitwear producers.

Eddie Doherty (www.handwoventweed.com; Front St)

John Molloy's (www.johnmolloy.com)

Kennedy's (Front St)

Triona Design (www.trionadesign.com; Main St)

If You Like... Scenic Drives

If you like the snaking switchbacks traversing the Glen Gesh Pass in southwestern Donegal (p280), try these other scenic routes on for size (but keep your eye on the road!):

1 **DUNFANAGHY TO GWEEDORE**
A spectacular coastal highway links these towns.

2 **INISHOWEN PENINSULA**
A stunning 100-mile loop of the isolated peninsula.

3 **HORN HEAD**
The Head's vertiginous heights offer fine views.

4 **THE LINGERING ARC**
Through stunning Glenveagh National Park.

Northwestern Donegal

Dunlewey & Around

POP 700

Blink and chances are you've missed the tiny hamlet of Dunlewy (Dún Lúiche) beside Lough Dunlewy. You won't miss the spectacular scenery, however, or pinnacle-shaped Mt Errigal, whose bare face towers over the surrounding area. Plan enough time to get out of your car and do some walking here, as it's a magical spot.

Sights & Activities

MT ERRIGAL Walking
The looming presence of Mt Errigal (752m) seemingly dares walkers to attempt the tough but beautiful climb to its pyramid-shaped peak. If you're keen to take on the challenge, pay close attention to the weather. It's a dangerous climb on misty or wet days, when the mountain is shrouded in cloud and visibility is minimal.

There are two paths to the summit: the easier route, which covers 5km and takes around two hours; and the more difficult 3.3km walk along the northwestern ridge, which involves scrambling over scree for about 2½ hours. Details of both routes are available at the Dunlewey Lakeside Centre.

POISONED GLEN Walking
Legend has it that the stunning ice-carved rock face of the Poisoned Glen got its sinister name when the ancient one-eyed giant king of Tory, Balor, was killed here by his exiled grandson, Lughaidh, whereupon the poison from his eye split the rock and poisoned the glen. The less interesting truth, however, lies in a cartographic gaffe. Locals were inspired to name it An Gleann Neamhe (the Heavenly Glen), but when an English cartographer mapped the area, he carelessly marked it An Gleann Neimhe – the Poisoned Glen.

The R251 has several viewpoints overlooking the glen. It's possible to walk through it, although the ground is rough

Don't Miss Maghery & The Glen Gesh Pass

On the northern edge of the peninsula, tiny Maghery has a picturesque waterfront. If you follow the strand westward, you'll get to a rocky promontory full of caves. During Cromwell's 17th-century destruction, 100 villagers sought refuge here, but all except one were discovered and massacred.

About 1.5km east of Maghery is the enchanting **Assarancagh Waterfall**, beyond which is the beginning of a 10km marked trail to the **Glen Gesh Pass** (Glean Géis, meaning 'Glen of the Swans'). It's almost alpine in appearance; cascading mountains and lush valleys are dotted with isolated farmhouses and small lakes. If you're driving or cycling, you can get to the pass directly from Glencolumbcille by following the road signs for Ardara.

and boggy. From the lakeside centre a return walk along the glen is 12km and takes two to three hours. Watch out for the green lady – the resident ghost!

Dunfanaghy & Around

POP 316

Clustered around the waterfront, Dunfanaghy's small, attractive town centre has a surprisingly wide range of accommodation and some of the finest dining options in the county's northwest. Glistening beaches, dramatic coastal cliffs, mountain trails and forests are all within a few kilometres.

Sights

HORN HEAD Scenic Drive

The towering headland of Horn Head has some of Donegal's most spectacular coastal scenery and plenty of birdlife. Its dramatic quartzite cliffs, covered with bog and heather, rear over 180m high, and the view from their tops is heart-pounding.

The road circles the headland; the best approach by bike or car is in a clockwise direction from the Falcarragh end of Dunfanaghy. On a fine day, you'll encounter tremendous views of Tory, Inishbofin, Inishdooey and tiny Inishbeg islands to the west; Sheep Haven Bay and the Rosguill Peninsula to the east; Malin Head to the northeast; and the coast of Scotland beyond. Take care in bad weather as the route can be perilous.

BEACHES Beaches

The wide, sandy and virtually empty **Killahoey Beach** leads right into the heart of Dunfanaghy village. **Marble Hill Beach**, about 3km east of town in Port-na-Blagh, is more secluded but usually crammed in summer. Reaching Dunfanaghy's loveliest spot, **Tramore Beach**, requires hiking 20 minutes through the grassy dunes immediately south of the village.

Sleeping

WHINS B&B **€€**

(☎074-913 6481; www.thewhins.com; s/d €50/74; P) The colourful, individually decorated rooms at the Whins have patchwork quilts, quality furniture and a real sense of character. A wide choice of superb breakfasts is served upstairs in a room overlooking Horn Head. The B&B is about 750m south of the village opposite the golf course.

ARNOLD'S HOTEL Hotel **€€**

(☎074-913 6208; www.arnoldshotel.com; Main St; s/d €70/100; Apr-Oct; P @) Open since 1922, this family-run hotel has comfortable but rather corporate rooms. The friendly staff, with their suggestions for local activities, helpful attitude and warm welcome, more than make up for this, though. The bar serves decent classic Irish dishes (mains €9 to €23).

MILL RESTAURANT & GUESTHOUSE Irish **€€€**

(☎074-913 6985; www.themillrestaurant.com; Figart, Dunfanaghy; 3-course menu €43.50; dinner Tue-Sun mid-Mar–mid-Dec; P) An exquisite country setting and perfectly composed meals make dining here a treat. Set in an old flax mill that was for many years the home of renowned watercolour artist Frank Eggington, it also has six high-class guestrooms (single/double €70/100). The mill is just south of the town on the Falcarragh road. Book in advance.

Getting There & Away

Feda O'Donnell (www.feda.ie) buses from Crolly (€7, 40 minutes) to Galway (€20, five hours) stop in Dunfanaghy square twice daily Monday to Saturday and three times on Friday and Sunday.

John McGinley (www.johnmcginley.com) buses stop in Dunfanaghy two to four times daily en route to Letterkenny (€7, one hour) and Dublin (€20, five hours).

The **Lough Swilly** (www.loughswillybusco.com) bus from Dungloe stops in Dunfanaghy once daily Monday to Friday en route to Letterkenny (€7, one hour) and Derry (€11.40, two hours).

Eastern Donegal

Lough Gartan

The patriarch of Irish monasticism, St Colmcille (or Columba), was born in a lovely setting near the glassy Lough Gartan, and some isolated stone structures and crosses remain from his lifetime. The lake is 17km northwest of Letterkenny. It's beautiful driving country, but there's no public transport.

Sights

GLEBE HOUSE Historic Building

(www.heritageireland.ie; Churchill; adult/child €3/1; 11am-6.30pm daily Easter, Jul & Aug, Sat-Thu Jun & Sep) The English painter Derrick Hill bought this historic house in 1953, providing him with a mainland base close to his beloved Tory Island. Before Hill arrived, the house served as a rectory and then a hotel. The 1828-built mansion is sumptuously decorated with an evident love of all things exotic, but its real appeal is Hill's astonishing art collection. In addition to paintings by Hill and Tory Island's 'naive' artists are works by Picasso, Landseer, Hokusai, Jack B Yeats and Kokoschka. The woodland gardens

GARETH McCORMACK / LONELY PLANET IMAGES ©

Don't Miss Glenveagh National Park

Lakes shimmer like dew in the mountainous valley of **Glenveagh National Park**. With great knuckles of rock, swaths of bog and scatterings of oak and birch forest, the 16,500 sq km protected area is magnificent walking country, featuring nature trails along lakes and through woods and bog, as well as a viewing point near the castle. You can get free maps and information on self-guided walks at the visitor centre. Excellent, themed **ranger-led walks** are held regularly between April and October but must be booked in advance.

The **Glenveagh Visitor Centre** has a 20-minute audiovisual display on the ecology of the park and the infamous Adair. The **cafe** (Easter & Jun-Sep) serves hot food and snacks, and reception sells the necessary midge repellent, as vital in summer as walking boots and waterproofs are in winter. Camping is not allowed.

The delightfully showy **Glenveagh Castle** was modelled on Scotland's Balmoral Castle. Access is by guided tour only, which lasts 30 minutes. The most eye-catching of the flamboyantly decorated rooms include the tartan-and-antler-covered music room and the pink candy-striped room demanded by Greta Garbo whenever she stayed here.

The last guided tours of the castle leave about 45 minutes before closing time. Cars are not allowed beyond the visitor centre. You can walk the scenic 3.6km route to the castle or take the **shuttle bus**.

THINGS YOU NEED TO KNOW

Glenveagh National Park (Páirc Náisiúnta Ghleann Bheatha; www.glenveaghnationalpark.ie; 10am-6pm mid-Mar–Oct, 9am-5pm Nov–mid-Mar)

Ranger-led walks (074-913 7090; adult/child €5/free)

Glenveagh Visitor Centre cafe (Easter & Jun-Sep)

Glenveagh Castle (adult/child €5/2)

Shuttle bus (adult single/return €2/3, child return €2; every 15 min)

are also wonderful. A guided tour of the house takes about 45 minutes.

Northeastern Donegal

Rosguill Peninsula

The best way to appreciate Rosguill's rugged splendour is by driving, cycling or even walking the 15km **Atlantic Drive**. It's signposted to your left as you come into the sprawling village of **Carrigart** (Carraig Airt) from the south. There are plenty of thirst-quenching pubs in the village, and a pretty, secluded beach at **Trá na Rossan**. On no account should you swim in Mulroy Bay or the surrounding areas, as it's unsafe. Perhaps this is why the summer crowds don't linger here. Most prefer to travel 4km northward to **Downings** (often written as Downies), where the beach is spectacular, though it's much more built-up and lined with rows of static caravans.

Activities

ROSAPENNA GOLF CLUB Golf

(www.rosapenna.ie; Downings; green fees €50) Designed by St Andrew's Old Tom Morris in 1891 and remodelled by Harry Vardon in 1906, the scenery at this renowned golf club is as spectacular as the layout, which can challenge even the lowest handicapper.

Fanad Peninsula

The second-most northerly point in Donegal, Fanad Head thrusts out into the Atlantic to the east of Rosguill. The peninsula curls around the watery expanses of Mulroy Bay to the west and Lough Swilly to the east, the latter trimmed by high cliffs and sandy beaches.

Most travellers stick to the peninsula's eastern flank, visiting the beautiful beach and excellent golf course at Portsalon, and the quiet heritage towns of Rathmelton and Rathmullan. Accommodation is relatively limited, so book ahead in summer.

Detour: Olde Glen Bar & Restaurant

Authentic down to its original 1700s uneven stone floor, this treasure of a traditional pub **(Glen, Carrigart; mains €18-24; dinner Tue-Sat late May–mid-Sep, Fri-Sun Easter-late May, Sat & Sun mid-Sep–Easter)** in the tiny hamlet of Glen serves a sensational pint. Out the back, its small farmhouse-style restaurant serves outstanding blackboard specials. It doesn't take reservations and is popular with locals – turn up by 5.30pm to get a table for the 6pm seating, or by 7pm for a table at the 8pm seating. By the time you leave, you'll feel like a local yourself.

PORTSALON & FANAD HEAD

Once named the second-most-beautiful beach in the world by British newspaper the *Observer*, the tawny-coloured Blue Flag **beach** in Ballymastocker Bay, which is safe for swimming, is the principal draw of tiny Portsalon (Port an tSalainn). For golfers, however, the main attraction is the marvellously scenic **Portsalon Golf Club** (**074-915 9459; www.portsalongolfclub.com; Portsalon; green fees weekdays/weekends €40/50**).

The peninsula has some crankin' surf – for lessons contact **Adventure One Surf School** (**074-915 0262; www.adventureone.net; Ballyheirnan Bay, Fanad**). Two-hour lessons, which include gear rental, cost €30.

Sleeping & Eating

RATHMULLAN HOUSE B&B **€€€**

(**074-915 8188; www.rathmullanhouse.com; r from €220; P @**) This country house might be large and luxurious but the welcome from the family owners is so warm that you feel like you're staying with friends. Sprawled over wooded gardens on the shores of Lough Swilly, the original house dates from the 1780s, but extensions are sympathetic and stylish. Higher-priced rooms have claw-foot baths and some open to balconies or terraces. There's a tennis court, two genteel bars, and a glass-paned restaurant, the Weeping Elm, utilising organic produce from the property's walled gardens (menus €45 to €55; ⏲Thursday to Sunday).

The **Lough Swilly** (☎074-912 2863) bus from Letterkenny runs to Rathmullan (€4.40, 45 minutes) once daily from Monday to Friday, twice on Saturday, en route to Milford.

Inishowen Peninsula

The Inishowen Peninsula reaches just far enough into the Atlantic to qualify as the northernmost point on the island of Ireland: Malin Head. It is remote, rugged, desolate and sparsely populated, making it a special and quiet sort of place. Ancient sites and ruined castles abound, as do traditional thatched cottages that aren't yet demoted to storage sheds.

Surrounded by vast estuarine areas and open seas, the Inishowen Peninsula naturally attracts a lot of birdlife. The variety is tremendous, with well over 200 species passing through or residing permanently on the peninsula. Inishowen regularly receives well-travelled visitors from Iceland, Greenland and North America. Irregular Atlantic winds mean rare and exotic species also blow in from time to time. Twitchers should check out *Finding Birds in Ireland,* by Eric Dempsey and Michael O'Clery, or visit www.birdsireland.com. For information on everything else, visit www.visitinishowen.com.

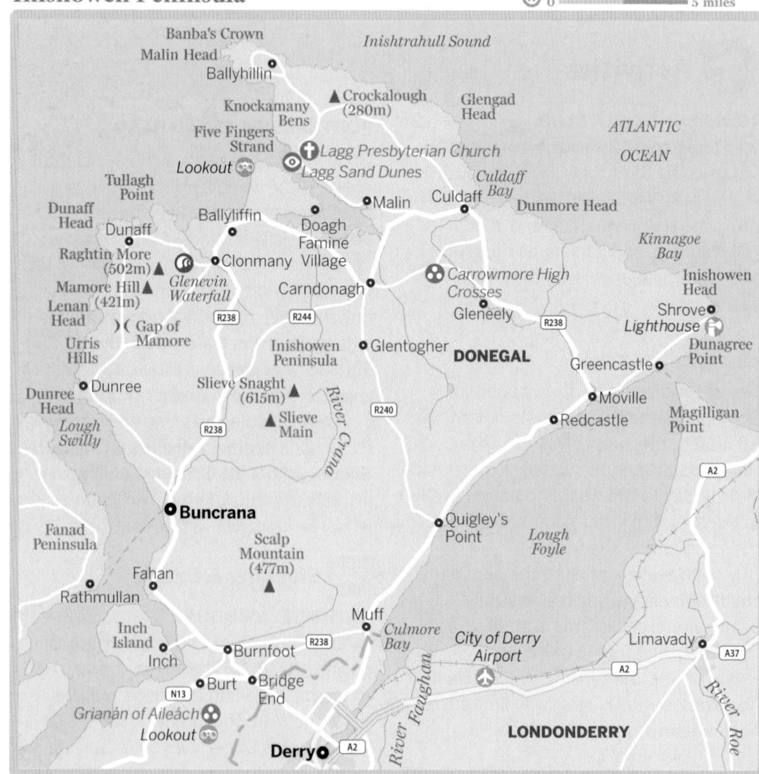

Buncrana

POP 3411

On the tame side of the peninsula, Buncrana is a busy but appealing town with its fair share of pubs and a 5km sandy beach on the shores of Lough Swilly. You'll find all the local services you'll need here before heading into the wilds further north.

Sleeping & Eating

WESTBROOK HOUSE B&B **€€**

(074-936 1067; www.westbrookhouse.ie; Westbrook Rd; s/d €40/70; P) A handsome Georgian house set in beautiful gardens, Westbrook offers old-world hospitality and charm by the bucket load. Chandeliers, antique furniture and cut glass give it a refined sophistication but the little trinkets and subtle florals make it very much a lived-in and loved home.

BEACH HOUSE Seafood **€€**

(074-936 1050; www.thebeachhouse.ie; The Pier, Swilly Rd; lunch mains €6.50-17.50, dinner mains €16-26; daily Jun-Aug, dinner Wed-Sun, lunch Sat & Sun Sep-Dec & Feb-May;) With plate-glass windows facing the lough, this aptly named cafe/restaurant projects an elegant simplicity. Although the menu is also intrinsically simple, the quality and preparation are a cut above: 'surf and turf', for example, comes with fillet steak, crab claws, langoustines and creamy bisque.

South of Buncrana

GRIANÁN OF AILEÁCH Fort

(10am-6pm; P) This amphitheatre-like stone **fort** encircles the top of Grianán Hill like a halo and offers eye-popping views of the surrounding loughs. On clear days you can see as far as Derry. Its mini-arena can resemble a circus whenever a tour bus rolls up and spills its load inside the 4m-thick walls.

The fort may have existed at least 2000 years ago, but it's thought that the site itself goes back to pre-Celtic times as a temple to the god Dagda. Between the 5th and 12th centuries it was the seat of the O'Neills, before being demolished by Murtogh O'Brien, king of Munster. Most of what you see now is a reconstruction built between 1874 and 1878.

The fort is 18km south of Buncrana near Burt, signposted off the N13.

The merry-go-round shaped **Burt Church** at the foot of the hill was modelled on the fort by Derry architect Liam McCormack and built in 1967.

Clonmany & Ballyliffin

POP 700

These two quaint villages and their surrounds have plenty to occupy visitors for a day or two. Both have post offices but no banks.

With two championship courses, **Ballyliffin Golf Club** (www.ballyliffingolfclub.

Malin Head cattle (p289)

PHOTOGRAPHER: © ILSE SCHRAMA / ALAMY

com; Ballyliffin; green fees €60-70) is among the best places to play a round of golf in Donegal. The scenery is so beautiful that it can distract even the most focused golfer. Its above-average restaurant, The Links, overlooks the fairways (lunch and dinner mains €9.50 to €20).

Sleeping & Eating

GLEN HOUSE B&B **€€**
(**074-937 6745; www.glenhouse.ie; Straid, Clonmany; s/d €60/90;**) Despite the grand surroundings and luxurious rooms, you'll find neither the pretension nor the high prices of many country house hotels at this gem of a guesthouse. The welcome couldn't be friendlier or more professional, the rooms are a lesson in restrained sophistication and the setting is incredibly tranquil. The walking trail to Glenevin Waterfall starts next door to the **tearoom** (**10am-6pm daily Jun-Aug, Sat & Sun Sep-May**), which opens to a timber deck. From September to May there's a minimum two-night stay.

Malin Head

Even if you've already seen Ireland's southernmost point and its westernmost point, you'll still be impressed when you clap your eyes on Malin Head, the island's northern extent. The head's rocky, weather-battered slopes feel like they're being dragged unwillingly into the sea. It's great for wandering on foot, absorbing the stark natural setting and pondering deep subjects as the wind tries to blow the clothes off your back. Bring cash with you, as there are no ATMs here.

On the northernmost tip, called **Banba's Crown**, stands a cumbersome cliff-top **tower** that was built in 1805 by the British admiralty and later used as a Lloyds signal station. Around it are unattractive concrete huts that were used by the Irish army in WWII as lookout posts. To the west from the fort-side car park, a path leads to **Hell's**

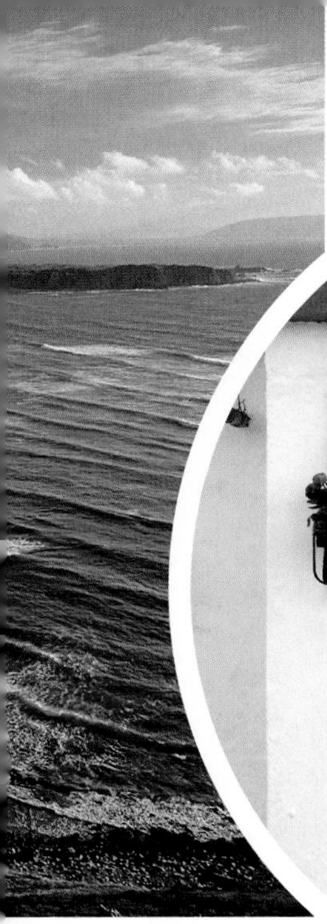

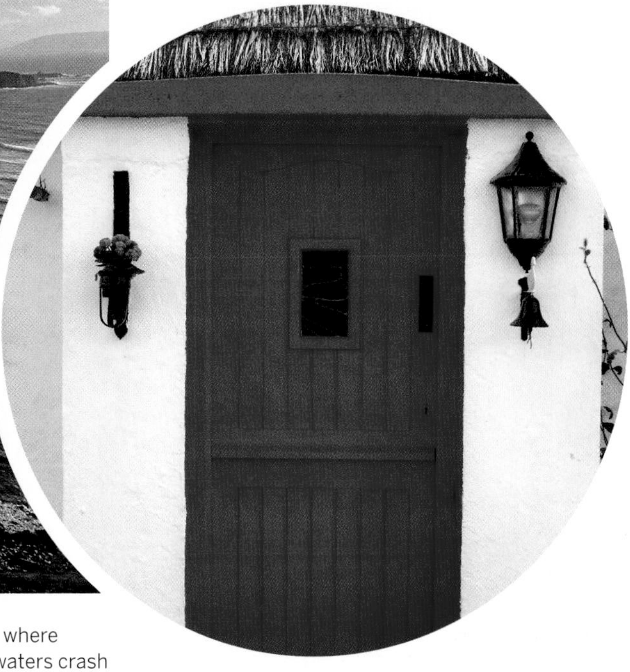

Left: Five Fingers Strand, Malin Head;
Below: Door of traditional thatched cottage, Malin Head

Hole, a chasm where the incoming waters crash against the rocky formations. To the east a longer headland walk leads to the **Wee House of Malin**, a hermit's cave in the cliff face.

Several endangered bird species thrive here, and this is one of the few places in Ireland where you can still hear the call of the endangered corncrake in summer. Other birds to look out for are choughs, snow buntings and puffins.

The Plantation village of **Malin**, on Trawbreaga Bay, 14km southeast of Malin Head, has a pretty movie-set quality. Walkers can head out from the tidy village green on a circular route that takes in **Knockamany Bens**, a local hill with terrific views, as well as **Lagg Presbyterian Church** (3km northwest from Malin), the oldest church still in use on the peninsula. The massive sand dunes at **Five Fingers Strand**, another 1km beyond the church, are a dog's dream.

Sleeping & Eating

VILLAGE B&B B&B **€€**
(074-937 0763; www.malinvillagebandb.com; The Green; s/d €45/70) Sitting right in the centre of the village, this lovely B&B has a choice of cosy rooms, some traditional with antique furniture and brocade armchairs, others more contemporary with white linen and pretty floral patterns. Although you'll get a hearty breakfast here, guests also have use of a kitchen and utility room so you can cook a meal or catch up on some laundry.

Belfast, Derry & the Antrim Coast

Once a byword for trouble, Northern Ireland has emerged from nearly four decades of sectarian conflict to finally take its place as one of the loveliest corners of the island, with as much to offer as any of Ireland's tourist havens.

The regional capital, Belfast, has shrugged off its bomb-scarred past and reinvented itself as one of the most exciting and dynamic cities in Britain – of which Northern Ireland remains a firm part. You can explore the tensions as they're expressed today in the iconic neighbourhoods of West Belfast or in the province's second city, Derry (or Londonderry), which is leading the north's cultural revival.

And it wouldn't be Ireland if it didn't have its fair share of stunning landscapes: from the Antrim coast and its world-famous Giant's Causeway to the mountains of Mourne in south County Down.

Houses in the Bogside (p323), Derry
PHOTOGRAPHER: MARTIN MOOS / LONELY PLANET IMAGES ©

Belfast, Derry & the Antrim Coast

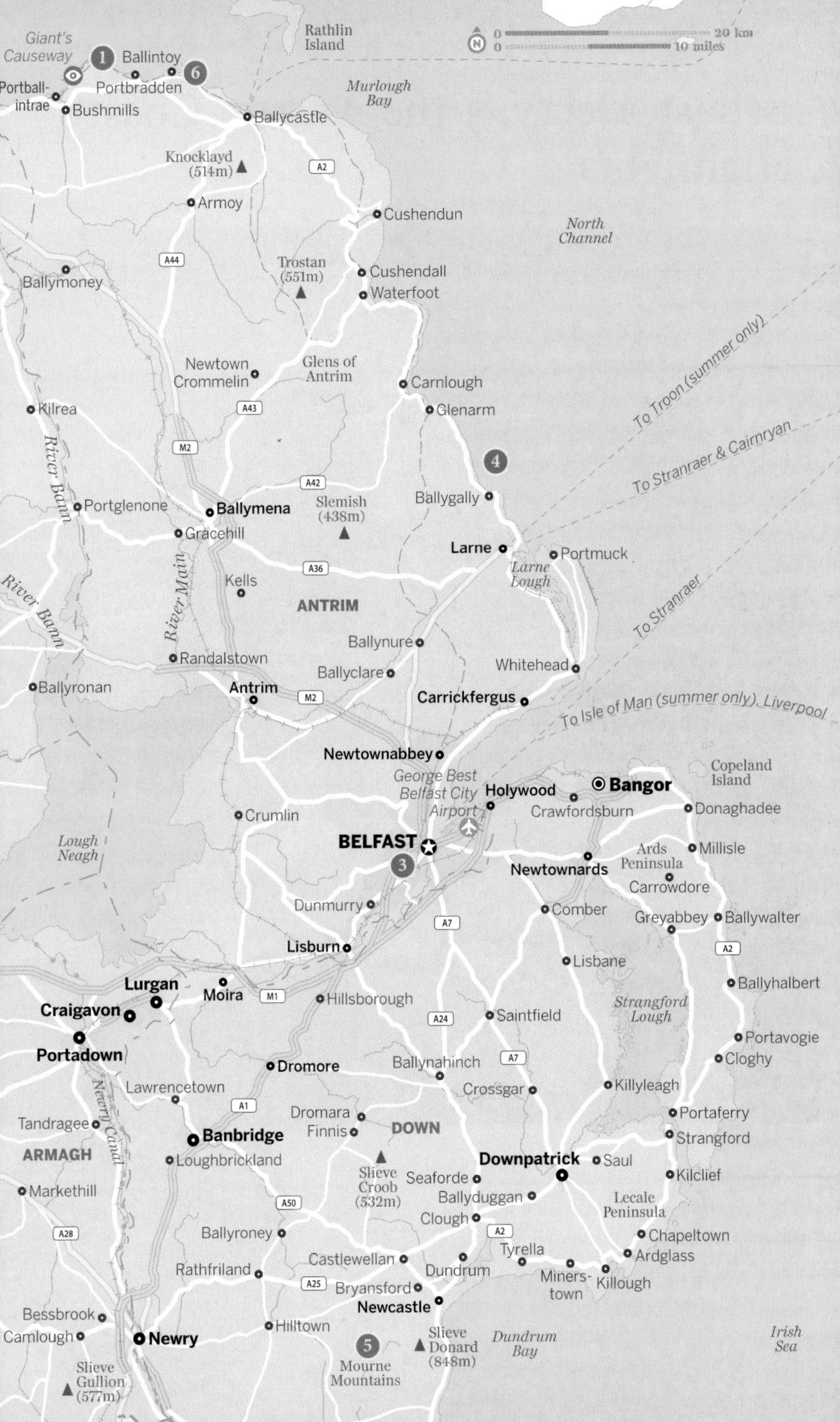

Rathlin Island
0 20 km
0 10 miles
Giant's Causeway
Ballintoy
Portballintrae
Portbradden
Bushmills
Murlough Bay
Ballycastle
Knocklayd (514m)
A2
Armoy
Cushendun
North Channel
A44
Trostan (551m)
Ballymoney
Cushendall
Waterfoot
Newtown Crommelin
Glens of Antrim
Carnlough
Kilrea
A43
Glenarm
To Troon (summer only)
River Bann
M2
To Stranraer & Cairnryan
A42
Ballygally
Portglenone
Ballymena
Slemish (438m)
Gracehill
Larne
Portmuck
Larne Lough
A36
Kells
River Bann
River Main
ANTRIM
To Stranraer
Ballynure
Randalstown
Whitehead
Ballyclare
Ballyronan
Antrim
M2
Carrickfergus
To Isle of Man (summer only), Liverpool
Newtownabbey
Copeland Island
George Best Belfast City Airport
Holywood
Bangor
Crawfordsburn
Donaghadee
Crumlin
Lough Neagh
BELFAST
Ards Peninsula
Millisle
Newtownards
Carrowdore
Dunmurry
Comber
Greyabbey
Ballywalter
A7
Lisburn
A2
Lisbane
Lurgan
Ballyhalbert
Moira
M1
Hillsborough
Craigavon
A24
Saintfield
Strangford Lough
Portadown
Portavogie
A7
Cloghy
Dromore
Ballynahinch
Newry Canal
Lawrencetown
Crossgar
Killyleagh
A1
Tandragee
Dromara
Portaferry
Finnis
DOWN
Banbridge
Strangford
ARMAGH
Loughbrickland
Downpatrick
Saul
Slieve Croob (532m)
Seaforde
Kilclief
Markethill
Ballyduggan
Lecale Peninsula
A50
Clough
A28
A2
Chapeltown
Ballyroney
Tyrella
Ardglass
Castlewellan
Rathfriland
Dundrum
Minerstown
Killough
A25
Bryansford
Newcastle
Bessbrook
Hilltown
Slieve Donard (848m)
Dundrum Bay
Irish Sea
Camlough
Newry
Mourne Mountains
Slieve Gullion (577m)

Belfast, Derry & the Antrim Coast's Highlights

1

Coastal Causeway Route

There is nothing better than driving along on a sunny day with the green Glens of Antrim on your left and the Irish Sea with views over to Scotland on your right – and as you turn each bend you get another spectacular view. Giant's Causeway, County Antrim

Need to Know

Best Time to Visit April to September. **Advance Planning** Book accommodation early, especially around the NorthWest 200. **For further coverage, see p321.**

Local Knowledge

Coastal Causeway Route Don't Miss List

BY JASON POWELL, CAUSEWAY COASTS & GLENS TOURISM (WWW.CAUSEWAYCOASTANDGLENS.COM)

1 GIANT'S CAUSEWAY

The **Giant's Causeway** (p321) is Northern Ireland's most popular attraction and my favourite place. The 40,000 basalt columns, the 400ft cliffs and the views all show the magnificence of Mother Nature. Best time to visit? When the weather is a bit stormy and the Atlantic waves crash in on the rocks!

2 RATHLIN ISLAND

There is no better place to get away from it all than **Rathlin Island** (p322; pictured above left). Just five miles from Ballycastle, it is a world away from the mainland. There are only a few cars on the island, so it is ideal for walking or cycling, and it is a great place to see sea birds as it is home to the largest sea bird colony in Northern Ireland.

3 MORTON'S FISH & CHIPS

Morton's (**☎ 028 2076 1100; 22 Bayview Rd, Ballycastle**) is tiny, but it serves the best fish and chips on the island. You have to wait about 10 minutes as they make it all fresh, but once you have your order, you can just sit out on the harbour and watch the fishing boats sailing around the harbour.

4 GLENARIFF FOREST PARK

Glenariff Forest Park is a great place to get back to nature with great walks that take you past three wonderful waterfalls. As you get to the higher ground, you will reach some magnificent mountain viewpoints.

5 NORTHWEST 200

When I first stood at the grid of the **NorthWest 200** (p43; www.northwest200.org), with the bikes revving ready to go, I could feel the tension and adrenaline of the country's biggest sporting event. The noise was unbelievable – I could feel the vibrations going right through my body. At that moment I was converted.

Bogside, Derry

The close-knit community of the Bogside has made the headlines for all the wrong reasons since the late 1960s, but the last decade has seen it return to its traditional strengths, and it is now one of the city's most interesting districts. **Below:** The Civil Rights Mural – The Beginning; **Top right:** Operation Motorman mural; **Bottom right:** The Petrol Bomber mural. Murals in Rossville St, Bogside, by the Bogside Artists.

Need to Know

Best Time to Visit Anytime! **Security Concerns** None – despite its troubled past, the Bogside is safe and well explored by curious visitors. **For further coverage, see p323.**

2

Local Knowledge

Bogside, Derry Don't Miss List

BY TOM KELLY, KEVIN HASSON & WILLIAM KELLY, BOGSIDE ARTISTS (WWW.BOGSIDEARTISTS.COM)

1 THE PEOPLE'S ART GALLERY

Our murals are the result of a vision from the start to tell our story in the form of a simple but edifying panorama, not just for locals but for anyone. **The People's Gallery** is without doubt the number one attraction in the Bogside.

2 FREE DERRY CORNER GABLE END

The **gable-end** is a significant feature of the Bogside. Its slogan was derived from Berkeley's famous 'You Are Now Entering Free Berkeley' and for years many people came forward to claim the inspired idea to be originally theirs! Still, it is a site of great importance for Bogsiders as a moment in their history, captured forever.

3 BLOODY SUNDAY MEMORIAL

This memorial lists the names of the 14 victims killed on 30 January 1972 by British soldiers. It is situated close to where most of the victims had been killed. It is visited by countless tourists each year and wreaths are often laid there on commemorative occasions.

4 LONG TOWER CHAPEL

The **Long Tower** is a true Bogside landmark: so many local people were baptised and married there. The pews and very bricks of the building have been sanctified by the sufferings and anguish of Bogside Catholics during the Troubles. If the walls could speak, they would moan.

5 THE PETROL BOMBER MURAL

Originally titled 'The Battle of the Bogside', our first mural was created to commemorate the events of August 1969, one of the first major confrontations of the Troubles. The mural shows a young boy in a gas mask – which he used to try to protect himself from the CS gas used by the RUC – holding a petrol bomb.

West Belfast

For more than three decades, West Belfast (p310) was synonymous with violence, sectarianism and the politics of hatred. And while divisions remain entrenched, the violence has long since abated and the two communities are openly welcoming of visitors eager to see in person what they would once only see on the news. Visitors also witness firsthand the extraordinary efforts being made to regenerate communities that not so long ago were literally dying on their feet. Republican political mural, Falls Rd, Belfast

3

5

Mourne Mountains

One of Northern Ireland's most magnificent corners is the humpbacked granite hills of the Mourne Mountains (p316), flecked with yellow gorse and dotted with whitewashed cottages and drystone walls. Some of the best walking in the province is in these gentle hills, especially around the magnificent Silent Valley Reservoir.

RICHARD CUMMINS / LONELY PLANET IMAGES ©

The Antrim Coast

4

It's a no brainer, but the number one tourist destination in Northern Ireland deserves all of the kudos it gets. The Antrim Coast (p322), though, is about more than just coastline: from the intoxicating charms of the Bushmill's Distillery (p319), to the more sedate pleasures of Rathlin Island (p322), there's something for everyone. Giant's Causeway, County Antrim

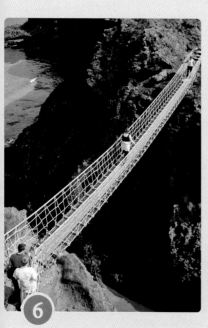

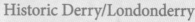

JOHN SONES / LONELY PLANET IMAGES ©

6

Carrick-a-Rede Rope Bridge

Crossing the 20 swaying metres of the Carrick-a-Rede Rope Bridge (p320) to the eponymous island is either breathtaking or frightening (depending on your head for heights); it's a short, stunning clamber that will linger long in the memory. It's on the Antrim Coast, between the Giant's Causeway and Ballycastle.

7

Historic Derry/Londonderry

Northern Ireland's second city (p322) – Ireland's only surviving walled city – is second to none in terms of history and character. A walk around the historic walls is one of the highlights of any trip, as is an exploration of the well-storied Bogside district, which, like West Belfast, was at the heart of the Troubles but is in the midst of restoring itself and its battered community to its rightful pride of place.

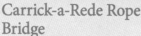

Belfast, Derry & the Antrim Coast's Best...

Spots to Lay Your Head

- **Malmaison Hotel** (p313) A successful conversion of two elegant Italianate warehouses.
- **Clarmont** (p318) Welcoming B&B in Portrush with great sea views.
- **Merchant's House** (p325) Superb Georgian-style B&B.
- **Whitepark House B&B** (p320) Handsome 18th-century home overlooking White Park Bay.

Cultural Stops

- **Ulster Folk Museum** (p316) 18th- and 19th-century living brought to life.
- **Ulster Transport Museum** (p316) See the ill-fated DeLorean car.
- **Ulster Museum** (p310) Superb collection.
- **Ormeau Baths Gallery** (p307) Northern Ireland's top-rated modern art gallery.
- **Museum of Free Derry** (p325) One of the best political museums in Europe.

Bites

- **Ginger** (p313) Small and unassuming, the food is outstanding.
- **Halo Pantry & Grill** (p326) Three floors of food, from snacks to formal dining.
- **Cayenne** (p314) Paul Rankin's culinary reputation just gets better.
- **55 Degrees North** (p318) Antrim Coast's best eatery.
- **Bushmills Inn** (p319) Superb restaurant attached to popular inn.

Scenic Walks

- **Mourne Mountains** (p316) Best walks in the province.
- **Cushendun** (p322) Bracing coastal walks.
- **Rathlin Island** (p322) Perfect island walk.
- **Derry City Walls** (p323) Walk the length of the 16th-century walls.

Left: Cushendun (p322) coastline, County Antrim; **Above:** Derry city walls (p323)

Need to Know

ADVANCE PLANNING

- **Two months before** Book your accommodation, especially along the Antrim Coast.
- **One month before** Read a book on Northern Ireland's turbulent history.
- **Two weeks before** Make reservations for the province's top restaurants.

RESOURCES

- **Discover Northern Ireland** (www.discovernorthernireland.com) Official website of Northern Ireland Tourism Bureau.
- **Antrim** (www.countyantrim.com) Attractions, accommodation and restaurants in Antrim.
- **Belfast Tourism** (www.gotobelfast.com) Belfast Welcome Centre.
- **Derry Tourism** (www.derryvisitor.com) City's official website.

GETTING AROUND

- **Bus** Excellent regional service on all main routes linking all towns and cities.
- **Train** Good between Belfast and Derry, serving the Antrim Coast.
- **Car** Probably the easiest way of getting around.

BE FOREWARNED

- **Sectarianism** Broad divisions still exist, especially in so-called 'interface' areas in parts of Belfast; these are best avoided, as is most of the province around the marching days of 11–12 July, when Loyalists march throughout the province.
- **Seasonal tourism** Many hotels and restaurants shut down between December and Easter.

Belfast, Derry & the Antrim Coast Itineraries

Northern Ireland is fascinating and beautiful. These itineraries cover its largest, most interesting city and its most scenic and best-loved stretch of coastline.

3 DAYS

BELFAST & THE MOURNE MOUNTAINS

Best of Belfast

This itinerary is all about the province's capital and biggest city, **(1) Belfast**. Start your visit with a free, guided tour of **City Hall**. Take a black taxi tour of the **West Belfast murals**, then ask the taxi driver to drop you off at the **John Hewitt Bar & Restaurant** for lunch. Catch a **Titanic tour** boat trip around the harbour, then walk across the bridge over the Lagan to cover the **Titanic Trail**, which is currently in the midst of a massive and ambitious programme of development. Round off the day with dinner at celebrity chef Paul Rankin's latest venture, **Cayenne**. On your second day, get outside the city centre, visiting the **(2) Ulster Folk and Transport museums**, which include the original design drawings for the world's most famous doomed ocean liner. On your return, take in a meal at the superb **Ginger**. On your final day, get to the **(3) Mourne Mountains** for a nice energetic walk; as you amble about, remember that Belfast-born CS Lewis based his vision of Narnia on the views before you.

Top Left: Exhibit at the Ulster Transport Museum (p316); **Top Right:** Rathlin Island (p322), County Antrim

5 DAYS

GLENS OF ANTRIM TO GIANT'S CAUSEWAY

The Antrim Coast

Most visitors naturally make their way to the Antrim Coast, the province's number one tourist destination and a favourite of many locals themselves. You could drive it in a couple of hours, but this five-day itinerary is all about taking a bit of time to enjoy it. Start north of Belfast at the **(1) Glens of Antrim**, making sure to visit the seaside village of **(2) Cushenden**, famous for its National Trust Cornish-style cottages. Take the **(3) Torr Head Scenic Rd** to Ballycastle, from which you can go on to explore the bird sanctuary of **(4) Rathlin Island** – guillemots, kittiwakes, razorbills and puffins from mid-April to August. If you're up for it, make the short but devilishly challenging crossing to **(5) Carrick-a-Rede Island**, for which you'll need real sea legs! Your next stop is the historic town of **(6) Bushmills** (p318), home of the famous distillery that should be a highlight of a visit here. And finally, clamber across the most famous site in all of Northern Ireland, the hexagonal natural wonders that make up the **(7) Giant's Causeway**. If you've taken the appropriate amount of time, five days will have flown by!

Discover Belfast, Derry & the Antrim Coast

At a Glance

- **Belfast** (p306) A metropolis growing in confidence and distractions after years of living under a violent shadow.
- **Derry/Londonderry** (p322) The province's second city has a more intimate character and plenty of history.
- **Antrim Coast** (p322) Scenic coastline stretching virtually the entire length of the north of the province, from just north of Belfast to just east of Derry.

Belfast City Hall

PHOTOGRAPHER: RICHARD CUMMINS / LONELY PLANET IMAGES ©

BELFAST

Once lumped with Beirut, Baghdad and Bosnia as one the four 'B's for travellers to avoid, Belfast has pulled off a remarkable transformation from bombs-and-bullets pariah to a hip hotels-and-hedonism party town.

Dangers & Annoyances

Even at the height of the Troubles, Belfast wasn't a particularly dangerous city for tourists, and today you're less at risk from crime here than you are in London. It's best, however, to avoid the so-called 'interface areas' – near the peace lines in West Belfast, Crumlin Rd and the Short Strand (just east of Queen's Bridge) – after dark; if in doubt about any area, ask at your hotel or hostel.

At the time of research dissident Republican groups had launched a bombing campaign aimed at police and military targets. Security alerts usually have no effect on visiting tourists (other than roads being closed), but be aware of the potential danger. You can follow the Police Service of Northern Ireland (PSNI) on Twitter (@policeserviceni) and receive immediate notification of any alerts.

If you want to take photos of fortified police stations, army posts or other military or quasi-military paraphernalia, get permission first, just to be on the safe side. In the Protestant and Catholic strongholds of West Belfast it's best not to photograph people without permission; always ask first and be prepared to accept a refusal. Taking pictures of the murals is not a problem.

Sights

City Centre

FREE **CITY HALL** Historic Building

(Map p308; www.belfastcity.gov.uk; Donegall Sq; guided tours 11am, 2pm & 3pm Mon-Fri,

2pm & 3pm Sat) The Industrial Revolution transformed Belfast in the 19th century, and its rapid rise to muck-and-brass prosperity is manifested in the extravagance of City Hall. Built in classical Renaissance style in fine, white Portland stone, it was completed in 1906 and paid for from the profits of the gas supply company.

FREE CROWN LIQUOR SALOON Historic Building
(Map p308; www.crownbar.com; 46 Great Victoria St; 11.30am-11pm Mon-Sat, 12.30-10pm Sun) There are not too many historical monuments that you can enjoy while savouring a pint of beer, but the National Trust's Crown Liquor Saloon is one of them.

The interior (1898) sports a mass of stained and cut glass, marble, ceramics, mirrors and mahogany, all atmospherically lit by genuine gas mantles. A long, highly decorated bar dominates one side of the pub, while on the other is a row of ornate wooden snugs. The snugs come equipped with gunmetal plates (from the Crimean War) for striking matches, and bell pushes that once allowed drinkers to order top-ups without leaving their seats (alas, no longer).

GRAND OPERA HOUSE Historic Building
(Map p308; www.goh.co.uk; Great Victoria St) One of Belfast's great Victorian landmarks is the Grand Opera House, across the road from the Crown Liquor Saloon. Opened in 1895, and completely refurbished in the 1970s, it suffered grievously at the hands of the IRA, having sustained severe bomb damage in 1991 and 1993. It was said that as the Europa Hotel next door was home to the media during the Troubles, the IRA brought the bombs to them so they wouldn't have to leave the bar.

FREE ORMEAU BATHS GALLERY Art Gallery
(Map p308; www.ormeaubaths.co.uk; 18A Ormeau Ave; 10am-5pm Tue-Sat) Housed in a converted 19th-century public bathhouse, the Ormeau Baths Gallery is Northern Ireland's principal exhibition space for contemporary visual art. The gallery stages changing exhibitions of work by Irish and international artists, and has hosted controversial showings of works by Gilbert and George, and Jake and Dinos Chapman. The gallery is a few blocks south of Donegall Sq.

Titanic Quarter

Belfast's former shipbuilding yards – the birthplace of RMS *Titanic* – stretch along the east side of the River Lagan, dominated by the towering yellow cranes known as **Samson and Goliath** (dating from the 1970s). The area is currently undergoing a £1 billion regeneration project known as **Titanic Quarter** **(www.titanicquarter.com)**, which plans to transform the long-derelict docklands over the next 15 to 20 years.

Queen's Rd strikes northeast from the Odyssey Complex into the heart of the Titanic Quarter, a massive redevelopment area that is part industrial wasteland, part building site and part hi-tech business park. Not much remains from the time when the *Titanic* was built, but what does has been restored, and the challenging modern outline of Titanic Belfast now forms the centrepiece of the district. A series of **information boards** along Queen's Rd describe items and areas of interest.

SS NOMADIC Historic Ship
(www.nomadicbelfast.com; Queens Rd) The **Hamilton Graving Dock** (off map p308), just northeast of the Odyssey Complex, is now the permanent berth of the SS *Nomadic* – the only surviving vessel of the White Star Line (the shipping company that owned the *Titanic*). In 2006 she was rescued from the breaker's yard and brought to Belfast. The little steamship once served as a tender ferrying 1st- and 2nd-class passengers between Cherbourg Harbour and the giant Olympic Class ocean liners (which were too big to dock at the French port); on 10 April 1912 she delivered 142 1st-class passengers to the ill-fated *Titanic*. She was still undergoing restoration work at the time of research, but should be open to the public by April 2012.

Central Belfast

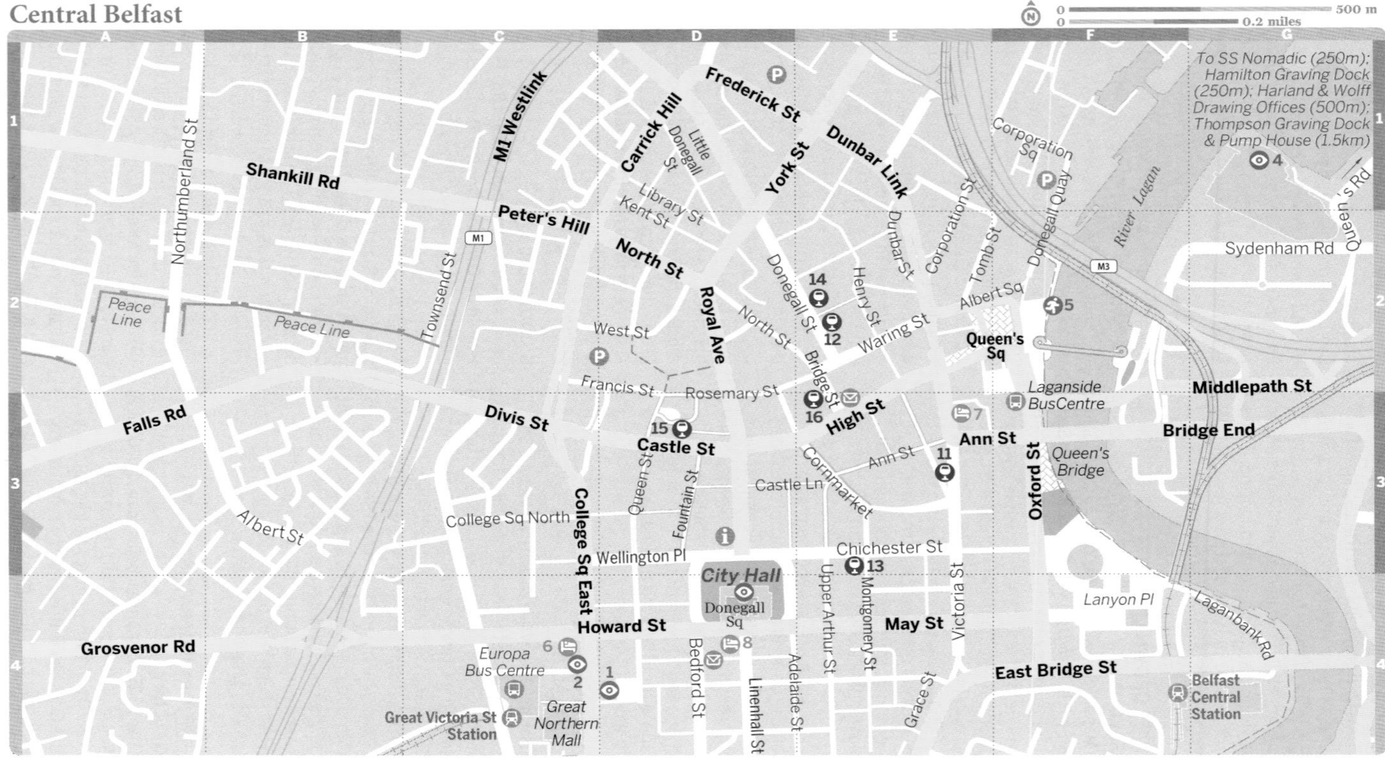
0 500 m
0 0.2 miles
To SS Nomadic (250m); Hamilton Graving Dock (250m); Harland & Wolff Drawing Offices (500m); Thompson Graving Dock & Pump House (1.5km)
Queen's Rd
Sydenham Rd
River Lagan
M3
Donegall Quay
Corporation Sq
Middlepath St
Bridge End
Laganside BusCentre
Queen's Bridge
Oxford St
Queen's Sq
Albert Sq
Tomb St
Corporation St
Dunbar St
Dunbar Link
Frederick St
York St
Henry St
Waring St
Donegall St
Bridge St
High St
Ann St
Victoria St
Lanyon Pl
Laganbank Rd
Belfast Central Station
East Bridge St
May St
Grace St
Montgomery St
Upper Arthur St
Adelaide St
Linenhall St
Chichester St
Cornmarket
Castle Ln
City Hall
Donegall Sq
Bedford St
Howard St
Wellington Pl
Fountain St
Queen St
Castle St
Rosemary St
North St
Royal Ave
Little Donegall St
Carrick Hill
Library St
Kent St
West St
Francis St
College Sq East
College Sq North
Divis St
Peter's Hill
M1 Westlink
M1
Townsend St
Peace Line
Shankill Rd
Northumberland St
Falls Rd
Albert St
Grosvenor Rd
Europa Bus Centre
Great Northern Mall
Great Victoria St Station

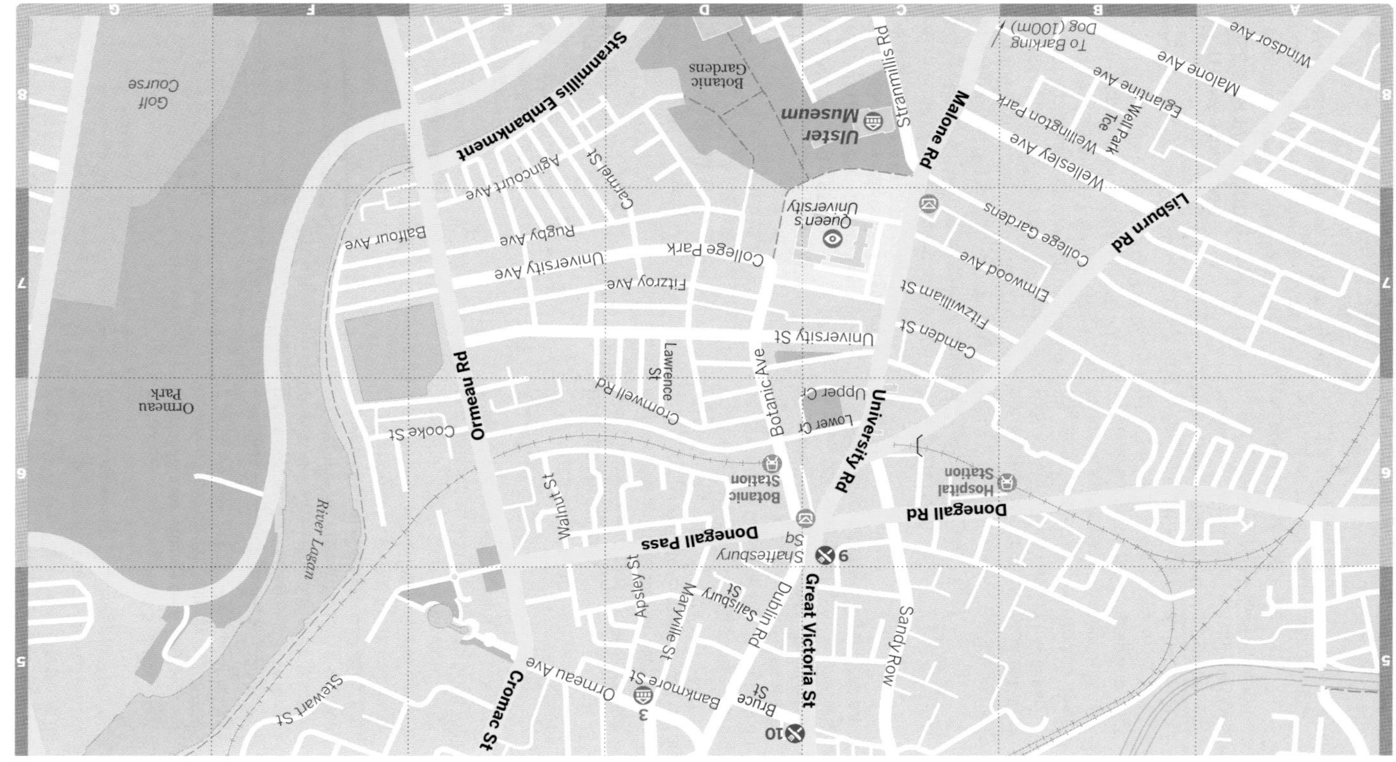
Ormeau Park
Golf Course
River Lagan
Stewart St
Cromac St
Ormeau Ave
Ormeau Rd
Cooke St
Balfour Ave
Rugby Ave
Agincourt Ave
Stranmillis Embankment
Carmel St
University Ave
Fitzroy Ave
College Park
Walnut St
Apsley St
Bankmore St
Maryville St
Salisbury St
Bruce St
Dublin Rd
Donegall Pass
Shaftesbury Sq
Great Victoria St
Cromwell Rd
Lawrence St
Botanic Station
Botanic Ave
Lower Cr
Upper Cr
University St
University Rd
Queen's University
Botanic Gardens
Ulster Museum
Stranmillis Rd
Malone Rd
Camden St
Fitzwilliam St
Elmwood Ave
College Gardens
Lisburn Rd
Wellesley Ave
Wellington Park
Well Park Tce
Eglantine Ave
Malone Ave
Windsor Ave
To Barking Dog (100m)
Sandy Row
Donegall Rd
Hospital Station
3
9
10

Central Belfast

HARLAND AND WOLFF DRAWING OFFICES Historic Building

(off map p308; Queen's Rd; open to guided tours only) Just along the road from the *Nomadic* are the original Harland and Wolff drawing offices, where the designs for the *Titanic* were first drawn up; you can only see inside as part of a guided tour. Behind the building, where the new Titanic Belfast attraction now sits (though best seen from a boat tour on the river), are the two massive **slipways** where the *Titanic* and her sister ship *Olympic* were built and launched.

FREE **THOMPSON PUMP HOUSE & GRAVING DOCK** Historic Site

(off map p308; Queens Rd; www.titanicsdock.com; admission to visitor centre free, guided tour adult/child €6/4; visitor centre 10.30am-4pm) At the far end of Queens Rd is the most impressive monument to the days of the great liners – the vast Thompson Graving Dock where the *Titanic* was fitted out. Its huge size gives you some idea of the scale of the ship, which could only just fit into it.

W5 Science Centre

(Map p308; www.w5online.co.uk; Odyssey Complex, Sydenham Rd; adult/child £7.70/5.70, 2 adults & 2 children £23; 10am-5pm Mon-Fri, 10am-6pm Sat, noon-6pm Sun, last admission 1hr before closing;) Also known as whowhatwherewhenwhy, and open during school terms only, W5 is an interactive science centre aimed at children of all ages. Kids can compose their own tunes by biffing the 'air harp' with a foam rubber bat, try to beat a lie detector, create cloud rings and tornadoes, and design and build their own robots and racing cars.

South Belfast (Queen's Quarter)

ULSTER MUSEUM Museum

(Map p308; www.nmni.com/um; Stranmillis Rd; admission free; 10am-5pm Tue-Sun;) Recently reopened after a major revamp, the Ulster Museum is now one of the North's don't-miss attractions. You could spend several hours browsing the beautifully designed displays, but if you're pressed for time don't miss the Armada Room; Takabuti, a 2500-year-old Egyptian mummy; the Bann Disc; and the Snapshot of an Ancient Sea Floor.

West Belfast (Gaeltacht Quarter)

Though scarred by three decades of civil unrest, the former battleground of West Belfast is one of the most compelling places to visit in Northern Ireland. Recent history hangs heavy in the air, but there is a noticeable spirit of optimism and hope for the future.

The main attractions are the powerful murals that chart the history of the conflict, as well as the political passions of the moment and, for visitors from mainland Britain, there is a grim fascination to be found in wandering through the former 'war zone' in their own backyard.

Despite its past reputation, the area is safe to visit. The best way to see West Belfast is on a **black taxi tour** (p313). The cabs visit the more spectacular murals as well as the Peace Line (where you can write a message on the wall) and other significant sites, while the drivers provide a colourful commentary on the history of the area.

There's nothing to stop you visiting under your own steam, either walking or using the shared black taxis that travel along the Falls and Shankill Rds. Alternatively, buses 10A to 10F from Queen St will take you along the Falls Rd; buses 11A to 11D from Wellington Pl go along Shankill Rd.

FALLS ROAD

Although the signs of past conflict are inescapable, the Falls today is an unexpectedly lively, colourful and optimistic place. Local people are friendly and welcoming, and community ventures such as Conway Mill, the Cultúrlann centre and black taxi tours have seen tourist numbers increase dramatically.

SHANKILL ROAD

Although the Protestant Shankill district (from the Irish *sean chill,* meaning 'old church') has received less media and tourist attention than the Falls, it also contains many interesting murals. The people here are just as friendly, but the Shankill has far fewer tourists than the Falls. Loyalist communities seem to have more difficulty in presenting their side of the story than the Republicans, who have a far more polished approach to public relations.

Tours

Boat Tours

LAGAN BOAT COMPANY History
(☎9033 0844; www.laganboatcompany.com; adult/child £10/8; ⏰12.30pm, 2pm & 3.30pm daily Apr-Sep, 12.30 & 2pm daily Oct, 12.30 & 2pm Sat & Sun Nov-Mar) The excellent **Titanic tour** explores the derelict docklands downstream of the weir, taking in the slipways where the liners *Titanic* and *Olympic* were launched and the huge dry dock where they could fit with just nine

Republican murals along Falls Rd

TONY WHEELER / LONELY PLANET IMAGES ©

Don't Miss Murals of Belfast

Belfast's tradition of political murals dates from 1908 when images of King Billy (William III, Protestant victor over the Catholic James II at the Battle of the Boyne in 1690; pictured above) were painted by Unionists protesting against home rule for Ireland. The tradition was revived in the late 1970s as the Troubles wore on, with murals used to mark out sectarian territory, make political points, commemorate historical events and glorify terrorist groups.

The first Republican murals appeared in 1981, when the hunger strike by Republican prisoners – demanding recognition as political prisoners – at the Maze Prison saw the emergence of dozens of murals of support. After the Good Friday Agreement of 1998, the murals came to demand police reform and the protection of nationalists from sectarian attacks. The main areas for Republican murals are Falls Rd, Beechmount Ave, Donegall Rd, Shaw's Rd and the Ballymurphy district in West Belfast; New Lodge Rd in North Belfast; and Ormeau Rd in South Belfast.

Loyalist murals have traditionally been more militaristic and defiant in tone than the Republican murals. The Loyalist battle cry of 'No Surrender!' is everywhere, along with red, white and blue painted kerbstones, paramilitary insignia and images of King Billy.

In recent years there has been a lot of debate about what to do with Belfast's murals. There's no doubt they have become an important tourist attraction, but there is now a move to replace the more aggressive and militaristic images with murals dedicated to local heroes and famous figures such as footballer George Best and *Narnia* novelist CS Lewis.

If you want to find out more about Northern Ireland's murals, look out for the books *Drawing Support* (three volumes) by Bill Rolston and *The Peoples' Gallery* by the Bogside Artists.

THINGS YOU NEED TO KNOW

Mural Directory www.cain.ulst.ac.uk/murals

inches to spare; departs from Donegall Quay near the *Bigfish* sculpture.

Taxi Tours

Black taxi tours of West Belfast's murals – known locally as the 'bombs and bullets' or 'doom and gloom' tours – are offered by a large number of taxi companies and local cabbies. For a one-hour tour expect to pay from £25 to £30 total for one or two people, and £8 to £10 per person for three to six. Call and they will pick you up from anywhere in the city centre.

The following are recommended:

Harpers Taxi Tours (☎07711 757178; www.harperstaxitours.co.nr)

Official Black Taxi Tours (☎9064 2264, toll-free 0800 052 3914; www.belfasttours.com)

Original Belfast Black Taxi Tours (☎07751 565359; taxitours@live.co.uk)

Sleeping

MALMAISON HOTEL Hotel ££
(Map p308; ☎9022 0200; www.malmaison-belfast.com; 34-38 Victoria St; r from £95, ste from £325; @ wifi) Housed in a pair of beautifully restored Italianate warehouses (originally built for rival firms in the 1850s), the Malmaison is a luxurious haven of king-size beds, deep leather sofas and roll-top baths big enough for two, all done up in a decadent decor of black, red, dark chocolate and cream. The massive, rock-star Samson suite has a giant bed (almost 3m long), a huge bathtub and, wait for it...a billiard table, with purple baize.

TEN SQUARE Hotel £££
(Map p308; ☎9024 1001; www.tensquare.co.uk; 10 Donegall Sq S; r from £139; @ wifi) A former bank building to the south of City Hall that has been given a designer feng-shui makeover, Ten Square is an opulent, Shanghai-inspired boutique hotel with friendly and attentive service. Magazines such as *Cosmopolitan* and *Conde Nast Traveller* drool over the dark lacquered wood, low-slung futon-style beds and sumptuous linen, and the list of former guests includes Bono and Brad Pitt.

FITZWILLIAM HOTEL Hotel £££
(Map p308; ☎9044 2080; www.fitzwilliamhotelbelfast.com; 1-3 Great Victoria St; r from £115; @ wifi) A new hotel in a truly central location, the Fitzwilliam pushes all the right style buttons with its use of designer fabrics, cool colours and mood lighting. Bedrooms have crisp linen sheets, fluffy bathrobes and powerful showers, and the staff are unstintingly helpful. There's an excellent restaurant, too.

iTours

Belfast iTours (belfastitours.com) offers nine self-guided video tours of the city that you can download to your smartphone or MP4 player; alternatively you can hire a preloaded MP4 player (£9 for 24 hours) from the Belfast Welcome Centre.

Eating

GINGER Bistro £££
(Map p308; ☎9024 4421; www.gingerbistro.com; 7-8 Hope St; mains £17-22; ⏰noon-3pm Tue-Sat & 5-9pm Mon-Sat) Ginger is one of those places you could walk right past without noticing, but if you do you'll be missing out. It's a cosy and informal little bistro with an unassuming exterior, serving food that is really anything but ordinary – the flame-haired owner/chef (hence the name) really knows what he's doing, sourcing top-quality Irish produce and turning out exquisite dishes such as such as scallops with crisp black pudding and chorizo butter. The lunch and pretheatre (5pm to 6.45pm Monday to Friday) menu offers main courses for £8 to £12.

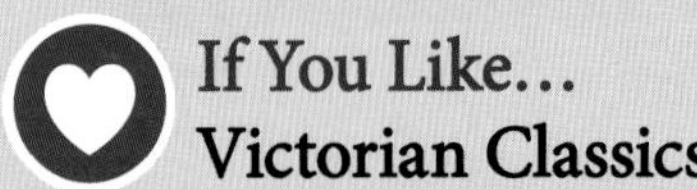

If You Like... Victorian Classics

If you like Victorian classics like the Crown Saloon, you should stick your head into these other beautiful Belfast bars:

1 **BITTLE'S BAR**
(Map p308; 103 Victoria St)

2 **DUKE OF YORK**
(Map p308; 11 Commercial Ct)

3 **KELLY'S CELLARS**
(Map p308; 1 Bank St)

4 **WHITE'S**
(Map p308; www.whitestavern.co.uk; 1-4 Wine Cellar Entry)

CAYENNE Irish **£££**
(Map p308; ☎9033 1532; www.cayenne-restaurant.co.uk; 7 Ascot House, Shaftesbury Sq; mains £18-25, 2-course lunch £12.50; ⊙noon-2.15pm Mon-Fri, to 4pm Sun, 5-11pm Wed-Mon) Behind an anonymous frosted-glass facade lurks this funky, award-winning restaurant operated by celebrity chef Paul Rankin. Grey and black walls lit with the glowing orange-red of the eponymous pepper provide an aura of sophistication. The menu concentrates on Irish produce prepared with an Asian or Mediterranean twist; the set three-course dinner menu (£23 or £28) is good value.

Drinking

CROWN LIQUOR SALOON Pub
(Map p308; www.crownbar.com; 46 Great Victoria St) Belfast's most famous bar has a wonderfully ornate Victorian interior. Despite being a tourist attraction (see p307), it still fills up with crowds of locals at lunchtime and in the early evening.

GARRICK BAR Pub
(Map p308; www.thegarrickbar.com; 29 Chichester St) Established in 1870 but recently refurbished, the Garrick hangs on to a traditional atmosphere with acres of dark wood panelling, tiled floors, a pillared bar and old brass oil lamps. There are snug booths with buttoned leather benches, and a real coal fire in each room. Traditional music sessions in the front bar at 9.30pm on Wednesday, 5pm Friday and 4pm Sunday.

WHITE'S TAVERN Pub
(Map p308; www.whitestavern.co.uk; 1-4 Wine Cellar Entry) Established in 1630 but rebuilt in 1790, White's claims to be Belfast's oldest tavern (unlike a pub, a tavern provided food and lodging). Downstairs is a traditional Irish bar with an open peat fire and live trad music Friday to Sunday; upstairs is like your granny's living room, stuffed with old armchairs and sofas, and hosting DJs and covers bands at the weekends.

JOHN HEWITT BAR & RESTAURANT Pub
(Map p308; www.thejohnhewitt.com; 51 Donegall St) Named for the Belfast poet and socialist, the John Hewitt is one of those treasured bars that has no TV and no gaming machines; the only noise here is the murmur of conversation. As well as Guinness, the bar serves Hilden real ales from nearby Lisburn, plus Hoegaarden and Erdinger wheat beers. There are regular sessions of folk, jazz and bluegrass from 9pm most nights.

Information

Tourist Information

Belfast Welcome Centre (☎9024 6609; www.gotobelfast.com; 47 Donegall Pl; ⊙9am-7pm Mon-Sat & 11am-4pm Sun Jun-Sep, 9am-5.30pm Mon-Sat & 11am-4pm Sun Oct-May) Provides information about the whole of Northern Irelan, and books accommodation anywhere in Ireland and Britain. Services include left luggage (not overnight), currency exchange and internet access.

Belfast Visitor Pass

VISITOR PASS

The Belfast Visitor Pass (per one/two/three days £6.50/10.50/14) allows unlimited travel on bus and train services in Belfast and around. It can be purchased at airports, main train and bus stations, the Metro kiosk on Donegall Sq, and the Belfast Welcome Centre.

Getting There & Away

Air

Belfast International Airport (Off-map p317; BFS; www.belfastairport.com) Located 30km northwest of the city; flights from Galway, UK, Europe and New York.

George Best Belfast City Airport (Map p317; BHD; www.belfastcityairport.com; Airport Rd) Situated 6km northeast of the city centre; flights from the UK, Cork and Paris.

Bus

Europa Bus Centre (Map p308; ☎9066 6630) Belfast's main bus station is behind the Europa Hotel and next door to Great Victoria St train station; it's reached via the Great Northern Mall beside the hotel. It's the main terminus for buses to Derry, Dublin and destinations in the west and south of Northern Ireland.

Laganside Bus Centre (Map p308; ☎9066 6630; Oxford St) This smaller bus station, near the river, is mainly for buses to County Antrim, eastern County Down and the Cookstown area.

Train

Belfast Central Station (Map p308; East Bridge St) East of the city centre; trains run to Dublin and all destinations in Northern Ireland. If you arrive by train at Central Station, your rail ticket entitles you to a free bus ride into the city centre.

Great Victoria St Station (Map p308; Great Northern Mall) Next to the Europa BusCentre; has trains for Portadown, Lisburn, Bangor, Larne Harbour and Derry.

If you arrive by train at Central Station, your rail ticket entitles you to a free bus ride into the city centre.

Getting Around

To/From the Airports

Belfast International Airport Airport Express 300 bus runs to the Europa Bus Centre (one way/return £7/10, 30 minutes) every 10 or 15 minutes between 7am and 8pm, every 30 minutes from 8pm to 11pm, and hourly

Crown Liquor Saloon (p314)

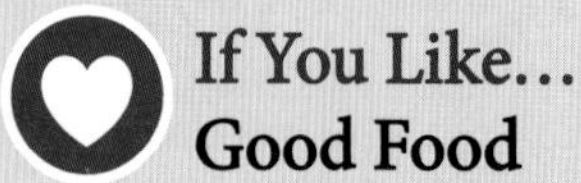

If You Like... Good Food

If you like the cuisine at Ginger (p313), try these other restaurants in County Down, all within easy reach of Belfast:

1 **PLOUGH INN**
(Hillsborough; ☎9268 2985; www.theploughhillsborough.co.uk; 3 The Square; mains bar £6-12, restaurant £13-23; ⏰bar lunches noon-2.30pm, restaurant 6-9.30pm) This fine old pub serves gourmet bar lunches and fine dining in the restaurant around the back.

2 **GRACE NEILL'S**
(Donaghedee; ☎9188 4595; www.graceneills.com; 33 High St; 2-/3-course lunch £14/18, dinner mains £15-25; ⏰food noon-3pm & 5.30-9pm Mon-Fri, noon-9.30pm Sat, 12.30-8pm Sun) At the back of Ireland's oldest pub is one of the North's best modern bistros, with a lunch menu described as upmarket comfort food.

3 **VANILLA**
(Newcastle; ☎4372 2268; www.vanillarestaurant.co.uk; 67 Main St; 2-course lunch £13, dinner mains £12-20; ⏰noon-3.30pm Thu-Tue, 5-8.30pm Sun-Tue & Thu, 6-9.30pm Fri & Sat) A sharply styled bistro that shamelessly promotes Irish produce in dishes such as flaky pastry seafood tart with mustard, cheddar and roast onions, and Irish ribeye steak with mushroom and smoked bacon croquettes.

through the night; a return ticket is valid for one month. A taxi costs about £25.

George Best Belfast City Airport Airport Express 600 bus runs to the Europa Bus Centre (one way/return £2/3, 15 minutes) every 15 or 20 minutes between 6am and 10pm. The taxi fare to the city centre is about £7.

AROUND BELFAST

Holywood

ULSTER FOLK MUSEUM Museum
(Map p317; www.nmni.com/uftm; Cultra, Holywood; adult/child £6.50/4, combined ticket to both museums £8/4.50; ⏰10am-5pm Tue-Sun Mar-Sep, 10am-4pm Tue-Fri & 11am-4pm Sat & Sun Oct-Feb) On the south side of the main road is the Folk Museum, where farmhouses, forges, churches and mills, and a complete village have been reconstructed, with human and animal extras combining to give a powerful impression of Irish life over the past few hundred years. From industrial times, there are red-brick terraces from 19th-century Belfast and Dromore. In summer, there are thatching and ploughing demonstrations and characters dressed in period costume.

ULSTER TRANSPORT MUSEUM Museum
(Map p317; www.nmni.com/uftm; Cultra, Holywood; adult/child £6.50/4, combined ticket to both museums £8/4.50; ⏰10am-5pm Tue-Sun Mar-Sep, 10am-4pm Tue-Fri & 11am-4pm Sat & Sun Oct-Feb) On the other side of the road is the Transport Museum, a sort of automotive zoo, with displays of captive steam locomotives, rolling stock, motorcycles, trams, buses and cars. The highlight of the car collection is the stainless steel–clad prototype of the ill-fated **DeLorean DMC**, made in Belfast in 1981. The car was a commercial disaster but achieved everlasting fame in the *Back to the Future* films.

Most popular is the **RMS Titanic display**, which includes the original design drawings for the *Olympic* and the *Titanic*, photographs of the ship's construction and reports of its sinking. At the time of research a new exhibition was being constructed in time for the Titanic centenary in April 2012.

Buses to Bangor stop nearby. Cultra Station on the Belfast to Bangor train line is within a 10-minute walk.

Mourne Mountains

The humpbacked granite hills of the Mourne Mountains dominate the horizon as you head south from Belfast towards Newcastle. This is one of the most beautiful corners of Northern Ireland, with a distinctive landscape of yellow gorse, grey granite and whitewashed cottages, the

Around Belfast

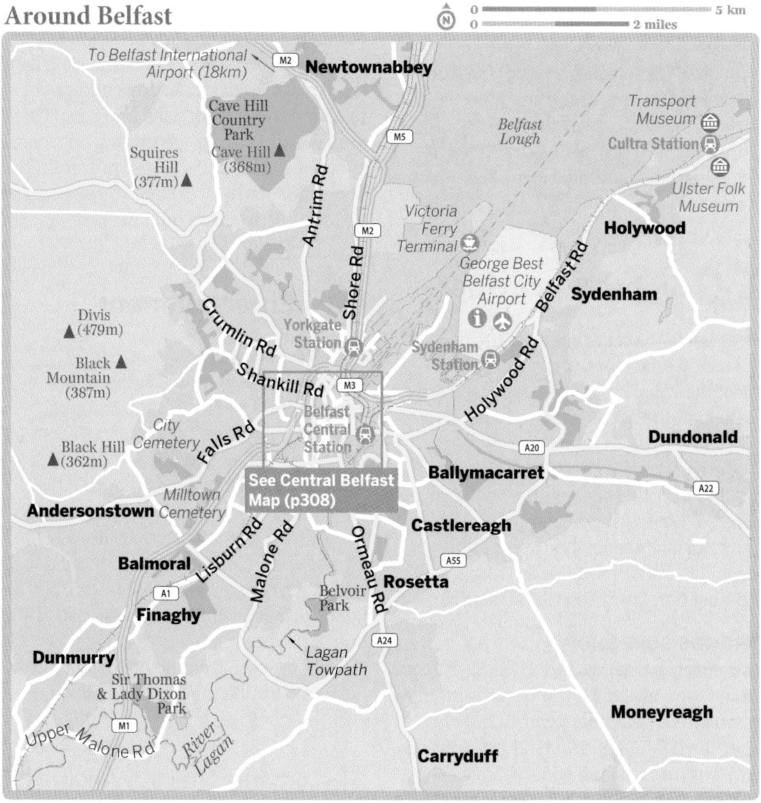

See Central Belfast Map (p308)

lower slopes of the hills latticed with a neat patchwork of drystone walls cobbled together from huge, rounded granite boulders.

Sights

SILENT VALLEY RESERVOIR Reservoir

(car/motorcycle £4.50/2, plus per adult/child £1.60/0.60; 10am-6.30pm Apr-Oct, to 4pm Nov-Mar) At the heart of the Mournes is the beautiful Silent Valley Reservoir, where the River Kilkeel was dammed in 1933. There are scenic, waymarked walks around the grounds, a **coffee shop (11am-5.30pm Sat & Sun Apr-Sep)** and an interesting exhibition on the building of the dam. From the car park, a shuttle bus (adult/child return £1.40/1) will take you another 4km up the valley to the Crom Dam. It runs daily in July and August, weekends only in May, June and September.

Getting There & Away

In July and August only, the Ulsterbus 405 Mourne Rambler service runs a circular route from Newcastle, calling at a dozen stops around the Mournes, including Bryansford (8 minutes), Meelmore (17 minutes), Silent Valley (40 minutes), Carrick Little (45 minutes) and Bloody Bridge (one hour). There are six buses daily – the first leaves at 9.30am, the last at 5pm; a £5.50 all-day ticket allows you to get on and off as many times as you like.

Bus 34A (July and August only) runs from Newcastle to the Silent Valley car park (45 minutes, two daily), calling at Donard Park (five minutes) and Bloody Bridge (10 minutes).

Portrush

POP 6300

The bustling seaside resort of Portrush (Port Rois) bursts at the seams with holidaymakers in high season and, not surprisingly, many of its attractions are focused unashamedly on good, old-fashioned family fun.

Sights & Activities

Portrush's main attraction is the beautiful sandy beach of **Curran Strand** that stretches for 3km to the east of the town, ending at the scenic chalk cliffs of White Rocks.

Portrush is the centre of Northern Ireland's surfing scene – the Portrush Open in March is a regular feature on the Irish Surfing Association competition calendar, and the UK Pro Surf Tour held a contest here for the first time in 2007.

TROGGS SURF SHOP Surf Shop
(www.troggssurfshop.co.uk; 88 Main St; ⏲10am-6pm) From April to November this friendly shop offers bodyboard/surfboard hire (per day £5/10) and wetsuit hire (per day £7), surf reports and general advice. A two-hour lesson including equipment hire costs £25 per person.

Sleeping

CLARMONT B&B **££**
(☎7082 2397; www.clarmont.com; 10 Landsdowne Cres; per person £35-45) Our favourite among several guesthouses on Landsdowne Cres, the Clarmont has great views and, from polished pine floors to period fireplaces, has a decor that tastefully mixes Victorian and modern styles. Ask for a room with a bay window.

Eating

55 DEGREES NORTH International **££**
(☎7082 2811; www.55-north.com; 1 Causeway St; mains £10-18; ⏲5-9pm Mon-Fri, 5-9.30pm Sat, 5-8.30pm Sun) One of the north coast's most stylish restaurants, 55 Degrees North boasts a wall of floor-to-ceiling windows allowing diners to soak up a spectacular panorama of sand and sea. The food is excellent, concentrating on clean, simple flavours and unfussy presentation. There's an early-bird menu (three courses £10 to £12) available 5pm to 7pm.

Entertainment

KELLY'S COMPLEX Club
(www.kellysportrush.co.uk; 1 Bushmills Rd; ⏲Wed & Sat) The North's top clubbing venue regularly features DJs from London and Manchester, and attracts clubbers from as far afield as Belfast and Dublin. Plain and small-looking from the outside, the TARDIS effect takes over as you enter a wonderland of five bars and three dance floors. It's been around since 1996, but **Lush! (admission £7-12; ⏲9pm-2am Sat)** is still one of the best club nights in Ireland.

The complex is on the A2 just east of Portrush, beside the Golf Links Holiday Park.

Getting There & Around

The bus terminal is near the Dunluce Centre. Bus 140 links Portrush with Coleraine (20 minutes) and Portstewart (20 to 30 minutes) every 30 minutes or so.

The train station is just south of the harbour. Portrush is served by trains from Coleraine (£2.20, 12 minutes, hourly Monday to Saturday, 10 on Sunday), where there are connections to Belfast or Derry.

For taxis, try Andy Brown's (☎7082 2223) or North West Taxis (☎7082 4446). A taxi to Kelly's is around £7, and it's £14 to the Giant's Causeway.

Bushmills

POP 1350

The small town of Bushmills has long been a place of pilgrimage for connoisseurs of Irish whiskey. A good youth hostel and a restored rail link with the Giant's Causeway have also made it an attractive stop for hikers exploring the Causeway Coast.

Sights

BUSHMILLS DISTILLERY Distillery
(www.bushmills.com; Distillery Rd; adult/child £6/3; 9.15am-5pm Mon-Sat year-round, 11am-5pm Sun Jul-Sep, noon-5.30pm Sun Mar-Jun & Oct) Bushmills is the world's oldest legal distillery, having been granted a licence by King James I in 1608. Bushmills whiskey is made with Irish barley and water from St Columb's Rill, a tributary of the River Bush, and matured in oak barrels. During ageing, the alcohol content drops from around 60% to 40%; the spirit lost through evaporation is known, rather sweetly, as 'the angels' share'. After a tour of the distillery you're rewarded with a free sample (or a soft drink), and four lucky volunteers get a whiskey-tasting session to compare Bushmills with other brands.

GIANT'S CAUSEWAY & BUSHMILLS RAILWAY Heritage Railway
(www.freewebs.com/giantscausewayrailway; adult/child return £7.50/5.50) Brought from a private line on the shores of Lough Neagh, the narrow-gauge line and locomotives (two steam and one diesel) follow the route of a 19th-century tourist tramway for 3km from Bushmills to below the Giant's Causeway visitor centre. Trains run hourly between 11am and 5.30pm, departing on the hour from the Causeway, on the half-hour from Bushmills, daily in July and August, weekends only from Easter to June and September and October.

Eating

BUSHMILLS INN Irish ££
(lunch mains £10-12, dinner mains £15-22; noon-9.30pm Mon-Sat, 12.30-9pm Sun;) The inn's excellent restaurant, with intimate wooden booths set in the old 17th-century stables, specialises in fresh Ulster produce and serves everything from sandwiches to full á-la-carte dinners.

Giant's Causeway to Ballycastle

Between the Giant's Causeway and Ballycastle lies the most scenic stretch of the Causeway Coast, with sea cliffs of

Portrush harbour

STEPHEN SAKS / LONELY PLANET IMAGES ©

contrasting black basalt and white chalk, rocky islands, picturesque little harbours and broad sweeps of sandy beach.

About 8km east of the Giant's Causeway is the meagre ruin of 16th-century **Dunseverick Castle**, spectacularly sited on a grassy bluff. Another 1.5km on is the tiny seaside hamlet of **Portbradden**, with half a dozen harbourside houses and the tiny, blue-and-white **St Gobban's Church**, said to be the smallest in Ireland. Visible from Portbradden and accessible via the next junction off the A2 is the spectacular **White Park Bay**, with its wide, sweeping sandy beach.

A few kilometres further on is **Ballintoy** (Baile an Tuaighe), another pretty village tumbling down the hillside to a picture-postcard harbour. The restored limekiln on the quayside once made quicklime using stone from the chalk cliffs and coal from Ballymoney.

The main attraction on this stretch of coast is the famous (or notorious, depending on your head for heights) **Carrick-a-Rede Rope Bridge** (www.ntni.org.uk; Ballintoy; adult/child £5.60/2.90; 10am-7pm Jun-Aug, to 6pm Mar-May, Sep & Oct). The 20m-long, 1m-wide bridge of wire rope spans the chasm between the sea cliffs and the little island of Carrick-a-Rede, swaying gently 30m above the rock-strewn water.

The island has sustained a salmon fishery for centuries; fishermen stretch their nets out from the tip of the island to intercept the passage of salmon migrating along the coast to their home rivers. The fishermen put the bridge up every spring as they have done for the last 200 years – though it's not, of course, the original bridge.

Crossing the bridge is perfectly safe, but it can be frightening if you don't have a head for heights, especially if it's breezy (in high winds the bridge is closed). Once on the island there are good views of Rathlin Island and Fair Head to the east. There's a small National Trust information centre and cafe at the car park.

Sleeping & Eating

WHITEPARK HOUSE B&B ££
(2073 1482; www.whiteparkhouse.com; 150 Whitepark Rd, Ballintoy; s/d £75/100; P @)
A beautifully restored 18th-century house overlooking White Park Bay, this B&B has traditional features such as antique furniture and a peat fire complemented by Asian artefacts gathered during the welcoming owners' oriental travels. There are three rooms – ask for one with a sea view.

ROARK'S KITCHEN Cafe £
(Ballintoy Harbour; mains £3-6; 11am-7pm Jun-Aug, Sat & Sun only May & Sep)
This cute little chalk-built tearoom on the quayside at Ballintoy serves teas,

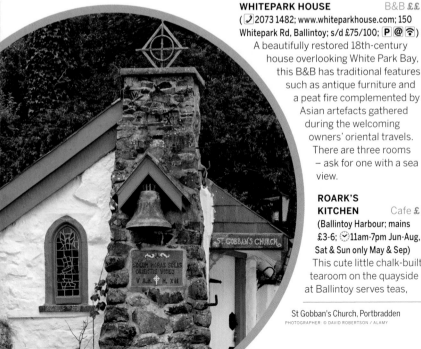

St Gobban's Church, Portbradden
PHOTOGRAPHER: © DAVID ROBERTSON / ALAMY

RICHARD CUMMINS / LONELY PLANET IMAGES ©

Don't Miss Giant's Causeway

The causeway's vast expanse of regular, closely packed, hexagonal stone columns dipping gently beneath the waves looks for all the world like the handiwork of giants. This spectacular rock formation – a national nature reserve and Northern Ireland's only Unesco World Heritage Site – is one of Ireland's most impressive and atmospheric landscape features. It is all too often swamped by visitors – around 750,000 each year. If you can, try to visit midweek or out of season to experience it at its most evocative. Sunset in spring and autumn is the best time for photographs.

From the car park, it's an easy 1km walk downhill on a tarmac road (wheelchair accessible) to the Giant's Causeway itself. However, a much more interesting approach is to follow the cliff-top path northeast for 2km to the **Chimney Tops** headland, which has an excellent view of the Causeway and the coastline to the west, including Inishowen and Malin Heads.

This pinnacled promontory was bombarded by ships of the Spanish Armada in 1588, who thought it was Dunluce Castle, and the wreck of the Spanish galleon *Girona* lies just off the tip of the headland. Return towards the car park and about halfway back descend the **Shepherd's Steps** (signposted) to a lower-level footpath that leads down to the Causeway. Allow 1½ hours for the round trip.

Alternatively, you can visit the Causeway first, then follow the lower coastal path as far as the **Amphitheatre** viewpoint at Port Reostan, passing impressive rock formations such as the **Organ** (a stack of vertical basalt columns resembling organ pipes), and return by climbing the Shepherd's Steps.

THINGS YOU NEED TO KNOW

Car park (£6 per car);

Minibuses (every 15 min; adult/child £2/1 return), with wheelchair access;

Guided tours (Jun to Aug only; £3.50/2.25 per adult/child).

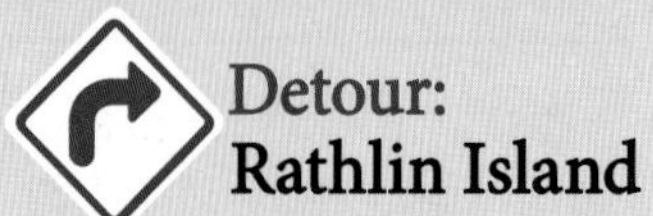

Detour: Rathlin Island

In spring and summer, rugged Rathlin Island (Reachlainn; www.rathlincommunity.org), 6km offshore from Ballycastle, is home to hundreds of seals and thousands of nesting seabirds. An L-shaped island just 6.5km long and 4km wide, Rathlin is famous for the coastal scenery and bird life at **Kebble National Nature Reserve** at its western end.

RSPB West Light Viewpoint (www.rspb.org.uk; admission free; 11am-3pm Apr-Aug) provides stunning views of the neighbouring sea stacks, thick with guillemots, kittiwakes, razorbills and puffins from mid-April to August. During the summer a minibus service runs there from the harbour; public toilets and binocular hire are available.

A **ferry** (2076 9299; www.rathlinballycastleferry.com; adult/child/bicycle return £11.20/5.60/3) operates daily from Ballycastle; advance booking is recommended in spring and summer. From April to September there are eight or nine crossings a day, half of which are fast catamaran services (20 minutes), the rest via a slower car ferry (45 minutes); in winter the service is reduced.

coffees, ice cream, home-baked apple tart and lunch dishes such as Irish stew or chicken-and-ham pie.

Glens of Antrim

The northeastern corner of Antrim is a high plateau of black basalt lava overlying beds of white chalk. Along the coast, between Cushendun and Glenarm, the plateau has been dissected by a series of scenic, glacier-gouged valleys known as the Glens of Antrim.

Cushendun

POP 350

The pretty seaside village of Cushendun is famous for its distinctive Cornish-style cottages, now owned by the National Trust. Built between 1912 and 1925 at the behest of the local landowner, Lord Cushendun, they were designed by Clough Williams-Ellis, the architect of Portmeirion in north Wales. There's a nice sandy **beach**, various short **coastal walks** (outlined on an information board beside the car park), and some impressive **caves** cut into the overhanging conglomerate sea cliffs south of the village (follow the trail around the far end of the holiday apartments south of the river mouth).

COUNTY DERRY

Derry/Londonderry

POP 83,700

Northern Ireland's second city comes as a pleasant surprise to many visitors. Derry (or Londonderry) may not be the prettiest of cities, and it certainly lags behind Belfast in terms of investment and redevelopment, but it has a great riverside setting, several fascinating historical sights and a determined air of can-do optimism that has made it the powerhouse of the North's cultural revival.

In preparation for Derry's year in the limelight as **UK City of Culture 2013** (www.cityofculture2013.com), the city centre was given a makeover, and an elegant new footbridge – the **Peace Bridge** – was built across the River Foyle. Confirmed events at the time of writing include a Cultural Olympiad in the run-up to the London Olympics in 2012, and the hosting of the Turner Prize in 2013.

Sights

Walled City

Derry's walled city is Ireland's earliest example of town planning. It is thought to have been modelled on the French Renaissance town of Vitry-le-François, designed in 1545 by Italian engineer Hieronimo Marino; both are based on the grid plan of a Roman military camp, with two main streets at right angles to each other, and four city gates, one at either end of each street.

Completed in 1619, Derry's **city walls** **(www.derryswalls.com)** are 8m high and 9m thick, with a circumference of about 1.5km, and are the only city walls in Ireland to survive almost intact.

TOWER MUSEUM Museum

(Union Hall Pl; adult/child £4.20/2.65; ⌚10am-5pm Tue-Sat, plus 11am-3pm Sun Jul & Aug) Inside the Magazine Gate is this award-winning museum, housed in a replica 16th-century tower house. Head straight to the 5th floor for a view from the top of the tower, then work your way down through the excellent **Armada Shipwreck** exhibition, which tells the story of *La Trinidad Valenciera* – a ship of the Spanish Armada that was wrecked at Kinnagoe Bay in Donegal in 1588. It was discovered by the City of Derry Sub-Aqua Club in 1971 and excavated by marine archaeologists. On display are bronze guns, pewter tableware and personal items – a wooden comb, an olive jar, a shoe sole – recovered from the site, including a 2.5-tonne siege gun bearing the arms of Phillip II of Spain showing him as king of England.

Bogside

The Bogside district, to the west of the walled city, developed in the 19th and early 20th centuries as a working-class, predominantly Catholic, residential area. By the 1960s its serried ranks of small, terrace houses had become an overcrowded ghetto of poverty and unemployment, a focus for the emerging civil rights movement and a hotbed of Nationalist discontent.

In August 1969 the three-day 'Battle of the Bogside' – a running street battle between local youths and the Royal Ulster Constabulary (RUC) – prompted the UK government to send British troops

Tower Museum, Derry city walls

STEPHEN SAKS / LONELY PLANET IMAGES ©

Derry

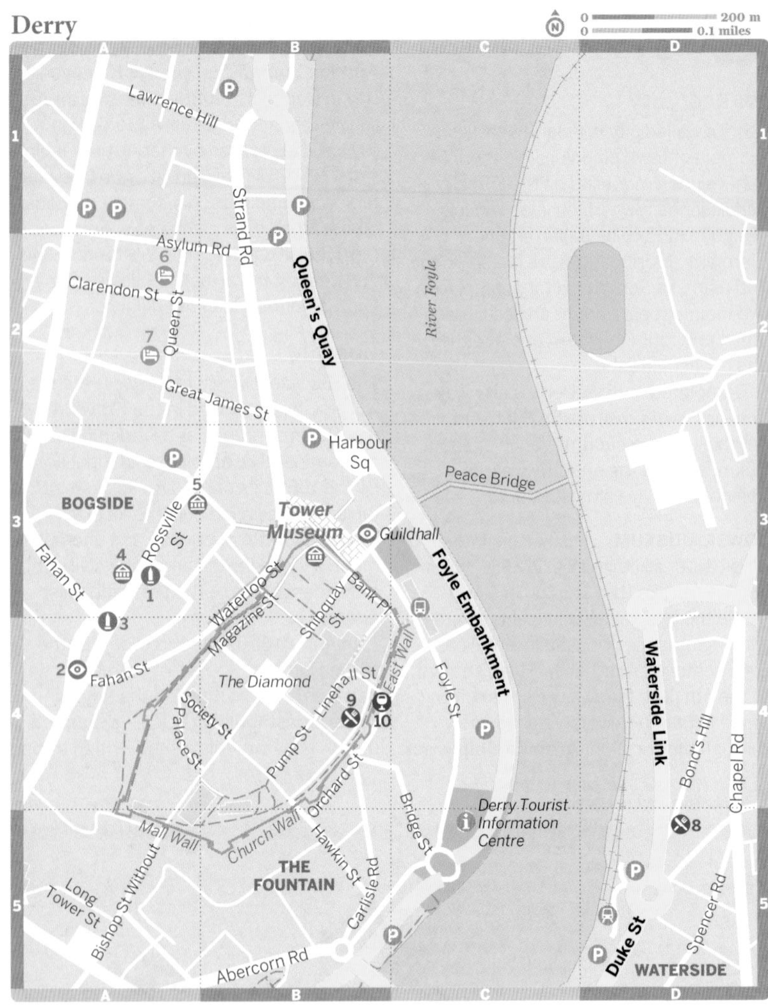

into Northern Ireland. The residents of the Bogside and neighbouring Brandywell districts – 33,000 of them – declared themselves independent from the civil authorities, and barricaded the streets to keep the security forces out. 'Free Derry', as it was known, was a no-go area for the police and army, its streets patrolled by IRA volunteers. In January of 1972 the area around Rossville St witnessed the horrific events of Bloody Sunday. 'Free Derry' ended with Operation Motorman on 31 July 1972, when thousands of British troops and armoured cars moved in to occupy the Bogside.

Since then the area has been extensively redeveloped, the old houses and flats demolished and replaced with modern housing, and the population is now down to 8000. All that remains of the old Bogside is **Free Derry Corner** at the intersection of Fahan and Rossville Sts, where the gable end of a house painted with the famous slogan 'You are Now Entering Free Derry' still stands.

Derry

Top Sights

Nearby is the H-shaped **Hunger Strikers' Memorial** and, a little further north along Rossville St, the **Bloody Sunday Memorial**, a simple granite obelisk that commemorates the 14 civilians who were shot dead by the British Army on 30 January 1972.

PEOPLE'S GALLERY MURALS Urban Art

(Rossville St) The 12 murals that decorate the gable ends of houses along Rossville St, near Free Derry Corner, are popularly referred to as the People's Gallery. They are the work of Tom Kelly, Will Kelly and Kevin Hasson, known as 'the Bogside Artists'. The three men have spent most of their lives in the Bogside, and lived through the worst of the Troubles.

Their murals, mostly painted between 1997 and 2001, commemorate key events in the Troubles, including the Battle of the Bogside, Bloody Sunday, Operation Motorman (the British Army's operation to retake IRA-controlled no-go areas in Derry and Belfast in July 1972) and the 1981 hunger strike. The most powerful images are those painted largely in monochrome, consciously evoking journalistic imagery, such as *Operation Motorman,* showing a British soldier breaking down a door with a sledgehammer; *Bloody Sunday,* with a group of men led by local priest Father Daly carrying the body of Jackie Duddy (the first fatality on that day); and *Petrol Bomber,* a young boy wearing a gas mask and holding a petrol bomb.

The murals can be seen online at www.cain.ulst.ac.uk/bogsideartists, and in the book *The People's Gallery* (available for purchase from the gallery shop and the artists' website).

MUSEUM OF FREE DERRY Museum

(www.museumoffreederry.org; 55-61 Glenfada Park; adult/child £3/2; 9.30am-4.30pm Mon-Fri year-round, 1-4pm Sat Apr-Sep, 1-4pm Sun Jul-Sep) Just off Rossville St, this museum chronicles the history of the Bogside, the civil rights movement and the events of Bloody Sunday through photographs, newspaper reports, film clips and the accounts of first-hand witnesses, including some of the original photographs that inspired the murals of the People's Gallery.

Sleeping

MERCHANT'S HOUSE B&B ££

(7126 9691; www.thesaddlershouse.com; 16 Queen St; s £35-50, d £50-60; @ wifi) Run by the same owners as the Saddler's House, this historic, Georgian-style town house is a gem of a B&B. It has an elegant lounge and dining room with marble fireplaces and antique furniture, TV, coffee-making facilities and even bathrobes in the bedrooms (only one has a private bathroom), and homemade marmalade at breakfast. Call at the Saddler's House first to pick up a key.

SADDLER'S HOUSE B&B ££

(7126 9691; www.thesaddlershouse.com; 36 Great James St; s £35-50, d £50-60; @ wifi) Centrally located within a five-minute walk of the walled city, this friendly B&B is set in a lovely Victorian town house. All seven rooms have private bathrooms, and you get to enjoy a huge breakfast in the family kitchen.

LABURNUM LODGE B&B ££
(7135 4221; www.laburnumlodge.com; 9 Rockfield, Madam's Bank Rd; s/d £40/55; P @) Readers have recommended this suburban villa on a quiet street on the northern edge of town, impressed by the friendly welcome, spacious bedrooms and hearty breakfasts. If you don't have your own transport, the owner can pick you up from the train or bus station.

Eating

HALO PANTRY & GRILL International ££
(7127 1567; 5 Market St; mains lunch £6-10, dinner £9-22; Pantry noon-10pm, Grill 5-10pm) Housed over three floors of a converted shirt factory decorated with local art and photography, Halo offers light meals and snacks (including superb homemade lasagne) in the Pantry, and more formal dinners (from steak to seafood) in the upstairs Grill.

BROWN'S RESTAURANT Modern Irish ££
(7134 5180; 1 Bond's Hill, Waterside; mains £13-21; noon-2.30pm Tue-Fri, 5.30-10pm Tue-Sat) From the outside Brown's may not have the most promising location, over the river in Waterside, but step inside and you're in a little art deco enclave of brandy-coloured banquettes and ornate metal light fittings, with the odd Rothko print adorning the walls. The ever-changing menu is a gastronome's delight, making creative use of fresh local produce in dishes such as wood pigeon wrapped in pastry, with creamed shallots, cranberries and red wine sauce.

Drinking

BADGERS BAR Pub
(16-18 Orchard St) A fine polished-brass and stained-glass Victorian pub crammed

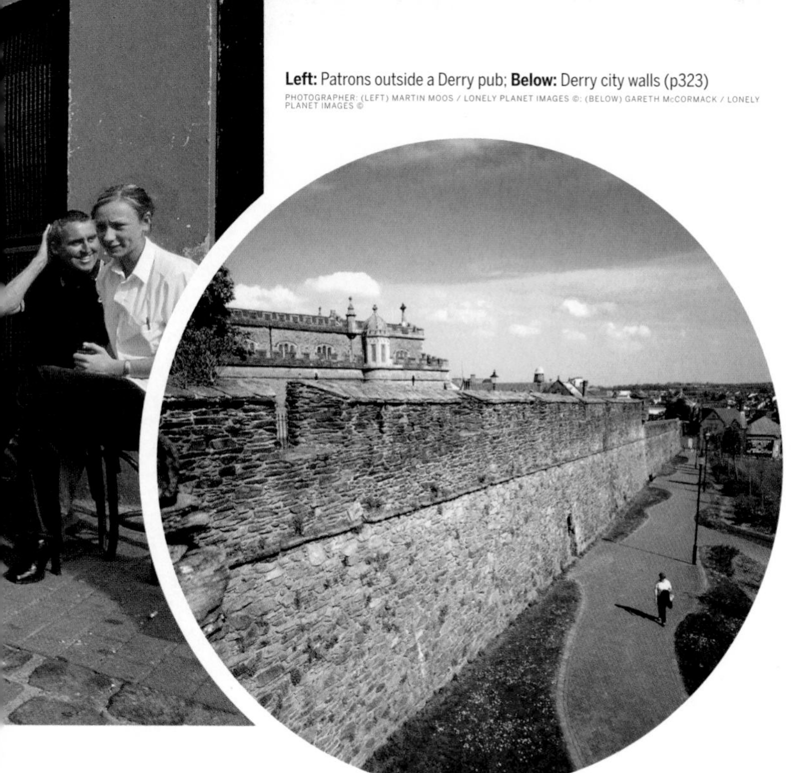

Left: Patrons outside a Derry pub; **Below:** Derry city walls (p323)

PHOTOGRAPHER: (LEFT) MARTIN MOOS / LONELY PLANET IMAGES ©; (BELOW) GARETH McCORMACK / LONELY PLANET IMAGES ©

with wood-panelled nooks and crannies, Badgers overflows at lunchtime with shoppers enjoying quality pub grub, and offers a quiet haven in the evenings when it attracts a crowd of more mature drinkers.

Information

Derry Tourist Information Centre (☎7126 7284; www.derryvisitor.com; 44 Foyle St; ⏰9am-7pm Mon-Fri, 10am-6pm Sat & 10am-5pm Jul-Sep, 9am-5pm Mon-Fri & 10am-5pm Sat Mar-Feb) Covers all of Northern Ireland and the Republic as well as Derry. Sells books and maps, can book accommodation throughout Ireland and has a bureau de change.

Getting There & Away

Air

City of Derry Airport (☎7181 0784; www.cityofderryairport.com) About 13km east of Derry along the A2 towards Limavady. Direct flights daily to Dublin (Aer Arann), London Stansted, London Luton, Liverpool, Birmingham and Glasgow Prestwick (Ryanair).

Bus

The **bus station** (☎7126 2261; Foyle St) is just northeast of the walled city.

Train

Derry's train station (always referred to as Londonderry in Northern Ireland timetables) is on the eastern side of the River Foyle; a free Rail Link bus connects with the bus station. There are trains to Belfast (£11, 2¼ hours, seven or eight daily Monday to Saturday, four on Sunday) and Coleraine (£8.20, 45 minutes, seven daily), with connections to Portrush (£10, 1¼ hours).

Ireland In Focus

Bluebells in County Derry (p322)

Ireland Today

belief systems
(% of population)

if Ireland were 100 people

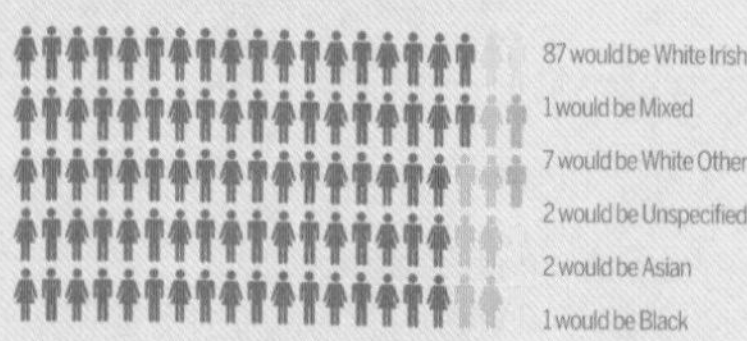

population per sq km

View of Custom House, Dublin (p51)

For the Love of God, Go

In 2011 Ireland went to the polls, elected a brand new government and welcomed both the Queen of England and President Barack Obama, who visited in the space of a frenzied week in May. Ireland finished eighth in the Eurovision Song Contest, which was pretty good given that they'd finished second-last the year before. But one overriding truth overshadowed everything.

In government since 1991, Fianna Fáil had taken credit for the Celtic Tiger but proved a little slippier when it came to taking the blame for the financial meltdown of 2008. Problem was the country had no difficulty pinning the blame on them, so the 2011 general election saw their worst electoral defeat in history – from 78 seats in the 144-seat Dáil to just 20. Their coalition partners, the Greens, fared even worse: not one of their candidates was elected.

RICHARD I'ANSON / LONELY PLANET IMAGES ©

Who's Really in Charge?

The new government is a coalition of centre-right Fine Gael (traditionally Ireland's political bridesmaids) and centre-left Labour, but their policies are hamstrung by the €85 billion bailout given to Ireland by the International Monetary Fund (IMF), the European Union (EU) and European Central Bank (ECB), which has to be repaid at a prohibitively high rate of interest and has resulted in some fairly savage cuts in public spending. In a few short years, Ireland went from being the poster-child for economic success to a terminal patient on financial life support: what happened?

Pop Goes the Bubble

Everyone has a theory as to why it all went south – you'll hear plenty of them on your travels. Basically, it was because of an unsustainable construction boom that saw far too many houses being built and far too many cheap loans given out to both build and buy them. When Lehmann Bros collapsed, taking the markets with it, Irish banks' source of cheap credit dried up and their exposure to their debtors was revealed: all six of the main Irish banks risked immediate collapse. Faced with financial Armageddon, the then-minister for finance, Brian Lenihan, guaranteed all deposits and bondholder investments in the six banks. That guarantee has been the most contentious and divisive decision made in Irish politics since independence. As it stands, Ireland will not be allowed near a money market until at least 2013–14.

Meanwhile, Life Goes On

In economic terms, conditions are tough. Unemployment is up, pay is down and tourism – one of Ireland's most important sources of revenue – fell by roughly 30% between 2008 and 2011. While the old cliché that Ireland is too well used to hard times to let them knock it out of its stride is ridiculously crude and simplistic, there is some truth in it. The Irish – fatalistic and pessimistic to the core – will shrug their shoulders and just get on with their lives. It's not a coincidence that, unlike in Greece, the Irish haven't taken to the streets to protest the restrictive austerity measures that resulted from the banking collapse.

History

Celtic crosses in County Sligo (p272)

GARETH McCORMACK / LONELY PLANET IMAGE

From pre-Celts to Celtic cubs, Ireland's history is a search for identity, which would be a little more straightforward if this small island hadn't been of such interest to so many invaders, especially the English. Indeed, Ireland's fractious relationship with its nearest neighbour has occupied much of the last 1000 years, and it is through the prism of that relationship that a huge part of the Irish identity is reflected.

Who the Hell are the Irish?

Hunters and gatherers may first have traversed the narrowing land bridge that once linked Ireland with Britain, but many more crossed the Irish Sea in small hide-covered boats. In the 8th century BC, Ireland came to the attention of the fearsome Celts, who, having fought their way across Central Europe, established permanent settlements on the island in the 3rd century BC. Despite the constantly shifting political situation, the Celts cre-

10,000–8000 BC

After the last Ice Age ends, the first humans arrive in Ireland.

ated the basis of what we now term 'Irish' culture: they devised a sophisticated code of law called the Brehon Law (which remained in use until the early 17th century), and their swirling, mazelike design style, evident on artefacts nearly 2000 years old, is considered the epitome of Irish design.

Getting into the Habit

Arguably the most significant import into Ireland came between the 3rd and 5th centuries AD, when Christian missionaries first brought the new religion of Rome. Everyone has heard of St Patrick, but he was merely the most famous of many who converted the local pagan tribes by cleverly fusing traditional pagan rituals with the new Christian teaching, creating an exciting hybrid known as Celtic (Insular) Christianity. The artistic and intellectual credentials of Ireland's Christians were the envy of Europe, and led to the moniker 'the land of saints and scholars'.

More Invaders

The Celts' lack of political unity made the island easy pickings for the next wave of invaders, Danish Vikings. Over the course of the 9th and 10th centuries, they established settlements along the east coast, intermarried with the Celtic tribes and introduced red hair and freckles to the Irish gene pool.

The '800 years' of English rule in Ireland began in 1171, when the English king Henry II sent a huge invasion force, at the urging of the pope, to bring the increasingly independent Christian missionaries to heel. It was also intended to

St Patrick

Ireland's patron saint, St Patrick (AD 389–461), remembered all around the world on 17 March, wasn't even Irish. This symbol of Irish pride hailed from what is now Wales, which at the time of his birth was under Roman occupation. Kidnapped by Irish raiders when he was 16 and made a slave, he found religion, escaped from captivity and returned to Britain. He returned to Ireland vowing to make Christians out of the Irish, and within 30 years of his return his dream had come true.

So next St Paddy's Day, as you're swilling Guinness, think of who the man really was.

700–300 BC
The Celtic culture and language arrive, ushering in 1000 years of cultural and political dominance.

AD 431–2
Arrival of the first Christian missionaries with Bishop Palladius and, a year later, St Patrick.

550–800
The great monastic teachers begin exporting their knowledge across Europe, ushering in Ireland's 'Golden Age'.

Beyond the Pale

The expression 'beyond the pale' came into use when the Pale – defined as a jurisdiction marked by a clear boundary – was the English-controlled part of Ireland, which stretched roughly from Dalkey, a southern suburb of Dublin, to Dundalk, north of Drogheda. Inland, the boundary extended west to Trim and Kells. To the British elite, the rest of Ireland was considered uncivilised.

curb the growing power of the Anglo-Norman lords, who had arrived in Ireland two years before Henry's army, and who had settled quite nicely into Irish life, becoming – as the old saying went – *Hiberniores Hibernis ipsis* (more Irish than the Irish themselves). By the 16th century, they had divided the country into their own fiefdoms and the English Crown's direct control didn't extend any further than a cordon surrounding Dublin, known as 'the Pale'.

Divorce, Dissolution & Destruction

Henry VIII's failure to get the pope's blessing for his divorce augured badly for the Irish, who sided with the Vatican. Henry retaliated by ordering the dissolution of all monasteries in Britain and Ireland, and had himself declared King of Ireland. His daughter Elizabeth I went even further, establishing jurisdiction in Connaught and Munster before crushing the last of the rebels, the lords of Ulster, led by the crafty and courageous Hugh O'Neill, Earl of Tyrone.

With the native chiefs gone, Elizabeth and her successor, James I, could pursue their policy of Plantation with impunity. Though confiscations took place all over the country, Ulster was most affected both because of its wealthy farmlands and as punishment for being home to the primary fomenters of rebellion.

Bloody Religion

At the outset of the English Civil War in 1641, the Irish threw their support behind Charles I against the Protestant parliamentarians in the hope that victory for the king would lead to the restoration of Catholic power in Ireland. When Oliver Cromwell and his Roundheads defeated the Royalists and took Charles' head off in 1649, Cromwell then turned his attention to the disloyal Irish. His nine-month campaign was effective and brutal; yet more lands were confiscated – Cromwell's famous utterance that the Irish could 'go to hell or to Connaught' seems odd given the province's beauty, but there wasn't much arable land out there – and Catholic rights restricted even more.

795–841

Vikings plunder Irish monasteries before establishing settlements throughout the country.

VIKING LONGSHIP, IRISH NATIONAL HERITAGE PARK, RICHARD CUMMINS / LONELY PLANET IMAGES ©

1171

King Henry II invades Ireland and forces Anglo-Norman warlords to accept him as their overlord.

The Boyne & Penal Laws

Catholic Ireland's next major setback came in 1690. Yet again the Irish had backed the wrong horse, this time supporting James II after his deposition in the Glorious Revolution by the Dutch Protestant King William of Orange (who was married to James' own daughter Mary). After James had unsuccessfully laid siege to Derry for 105 days (the loyalist cry of 'No Surrender!', in use to this day, dates from the siege), in July he fought William's armies by the banks of the Boyne in County Louth and was roundly defeated.

The final ignominy for Catholic Ireland came in 1695 with the passing of the Penal Laws, known collectively as the 'popery code', which prohibited Catholics from owning land or entering any higher profession. Irish culture, music and education were banned in the hope that Catholicism would be eradicated. Most Catholics continued to worship at secret locations, but some prosperous Irish converted to Protestantism to preserve their careers and wealth. Land was steadily transferred to Protestant owners, and a significant majority of the Catholic population became tenants living in wretched conditions. By the late 18th century, Catholics owned barely 5% of the land.

If at First You Don't Succeed...

With Roman Catholics rendered utterly powerless, the seeds of rebellion against autocracy were planted by a handful of liberal Protestants, inspired by the ideologies of the Enlightenment and the unrest provoked by the American War of Independence and then the French Revolution.

The first of these came in 1798, when the United Irishmen, led by a young Dublin Protestant, Theobald Wolfe Tone (1763–98), took on the British at the Battle of Vinegar Hill in County Wexford – their defeat was hastened by the failure of the French to land an army of succour in 1796 in Bantry Bay.

The Liberator

The Act of Union, passed in 1801, was the British government's vain attempt to put an end to any aspirations towards Irish independence, but the nationalist genie was out of the bottle, not least in the body of a Kerry-born Catholic named Daniel O'Connell (1775–1847). In 1823 O'Connell founded the Catholic Association with the aim of achieving political equality for Catholics, which he did (in part) by forcing the passing of the 1829 Act of Catholic Emancipation, allowing some well-off Catholics voting rights and the right to be elected as MPs.

O'Connell's campaign now switched to the repeal of the Act of Union, but the 'Liberator' came to a sorry end in 1841 when he meekly stood down in face of a government order banning one of his rallies. His capitulation was deemed unforgivable given that Ireland was in the midst of the Potato Famine.

1366

Statutes of Kilkenny outlaw intermarriage and a host of Irish customs to stop Anglo-Norman assimilation.

1534–41

Henry VIII declares war on the Irish Church and declares himself King of Ireland.

1594

Hugh O'Neill, Earl of Tyrone, instigates open conflict with England and starts the Nine Years' War.

The Great Famine

As a result of the Great Famine of 1845–51, a staggering three million people died or were forced to emigrate from Ireland. This great tragedy is all the more inconceivable given that the scale of suffering was attributable to selfishness as much as to natural causes. Potatoes were the staple food of a rapidly growing, desperately poor population and, when a blight hit the crops, prices soared. The repressive Penal Laws ensured that farmers, already crippled with high rents, could ill afford the limited harvest of potatoes not affected by blight or imported from abroad to sell to the Irish. Inevitably, most tenants fell into arrears with little or no concession given by the mostly indifferent landlords and were evicted or sent to the dire conditions of the workhouses.

Shamefully, during this time there were abundant harvests of wheat and dairy produce – the country was producing more than enough grain to feed the entire population and it's said that more cattle were sold abroad than there were people on the island. But while millions of its citizens were starving, Ireland was forced to export its food to Britain and overseas.

The Poor Laws, in place at the height of the Famine, deemed landlords responsible for the maintenance of their poor and encouraged many to 'remove' tenants from their estates by paying their way to America. Many Irish were sent unwittingly to their deaths on board the notoriously scourged 'coffin ships'. British prime minister Sir Robert Peel made well-intentioned but inadequate gestures at famine relief, and some – but far too few – landlords did their best for their tenants.

Mass emigration continued to reduce the population during the next 100 years and huge numbers of Irish emigrants who found their way abroad, particularly to the USA, carried with them a lasting bitterness.

The Uncrowned King of Ireland

The baton of moderate opposition to British rule was then taken up by the extraordinary Charles Stewart Parnell (1846–91), who instigated the strategy of 'boycotting' (named after one particularly unpleasant agent named Charles Boycott) tenants, agents and landlords who didn't get on board with the demands of the Land League, an organisation set up to agitate for land reform, arguably the most important feature of the Irish struggle against British rule. The Land Act of 1881 improved life immeasurably for tenants, creating fair rents and the possibility of tenants owning their land.

Parnell's other assault on British rule was on agitating for Home Rule, a limited form of autonomy for Ireland. As leader of the Irish Parliamentary Party (IPP), he formed

1601
O'Neill surrenders after Battle of Kinsale and Irish rebellion against the Crown is broken.

1649–53
Oliver Cromwell lays waste throughout Ireland after the Irish support Charles I.

1690
Catholic King James II defeated by William of Orange in the Battle of the Boyne on 12 July.

alliances with William Gladstone's Liberal Party in return for the introduction of a Home Rule Bill, which came (but was defeated) in 1886 and 1892 – although Parnell was not around for the second bill: in 1890 he was embroiled in a divorce scandal, was forced to resign and died a broken man in 1891.

Rebellion Once Again

Ireland's struggle for some kind of autonomy picked up pace in the second decade of the 20th century. The radicalism that had always been at the fringes of Irish nationalist aspirations was once again beginning to assert itself, partly in response to a hardening of attitudes in Ulster. Mass opposition to any kind of Irish independence had resulted in the formation of the Ulster Volunteer Force (UVF), a loyalist vigilante group whose 100,000-plus members swore to resist any attempt to impose Home Rule on Ireland. Nationalists responded by creating the Irish Volunteer Force (IVF), and a showdown seemed inevitable.

Home Rule was finally passed in 1914, but the outbreak of WWI meant that its enactment was shelved for the duration. For most Irish, the suspension was

Ancient ruins, County Wexford (p152)

1798
A rising by the United Irishmen and Wolfe Tone ends in defeat and Tone's suicide.

1801
The Act of Union unites Ireland politically with Britain, ending Irish 'independence'.

1828–29
Prime Minister passes the Catholic Emancipation Act, giving limited rights to Catholics.

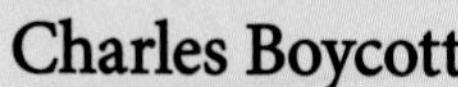

Charles Boycott

Poor Charles C Boycott. A County Mayo land agent, he was the (some would say deserving) victim of Parnell's 1880 policy of completely ostracising anyone who was seen to perpetuate the unjust practices that kept the vast majority of the Irish peasantry in landless penury. Boycott was no worse than hundreds of other such agents, but it was his name given to the uncomfortable practice of boycotting!

disappointing but hardly unreasonable and the majority of the volunteers enlisted to help fight the Germans.

The Easter Rising

A few, however, did not heed the call. Two small groups – a section of the Irish Volunteers under Pádraig Pearse and the Irish Citizens' Army led by James Connolly – conspired in a rebellion that took the country by surprise. A depleted Volunteer group marched into Dublin on Easter Monday 1916 and took over a number of key positions in the city, claiming the General Post Office on O'Connell St as its headquarters. From its steps, Pearse read out to passers-by a declaration that Ireland was now a republic and that his band was the provisional government. Less than a week of fighting ensued before the rebels surrendered to the superior British forces. The rebels weren't popular and had to be protected from angry Dubliners as they were marched to jail.

The Easter Rising would probably have had little impact on the Irish situation had the British not made martyrs of the rebel leaders. Of the 77 given death sentences, 15 were executed, including the injured Connolly, who was shot while strapped to a chair. This brought about a sea change in public attitudes and support for the Republicans rose dramatically.

War with Britain

By the end of WWI, Home Rule was far too little, far too late. In the 1918 general election, the Republicans stood under the banner of Sinn Féin and won a large majority of the Irish seats. Ignoring London's Parliament, where technically they were supposed to sit, the newly elected Sinn Féin deputies – many of them veterans of the 1916 Easter Rising – declared Ireland independent and formed the first Dáil Éireann (Irish assembly or lower house), which sat in Dublin's Mansion House under the leadership of Éamon de Valera (1882–1975). The Irish Volunteers became the Irish Republican Army (IRA) and the Dáil authorised it to wage war on British troops in Ireland.

1845–51
Between 500,000 and one million die during Potato Famine; two million more emigrate.

1879–82
The Land War sees tenant farmers defying their landlords en masse.

1916
The Easter Rising rebels surrender to superior British forces in less than a week.

As wars go, the War of Independence was pretty small fry. It lasted 2½ years and cost around 1200 casualties. But it was a pretty nasty affair, as the IRA fought a guerrilla-style, hit-and-run campaign against the British, their numbers swelled by returning veterans of WWI known as Black and Tans (on account of their uniforms, a mix of army khaki and police black), most of whom were so traumatised by their wartime experiences that they were prone to all kinds of brutality.

The Best... Irish History Museums

1 Kilmainham Gaol (p75)

2 National 1798 Rebellion Centre (p156)

3 Donegal Castle (p277)

4 Derrynane National Historic Park (p208)

5 Ulster Folk Museum (p316)

A Kind of Freedom

A truce in July 1921 led to intense negotiations between the two sides. The resulting Treaty, signed on 6 December 1921, created the Irish Free State, made up of 26 of 32 Irish counties. The remaining six – all in Ulster – remained part of the UK. The Treaty was an imperfect document: not only did it cement the geographic divisions on the island that 50 years later would explode into the Troubles, but it caused a split among nationalists – between those who believed the Treaty to be a necessary stepping stone toward full independence and those who saw it as capitulation to the British and a betrayal of Republican ideals. This division was to determine the course of Irish political affairs for virtually the remainder of the century.

Civil War

The Treaty was ratified after a bitter debate and the June 1922 elections resulted in a victory for the pro-Treaty side. But the anti-Treaty forces rallied behind de Valera, who, though president of the Dáil, had not been a member of the Treaty negotiating team (affording him, in the eyes of his critics and opponents, maximum deniability should the negotiations go pear-shaped) and objected to some of the Treaty's provisions, most notably the oath of allegiance to the English monarch.

Within two weeks of the elections, civil war broke out between comrades who, a year previously, had fought alongside each other. The most prominent casualty of this particularly bitter conflict was Michael Collins (1890–1922), mastermind of the IRA's campaign during the War of Independence and a chief negotiator of the Anglo-Irish Treaty – shot in an ambush in his native Cork. Collins himself had presaged the bitterness that would result from the Treaty: upon signing it he is said to have declared, 'I tell you, I have signed my own death warrant.'

1919

The Irish War of Independence begins in January.

1921

War ends in a truce on 11 July; Anglo-Irish Treaty is signed on 6 December.

STATUE FOR VICTIMS OF POTATO FAMINE, DOUG McKINLAY / LONELY PLANET IMAGES ©

The Best... Places Where History Happened

1 General Post Office (p79)

2 Vinegar Hill (p156)

3 Battle of the Boyne Site (p127)

4 Tara (p129)

5 Kinsale (p191)

The Making of a Republic

The Civil War ground to an exhausted halt in 1923 with the victory of the pro-Treaty side, who governed the new state until 1932. Defeated but unbowed, de Valera founded a new party in 1926 called Fianna Fáil (Soldiers of Ireland) and won a majority in the 1932 elections – they would remain in charge until 1948. In the meantime, de Valera created a new constitution in 1937 that did away with the hated oath of allegiance, reaffirmed the special position of the Catholic Church and once again laid claim to the six counties of Northern Ireland. In 1948 Ireland officially left the Commonwealth and became a Republic, but as historical irony would have it, it was Fine Gael, as the old pro-Treaty party were now known, that declared it – Fianna Fáil had surprisingly lost the election that year. After 800 years Ireland – or at least a substantial chunk of it – was independent.

Growing Pains & Roaring Tigers

Unquestionably the most significant figure since independence, Éamon de Valera's contribution to an independent Ireland was immense but, as the 1950s stretched into

1798 Rebellion memorial at Vinegar Hill (p156), Enniscorthy
PHOTOGRAPHER: © MAURICE SAVAGE / ALAMY

1921–22
Treaty grants independence to 26 counties, allowing six Ulster counties to remain part of Great Britain.

1922–23
Brief and bloody civil war between pro-Treaty and anti-Treaty forces results in victory for former.

1932
De Valera leads his Fianna Fáil party into government for the first time.

the 1960s, his vision for the country was mired in a conservative and traditional orthodoxy that was patently at odds with the reality of a country in desperate economic straits, where chronic unemployment and emigration were but the more visible effects of inadequate policy. De Valera's successor as Taoiseach was Sean Lemass, whose tenure began in 1959 with the dictum 'a rising tide lifts all boats'. By the mid-1960s his economic policies had halved emigration and ushered in a new prosperity that was to be mirrored 30 years later by the Celtic Tiger.

Partners in Europe

In 1972 the Republic (along with Northern Ireland) became a member of the European Economic Community (EEC), which brought an increased measure of prosperity thanks to the benefits of the Common Agricultural Policy, which set fixed prices and guaranteed quotas for Irish farming produce. Nevertheless, the broader global depression, provoked by the oil crisis of 1973, forced the country into yet another slump and emigration figures rose again, reaching a peak in the mid-1980s.

From Celtic Tiger...

In the early 1990s, European funds helped kick start economic growth. Huge sums of money were invested in education and physical infrastructure, while the policy of low corporate tax rates coupled with attractive incentives made Ireland very appealing to high-tech businesses looking for a door into EU markets. In less than a decade, Ireland went from being one of the poorest countries in Europe to one of the wealthiest: unemployment fell from 18% to 3.5%, the average industrial wage somersaulted to the top of the European league and the dramatic rise in GDP meant that the government had far more money than it knew what do with. Ireland became synonymous with the Celtic Tiger, an economic model of success that was the envy of the entire world.

The Victor's Version

Neil Jordan's epic film *Michael Collins* tells the story of the 'long fellow', idolised during his life and unquestionably one of the outstanding Irishmen of the 20th century.

Yet for much of that century Collins was seen by many as a traitor to the cause of Irish freedom, partly because he was a signatory of the Anglo-Irish Treaty, but mostly because his greatest political rival was Éamon de Valera, the embodiment of the Irish state from its foundation until the end of his life – when he left public life in 1973, aged 91, as the oldest head of state in the world.

1948
The new Fine Gael declares the Free State to be a republic.

1972
The Republic (and the UK) join the EEC; 13 civilians are killed by soldiers in Derry.

1993
Downing Street Declaration signed by British prime minister John Major and Irish *Taoiseach* Albert Reynolds.

...to Rescue Cat

From 2002, the Irish economy was kept buoyant by a gigantic construction boom that was completely out of step with any measure of responsible growth forecasting. The out-of-control international derivatives market flooded Irish banks with cheap money, and they were only too happy to lend it to anyone who wanted. And in Ireland, everyone wanted.

Then Lehman Brothers and the credit crunch happened. The Irish banks nearly went to the wall, were bailed out at the last minute and before Ireland could draw breath, the International Monetary Fund (IMF) and the European Union held the chits of the country's mid-term economic future. Ireland found itself yet again confronting the demons of its past: high unemployment, limited opportunity and massive emigration.

It's (Not So) Grim up North

Making sense of Northern Ireland isn't that easy. It's not because the politics are so entrenched (they are), or that the two sides are at such odds with each other (they are): it's because the fight is so old.

It began in the 16th century, with the first Plantations of Ireland ordered by the English Crown, whereby the confiscated lands of the Gaelic and Hiberno-Norman gentry were awarded to English and Scottish settlers of good Protestant stock. The policy was most effective in Ulster, where the newly arrived Protestants were given an extra leg-up by the Penal Laws, which successfully reduced the now landless Catholic population to second-class citizens with little or no rights.

Women of the Revolution

The 1916 Proclamation was a radical document for its day, and called for equal rights between men and women (Britain only gave women full suffrage in 1928). This was thanks to Countess Markievicz (1868–1927) and Maud Gonne (1865–1953), two Englishwomen who inspired a generation of revolutionaries. Countess Markievicz was a committed Republican and socialist, as well as one of the military leaders of the 1916 Rising. Maud Gonne was also a staunch Republican but is perhaps better known as WB Yeats' gorgeous muse (and desperately unrequited love).

1994
Sinn Féin leader Gerry Adams announces a cessation of IRA violence on 31 August.

mid-1990s
The 'Celtic Tiger' economy transforms Ireland into one of Europe's wealthiest countries.

Irish Apartheid

But fast-forward to 1921, when the notion of independent Ireland moved from aspiration to actuality. The new rump state of Northern Ireland was governed until 1972 by the Protestant-majority Ulster Unionist Party, backed up by the overwhelmingly Protestant Royal Ulster Constabulary (RUC) and the sectarian B-Specials militia. As a result of tilted economic subsidies, bias in housing allocation and wholesale gerrymandering, Northern Ireland was, in effect, an apartheid state, leaving the roughly 40% Catholic and Nationalist population grossly underrepresented.

Defiance of Unionist hegemony came with the Civil Rights Movement, founded in 1967 and heavily influenced by its US counterpart. In October 1968 a mainly Catholic march in Derry was violently broken up by the RUC amid rumours that the IRA had provided 'security' for the marchers. Nobody knew it at the time, but the Troubles had begun.

The Troubles

Conflict escalated quickly: clashes between the two communities increased and the police openly sided with the Loyalists against a Nationalist population made increasingly militant by the resurgence of the long-dormant IRA. In August 1969 British troops

Peace mural, Belfast (p306)

1998

After the Good Friday Agreement, the 'Real IRA' detonates a bomb in Omagh, killing 29 people and injuring 200.

2005

The IRA orders all of its units to commit to exclusively democratic means.

2007

The Northern Ireland Assembly resumes after a five-year break as Unionists and Nationalists resolve differences.

went to Derry and then Belfast to maintain law and order; they were initially welcomed in Catholic neighbourhoods but within a short time they too were seen as an army of occupation: the killing of 13 innocent civilians in Derry on Bloody Sunday (30 January 1972) set the grim tone for the next two decades, as violence, murder and reprisal became the order of the day in the province and, occasionally, on the British mainland.

Overtures of Peace

In the 1990s external circumstances started to alter the picture. Membership of the EU, economic progress in Ireland and the declining importance of the Catholic Church in the South started to reduce differences between the North and the Republic. Also, American interest added an international dimension to the situation.

A series of negotiated statements between the Unionists, Nationalists and the British and Irish governments eventually resulted in the historic Good Friday Agreement of 1998, which established the power-sharing Northern Ireland Assembly.

The agreement called for the devolution of legislative power from Westminster (where it had been since 1972) to a new Northern Ireland Assembly, but posturing, disagreement, sectarianism and downright pigheadedness made slow work of progress, and the assembly was suspended four times – the last from October 2002 until May 2007.

During this period, the politics of Northern Ireland polarised dramatically, resulting in the falling away of the more moderate UUP and the emergence of the hardline Democratic Unionist Party (DUP), led by Ian Paisley; and, on the Nationalist side, the emergence of the IRA's political wing, Sinn Féin, as the main torch-bearer of Nationalist aspirations, under the leadership of Gerry Adams and Martin McGuinness.

The Best... Books About Ireland

1 *The Course of Irish History* (TW Moody & FX Martin)

2 *The Great Hunger* (Cecil Woodham-Smith)

3 *The Irish in America* (Michael Coffey)

4 *For the Cause of Liberty: A Thousand Years of Ireland's Heroes* (Terry Golway)

5 *A History of Ulster* (Jonathon Bardon)

2008
The Irish banking system is declared virtually bankrupt following the collapse of Lehman Brothers.

2010
Ireland surrenders financial sovereignty to IMF and EU in exchange for bailout package of €85bn.

2011
Queen Elizabeth II is the first British monarch to visit the Republic of Ireland.

The Irish Way of Life

Crowds in Quay St, Galway City (p230)

CHRIS MELLOR / LONELY PLANET IMAGES ©

The Irish are renowned for their easygoing, affable nature, but they're no strangers to grumbling – about work, the weather and those feckin' eejits in government. No matter what, their greatest comfort is humour – often black, but always entertaining. They prefer informality to stuffiness, but can be quick to take offence if certain rules are not abided by – usually to do with courtesy, not talking yourself up and, most importantly, failing to buy a pint when it's your turn to do so.

The National Psyche

Like anyone, the Irish are a complicated, contradictory bunch, but one characteristic gets to the very essence of the Irish personality. Slagging – the Irish version of teasing – is an art form, which may seem caustic to unfamiliar ears, but is quickly revealed as an intrinsic element of how the Irish relate to one another. It is commonly assumed that the mettle of friendship is proven by how well you can take a joke rather than by the payment of a cheap compliment.

The Irish aren't big on talking themselves up, preferring their actions to speak for themselves. They also admire the peculiar art of self-deprecation, known locally as *an beál bocht a chur ort,* or 'putting on the poor mouth', the mildly pejorative practice of making out that things are far worse than they really are in order to evoke sympathy

If I Should Fall From Grace

Once the poster child for devout Catholicism, Ireland has become largely estranged from the church that used to play such a central role in its culture and lifestyle. Globalisation, increased prosperity and a general loosening of moral codes – which brought contraception and divorce to a country once vehemently opposed to them – are important factors, but overshadowing them all are the revelations of widespread clerical abuse of minors and the systematic cover-up by church authorities that protected the worst offenders. For a nation that once saw Mass attendance as an integral part of life, the sense of betrayal by a church seen to have abandoned its flock has been profound and far-reaching.

or the forbearance of creditors, of vital importance in the days when the majority of the Irish were at the mercy of an unforgiving landlord system. As a result, the Irish also have the trait of begrudgery – although it's something only recognised by them and generally kept within the wider family. It's kind of amusing, though, to note that someone like Bono is subject to more intense criticism in Ireland than anywhere else in the world.

Beneath all of the garrulous sociability and self-deprecating twaddle lurks a dark secret, which is that at heart the Irish are low on self-esteem. They're therefore very suspicious of praise and tend not to believe anything nice that's ever said about them. The Irish wallow in false modesty like a sport.

This goes some way towards explaining the fractious relationship Ireland has with alcohol. The country regularly tops the list of the world's biggest binge drinkers, and while there is an increasing awareness of, and alarm at, the devastation caused by alcohol to Irish society (especially to young people), drinking remains the country's most popular social pastime, with no sign of letting up. Spend a weekend night walking around any town in the country and you'll get a firsthand feel of the influence and effect of the booze.

Nevertheless, the prosperity of the last two decades and the radical lifestyle shifts it entailed has imbued the Irish with a renewed sense of confidence and a conviction that they are deserving of a seat at anyone's table. For the first time, the Irish, particularly the under-30s, have no problem relaying their achievements and successes, in contrast to the older generation who were brought up in the belief that telling anyone they were doing well was unseemly and boastful!

As Ireland adjusts to the new, post-crash economic realities, an interesting gap in perspective has emerged: the younger generation, raised on boundless possibility, have struggled to adjust to circumstances that are oh-so-familiar to their parents, who were brought up in a time when unemployment, emigration and a cap on ambition were basic facts of life.

While Ireland's economic woes may be depressingly familiar to the older generation and forced many of the country's younger people to try their luck elsewhere, this is *not* the Ireland of yesteryear. The two decades since 1990 have transformed the country immeasurably, with prosperity, modernity and multiculturalism helping shift traditional attitudes and social mores.

The Irish People

Traditional Ireland – of the large family, closely linked to church and community – is quickly disappearing as the nation's increased urbanisation continues to break up the social fabric of community interdependence that was a necessary element of relative poverty. Contemporary Ireland is therefore not altogether different from any other European country, and you have to travel further to the margins of the country – the islands and the isolated rural communities – to find an older version of society.

Nevertheless, Ireland's birth rate – the highest in the EU at 17.2 births per 1000 people – grew by a massive 9.4% in 2008, although it's a sign of the times that about a third of the babies born in 2008 were born outside of marriage (even if roughly half of those were registered as having both parents living together). And while the number of couples getting married is down, it is only slightly so, hovering around five marriages per 1000 people over the last decade.

The attitude towards gay people has also been transformed, courtesy of a general liberalisation of the country's mores and the enactment of protective legislation against any kind of sexual discrimination. The passing of the Civil Partnership Act in 2011, which recognised civil unions between same-sex couples but did not grant them full marriage rights, was seen as a further step in the right direction, though not nearly far enough by the LGBT community. Same-sex couples in Northern Ireland do have the rights and responsibilities of full civil marriage, courtesy of the UK's 2004 Civil Partnership Act.

Ireland has long been a pretty homogenous country, but the arrival of thousands of immigrants from all over the world – 10% of the population is foreign-born – has challenged the mores of racial tolerance and integration. To a large extent it has been successful, although if you scratch beneath the surface, racial tensions can be exposed. So long as the new arrivals take on the jobs that many Irish wouldn't bother doing anymore, everything is relatively hunky-dory; it's when the second generation of immigrants begin competing for the middle-class jobs that Ireland's tolerance credentials will truly be tested.

The Best... Irish Attractions

1 National Museum (p73)

2 Guinness Storehouse (p74)

3 Kilkenny Castle (p149)

4 Skellig Michael (p209)

5 Dún Aengus (p237)

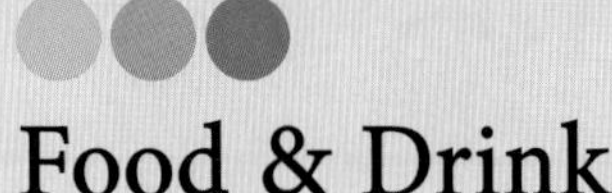

Food & Drink

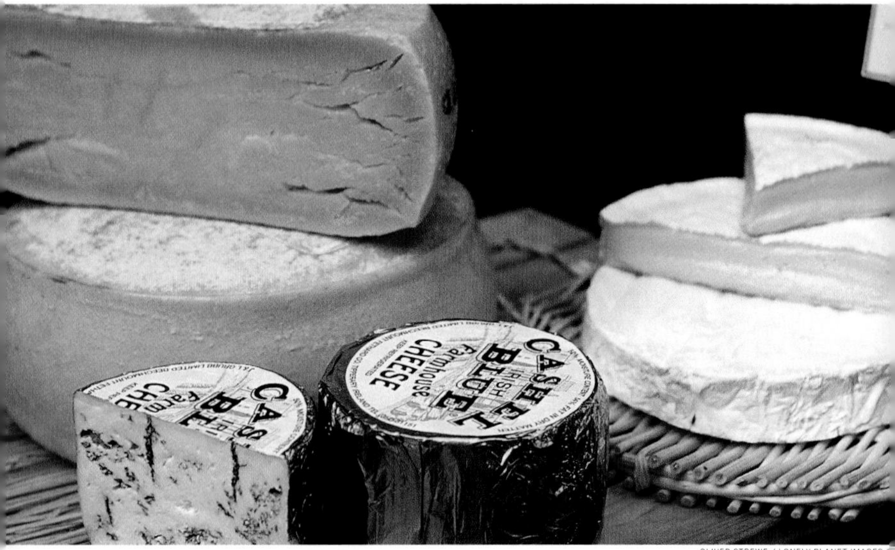

A selection of Irish cheeses

OLIVER STREWE / LONELY PLANET IMAGES ©

Ireland's recently acquired reputation as a gourmet destination is thoroughly deserved, as a host of chefs and producers are leading a foodie revolution that, at its heart, is about bringing to the table the kind of meals that have always been taken for granted on well-run Irish farms. Coupled with the growing sophistication of the Irish palate – by now well-used to the varied flavours of the world's range of ethnic cuisines – it's now relatively easy to eat well in all budgets.

Local Specialities

To Eat...

Potatoes

It's a wonder the Irish retain their good humour amid the perpetual potato-baiting they endure. But, despite the stereotyping, and however much we'd like to disprove it, potatoes are still paramount here and you'll see lots of them on your travels. The mashed potato dishes colcannon and champ (with cabbage and spring onion respectively) are two of the tastiest recipes in the country.

Meat & Seafood

Irish meals are usually meat based, with beef, lamb and pork common options. Seafood, long neglected, is finding a place on the table in Irish homes. It's widely available in restaurants and is often excellent, especially in the west. Oysters, trout and salmon are delicious, particularly if they're direct from the sea or a river rather than a fish farm. The famous Dublin Bay prawn isn't actually a prawn but a lobster. At its best, the Dublin Bay prawn is superlative, but it's priced accordingly. If you're going to splurge, do so here – but make sure you choose live Dublin Bay prawns because once these fellas die, they quickly lose their flavour.

Soda Bread

The most famous Irish bread, and one of the signature tastes of Ireland, is soda bread. Irish flour is soft and doesn't take well to yeast as a raising agent, so Irish bakers of the 19th century leavened their bread with bicarbonate of soda. Combined with buttermilk, it makes a superbly light-textured and tasty bread, and is often on the breakfast menus at B&Bs.

Cheese

Ireland has some wonderful cheeses, such as the flavoursome farmhouse **Ardrahan** with a rich nutty taste; the subtle **Corleggy**, a pasteurised goats cheese from County Cavan; **Durrus**, a creamy, fruity cheese; creamy **Cashel Blue** from Tipperary and the award-winning Camembert-style cheese, **Cooleeney**.

The Fry

Perhaps the most feared Irish speciality is the fry – the heart attack on a plate that is the second part of so many B&B deals. In spite of the hysterical health fears, the fry is still one of the most common traditional meals in the country. Who can say no to a plate of fried bacon, sausages, black pudding, white pudding, eggs and tomatoes? For the famous Ulster fry, common throughout the North, simply add fadge (potato bread).

To Drink...

Stout

While Guinness has become synonymous with stout the world over, few outside Ireland realise that there are two other major producers competing for the favour of the Irish drinker: Murphy's and Beamish & Crawford, both based in Cork city.

Tea

The Irish drink more tea, per capita, than any other nation in the world and you'll be offered a cup as soon as you cross the threshold of any Irish home. Taken with milk (and sugar, if you want) rather than lemon, preferred blends are very strong, and nothing like the namby-pamby versions that pass for Irish breakfast tea elsewhere.

Whiskey

At last count, there were almost 100 different types of Irish whiskey, brewed by only three distilleries – Jameson's,

Vegetarians & Vegans

Vegies can take a deep breath. And then exhale. Calmly. For Ireland has come a long, long way since the days when vegetarians were looked upon as odd creatures; nowadays, even the most militant vegan will barely cause a ruffle in all but the most basic of rustic kitchens. Which isn't to say that travellers with plant-based diets are going to find the most imaginative range of options on menus outside the bigger towns and cities – or in the plethora of modern restaurants that have opened in the last few years – but you can rest assured that the overall quality of the homegrown vegetable is top-notch and most places will have at least one dish that you can tuck into comfortably.

Dare to Try

Ironically, while the Irish palate has become more adventurous, it is the old-fashioned Irish menu that features some fairly interesting dishes:

- **Black pudding** Made from congealed pork blood, suet and other fillings, it is a ubiquitous part of an Irish cooked breakfast.
- **Boxty** A Northern Irish starchy potato cake made with a half-and-half mix of cooked mashed potatoes and grated, strained raw potato.
- **Carrageen** The typical Irish seaweed that can be found in dishes as diverse as salad and ice cream.
- **Corned beef tongue** Usually accompanied by cabbage, this dish is still found on a traditional Irish menu
- **Lough Neagh eel** A speciality of Northern Ireland typically eaten around Halloween; it's usually served in chunks and with a white onion sauce
- **Poitín** It's rare enough that you'll be offered a drop of the 'cratur', as illegally distilled whiskey (made from malted grain or potatoes) is called here. Still, there are pockets of the country with secret stills – in Donegal, Connemara and West Cork.

Bushmills and Cooley's. A visit to Ireland reveals a depth of excellence that will make the connoisseur's palate spin, while winning over many new friends to what the Irish call *uisce beatha* (water of life).

Other Irish Beers

For something a little different, try **Beamish Ale**, a sweet and palatable traditional red ale brewed in Cork city; **Caffrey's Irish Ale**, a robust cross between a stout and an ale brewed in County Antrim; **Kinsale Irish Lager**, a golden-coloured lager brewed in the eponymous County Cork town, with a slightly bitter taste that fades after a few sips; the hard to come by but worthy **McCardles Traditional Ale**, a wholesome dark nutty ale or **Smithwick's**, a lovely refreshing full scoop brewed in Kilkenny on the site of the 14th-century St Francis Abbey, Ireland's oldest working brewery.

When to Eat

Irish eating habits have changed over the last couple of decades, and there are differences between urban and rural practices.

Breakfast

An important meal given the Irish tendency toward small lunches. Usually eaten before 9am (although hotels and B&Bs will serve until 11am Monday to Friday, to noon at weekends) as most people rush off to work. Weekend brunch is popular in bigger towns and cities, although it pretty much copies traditional rural habits of eating a large, earthy breakfast late in the morning.

Lunch

Once the biggest meal of the day, lunch is now one of the more obvious rural/urban divides. Urban workers have succumbed to the eat-on-the-run restrictions of nine-to-five, with most eating a sandwich or a light meal between 12.30pm and 2pm (most restaurants don't begin to serve lunch until at least midday) in urban areas. At weekends, especially Sunday, the midday lunch is skipped in favour a substantial mid-afternoon meal (called dinner), usually between 2pm and 4pm.

Tea

No, not the drink, but the evening meal – also confusingly called dinner. For urbanites, this is the main meal of the day, usually eaten around 6.30pm. Rural communities eat at the same time but a more traditional tea of bread, cold cuts and, yes, tea. Restaurants follow more international habits, with most diners not eating until at least 7.30pm.

Supper

A before-bed snack of tea and toast or sandwiches, still enjoyed by many Irish although urbanites increasingly eschew it for health reasons. Not a practice in restaurants.

The Best... Memorable Meals

1 Restaurant Patrick Guilbaud (p85)

2 Fishy Fishy Cafe (p192)

3 Tannery (p162)

4 Ginger (p313)

5 55 Degrees North (p318)

Dining Etiquette

The Irish aren't big on restrictive etiquette, preferring friendly informality to any kind of stuffy formality. Still, there are a few tips to dining with the Irish.

All restaurants welcome kids up to 7pm, but pubs and some smarter restaurants don't allow them in the evening. Family restaurants have children's menus, others have reduced portions of regular menu items.

A dish of colcannon

If the food is not to your satisfaction, it's best to politely explain what's wrong with it as soon as you can; any respectable restaurant will endeavour to replace the dish immediately.

If you insist on paying the bill, be prepared for a first, second and even third refusal to countenance such an *exorbitant* act of generosity. But don't be fooled: the Irish will refuse something several times even if they're delighted with it. Insist gently but firmly and you'll get your way!

A local repast: lobsters, bread and Guinness, Galway
OLIVER STREWE / LONELY PLANET IMAGES ©

The Pub

Locals outside a Kinsale (p191) pub, County Cork

RICHARD CUMMINS / LONELY PLANET IMAGES ©

Simply put, the pub is the heart of Ireland's social existence, and we're guessing that experiencing it ranks pretty high on your list of things to do while you're here. But let's be clear: we're not just talking about a place to get a drink. Oh no. You can get a drink in a restaurant or a hotel, or wherever there's someone with a bottle of something strong. The pub is something far more than just that.

Role

The pub is the broadest window through which you can examine and experience the very essence of the nation's culture, in all its myriad of forms. It's the great leveller, where status and rank hold no sway, where generation gaps are bridged, inhibitions lowered, tongues loosened, schemes hatched, songs sung, stories told and gossip embroidered. It's a unique institution: a theatre and a cosy room, a centre stage and a hideaway, a debating chamber and a place for silent contemplation. It's whatever you want it to be, and that's the secret of the great Irish pub.

Talk

Talk – whether it is frivolous, earnest or incoherent – is the essential ingredient. Once tongues are loosened and the cogs of thought oiled, the conversation can go

anywhere and you should let it flow to its natural conclusion. An old Irish adage suggests you should never talk about sport, religion or politics in unfamiliar company. But as long as you're mindful, you needn't restrict yourself too much. While it's a myth to say you can walk into any pub and be befriended, you probably won't be drinking on your own for long – unless that's what you want of course. There are few more spiritual experiences than a solitary pint in an old country pub in the mid-afternoon.

The Best... Traditional Music Pubs

1 O'Donoghue's (p90)

2 Cobblestone (p91)

3 Cíaran's Bar (p245)

4 Tig Cóilí (p233)

5 O'Friel's Bar (p250)

Tradition

Aesthetically, there is nothing better than the traditional haunt, populated by flat-capped pensioners bursting with delightful anecdotes and always ready to dispense a kind of wisdom distilled through generations' worth of experience. The best of them have stone floors and a peat fire; the chat barely rises above a respectful murmur save for appreciative laughter; and most of all, there's no music save the kind played by someone sitting next to you. Pubs like these are a disappearing breed, but there are still plenty of them around to ensure that you will find one, no matter where you are.

Etiquette

The rounds system – the simple custom where someone buys you a drink and you buy one back – is the bedrock of Irish pub culture. It's summed up in the Irish saying: 'It's impossible for two men to go to a pub for one drink.' Nothing will hasten your fall from social grace here like the failure to uphold this pub law.

Another golden rule about the system is that the next round starts when the first person has finished (preferably just about to finish) their drink. It doesn't matter if you're only halfway through your pint – if it's your round, get your order in.

Irish Mythological Symbols

Shamrocks (three-leafed clover)

JOHN SONES / LONELY PLANET IMAGES ©

Ireland's collection of icons serves to exemplify the country – or a simplistic version of it – to an astonishing degree. It's referred to by the Irish as Oirishness, which is what happens when you take a spud, shove it in a pint of Guinness and garnish it with shamrock; you'll see it throughout the world, as the hyphenated Irish join with the nation's native sons and daughters to celebrate St Patrick's Day, their eyes made bleary by more than just emotion.

The Shamrock

Ireland's most enduring symbol is the shamrock, a three-leafed white clover known diminutively in Irish as *seamróg*, which was anglicised as 'shamrock'. According to legend, when St Patrick was trying to explain the mystery of the Holy Trinity to the recently converted Celtic chieftains, he plucked the modest little weed and used its three leaves to explain the metaphysically challenging concept of the Father, the Son and the Holy Spirit as being separate but part of the one being. This link is what makes the shamrock a ubiquitous part of the St Patrick's Day celebrations.

The Celtic Cross

Everywhere you go, you will see examples of the Celtic cross – basically, a cross surrounded by a ring. Its origins weren't simply a question of aesthetic design but more of practical necessity. The cross was a clever fusing of new Christian teaching (the cross itself) with established pagan beliefs, in this, case sun worship (marked by the circle).

Some of the most famous crosses in Ireland are in Monasterboice, County Louth and Clonmacnoise, County Offaly.

The Best... Irish Crafts & Memorabilia

1 Avoca Handweavers (p93)

2 Kilkenny Shop (p93)

3 Thomas Dillon's Claddagh Gold (p234)

4 Ardara Heritage Centre (p281)

5 Long Room, Trinity College (p62)

The Leprechaun

The country's most enduring cliché is the myth of the mischievous leprechaun and his pot of gold, which he jealously guards from the attentions of greedy humans. Despite the twee aspect of the legend, their origin predates the Celts and belongs to the mythological Tuatha dé Danann (peoples of the Goddess Danu), who lived in Ireland 4000 years ago. When they were eventually defeated, their king Lugh (the demi-God father of Cúchulainn) was forced underground, where he became known as Lugh Chromain, or 'little stooping Lugh' – the origin of leprechaun.

The Irish can get visibly irritated if asked whether they believe in leprechauns (you might as well ask them if they're stupid), but many rural dwellers are a superstitious lot. They mightn't necessarily *believe* that malevolent sprites who dwell in faerie forts actually exist, but they're not especially keen to test the theory either, which is why there still exist trees, hills and other parts of the landscape that are deemed to have, well, supernatural qualities, and as such will never be touched.

The Harp

The Celtic harp, or *clársach*, is meant to represent the immortality of the soul, which is handy given that it's been a symbol of Ireland since the days of Henry VIII and the first organised opposition to English rule. The harp was the most popular instrument at the Celtic court, with the harpist (usually blind) being ranked only behind the chief and bard in order of importance. In times of war, the harpist played a special, jewel-encrusted harp and served as the cheerleading section for soldiers heading into battle.

During the first rebellions against the English, the harp was once again an instrument of revolutionary fervour, prompting the crown to ban it altogether; this eventually led to its decline as the instrument of choice for Irish musicians but ensured its status as a symbol of Ireland.

The Claddagh Ring

The most famous of all Irish jewellery is the Claddagh ring, made up of two hands (friendship) clasping a heart (love) and usually surmounted by a crown (loyalty). Made in the eponymous fishing village of County Galway since the 17th century, the symbolic origins are much older and belong to a broader family of rings popular since Roman times known as the *fede* rings (from *mani in fede,* or 'hands in trust'), which were used

The Luck of the Irish?

Nearly a millennium of occupation, a long history of oppression and exploitation, a devastating famine, mass emigration...how *exactly* are the Irish 'lucky'? Well, they're not – or at least not any more so than anybody else. The expression was born in the mid-19th century United States during the gold and silver rush, when some of the most successful miners were Irish or of Irish extraction. It didn't really seem to matter that the Irish – recent escapees from famine and destitution in Ireland – were over-represented among the miners; the expression stuck. Still, the expression was always a little derisory, as though the Irish merely stumbled across good fortune.

to symbolise marriage. Nevertheless, their popularity is relatively recent, and almost entirely down to their wearing by expat Americans who use them to demonstrate their ties to their Irish heritage (see p234).

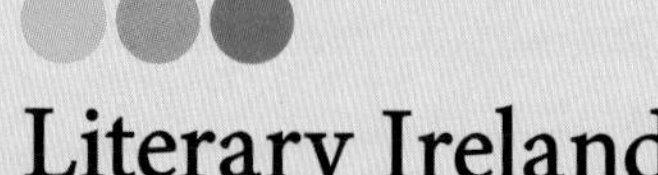

Literary Ireland

A Bloomsday reading (p82) at the James Joyce Cultural Centre

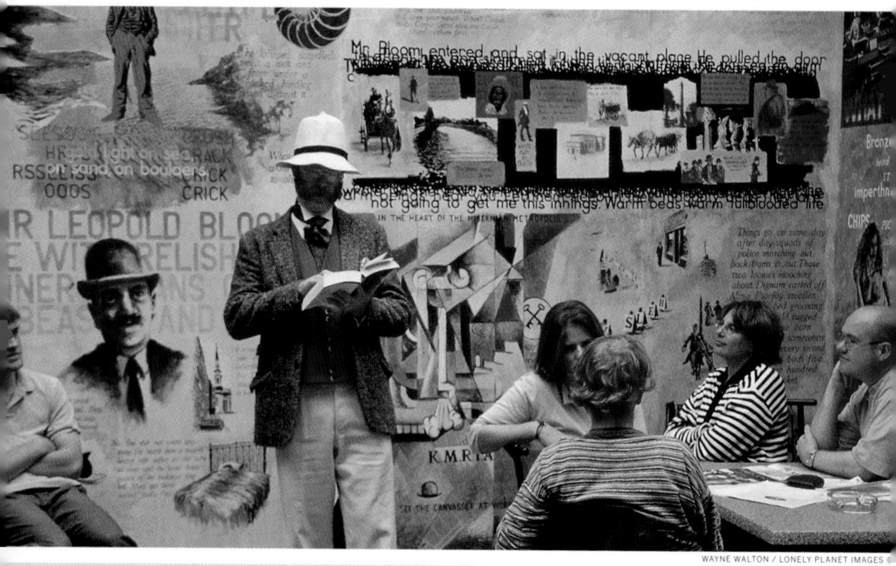

Of all their national traits, characteristics and cultural expressions, it's perhaps the way the Irish speak and write that best distinguishes them. Their love of language and their great oral tradition have contributed to Ireland's legacy of world-renowned writers and storytellers. All this in a language imposed on them by a foreign invader; the Irish responded to this act of cultural piracy by mastering a magnificent hybrid– an English that has been flavoured and enriched by the rhythms, pronunciation patterns and grammatical peculiarities of Irish.

The Mythic Cycle

Before there was anything like modern literature, there was the Ulaid (Ulster) Cycle – Ireland's version of the Homeric epic – written down from oral tradition between the 8th and 12th centuries. The chief story is the Táin Bó Cúailnge (Cattle Raid of Cooley), about a battle between Queen Maeve of Connaught and Cúchulainn, the principal hero of Irish mythology. Cúchulainn appears in the work of Irish writers right up to the present day, from Samuel Beckett to Frank McCourt.

Modern Literature

From the mythic cycle, zip forward 1000 years, past the genius of Jonathan Swift (1667–1745) and his *Gulliver's Travels;* stopping to acknowledge acclaimed dramatist Oscar Wilde (1854–1900); *Dracula* creator Bram Stoker (1847–1912) – some have optimistically claimed that the name of the count may have come from the Irish *droch fhola* (bad blood); and the literary giant that was James Joyce (1882–1941), whose name and books elicit enormous pride in Ireland (although we've yet to meet five people who have read all of *Ulysses*!).

The majority of Joyce's literary output came when he had left Ireland for the artistic hotbed that was Paris, which was also true for another great experimenter of language and style, Samuel Beckett (1906-89). Influenced by the Italian poet Dante and French philosopher Descartes, Joyce's work centres on fundamental existential questions about the human condition and the nature of self. He is probably best known for his play *Waiting for Godot*, but his unassailable reputation is based on a series of stark novels and plays.

Of the dozens of 20th-century Irish authors to have achieved published renown, some names to look out for include playwright and novelist Brendan Behan (1923-64), who wove tragedy, wit and a turbulent life into his best works, including *Borstal Boy*, *The Quare Fellow* and *The Hostage*. Inevitably, as life imitated art, Behan died young of alcoholism.

Belfast-born CS Lewis (1898–1963) died a year earlier, leaving us *The Chronicles of Narnia*, a series of allegorical children's stories, three of which have been made into films – the third (*The Voyage of the Dawn Treader*) came out in 2010. Other Northern writers have, not surprisingly, featured the Troubles in their work: Bernard McLaverty's *Cal* (also made into a film) and his more recent *The Anatomy School* are both wonderful.

Contemporary Scene

"I love James Joyce. Never read him, but he's a true genius." Yes, the stalwarts are still great, but ask your average Irish person who their favourite home-grown writer is and they'll most likely mention someone *who's still alive*.

They might mention Roddy Doyle (b 1958), whose mega-successful Barrytown quartet – *The Commitments*, *The Snapper*, *The Van* and *Paddy Clarke, Ha Ha Ha* – have all been made into films. Most recently, he's turned to social and political history with a new trilogy, beginning with *A Star Called Henry* (2000), a story of an IRA hit-man called Henry Smart; followed by *Oh, Play That Thing!* (2004) and *The Dead Republic* (2010), both of which follow Henry on his adventures in the United States.

Sebastian Barry (b 1955) started his career as a poet with *The Water Colorist* (1983), became famous as a playwright, but achieved his greatest success as a novelist: he was shortlisted for the Man Booker Prize twice, in 2005 for his WWI drama *A Long Way Down* and in 2008 for the absolutely compelling *The Secret Scripture*,

The Gaelic Revival

While Home Rule was being debated and shunted, something of a revolution was taking place in Irish arts, literature and identity. The poet William Butler Yeats and his coterie of literary friends (including Lady Gregory, Douglas Hyde, John Millington Synge and George Russell) championed the Anglo-Irish literary revival, unearthing old Celtic tales and writing with fresh enthusiasm about a romantic Ireland of epic battles and warrior queens. For a country that had suffered centuries of invasion and deprivation, these images presented a much more attractive version of history.

about a 100-year-old inmate of a mental hospital who decides to write an autobiography. It was the Costa Book of the Year in 2008 and won the prestigious James Tait Black Memorial Prize in 2009.

Anne Enright (b 1962) did nab the Man Booker for *The Gathering* (2007), a zeitgeist tale of alcoholism and abuse; her latest novel is *The Forgotten Waltz* (2011). John Banville (b 1945) also won the Booker for *The Sea* (2009); we recommend either *The Book of Evidence* (1989) or the masterful roman á clef *The Untouchable* (1998). Banville's precise and often cold prose divides critics, who consider him either the English language's greatest living stylist or an unreadable intellectual; if you're of the latter inclination then you should check out his highly readable crime novels, written under the pseudonym of Benjamin Black: his most recent is *Elegy for April* (2010).

Another big hitter is Wexford-born but Dublin-based Colm Tóibin (b 1955), who spent four years looking for a publisher for his first novel *The South* (1990), but has gone on to become a hugely successful novelist and scholar – *The Master* (2004) and *Brooklyn* (2009) were both very well received; his latest novel, *The Empty Family* (2011) is a collection of short stories. Of the host of younger writers making names for themselves,

The Best... Contemporary Fiction

1 *The Empty Family* (Colm Tóibín)

2 *Ghost Light* (Joseph O'Connor)

3 *The Forgotten Waltz* (Anne Enright)

4 *Room* (Emma Donoghue)

5 *John The Revelator* (Peter Byrne)

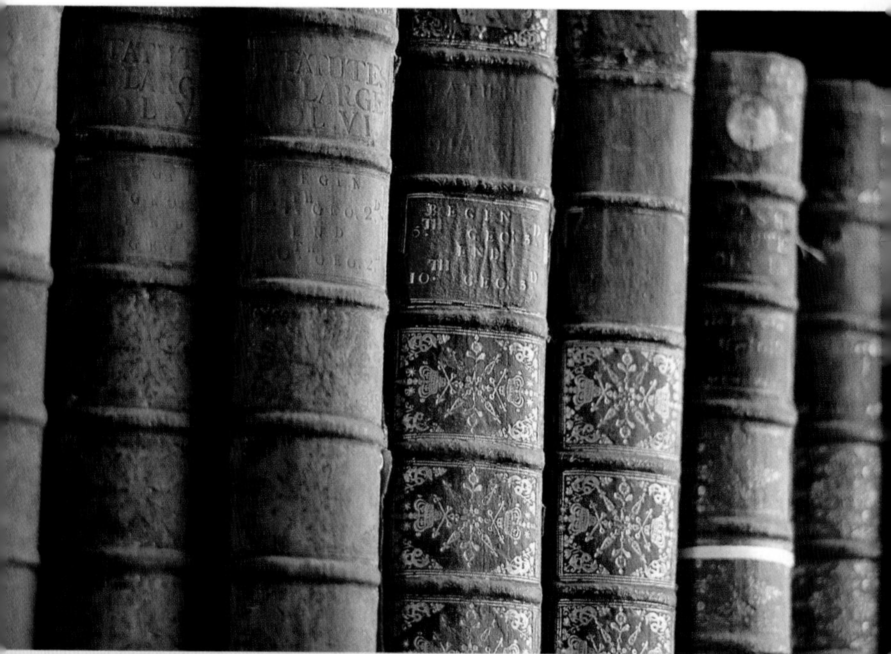

Antique books in Marsh's Library (p80), Dublin

we recommend the work of Claire Kilroy (b 1973), whose three novels – *All Summer* (2003), *Tenderwire* (2006) and *All the Names Have Been Changed* (2009) – have established her as a genuine talent.

Like some of their famous antecedents, some Irish novelists have gone abroad to write and find success. Joseph O'Neill (b 1964) won the PEN/Faulkner Award for fiction for his post-9/11 novel *Netherland* (2009), while Colum McCann (b 1965), who also tackled 9/11 but in a far more allegorical fashion, picked up the National Book Award for *Let the Great World Spin* (2009).

Chick Lit

Authors hate the label and publishers profess to disregard it, but chick lit is big business and few have mastered it as well as the Irish. Doyenne of them all is Maeve Binchy (b 1940) whose mastery of the style has seen her outsell most of the literary greats – her latest in a long line of bestsellers is *Heart And Soul* (2008). Hot on her heels is Marion Keyes (b 1963), author of 11 bestsellers that tackle themes like alcoholism and mental health, issues that Keyes has battled with herself. Her latest book is *The Brightest Star in the Sky* (2009). Former agony aunt Cathy Kelly (b 1966) has written 13 novels, each more successful than the last – in 2010 she published two, *The Perfect Holiday* and *Homecoming*.

Traditional Music

Traditional music at a Dublin pub

DOUG McKINLAY / LONELY PLANET IMAGES ©

Irish music (known as traditional music, or just trad) has maintained a vibrancy not found in other traditional European forms, which have lost out to the overbearing influence of pop music. While Irish music has retained many of its traditional aspects, it has also influenced many forms of music, most notably US country and western – a fusion of Mississippi Delta blues and Irish traditional tunes, combined with other influences like Gospel, is at the root of rock & roll.

Trad music's current success is also due to the willingness of its exponents to update the way it's played (in ensembles rather than the customary *céilidh* – communal dance – bands), the habit of pub sessions (introduced by returning migrants) and the economic good times that encouraged the Irish to celebrate their culture rather than trying to replicate international trends. And then, of course, there's *Riverdance*, which made Irish dancing sexy and became a worldwide phenomenon, despite the fact that most aficionados of traditional music are seriously underwhelmed by its musical worth.

Instruments

Despite popular perception, the harp isn't widely used in traditional music; the *bodhrán* (*bow*-rawn) goat-skin drum is much more prevalent. The uillean pipes, played by squeezing bellows under the elbow, provide another distinctive sound although you're not likely to see them in a pub. The fiddle isn't unique to Ireland but it is one of the main instruments in the country's indigenous music, along with the flute, tin whistle, accordion and bouzouki (a version of the mandolin). Music fits into five main categories (jigs, reels, hornpipes, polkas and slow airs), while the old style of singing unaccompanied versions of traditional ballads and airs is called *sean-nós*.

The Best... Traditional Albums

1 *The Quiet Glen* (Tommy Peoples)

2 *Paddy Keenan* (Paddy Keenan)

3 *Compendium: The Best of Patrick Street* (Various)

4 *The Chieftains 6: Bonaparte's Retreat* (The Chieftains)

5 *Old Hag You Have Killed Me* (The Bothy Band)

Tunes

Traditionally, music was performed as a background to dancing, and while this has been true ever since Celtic times, the many thousands of tunes that fill up the repertoire aren't nearly as ancient as that; most aren't much older than a couple of hundred years. Because much of Irish music is handed down orally and aurally, there are myriad variations in the way a single tune is played, depending on the time and place of its playing. The blind itinerant harpist Turlough O'Carolan (1680-1738), for example, wrote more than 200 tunes – it's difficult to know how many versions their repeated learning has spawned.

Popular Bands

More folksy than traditional, the Dubliners, fronted by the distinctive gravel voice and grey beard of Ronnie Drew (1934-2008), made a career out of bawdy drinking songs that got *everybody* singing along. Other popular bands include the Fureys, comprising four brothers originally from the travelling community (no, not like the Wilburies) along with guitarist Davey Arthur. And if it's rousing renditions of Irish rebel songs you're after, you can't go past the Wolfe Tones.

Since the 1970s, various bands have tried to blend traditional with more progressive genres, with mixed success. The first band to pull it off was Moving Hearts, led by Christy Moore, who went on to become the greatest Irish folk musician ever.

Family Travel

Park by the River Corrib, Galway (p230)

WAYNE WALTON / LONELY PLANET IMAGES

Ireland is generally a pretty good place to bring kids. The Irish love them – it's not so long ago since the average Irish family numbered four, five, six or more children – and they have a pretty easygoing approach to the noise and mayhem that they often bring in their wake. The quality and availability of services for children vary, however, and can be completely lacking outside of bigger towns and cities.

Restaurants & Hotels

On the whole you'll find that restaurants and hotels will go out of their way to cater for you and your children. Hotels will provide cots at no extra charge and most restaurants have highchairs. Bear in mind that under-16s are banned from pubs after 7pm – even if they're accompanied by their parents.

Transport

Under-fives travel free on all public transport and most admission prices have an under-16s reduced fee. It's always a good idea to talk to fellow travellers with (happy) children and locals on the road for tips on where to go.

Car seats (around €50/£25 per week) are mandatory for children in hire cars between the ages of nine months and four years. Bring your own seat for infants under about nine months as only larger, forward-facing child seats are generally available. Remember not to place baby seats in the front if the car has an airbag.

Feeding & Changing

Although breast-feeding is not a common sight (Ireland has one of the lowest rates of it in the world), you can do so with impunity pretty much everywhere without getting so much as a stare. Diaper-changing facilities are generally only found in the newer, larger shopping centres – otherwise you'll have to make do with a public toilet.

Parks & Gardens

As far as parks, gardens and green spaces, Ireland has an abundance of them, but very few amenities such as designated playgrounds and other exclusively child-friendly spots. In Dublin, St Stephen's Green has a popular playground in the middle of it, but it is the exception rather than the rule.

For further general information see Lonely Planet's *Travel with Children*. Also check out www.eumom.ie for pregnant women and parents with young children; and www.babygoes2.com, a travel site about family-friendly accommodation worldwide.

The Best... Distractions for the Kids

1 National Museum of Ireland – Natural History (p73)

2 Ulster Museum (p310)

3 Killary Adventure Centre (p242)

4 Aillwee Caves |(p256)

5 Fin McCool Surf School (p279)

Need to Know

- **Car Seats** Mandatory in hire cars for children aged nine months to four years (around €50/£25 per week)
- **Changing Facilities** Practically non-existent, even in big cities
- **Cots** Usually available at all accommodations but the most basic B&Bs
- **Health** As you would do at home
- **Highchairs** Ask and most restaurants will usually provide
- **Nappies** Sold in every supermarket and convenience store
- **Pubs** Children are not allowed in after 7pm
- **Transport** Look out for family passes and kids' discounts on trains and buses

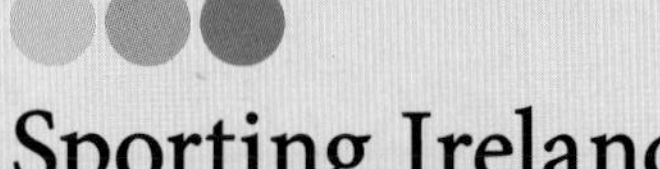

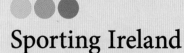

Sporting Ireland

Cork women's hurling team

WADE EAKLE / LONELY PLANET IMAGES ©

Sport has a special place in the Irish psyche, probably because it's one of the few occasions when an overwhelming expression of emotion won't cause those around you to wince in discomfort. The Irish treat their sport – both watched and played – like a religion. For some, it's all about faith through good works, like jogging, amateur football and yoga; for most everyone else, observance is enough, especially from the living room armchair or the pub stool.

Gaelic Football & Hurling

Gaelic games are at the core of 'Irishness'; they are enmeshed in the fabric of Irish life and hold a unique place in the heart of its culture. Their resurgence towards the end of the 19th century was entwined with the whole Gaelic revival and the march towards Irish independence. The beating heart of Gaelic sports is the Gaelic Athletic Association (GAA), set up in 1884 'for the preservation and cultivation of National pastimes'. The GAA is still responsible for fostering these amateur games and it warms our hearts to see that after all this time – and amid the onslaught of globalisation and the general commercialisation of sport – they are still far and away the most popular sports in Ireland.

Gaelic games are fast, furious and not for the faint-hearted. Challenges are fierce, and contact between players is extremely aggressive. Both sports are county-based games. The dream of every club player is to represent his county, with the hope of perhaps playing in an All-Ireland final in September at Croke Park in Dublin, the climax of a knockout championship that is played first at a provincial and then interprovincial level.

Football (Soccer)

There is huge support in Ireland for the 'world game', although fans are much more enthusiastic about the likes of Manchester United, Liverpool and the two Glasgow clubs (Rangers and Celtic) than the struggling pros and part-timers who make up the **National League** (www.fai.ie) in the Republic and the **Irish League** (www.irishfa.com) in Northern Ireland. It's just too difficult for domestic teams to compete with the multimillionaire glitz and glamour of the English Premiership, which has always drawn the cream of Irish talent.

At an international level, the Republic and Northern Ireland field separate teams; in 2011 both were performing adequately but with limited success, a far cry from their relative moments of glory – the 1980s for Northern Ireland and 1988 to 2002 for the Republic.

To distinguish it from Gaelic Football, you'll often hear it referred to as 'soccer,' especially in Gaelic strongholds that by doing so imply scorn on so-called 'garrison sports,' which will allay American confusion but only irritate the Brits. But Irish fans of Association Football (the official name of the sport) will always call it football and the other Gaelic Football or, in Dublin, gah – which is just a pronunciation of the letters GAA.

Rugby

Although traditionally the preserve of Ireland's middle classes, rugby captures the mood of the whole island in February and March during the annual Six Nations Championships, because the Irish team is drawn from both sides of the border and is supported by both Nationalists and Unionists. In recognition of this, the Irish national anthem is no longer played at internationals, replaced by the slightly dodgy but thoroughly inoffensive *Ireland's Call,* a song written especially for the purpose – although

Rules of the Games

Both football and hurling are played by two teams of 15 players whose aim is to get the ball through what resembles a rugby goal: two long vertical posts joined by a horizontal bar, below which is a soccer-style goal, protected by a goalkeeper. Goals (below the crossbar) are worth three points, whereas a ball placed over the bar between the posts is worth one point. Scores are shown thus: 1-12, meaning one goal and 12 points, giving a total of 15 points.

Gaelic football is played with a round, soccer-size ball, and players are allowed to kick it or hand-pass it, like Aussie Rules. Hurling, which is considered by far the more beautiful game, is played with a flat stick or bat known as a hurley or *camán*. The small leather ball, called a *slíothar,* is hit or carried on the hurley; handpassing is also allowed. Both games are played over 70 action-filled minutes.

nobody seemed to mind it in 2009 when Ireland won its first Grand Slam (a clean sweep of victories in one campaign) since 1948.

Rugby is arguably more exciting at a provincial level, where Leinster and Munster have an ongoing rivalry (both have won the Heineken Cup, Europe's premier competition, twice; Leinster most recently in 2009 and 2011) and Ulster are just a step behind them. Rugby isn't big in the west, so Connaught aren't very good.

Horse Racing & Greyhound Racing

A passion for horse racing is deeply entrenched in Irish life and comes without the snobbery of its English counterpart. If you fancy a flutter on the gee-gees, you can watch racing from around Ireland and England on the TV in bookmakers shops every day. No money ever seems to change hands in the betting, however, and every Irish punter will tell you they 'broke even'.

Ireland has a reputation for producing world-class horses for racing and other equestrian events like show jumping, also very popular, albeit in a much less egalitarian kind of way. Major annual races include the Irish Grand National (Fairyhouse, April), Irish Derby (the Curragh, June) and Irish Leger (the Curragh, September). For more information on events, contact **Horse Racing Ireland** (www.hri.ie).

Traditionally the poor-man's punt, greyhound racing ('the dogs'), has been smartened up in recent years and partly turned into a corporate outing. It offers a cheaper, more accessible and more local alternative to horse racing. There are 20 tracks across the country, administered by the **Irish Greyhound Board** (www.igb.ie).

The Best... Current Sporting Heroes

1 Rory McIlroy (Golf)

2 Brian O'Driscoll (Rugby)

3 Henry Shefflin (Hurling)

4 Colm 'Gooch' Cooper (Gaelic Football)

5 Aiden O'Brien (Horse Racing)

Road Bowling

The object of this sport is to throw an 800g cast-iron ball along a public road (normally one with little traffic) for a designated distance, usually 1km or 2km. The person who does it in the least number of throws is the winner. The main centre is Cork, which has 200 clubs, and, to a lesser extent, Armagh. Competitions take place throughout the year, attracting considerable crowds. The sport has been taken up in various countries around the world, including the USA, Germany and the Netherlands and a world championship competition has been set up (see www.irishroadbowling.ie).

Survival Guide

Signs along the road to the Ring of Kerry (p204)

Directory

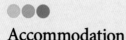

Price Ranges

Throughout this book, reviews of places to stay use the following price ranges, all based on double room with private bathroom in high season.

BUDGET	REPUBLIC	NORTHERN IRELAND
Budget (€/£)	<€60	<£40
Midrange (€€/££)	€60-150	£40-100
Top end (€€€/£££)	>€150	>£100

Accommodation

B&BS & GUESTHOUSES

Bed and breakfasts are small, family-run houses, farmhouses and period country houses with fewer than five bedrooms. Standards vary enormously, but most have some bedrooms with private bathroom at a cost of roughly €35 to €40 (£20 to £25) per person per night. In luxurious B&Bs, expect to pay €55 (£38) or more per person.

Guesthouses are like upmarket B&Bs but bigger – the Irish equivalent of a boutique hotel. Facilities are usually better and sometimes include a restaurant.

Other tips:

- Facilities in B&Bs range from basic (bed, bathroom, kettle) to beatific (whirlpool baths, LCD TVs, wi-fi) as you go up in price.
- Most B&Bs take credit cards but the occasional rural one might not have facilities; check when you book.
- Advance reservations are strongly recommended, especially in peak season (June to September).
- If full, B&B owners may recommend another house in the area (possibly a private house taking occasional guests, not in tourist listings).

HOTELS

Hotels range from the local pub to medieval castles. In most cases, you'll get a better rate than the one published if you go online or negotiate directly with the hotel, especially out of season. The explosion of bland midrange chain hotels (many Irish-owned) has proved a major challenge to the traditional B&B or guesthouse: they might not have the same personalised service but their rooms are clean and their facilities generally quite good.

HOUSE SWAPPING

House swapping has become a popular and affordable way to visit a country and enjoy a real home away from home. There are several agencies in Ireland that, for an annual fee, facilitate international swaps. The fee pays for access to a website and a book giving house descriptions, photographs and the owner's details. After that, it's up to you to make arrangements. Use of the family car is sometimes included.

A 'Standard' Hotel Rate?

There is no such thing. Prices vary according to demand – or have different rates for online, phone or walk-in bookings. B&B rates are more consistent, but virtually every other accommodation will charge wildly different rates depending on the time of year, day, festival schedule and even your ability to do a little negotiating.

Homelink International House Exchange (www.homelink.ie)

Intervac International Holiday Service (www.intervac-homeexchange.com)

RENTAL ACCOMMODATION

Self-catering accommodation is often rented on a weekly basis and usually means an apartment or house where you look after yourself. The rates vary from one region and season to another. Fáilte Ireland publishes a guide for registered self-catering accommodation; you can check listings at their website www.discoverireland.ie.

Activities

Activities open up Ireland in a way that can be both cheap and relaxing, and offer a unique experience of the country.

BIRDWATCHING

The variety and size of the flocks that visit or breed in Ireland make it of particular interest to birdwatchers. It's also home to some rare and endangered species.

There are more than 70 reserves and sanctuaries in Ireland, but some aren't open to visitors and others are privately owned, so you'll need permission from the proprietors before entering.

Some useful publications on birdwatching are Dominic Couzens' *Collins Birds of Britain and Ireland* and the slightly out-of-date *Where to Watch Birds in Ireland* by Clive Hutchinson.

More information on birdwatching can be obtained from the tourist boards and from the following organisations:

Birds of Ireland News Service (☎ 01-830 7364; www.birdsireland.com)

BirdWatch Ireland (☎ 01-281 9878; www.birdwatchireland.ie) Runs birdwatching field courses, all of which take place on Cape Clear Island in County Cork.

National Parks & Wildlife Service (☎ 01-888 2000; www.npws.ie)

Royal Society for the Protection of Birds (RSPB; ☎ 9049 1547; www.rspb.org.uk; Belvoir Park Forest, Belfast)

CYCLING

Cyclists, alas, will have to share the road with the motorised bully, but they can find solace in the scenic routes that wend their way through sparsely populated countryside or along rugged coasts. The tourist boards can supply you with a list of operators who organise cycling holidays. For more on the practicalities of travelling around Ireland with a bike, see p380.

For organised cycling tours, you can try:

Go Ireland (☎ 066-976 2094; www.goactivities.com;

Book Accommodation Online

For more accommodation reviews and recommendations by Lonely Planet authors, check out the online booking service at www.lonelyplanet.com. You'll find the true, insider lowdown on the best places to stay on the island. Reviews are thorough and independent. Best of all, you can book online.

Other online resources include:

- **www.daft.ie** Online classified paper for short- and long-term rentals.
- **www.elegant.ie** Specialises in self-catering castles, period houses and unique properties.
- **www.familyhomes.ie** Lists (you guessed it) family-run guesthouses and self-catering properties.
- **www.gulliver.ie** Fáilte Ireland and the Northern Ireland Tourist Board's web-based accommodation reservation system.
- **www.irishlandmark.com** Not-for-profit conservation group that rents self-catering properties of historical and cultural significance, such as castles, gate lodges and lighthouses.
- **www.stayinireland.com** Lists guesthouses and self-catering options.

Something Different

An alternative to normal caravanning is to hire a horse-drawn caravan with which to wander the countryside. In high season you can hire one for around €800 a week. Search Fáilte Ireland's www.discoverireland.ie for a list of operators, or see www.irishhorsedrawncaravans.com.

Another unhurried and pleasurable way to see the countryside (with slightly less maintenance) is by barge on one of the country's canal systems. As above, contact Fáilte Ireland for a list of rental companies.

Another option is to hire a boat, which you can live aboard while cruising Ireland's inland waterways. One company offering boats for hire on the Shannon-Erne Waterway is **Emerald Star** (☎ 071-962 0234; www.emeraldstar.ie).

Old Orchard House, Killorglin, Co Kerry)

Irish Cycling Safaris (☎ 01-260 0749; www.cyclingsafaris.com; Belfield Bike Shop, UCD, Dublin)

FISHING

Ireland is justly famous for its generally no-fee coarse fishing, covering bream, pike, perch, roach, rudd, tench, carp and eel. Killing of pike over 6.6lb (3kg) in weight is prohibited, so anglers are limited to one pike; killing of coarse fish is frowned upon and anglers are encouraged to return coarse fish alive. Freshwater game fish include salmon, sea trout and brown trout. Some managed fisheries also stock rainbow trout.

Licences in the Republic are available from the local tackle shop or direct from the **Central Fisheries Board** (☎ 01-884 2600; www.fishinginireland.info).

In the North, rod licences for coarse and game fishing are obtainable from the **Foyle, Carlingford & Irish Lights Commission** (☎ 7134 2100; www.loughs-agency.org) for the Foyle and Carlingford areas, and from the **Fisheries Conservancy Board** (☎ 3833 4666; www.fcbni.com) for all other regions. You also require a permit from the owner, which is usually the **Department of Culture, Arts & Leisure, Inland Waterways & Inland Fisheries Branch** (☎ 9025 8825; www.dcalni.gov.uk).

GOLF

There are over 300 golf courses and links in Ireland. Despite the spread of new, American-style parkland courses over the last decade, golf in Ireland is best played on a links course, which can be found along the entirety of its coastline. Contact Fáilte Ireland, the NITB, the **Golfing Union of Ireland** (☎ 01-505 4000; www.gui.ie), or the **Irish Ladies Golf Union** (☎ 01-293 4833; www.ilgu.ie) for information on golfing holidays.

Green fees for 18 holes start from around €25 (£15) on weekdays, but top-notch places charge up to €200 (£150). Courses are tested for their level of difficulty; many are playable year round, especially links.

HORSE RIDING

Unsurprisingly, considering the Irish passion for horses, riding is a popular pastime. There are dozens of centres throughout Ireland, offering possibilities ranging from hiring a horse for an hour (from €25/£15) to fully packaged, residential equestrian holidays.

Recommended outfits are Canadian-based **Hidden Trails** (www.hiddentrails.com) and **Ballycumisk Riding School** (☎ 028-37246, 087 961 6969; Ballycumisk, Schull, Co Cork)

WALKING

There are many superb walks in Ireland, including 31 'waymarked ways' or designated long-distance paths of varying lengths. Individual chapters have details of recommended walks.

The maintenance and development of the ways is administered in the Republic by the **National Trails Office** (☎ 01-860 8800; www.walkireland.ie) and in the North by **Countryside Access & Activities Network** (CAAN; ☎ 9030 3930; www.countrysiderecreation.com).

Some useful guides are Lonely Planet's *Walking in Ireland*, Michael Fewer's *Irish Long-Distance Walks* or *Best Irish Walks* by Joss Lynam.

For mountain rescue call ☎999.

Maps

EastWest Mapping (☎053-937 7835; www.eastwestmapping.ie) has good maps of long-distance walks in the Republic and the North. Tim Robinson of **Folding Landscapes** (☎095-35886; www.foldinglandscapes.com) produces superbly detailed maps of the Burren, the Aran Islands and Connemara. His and Joss Lynam's *Mountains of Connemara: A Hill Walker's Guide* contains a useful detailed map.

Organised Walks

If you don't have a travelling companion you could consider joining an organised walking group:

Go Ireland (☎066-976 2094; www.goactivities.com; Old Orchard House, Killorglin, Co Kerry) Offers walking tours of the west.

South West Walks Ireland (☎066-712 8733; www.southwestwalksireland.com; 6 Church St, Tralee, Co Kerry) Provides a series of guided and self-guided walking programs around the southwest, northwest and Wicklow.

ROCK CLIMBING

Ireland's mountain ranges aren't high – Mt Carrantuohil in Kerry's Macgillycuddy's Reeks is the tallest mountain in Ireland at only 1039m – but they're often beautiful and offer some excellent climbing possibilities. The highest mountains are in the southwest.

Adventure centres around the country run courses and organise climbing trips. For further information contact the **Mountaineering Council of Ireland** (☎01-625 1115; www.mountaineering.ie), which also publishes climbing guides and the quarterly magazine *Irish Mountain Log*, or check the forums on **Irish Climbing Online** (www.climbing.ie).

WATER SPORTS

Scuba Diving

With little sewage from cities to obscure the waters, Ireland's west coast has some of the best scuba diving in Europe. The offshore islands and rocks host especially rich underwater life. The best period for diving is roughly March to October. Visibility averages more than 12m, but can increase to 30m on good days.

For more details about scuba diving in Ireland, contact Comhairle Fó-Thuinn (CFT), also known as the **Irish Underwater Council** (☎01-284 4601; www.cft.ie); Ireland's diving regulatory body, it publishes the dive magazine *SubSea* (also available online).

Swimming & Surfing

Ireland has some magnificent coastline and some great sandy beaches: the cleaner, safer ones have EU Blue Flag awards. Get a list from the government agency **An Taisce** (National Trust for Ireland; ☎01-454 1786; www.antaisce.org) or check online with the **Blue Flag Programme** (www.blueflag.org).

Surfers should visit www.surfingireland.net or www.victorkilo.com for beach reports and forecasts.

Donegal Adventure Centre (☎074-984 2418; www.donegal-holidays.com; Bay View Ave, Bundoran, Co Donegal) is an excellent youth-oriented surf school and **Bundoran Surf Co** (☎984 1968; www.bundoransurfco.com; Bundoran, Co Donegal) conduct surf lessons, kite-surfing and power-kiting.

The best months for surfing in Ireland – when the swells are highest – are September (when the water is warmest because of the Gulf Stream) and October.

Business Hours

Hours in both the Republic and Northern Ireland are roughly the same. Throughout this book we don't list opening and closing hours unless they differ significantly from those listed here:

Banks 10am to 4pm Monday to Friday (to 5pm Thursday)

Offices 9am to 5pm Monday to Friday

Post offices Northern Ireland 9am to 5.30pm Monday to Friday, 9am to 12.30pm Saturday; Republic 9am to 6pm Monday to Friday, 9am to 1pm Saturday. Smaller post offices may close at lunch and one day per week.

Pubs Northern Ireland 11.30am to 11pm Monday to Saturday, 12.30pm to 10pm Sunday. Pubs with late licences open until 1am Monday to Saturday, and midnight Sunday; Republic 10.30am to 11.30pm Monday to Thursday, 10.30am to 12.30am Friday and Saturday, noon to 11pm Sunday (30 minutes 'drinking up' time allowed). Pubs with bar extensions open to 2.30am Thursday to Saturday. All pubs close Christmas Day and Good Friday.

Restaurants Noon to 10.30pm; many close one day of the week.

Shops 9am to 5.30pm or 6pm Monday to Saturday (until 8pm on Thursday & sometimes Friday), noon to 6pm Sunday (in bigger towns only). Shops in rural towns may close at lunch and one day per week.

Tourist offices 9am to 5pm Monday to Friday, 9am to 1pm Saturday. Many extend their hours in summer, and open fewer hours/days or close from October to April.

Customs

Both the Republic of Ireland and Northern Ireland have a two-tier customs system: one for goods bought duty-free outside the European Union (EU); the other for goods bought in another EU country where tax and duty is paid. There is technically no limit to the amount of goods transportable within the EU, but customs will use certain guidelines to distinguish personal use from commercial purpose. Allowances are as follows:

Duty free For duty-free goods from outside the EU, limits include 200 cigarettes, 1L of spirits or 2L of wine, 60ml of perfume and 250ml of eau de toilette.

Tax and duty paid Amounts that officially constitute personal use include 3200 cigarettes (or 400 cigarillos, 200 cigars or 3kg of tobacco) and either 10L of spirits, 20L of fortified wine, 60L of sparkling wine, 90L of still wine or 110L of beer.

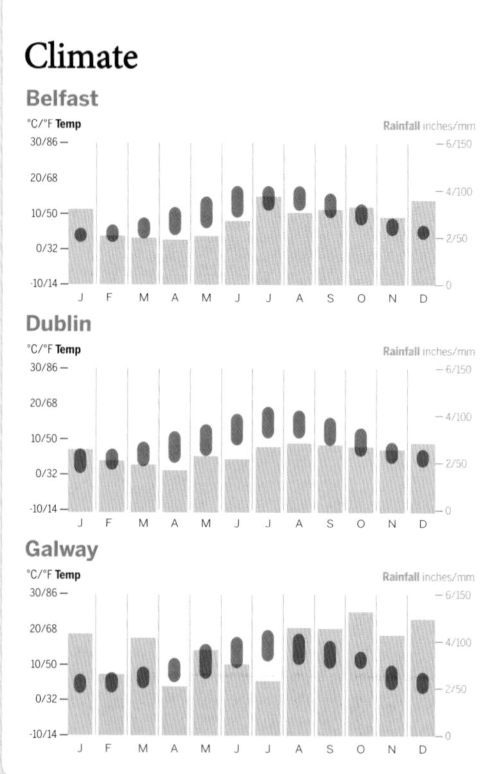

CATS & DOGS

Cats and dogs from anywhere outside Ireland and the UK are subject to strict quarantine laws. The EU Pet Travel Scheme, whereby animals are fitted with a microchip, vaccinated against rabies and blood-tested six months *prior* to entry, is in force in the UK and the Republic of Ireland. No preparation or documentation is necessary for the movement of pets directly between the UK and the Republic. Contact the **Department of Agriculture, Food & Rural Development** (☎ 01-607 2000; www.agriculture.gov.ie) in Dublin for further details.

Electricity

120V/60Hz

Gay & Lesbian Travellers

Ireland is a pretty tolerant place for gays and lesbians. Bigger cities like Dublin, Galway and Cork have well-established gay scenes, as do Belfast and Derry in Northern Ireland. That said, you'll still find pockets of homophobia throughout the island, particularly in smaller towns and rural areas. Resources include the following:

Gaire (www.gaire.com) Message board and info for a host of gay-related issues.

Gay & Lesbian Youth Northern Ireland (www.glyni.org.uk)

Gay Men's Health Project (☎ 01-660 2189; www.hse.ie) Practical advice on men's health issues.

National Lesbian & Gay Federation (NLGF; ☎ 01-671 9076; www.nlgf.ie) Publishes the monthly *Gay Community News* (www.gcn.ie).

Northern Ireland Gay Rights Association (Nigra; ☎ 9066 5257)

Outhouse (☎ 01-873 4932; www.outhouse.ie; 105 Capel St, Dublin) A gay, lesbian and transgender community centre.

Health

No jabs are required to travel to Ireland. Excellent health care is readily available. For minor, self-limiting illnesses, pharmacists can give valuable advice and sell over-the-counter medication. They can also advise when more specialised help is required and point you in the right direction.

EU citizens equipped with a European Health Insurance Card (EHIC), available from health centres or, in the UK, post offices, will be covered for most medical care – but not non-emergencies or emergency repatriation. While other countries, such as Australia, also have reciprocal agreements with Ireland and Britain, many do not.

In Northern Ireland, everyone receives free emergency treatment at accident and emergency (A&E) departments of state-run NHS hospitals, irrespective of nationality.

Insurance

Insurance is important: it covers you for everything from medical expenses and luggage loss to cancellations or delays in your travel arrangements, depending on your policy.

While EU citizens have most medical care covered with a EHIC card, an additional insurance policy for all other issues is recommended.

Worldwide travel insurance is available at www.lonelyplanet.com/travel_services. You can buy, extend and claim online at any time – even if you're already on the road.

All cars on public roads must be insured. If you are bringing your own vehicle check that your insurance will cover you in Ireland.

Internet Access

With the advent of 3G and wi-fi networks, internet cafes are increasingly disappearing from Irish towns. The ones that are left generally charge up to €6/£5 per hour.

If you'll be using your laptop or mobile device to get online, most hotels, an increasing number of B&Bs, hostels, bars and restaurants offer wi-fi access, charging anything from nothing to €5/£5 per hour.

Otherwise, most hotels and hostels in larger towns and cities have internet access via a desktop for customer use.

Legal Matters

Illegal drugs are widely available, especially in clubs. The possession of small quantities of marijuana attracts a fine or warning, but harder drugs are treated more seriously. Public drunkenness is illegal but commonplace – the police will usually ignore it unless you're causing trouble.

Contact the following for assistance:

Legal Aid Board (☎ 066-947 1000; www.legalaidboard.ie) Has a network of local law centres.

Northern Ireland Legal Services Commission (www.nilsc.org.uk)

Money

The currency in the Republic of Ireland is the euro (€); Northern Ireland uses the pound sterling (£). Although notes issued by Northern Irish banks are legal tender throughout the UK, many businesses outside of Northern Ireland refuse to accept them and you'll have to swap them in British banks.

ATMS

Usually called 'cash machines', ATMs are easy to find in cities and all but the smallest of towns. Watch out for ATMs that have been tampered with; card-reader scams ('skimming') have become a real problem.

CREDIT & DEBIT CARDS

Visa and MasterCard credit and debit cards are widely accepted in Ireland. Smaller businesses, like pubs or some B&Bs, prefer debit cards (and will charge a fee for credit cards). Nearly all credit and debit cards use the chip-and-PIN system: if your card isn't PIN enabled you should be able to sign in the usual way, but an increasing number of places will not accept your card.

TAXES & REFUNDS

Non-EU residents can claim Value Added Tax (VAT – a sales tax, 21% of the purchase price of luxury goods except for books, children's clothing or educational items) back on their purchases so long as the store operates either the Cashback or Taxback refund programme (they should display a sticker). You'll get a voucher with your purchase that must be stamped at the *last point of exit* from the EU. If you're travelling on to Britain or mainland Europe from Ireland, hold on to your voucher until you pass through your final customs stop in the EU; it can then be stamped and you can post it back for a refund of duty paid.

VAT in Northern Ireland is 20%; shops participating in the Tax-Free Shopping refund scheme will give you a form or invoice on request to be presented to customs when you leave. After customs have certified the form, it will be returned to the shop for a refund and the cheque sent to you at home.

TIPPING

You're not obliged to tip if the service or food was unsatisfactory (even if it's been automatically added to your bill as a 'service charge').

Hotels Only for bellhops who carry luggage, then €1/£1 per bag

Pubs Not expected unless table service is provided, then €1/£1 for a round of drinks

Restaurants 10% for decent service, up to 15% in more expensive places

Taxis 10% or rounded up to the nearest euro/pound

Toilet attendants €0.50/50p

TRAVELLERS CHEQUES

Safer than cash but hardly ever used: travellers cheques have become increasingly rare as credit/debit cards have become the method of choice. They are rarely accepted for purchases so for cash you'll still have to go to a bank or a change bureau.

Public Holidays

Public holidays can cause road chaos as everyone tries to get somewhere else for the break. It's wise to book accommodation in advance around these times.

Public holidays in both the Republic and Northern Ireland:

New Year's Day 1 January

St Patrick's Day 17 March

Easter (Good Friday to Easter Monday inclusive) March/April

May Holiday 1st Monday in May

Christmas Day 25 December

St Stephen's Day (Boxing Day) 26 December

St Patrick's Day and St Stephen's Day holidays are taken on the following Monday when they fall on a weekend. In the Republic, nearly everywhere closes on Good Friday even though it isn't an official public holiday. In the North, most shops open on Good Friday but close the following Tuesday.

NORTHERN IRELAND

Spring Bank Holiday Last Monday in May

Orangeman's Day 12 July

August Holiday Last Monday in August

REPUBLIC

June Holiday 1st Monday in June

August Holiday 1st Monday in August

October Holiday Last Monday in October

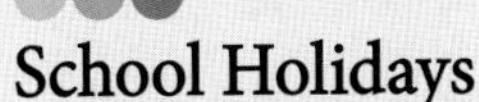

School Holidays

In the Republic, exact dates vary but are roughly:

Easter Holiday Week before and week after Easter

Summer Holiday July and August for primary schools, also June for secondary schools

Christmas Holiday Week before Christmas to week after New Year

There are also two midterm breaks, usually in October and February. For specific dates, check out www.citizensinformation.ie.

In the North, holidays for primary and secondary schools vary. Visit www.deni.gov.uk for more comprehensive information.

Safe Travel

Ireland is safer than most countries in Europe, but normal precautions should be observed.

Northern Ireland is as safe as anywhere else, but there are areas where the sectarian divide is bitterly pronounced, most notably in parts of Belfast. For the foreseeable future, it's probably best to ensure your visit to Northern Ireland doesn't coincide with the climax of the Orange marching season on 12 July; sectarian passions are usually inflamed and even many Northerners leave the province at this time.

Telephone

In this book, area codes and individual numbers are listed together, separated by a hyphen. Area codes in the Republic have three digits and begin with a 0, eg 021 for Cork, 091 for Galway and 061 for Limerick. The only exception is Dublin, which has a two-digit code (01). Always use the area code if calling from a mobile phone, but you don't need it if calling from a fixed-line number within the area code.

In Northern Ireland, the area code for all fixed-line numbers is 028, but you only need to use it if calling from a mobile phone or from outside Northern Ireland. To call Northern Ireland from the Republic, use 048 instead of 028 – without the international dialling code.

Other codes:

- 1550 or 1580 – premium rate
- 1890 or 1850 – lo-call or shared rate
- 0818 – calls at local rate, wherever you're dialling from within the Republic
- 1800 – free calls

Free call and lo-call numbers are not accessible from outside the Republic. Other tips:

- Prices are lower during evenings after 6pm and weekends.

Important Numbers

Include code only when outside area or from a mobile phone. Drop initial 0 when abroad.

Country Code	+353 Republic +44 Northern Ireland
International Access Code	00
Emergency (police, fire, ambulance)	999

- If you can find a public phone that works, local calls in the Republic cost €0.30 for around three minutes (around €0.60 to a mobile), regardless of when you call.
- Pre-paid phonecards can be purchased at both newsagencies and post offices, and work from all payphones for both domestic and international calls.

DIRECTORY ENQUIRIES

For directory enquiries, a number of agencies compete for your business.

- In the Republic, dial 11811 or 11850; for international enquiries it's 11818.
- In the North, call 118118, 118192, 118 500 or 118811.

INTERNATIONAL CALLS

To call out from Ireland dial 00, then the country code (1 for USA, 61 Australia etc), the area code (you usually drop the initial zero) then the number. Ireland's international dialling code is 353.

MOBILE PHONE

- Ireland uses the GSM 900/1800 cellular phone system, which is compatible with European and Australian, but not North American or Japanese, phones.
- SMS ('texting') is a national obsession – most people under 25 communic8 mostly by txt.
- Pay-as-you-go mobile phone packages with any of the main providers start at around €40 and usually include a basic handset and credit of around €10.
- SIM-only packages are also available, but make sure your phone is compatible with the local provider.

Time

In winter, Ireland is on Greenwich Mean Time (GMT), also known as Universal Time Coordinated (UTC), the same as Britain. In summer, the clock shifts to GMT plus one hour, so when it's noon in Dublin and London, it's 4am in Los Angeles and Vancouver, 7am in New York and Toronto, 1pm in Paris, 7pm in Singapore, and 9pm in Sydney.

Tourist Information

In both the Republic and the North there's a tourist office in almost every big town; most can offer a variety of services including accommodation and attraction reservations, currency-changing services, map and guidebook sales and free publications.

In the Republic, the tourism purview falls to **Fáilte Ireland** (Republic 1850 230 330, the UK 0800 039 7000; www.discoverireland.ie). It also has six regional offices:

Cork & Kerry (021-425 5100; Cork Kerry Tourism, Áras Discover, Grand Pde, Cork)

Dublin (01-605 7700; www.visitdublin.com; Dublin Tourism Centre, St Andrew's Church, 2 Suffolk St, Dublin)

East Coast & Midlands (044-934 8761; East Coast & Midlands Tourism, Dublin Rd, Mullingar) For Kildare, Laois, Longford, Louth, Meath, North Offaly, Westmeath and Wicklow.

Ireland North West & Lakelands (071-916 1201; Temple St, Sligo) For Cavan, Donegal, Leitrim, Monaghan and Sligo.

Ireland West (091-537 700; Ireland West Tourism, Áras Fáilte, Forster St, Galway) For Galway, Roscommon and Mayo.

Shannon Region (061-361 555; Shannon Development, Shannon, Clare) For Clare, Limerick, North Tipperary and South Offaly.

South East (051-875 823; South East Tourism, 41 The Quay, Waterford) For Carlow, Kilkenny, South Tipperary, Waterford and Wexford.

In Northern Ireland, it's the **Northern Irish Tourist Board** (NITB; head office 028-9023 1221; www.discovernorthernireland.com). Outside Ireland, Fáilte Ireland and the NITB unite under the banner Tourism Ireland. More information about offices around the world can be found at the international website, www.discoverireland.com.

Travellers with Disabilities

All new buildings have wheelchair access, and many hotels have installed lifts, ramps and other facilities. Others, especially B&Bs, have not adapted as successfully so you'll have far less choice. Fáilte Ireland

and NITB's accommodation guides indicate which places are wheelchair accessible.

In big cities, most buses have low-floor access and priority space on board, but the number of kneeling buses on regional routes is still relatively small.

Trains are accessible with help. In theory, if you call ahead, an employee of Iarnród Éireann (Irish Rail) will arrange to accompany you to the train. Newer trains have audio and visual information systems for visually impaired and hearing-impaired passengers.

The **Citizens' Information Board** (☎ 01-605 9000; www.citizensinformationboard.ie) in the Republic and **Disability Action** (☎ 028-9066 1252; www.disabilityaction.org) in Northern Ireland can give some advice to travellers with disabilities. Travellers to Northern Ireland can also check out the website www.allgohere.com.

Visas

If you're a European Economic Area (EEA) national, you don't need a visa to visit (or work in) either the Republic or Northern Ireland. Citizens of Australia, Canada, New Zealand, South Africa and the US can visit the Republic for up to three months and Northern Ireland for up to six months. They are not allowed to work unless sponsored by an employer.

Full visa requirements for visiting the Republic are available online at www.dfa.ie; for Northern Ireland's visa requirements see www.ukvisas.gov.uk.

Women Travellers

Ireland should pose no problems for women travellers. Finding contraception is not the problem it once was, although anyone on the pill should bring adequate supplies.

Rape Crisis Network Ireland (☎ 1800-77 88 88; www.rcni.ie) In the Republic. Runs a 24-hour helpline.

Rape Crisis & Sexual Abuse Centre (☎ 028-9032 9002; www.rapecrisisni.com) In Northern Ireland.

Transport

Getting There & Away

ENTERING THE COUNTRY

Dublin is the main point of entry for most visitors. In recent years, the growth of no-frills airlines means more routes and cheaper prices between Ireland and other European countries. If arriving in the Republic of Ireland:

- The overwhelming majority of airlines serving Ireland fly into the capital.
- Dublin is also home to two seaports that serve as the main points of sea transport with Britain; ferries from France arrive in the southern port of Rosslare.
- Dublin is also the nation's primary rail hub.

The border between the Republic of Ireland and Northern Ireland still exists as a political reality, albeit an invisible one – there are no checkpoints left and crossing

Climate Change & Travel

Every form of transport that relies on carbon-based fuel generates CO2, the main cause of human-induced climate change. Modern travel is dependent on aeroplanes, which might use less fuel per kilometre per person than most cars but travel much greater distances. The altitude at which aircraft emit gases (including CO2) and particles also contributes to their climate change impact. Many websites offer 'carbon calculators' that allow people to estimate the carbon emissions generated by their journey and, for those who wish to do so, to offset the impact of the greenhouse gases emitted with contributions to portfolios of climate-friendly initiatives throughout the world. Lonely Planet offsets the carbon footprint of all staff and author travel.

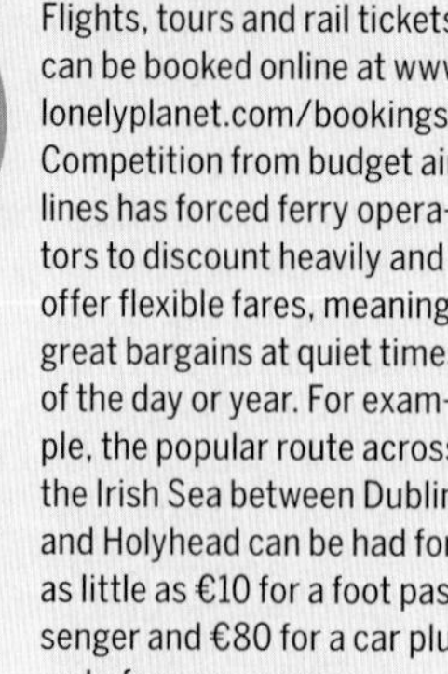

from one jurisdiction to another is barely noticeable. For information on visa requirements, see p379.

Flights, tours and rail tickets can be booked online at www.lonelyplanet.com/bookings.

Competition from budget airlines has forced ferry operators to discount heavily and offer flexible fares, meaning great bargains at quiet times of the day or year. For example, the popular route across the Irish Sea between Dublin and Holyhead can be had for as little as €10 for a foot passenger and €80 for a car plus up to four passengers.

Getting Around

The big decision in getting around Ireland is to go by car or use public transportation. Your own car will make the best use of your time and help you reach even the most remote of places via the spidery network of secondary and tertiary roads, but hire and fuel costs can be expensive for budget travellers – while parking hassles and traffic jams in most urban centres affect everyone – so public transport is often the better choice.

The bus network, made up of a mix of public and private operators, is extensive and generally quite competitive, although journey times can be slow. The rail network is quicker but more limited, serving only major towns and cities, and can be quite costly. Both buses and trains get busy during peak times; you'll need to book in advance to be guaranteed a seat.

 AIR

Ireland's size makes domestic flying unnecessary unless you're in a hurry, but there are flights between Dublin and Belfast, Cork, Derry, Donegal, Galway, Kerry, Shannon and Sligo, as well as a Belfast–Cork service. Most flights within Ireland take around 30 to 50 minutes.

Domestic carriers:

Aer Árann (www.aerarann.com)

Aer Lingus (www.aerlingus.com)

Ryanair (www.ryanair.com)

 BICYCLE

Ireland's compact size, relative flatness and scenery-around-every-corner landscapes make it an ideal cycling destination. Dodgy weather and the occasional uneven road surface are the only concerns. A good tip for cyclists in the west is that the prevailing winds make it easier to cycle from south to north.

Buses will carry bikes, but only if there's room. For trains, bear in mind:

- Intercity trains charge up to €10 per bike.
- Bikes are transported in the passenger compartment.
- Book in advance (www.irishrail.ie), as there's only room for three bikes per service.

Organisations that arrange cycle tours throughout Ireland:

Go Ireland (☎ 066-976 2094; www.govisitireland.com; Old Orchard House, Killorglin, Co Kerry)

Irish Cycling Safaris (☎ 01-260 0749; www.cyclingsafaris.com; Belfield Bike Shop, UCD, Dublin)

> **Fare Go**
>
> Travel costs throughout this book are for single (one-way) adult fares, unless otherwise stated.

 BOAT

Ireland's offshore islands are all served by boat, including the Aran and Skellig Islands to the west, the Saltee Islands to the southeast and Tory and Rathlin Islands to the north.

Ferries also operate across rivers, inlets and loughs, providing useful short cuts, particularly for cyclists.

Cruises are very popular on the 258km-long Shannon–Erne Waterway and on a variety of other lakes and loughs. The tourist offices only recommend operators that are registered with them. Details of non-tourist-board-affiliated boat trips are given under the relevant sections throughout this book.

BORDER CROSSINGS

Security has been progressively scaled down in Northern Ireland in recent years and all border crossings with the Republic are now open and generally unstaffed. Permanent checkpoints have been removed and ramps levelled. On major routes your only indication that you have crossed the border will be a change in road signs and the colour of number plates and postboxes.

BUS

The main bus services in Ireland:

Bus Éireann (01-836 6111; www.buseireann.ie) The Republic's bus line.

Dublin Bus (01-872 000; www.dublinbus.ie) Dublin's bus service.

Metro (9066 6630; www.translink.co.uk) Belfast's bus service.

Ulsterbus (028-9066 6600; www.ulsterbus.co.uk) Northern Ireland's bus service.

Private buses compete – often very favourably – with Bus Éireann in the Republic and also run where the national buses are irregular or absent.

Distances are not especially long: no bus journey will last longer than five hours. A typical fare on a popular route like Dublin to Cork is about €12 one way: distance and competitiveness will reflect pricing, but you can also find higher fares on routes that are shorter but less frequented.

Ferry & Fast Boat Routes

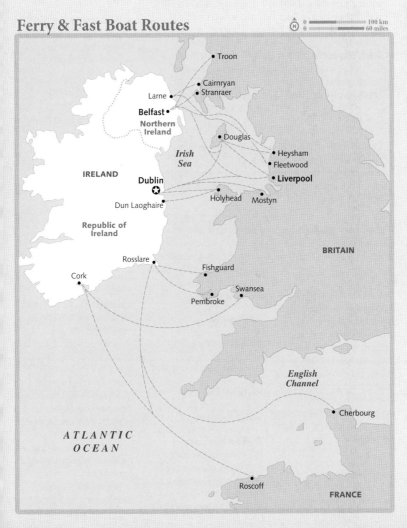

Bus & Rail Passes

There are a number of bus- or train-only and bus-and-rail passes worth considering if you plan on doing a lot of travel using public transportation:

Emerald Card (Bus & Rail) Eight days' travel out of 15 consecutive days (€218) to 15 days out of 30 (€375) on all national and local services within the Republic and Northern Ireland.

Irish Rambler (Bus) Three days' travel out of eight consecutive days (€53) to 15 days out of 30 (€168) on all Bus Éireann services.

Irish Rover (Bus) Three days' travel out of eight consecutive days (€68) to 15 days out of 30 on all Bus Éireann and Ulster Bus services, as well as local services in Cork, Galway, Limerick, Waterford and Belfast.

Irish Explorer (Bus & Rail) Eight days' travel out of 15 consecutive days (€194) on trains and buses within the Republic.

Irish Explorer (Rail) Five days' travel out of 15 consecutive days (€115.50) on trains in the Republic.

Children aged under 16 pay half-price for all these passes and for all normal tickets. Children aged under three travel for free on public transport. You can buy the above passes at most major train and bus stations in Ireland.

Bus Éireann bookings can be made online, but you can't reserve a seat for a particular service.

CAR & MOTORCYCLE

Travelling by car or motorbike means greater flexibility and independence. The road system is extensive, and the constantly growing network of motorways has cut driving times considerably. Downsides include traffic jams, problems with parking in urban centres and the high cost of petrol.

HIRE

Compared with many countries (especially the USA), hire rates are expensive in Ireland; you should expect to pay around €250 a week for a small car (unlimited mileage) but rates go up at busy times and drop off in quieter seasons. The main players:

Avis (www.avis.ie)

Budget (www.budget.ie)

Europcar (www.europcar.ie)

Hertz (www.hertz.ie)

Sixt (www.sixt.ie)

Thrifty (www.thrifty.ie)

The major car hire companies have different web pages on their websites for different countries, so the price of a car on the Irish page can differ from the same car's price on the USA or Australia page. You have to surf a lot of sites to get the best deals. **Nova Car Hire** (www.novacarhire.com) acts as an agent for Alamo, Budget, European and National and offers greatly discounted rates.

Other tips:

- Most cars are manual; automatic cars are available, but they're more expensive to hire.
- If you're travelling from the Republic into Northern Ireland, it's important to be sure that your insurance covers journeys to the North.
- The majority of hire companies won't rent you a car if you're under 23 and haven't had a valid driving licence for at least a year.
- Some companies in the Republic won't rent to you if you're aged 74 or over; there's no upper age limit in the North.
- Motorbikes and mopeds are not available for rent in Ireland.

PARKING

All big towns and cities have covered short-stay car parks that are conveniently signposted.

On-street parking is usually by 'pay and display' tickets available from on-street machines or disc parking (discs, which rotate to display the time you park your car, are available from newsagencies). Costs range from €1.50 to €4.50 per hour; all-day parking in a car park will cost around €24.

Yellow lines (single or double) along the edge of the

Motoring Organisations

The two main motoring organisations:

- **Automobile Association** (AA; www.aaireland.ie) Northern Ireland (☎0870-950 0600, breakdown assistance 0800-667 788); Republic (☎in Dublin 01-617 9999, in Cork 021-425 2444, breakdown assistance 1800 667 788)
- **Royal Automobile Club** (RAC; www.rac.ie) Northern Ireland (☎0800 029 029, breakdown assistance 0800 828 282); Republic (☎1890 483 483)

road indicate restrictions – usually you can park on single yellow lines between 7pm and 8am while double yellow lines means no parking at any time. Always look for the nearby sign that spells out when you can and cannot park.

In Dublin, Cork and Galway, clamping is rigorously enforced: it'll cost you €85 to have the yellow beast removed. In Northern Ireland, the fee is £100 for removal.

ROADS & RULES

Motorways (marked by M+number on a blue background) and primary roads (N+number on a green background) are the fastest way to get around and will deliver you quickly from one end of the country to another. Secondary and tertiary roads (marked as R+number) are much more scenic and fun, but they can be very winding and exceedingly narrow – perfect for going slowly and enjoying the views.

- EU licenses are treated like Irish licences.
- Non-EU licences are valid in Ireland for up to 12 months.
- You must carry your driving licence at all times.
- If you plan to bring a car from Europe, it's illegal to drive without at least third-party insurance.

The basic rules of the road:

- Drive on the left; overtake to the right.
- Safety belts must be worn by the driver and all passengers.
- Children aged under 12 aren't allowed to sit in the front passenger seat.
- Motorcyclists and their passengers must wear helmets.
- When entering a roundabout, give way to the right.

In the Republic, speed-limit and distance signs are in kilometres (although the occasional older white sign shows distances in miles); in the North, speed-limit and distance signs are in miles. Speed limits:

Republic 120km/h on motorways, 100km/h on national roads, 80km/h on regional and local roads, and 50km/h or as signposted in towns.

Northern Ireland 70mph on motorways, 60mph on main roads, 30mph in built-up areas.

Drinking and driving is taken very seriously; in both the Republic and Northern Ireland you're allowed a maximum blood-alcohol level of 80mg/100mL (0.08%) – and campaigners want it reduced to 50mg/100mL.

LOCAL TRANSPORT

Dublin and Belfast have comprehensive local bus networks, as do some other larger towns.

The Dublin Area Rapid Transport (DART) line runs roughly the length of Dublin's coastline, while the Luas tram system has two popular lines.

Taxis tend to be expensive – for daytime rates, flagfall is €4.10 and fares start at €1.03 per km after that (night-time rates are a bit higher). More details are available in the relevant sections throughout this book.

TOURS

Organised tours are a convenient way of exploring the country's main highlights if your time is limited. Tours can be booked through travel agencies, tourist offices in the major cities or directly through the tour companies themselves. Some of the most reputable operators:

Bus Éireann (www.buseireann.ie) Runs day tours to various parts of the Republic and the North.

CIE Tours International (www.cietours.ie) Runs four- to 11-day coach tours of the Republic and the North, including accommodation and meals.

Grayline Tours (www.irishcitytours.com) Dublin-based company offering half- and full-day tours of attractions around Dublin as well as the Ring of Kerry.

Paddywagon Tours (www.paddywagontours.com) Activity-filled three- and six-day tours all over Ireland with friendly tour guides. Accommodation is in IHH hostels.

Railtours Ireland (☎ 01-856 0045; www.railtoursireland.com) For train enthusiasts, organises a series of one- and two-day train trips in association with Iarnród Éireann.

Train Routes

Ulsterbus Tours (www.ulsterbus.co.uk) Runs a large number of day trips throughout the North and the Republic.

TRAIN

Given Ireland's relatively small size, train travel is an expensive luxury. All of the Republic's major towns and cities are on the limited rail network, which is operated by **Iarnród Éireann** (Irish Rail; ☎ 1850 366 222; www.irishrail.ie) and fans out from Dublin in such a way that connections between destinations not on the same line usually involve an out-of-the-way trip to the capital. There's no north–south route along the western coast, no network in Donegal and no direct connections from Waterford to Cork or Killarney.

Fares are high. A mid-week one-way ticket from Dublin to Cork will cost around €65; the return fare is only marginally more expensive – a feature designed to incentivise rail travel but making for poor-value one-way fares. The cheapest fares are always online.

Northern Ireland Railways (NIR; ☎ 028-9089 9411; www.nirailways.co.uk; Belfast Central Station) runs four routes from Belfast:

- one links with the system in the Republic via Newry to Dublin
- the other three go east to Bangor, northeast to Larne and northwest to Derry via Coleraine (see map p384).

Language

Irish (Gaeilge) is Ireland's official language. In 2003 the government introduced the Official Languages Act, whereby all official documents, street signs and official titles must be either in Irish or in both Irish and English. Despite its official status, Irish is really only spoken in pockets of rural Ireland known as the Gaeltacht, the main ones being Cork *(Corcaigh)*, Donegal *(Dún na nGall)*, Galway *(Gaillimh)*, Kerry *(Ciarraí)* and Mayo *(Maigh Eo)*.

Ask people outside the Gaeltacht if they can speak Irish and nine out of 10 of them will probably reply *'ah, cupla focal'* (a couple of words) – and they generally mean it. Irish is a compulsory subject in schools for those aged six to 15, but Irish classes have traditionally been rather academic and unimaginative, leading many students to resent it as a waste of time. As a result, many adults regret not having a greater grasp of it. In recent times, at long last, a new Irish curriculum has been introduced cutting the hours devoted to the subject but making the lessons more fun, practical and celebratory.

For in-depth language information and a witty insight into the quirks of language in Ireland, check out Lonely Planet's *Irish Language & Culture*. To enhance your trip with this title or a phrasebook, visit **lonelyplanet.com**. Lonely Planet iPhone phrasebooks are available through the Apple App store.

PRONUNCIATION

Irish divides vowels into long (those with an accent) and short (those without an accent), and distinguishes between broad (**a**, **á**, **o**, **ó**, **u**) and slender (**e**, **é**, **i** and **í**) vowels, which can affect the pronunciation of preceding consonants.

Other than a few odd-looking clusters, like **mh** and **bhf** (both pronounced as 'w'), consonants are generally pronounced as they are in English.

Irish has three main dialects: Connaught Irish (in Galway and northern Mayo), Munster Irish (in Cork, Kerry and Waterford) and Ulster Irish (in Donegal). The pronunciation guides given here are an anglicised version of modern standard Irish, which is essentially an amalgam of the three – if you read them as if they were English, you'll be able to get your point across in Gaeilge without even having to think about the specifics of Irish pronunciation or spelling.

BASICS

Hello. (greeting)
Dia duit. — deea gwit

Hello. (reply)
Dia is Muire duit. — deeas moyra gwit

Good morning.
Maidin mhaith. — mawjin wah

Good night.
Oíche mhaith. — eekheh wah

Goodbye. (when leaving)
Slán leat. — slawn lyat

Goodbye. (when staying)
Slán agat. — slawn agut

Excuse me.
Gabh mo leithscéal. — gamoh lesh scale

I'm sorry.
Tá brón orm. — taw brohn oruhm

Thank you (very) much.
Go raibh (míle) maith agat. — goh rev (meela) mah agut

Do you speak Irish?
An bhfuil Gaeilge agat? — on wil gaylge oguht

I don't understand.
Ní thuigim. — nee higgim

What is this?
Cad é seo? — kod ay shoh

What is that?
Cad é sin? — kod ay shin

I'd like to go to ...
Ba mhaith liom dul go dtí . . . — baw wah lohm dull go dee . . .

I'd like to buy ...
Ba mhaith liom . . . a cheannach. — bah wah lohm . . . a kyanukh

..., (if you) please.
. . . más é do thoil é. — . . . maws ay do hall ay

Yes.	*Tá.*	taw
No.	*Níl.*	neel
It is.	*Sea.*	sheh
It isn't.	*Ní hea.*	nee heh
another/ one more	*ceann eile*	kyawn ella
nice	*go deas*	goh dyass

MAKING CONVERSATION

Welcome.
Ceád míle fáilte. kade meela fawlcha
(lit: 100,000 welcomes)

How are you?
Conas a tá tú? kunas aw taw too

I'm fine.
Táim go maith. thawm go mah

What's your name?
Cad is ainm duit? kod is anim dwit

My name is (Sean Frayne).
(Sean Frayne) is ainm dom. (shawn frain) is anim dohm

Impossible!
Ní féidir é! nee faydir ay

Nonsense!
Ráiméis! rawmaysh

That's terrible!
Go huafásach! guh hoofawsokh

Take it easy.
Tóg é gobogé. tohg ay gobogay

Cheers!
Slainte! slawncha

I'm never ever drinking again!
Ní ólfaidh mé go brách arís! knee ohlhee mey gu brawkh ureeshch

Bon voyage!
Go n-éirí an bóthar leat! go nairee on bohhar lat

SIGNS

Fir	*fear*	Men
Gardaí	*gardee*	Police
Leithreas	*lehrass*	Toilet
Mna	*mnaw*	Women
Oifig An Phoist	*iffig ohn fwisht*	Post Office

Happy Christmas!
Nollaig shona! nuhlig hona

Happy Easter!
Cáisc shona! kawshk hona

DAYS OF THE WEEK

Monday	*Dé Luaín*	day loon
Tuesday	*Dé Máirt*	day maart
Wednesday	*Dé Ceádaoin*	day kaydeen
Thursday	*Déardaoin*	daredeen
Friday	*Dé hAoine*	day heeneh
Saturday	*Dé Sathairn*	day sahern
Sunday	*Dé Domhnaigh*	day downick

NUMBERS

1	*haon*	hayin
2	*dó*	doe
3	*trí*	tree
4	*ceathaír*	kahirr
5	*cúig*	kooig
6	*sé*	shay
7	*seacht*	shocked
8	*hocht*	hukt
9	*naoi*	nay
10	*deich*	jeh
20	*fiche*	feekhe

Behind the Scenes

Our Readers

Many thanks to the travellers who used the last edition and wrote to us with helpful hints, useful advice and interesting anecdotes:

Anna, Bill Bentley, Markus Deutsch, Petra Fetting, Mary H Hood, Kevin O'Dwyer, Selva Schrem Matas.

Author Thanks

FIONN DAVENPORT

Thanks to Glenn, Cat and all at Lonely Planet; to my fellow authors who make me want to visit the places they've written about and to the various tourist authorities, B&B owners, hoteliers and restaurateurs for providing information, sustenance and decent pillows along my travels.

Acknowledgments

Climate map data adapted from Peel MC, Finlayson BL & McMahon TA (2007) 'Updated World Map of the Köppen-Geiger Climate Classification', *Hydrology and Earth System Sciences*, 11, 163344.
Illustrations pp64-5, pp70-1, pp114-15 by Javier Zarracina
Cover photographs
Front: St Colman's Cathedral, Cobh, Richard Cummins / Lonely Planet Images ©
Back: Giant's Causeway ancient rock formation, Gareth Mc Cormack / Lonely Planet Images ©
Many of the images in this guide are available for licensing from Lonely Planet Images: www.lonelyplanetimages.com.

This Book

This 2nd edition of *Discover Ireland* was coordinated by Fionn Davenport, and researched and written by Fionn Davenport, Catherine Le Nevez, Etain O'Carroll, Ryan Ver Berkmoes and Neil Wilson. The previous edition was also coordinated by Fionn Davenport. This guidebook was commissioned in Lonely Planet's London office, and produced by the following:
Commissioning Editors Catherine Craddock, Katie O'Connell, Glenn van der Knijff, Clifton Wilkinson
Coordinating Editor Sonya Mithen
Coordinating Cartographer Jennifer Johnston
Coordinating Layout Designer Carol Jackson
Assisting Layout Designer Kerrianne Southway
Managing Editor Brigitte Ellemor
Managing Cartographer Mandy Sierp
Managing Layout Designer Chris Girdler
Assisting Editors Elizabeth Anglin, Judith Bamber, Rebecca Chau, Gabrielle Innes, Ali Lemer, Saralinda Turner, Jeanette Wall, Kate Whitfield
Assisting Cartographer Csanad Csutoros
Cover Research Naomi Parker
Internal Image Research Aude Vauconsant
Language Content Annelies Mertens, Branislava Vladisavljevic

Thanks to Yvonne Bischofberger, Melanie Dankel, Ryan Evans, Yvonne Kirk, Trent Paton, Gerard Walker, Wendy Wright

SEND US YOUR FEEDBACK

We love to hear from travellers – your comments keep us on our toes and help make our books better. Our well-travelled team reads every word on what you loved or loathed about this book. Although we cannot reply individually to postal submissions, we always guarantee that your feedback goes straight to the appropriate authors, in time for the next edition. Each person who sends us information is thanked in the next edition, and the most useful submissions are rewarded with a free book.

Visit **lonelyplanet.com/contact** to submit your updates and suggestions or to ask for help. Our award-winning website also features inspirational travel stories, news and discussions.

Note: We may edit, reproduce and incorporate your comments in Lonely Planet products such as guidebooks, websites and digital products, so let us know if you don't want your comments reproduced or your name acknowledged. For a copy of our privacy policy visit lonelyplanet.com/privacy.

Index

A

B

C

000 Map pages

E

000 Map pages

F

G

H

I

J

K

L

M

000 Map pages

N

000 Map pages

How to Use This Book

These symbols will help you find the listings you want:

- Sights
- Activities
- Courses
- Tours
- Festivals & Events
- Sleeping
- Eating
- Drinking
- Entertainment
- Shopping
- Information/ Transport

These symbols give you the vital information for each listing:

- Telephone Numbers
- Opening Hours
- Parking
- Nonsmoking
- Air-Conditioning
- Internet Access
- Wi-Fi Access
- Swimming Pool
- Vegetarian Selection
- English-Language Menu
- Family-Friendly
- Pet-Friendly
- Bus
- Ferry
- Metro
- Subway
- London Tube
- Tram
- Train

Reviews are organised by author preference.

Look out for these icons:

FREE No payment required

A green or sustainable option

Our authors have nominated these places as demonstrating a strong commitment to sustainability – for example by supporting local communities and producers, operating in an environmentally friendly way, or supporting conservation projects.

Map Legend

Sights

- Beach
- Buddhist
- Castle
- Christian
- Hindu
- Islamic
- Jewish
- Monument
- Museum/Gallery
- Ruin
- Winery/Vineyard
- Zoo
- Other Sight

Activities, Courses & Tours

- Diving/Snorkelling
- Canoeing/Kayaking
- Skiing
- Surfing
- Swimming/Pool
- Walking
- Windsurfing
- Other Activity/ Course/Tour

Sleeping

- Sleeping
- Camping

Eating

- Eating

Drinking

- Drinking
- Cafe

Entertainment

- Entertainment

Shopping

- Shopping

Information

- Bank
- Embassy/ Consulate
- Hospital/Medical
- Internet
- Police
- Post Office
- Telephone
- Toilet
- Tourist Information
- Other Information

Transport

- Airport
- Border Crossing
- Bus
- Cable Car/ Funicular
- Cycling
- Ferry
- Metro
- Monorail
- Parking
- Petrol Station
- Taxi
- Train/Railway
- Tram
- Other Transport

Routes

- Tollway
- Freeway
- Primary
- Secondary
- Tertiary
- Lane
- Unsealed Road
- Plaza/Mall
- Steps
- Tunnel
- Pedestrian Overpass
- Walking Tour
- Walking Tour Detour
- Path

Geographic

- Hut/Shelter
- Lighthouse
- Lookout
- Mountain/Volcano
- Oasis
- Park
- Pass
- Picnic Area
- Waterfall

Population

- Capital (National)
- Capital (State/Province)
- City/Large Town
- Town/Village

Boundaries

- International
- State/Province
- Disputed
- Regional/Suburb
- Marine Park
- Cliff
- Wall

Hydrography

- River/Creek
- Intermittent River
- Swamp/Mangrove
- Reef
- Canal
- Water
- Dry/Salt/ Intermittent Lake
- Glacier

Areas

- Beach/Desert
- Cemetery (Christian)
- Cemetery (Other)
- Park/Forest
- Sportsground
- Sight (Building)
- Top Sight (Building)

Our Story

A beat-up old car, a few dollars in the pocket and a sense of adventure. In 1972 that's all Tony and Maureen Wheeler needed for the trip of a lifetime – across Europe and Asia overland to Australia. It took several months, and at the end – broke but inspired – they sat at their kitchen table writing and stapling together their first travel guide, *Across Asia on the Cheap*. Within a week they'd sold 1500 copies. Lonely Planet was born.

Today, Lonely Planet has offices in Melbourne, London and Oakland, with more than 600 staff and writers. We share Tony's belief that 'a great guidebook should do three things: inform, educate and amuse'.

Our Writers

FIONN DAVENPORT

Coordinating Author, Dublin, Wicklow & Eastern Ireland, Cork & the Ring of Kerry Despite its myriad economic problems, Ireland has proven itself to be undaunted, beautiful and just as bloody interesting as it ever was. Fionn suspected as much, but he needed to traipse through his hometown of Dublin and explore the wilds of west Cork to have it confirmed in spades.

CATHERINE LE NEVEZ

Cork & the Ring of Kerry, Kilkenny & the Southeast, Wicklow & Eastern Ireland Since the age of four Catherine's been hitting the road at every opportunity. Along the way she completed her Doctorate of Creative Arts in Writing, Masters in Professional Writing and post-grad qualifications in Editing and Publishing. With Celtic connections (and a love of Guinness!), Catherine's travelled throughout every county in the emerald isle and has covered 20 of them for Lonely Planet, including several editions of *Ireland*.

ETAIN O'CARROLL

Galway, Clare & the West, Sligo & Donegal Born and bred in the Irish midlands, Etain escaped to become a travel writer and photographer, but despite criss-crossing the globe the lure of the old sod never quite went away. She now writes about her homeland for a variety of publications and has worked on several editions of Lonely Planet *Ireland*. Savouring pristine beaches and remote pubs was one of the sheer joys of research.

Read more about Etain at:
lonelyplanet.com/members/etainocarroll

RYAN VER BERKMOES

Galway, Clare & the West From Galway to Wexford, Ryan has delighted in the great swath of Ireland. He first visited Galway in 1985 when he remembers a grey place where the locals wandered the muddy tidal flats for fun. Times have changed! From lost rural pubs to lost memory, he's revelled in a place where his first name brings a smile and his surname brings a 'huh?'

NEIL WILSON

Belfast, Derry & the Antrim Coast Neil first visited Northern Ireland in 1994 and his interest in the history and politics of the place intensified when he found out that many of his ancestors were from Ulster. Working on the *Ireland* guidebook has allowed him to witness first-hand the progress being made towards a lasting peace, as well as enjoying some excellent hiking and biking in the Ring of Gullion and the Mourne Mountains.

Read more about Neil at:
lonelyplanet.com/members/neilwilson

Published by Lonely Planet Publications Pty Ltd
ABN 36 005 607 983
2nd edition – March 2012
ISBN 978 1 74220 118 4

10 9 8 7 6 5 4 3 2 1
Printed in China